MANAGED DISSENT

The mass street demonstrations that followed the 2020 police murder of George Floyd were perhaps the largest in American history. These events confirmed that even in a digital era, people rely on public dissent to communicate grievances, change public discourse, and stand in collective solidarity with others. However, the demonstrations also showed that the laws and practices surrounding public protest make public contention more dangerous, more costly, and less effective. Police fired tear gas into peaceful crowds, used physical force against compliant demonstrators, imposed broad curfews, limited the places where protesters could assemble, and abused "unlawful assembly" and other public disorder laws. These and other pathologies epitomize a system in which public protest is tightly constrained in the name of public order. *Managed Dissent* argues that, in order to preserve the venerable tradition of public protest in the United States, we must reform several aspects of the law of public protest.

Timothy Zick is the John Marshall Professor of Government and Citizenship at William & Mary Law School. Professor Zick is the author of *Speech Out of Doors: Preserving First Amendment Liberties in Public Places*; *The Cosmopolitan First Amendment: Protecting Transborder Expressive and Religious Liberties*; *The Dynamic Free Speech Clause: Free Speech and its Relation to Other Constitutional Rights*; and *The First Amendment in the Trump Era*. He is also the co-author of a First Amendment casebook, *The First Amendment: Cases and Theory*.

CAMBRIDGE STUDIES ON CIVIL RIGHTS AND CIVIL LIBERTIES

This series is a platform for original scholarship on US civil rights and civil liberties. It produces books on the normative, historical, judicial, political, and sociological contexts for understanding contemporary legislative, jurisprudential, and presidential dilemmas. The aim is to provide experts, teachers, policymakers, students, social activists, and educated citizens with in-depth analyses of theories, existing and past conditions, and constructive ideas for legal advancements.

General Editor: Alexander Tsesis, *Loyola University, Chicago*

Managed Dissent

THE LAW OF PUBLIC PROTEST

TIMOTHY ZICK

William & Mary Law School

CAMBRIDGE
UNIVERSITY PRESS

CAMBRIDGE
UNIVERSITY PRESS

Shaftesbury Road, Cambridge CB2 8EA, United Kingdom

One Liberty Plaza, 20th Floor, New York, NY 10006, USA

477 Williamstown Road, Port Melbourne, VIC 3207, Australia

314–321, 3rd Floor, Plot 3, Splendor Forum, Jasola District Centre, New Delhi – 110025, India

103 Penang Road, #05–06/07, Visioncrest Commercial, Singapore 238467

Cambridge University Press is part of Cambridge University Press & Assessment, a department of the University of Cambridge.

We share the University's mission to contribute to society through the pursuit of education, learning and research at the highest international levels of excellence.

www.cambridge.org
Information on this title: www.cambridge.org/9781316519561

DOI: 10.1017/9781009024372

First published 2023

A catalogue record for this publication is available from the British Library.

A Cataloging-in-Publication data record for this book is available from the Library of Congress.

ISBN 978-1-316-51956-1 Hardback
ISBN 978-1-009-01070-2 Paperback

Contents

Figure

Tables

Preface

Today there are ample opportunities to express oneself online. So why *do* people continue to assemble in the streets to protest and demonstrate? What value do traditional public protest and dissent have if, as Justice Anthony Kennedy recently wrote for the Supreme Court, the "most important" forums for speech are now social media platforms – the "modern public square"?[1] These questions are as pertinent today as they were when I published my first book, *Speech Out of Doors*, more than a decade ago.[2] Despite the explosion of digital outlets, millions of Americans continue to organize, participate in, and support protests, demonstrations, and rallies. In fact, as Greg Magarian has observed, "In this age of Black Lives Matter [BLM], the Dakota Access Pipeline protests, and the Women's March, public protest and collective political action matter more than at any other time in the past fifty years."[3]

An estimated 15 to 26 million protesters gathered in the streets after George Floyd's murder, in what were likely the largest public protests in American history.[4] Between January 2020 and June 2021, there were more than 30,000 public demonstrations in the United States.[5] Not even a deadly global pandemic could stop Americans from assembling to protest police violence, government pandemic restrictions, and other policies. Recent demonstrations, including those following the Supreme Court decision derecognizing the right to abortion, have confirmed that even in a digital age, public protest remains critically important as an act of expression, self-government, autonomy, and solidarity with others. As the most tangible example of politics "out of doors," as opposed to through more conventional means, public protests are vital to our democratic system.[6] For individuals and groups across the political spectrum, they remain a central component of American political and social contention.

Modern-day protests are part of a long and venerable tradition of American public contention. Revolutionary activism, which included disruptive and sometimes violent public protests, propelled the people's revolution against Britain. Early protesters and dissenters included those advocating the abolition of slavery, suffrage for women, and fair treatment of Native Americans and immigrants. Americans have participated in public protests concerning every war the United States has been involved in. During the twentieth century, protesters demanded "workers' rights, women's rights, Black equality, the prohibition of alcohol, reproductive rights, and gay rights. During the early part of the twenty-first century, there were protests concerning abortion rights, globalization, the North American Free Trade Agreement, bank bailouts, and healthcare reform."[7]

As deep as these historical roots run, we ought not to take the continued vitality or even the existence of public protests for granted. Public and official attitudes toward protest have ranged from lukewarm to overtly hostile. Too often, governments have responded to peaceful public protests with aggression, escalated force, and other repressive tactics. There are myriad limits on where, when, and how protests can occur. Police enforce a bevy of broad and sometimes vague public disorder laws against public protest organizers and participants, who are also subject to significant costs and civil liabilities – sometimes for vandalism and violence they did not participate in or encourage.

While most protests are peaceful gatherings, some are tense, dangerous, destructive, and even violent. Security and safety concerns regarding public protests are real. Because public protests take place in public venues and often involve large gatherings and counter-protests, they raise acute safety and security concerns. The potential for violence and vandalism, whether it comes from protesters, counter-protesters, provocateurs, or the police, cannot be ignored. A recent increase in the incidence of political violence and the presence of openly carried firearms and other weapons at protests have added to these concerns. If public protests cannot be made safe – from both the aggression of law enforcement and the threats from other sources – there is a risk Americans will cease to participate in them.

These challenges, and others, were all on display during the recent BLM protests across the nation. Although the protests were widely popular and predominantly peaceful (according to one study, 96 percent of the events involved no violence or property destruction),[8] participants were frequently subjected to aggressive protest policing: use of non-lethal force as a first response, mass arrests, and arbitrary enforcement of "unlawful assembly" and other public order laws. The degree of police misconduct and aggression was so egregious in New York that the state's Attorney General took the highly unusual step of suing the New York City Police Department. She alleged that officers beat protesters with batons, rammed them with bicycles, resorted to dangerous crowd containment strategies, used tear gas and other "non-lethal" force against peaceful assemblies, and unlawfully arrested legal observers, including members of the press. New York's officers were hardly outliers in terms of their use of force and other unlawful tactics. In fact, the pattern was distressingly common across the nation. As a result, thousands who attended demonstrations were arrested and injured. In many locations, racial justice protesters were met by armed counter-protesters, sometimes with fatal results.

In response to widespread civil unrest, officials across the country enacted strict curfews, restricted access to protest venues, and dispersed peaceful gatherings – often, as in New York, through aggression and force. Meanwhile, federal law enforcement officers from various agencies were dispatched to Portland, the District of Columbia, and other locations, ostensibly to "keep the peace" and maintain "law and order." But these officials, many of whom were not properly identified as federal agents and had no training in domestic crowd control, also resorted to force and unlawfully detained protesters. In response to the mass protests, Mark Esper, former President Donald Trump's Secretary of Defense, maintained "we need to dominate the battlespace."[9] According to Esper, the former president suggested deploying thousands of U.S. troops to the Capitol and, more shocking still, ordering them to *shoot* BLM protesters demonstrating in the wake of George Floyd's murder (Trump has denied these claims).[10]

Recent pro-choice protests, which erupted after the Supreme Court overturned *Roe v. Wade*, were also largely peaceful. Still, in several instances, law enforcement used tear gas and other aggressive means of controlling peaceful assemblies.[11] In Cedar Rapids, Iowa, one woman was hospitalized when someone drove a truck through a group of pro-choice protesters. Like other states, Iowa recently enacted a law that protects drivers who collide with protesters from legal liability under certain circumstances.[12] There has been an alarming increase in the number of such collisions.[13]

Not all protesters have faced this degree of aggression and hostility. On January 6, 2021, after attending a public rally, rioters stormed the U.S. Capitol to prevent the peaceful transition of presidential power after the 2020 election. In that instance, however, law enforcement seemed wholly unprepared to manage the throngs that descended on the House and Senate buildings. Rioters breached security, assaulted officers, and vandalized the Capitol. The Capitol riot raised questions about the fundamental difference between peaceful protest and violent insurrection, the culpability of those (including the former president) who may have encouraged the rioters, and the delicate balance between liberty and security during protests. At the same time, the relative restraint exercised by law enforcement against predominantly white rioters on January 6 raised longstanding questions about law enforcement's racially and ideologically discriminatory actions against protesters.[14]

In sum, responses to the BLM protests by local, state, and federal law enforcement signaled a willingness to maintain public order at the cost of civil liberties, particularly those of Black citizens. Over time, public support for the protests began to wane and calls for "law and order" became a rallying cry on the political right. Many states responded to that call by enacting new restrictions on public protest including limits on spontaneous demonstrations, more expansive definitions of "riot" and other criminal offenses, and increased criminal punishments for even minor acts of civil disobedience.[15]

We can and should draw important lessons from recent protest actions and movements. However, we ought to be careful not to view these events as evidence that the rights to protest and collective dissent rest on firm legal and other foundations. As recent BLM and pro-choice demonstrations showed, demonstrators can avoid some of the restrictions on public protest activity when they spontaneously gather and march in the streets.[16] But protest movement organizers and participants still face a daunting array of obstacles to the effective exercise of constitutionally protected rights to speak and peaceably assemble in public. These limits are not unique to nationwide demonstrations, widespread civil unrest, or public emergencies. Rather, they are manifestations of a deeply rooted desire to manage protest and dissent in the name of public order – even during much calmer periods.

Recent events should prompt us to consider how best to preserve the American tradition of public contention in the face of deeply rooted legal, constitutional, political, and social obstacles. In contrast to the history-making BLM protests, the ordinary public protest movement lacks the degree of spontaneous participation, public sympathy, and press attention that facilitated mass demonstrations during the summer of 2020. The question is how to preserve a tradition of peaceful but disruptive protest for those who want to engage in collective expression and politics out of doors.

Given the nation's recent experience with civil unrest, it may seem counterintuitive to argue, as this book does, that we ought to be concerned about not having *enough* public protest activity in the U.S. or the lack of adequate protection for protests and demonstrations. Judging from opinion polls, public discourse, and legislation, some Americans believe there is already *too much* protest activity in our streets and demonstrators' rights need to be further curtailed.

Americans now stand at a critical inflection point. Public protest rights occupy a precarious position – lauded by many as part of a tradition of rising up and speaking out, but derided by others as a form of "mob rule" that threatens public order. Public protest and dissent must be managed to some degree to maintain basic order and preserve public safety. However, as this book will show, the law of public protest allows officials and others to manage dissent far beyond these fundamental concerns – and, in some respects, to do so in ways that target or disparately affect certain types of messages and particular protest communities.[17] In important respects, the law of public protest fails to adequately protect Americans' exercise of fundamental First Amendment rights.

Acknowledgments

I have been thinking about the "law of public protest" and this project since I published my first book, *Speech Out of Doors: Preserving First Amendment Liberties in Public Places* (Cambridge University Press, 2008). That book focused on the law's problematic conception of "place" and how it has affected public contention and dissent. The mass protests that followed George Floyd's murder convinced me that the time was right to examine in more depth the various facets of the law of public protest.

I owe a special debt of gratitude to Alex Tsesis, editor of the Cambridge Studies on Civil Rights and Civil Liberties series, for supporting this project. I would also like to thank Matt Gallaway at Cambridge University Press for recognizing the merits of the project. I have learned much from the Civil Rights and Civil Liberties series over the years and am honored to contribute to it.

I am deeply indebted to William & Mary Law School and Dean Benjamin Spencer for providing financial and other support that made this book possible, including through the award of the William H. Cabell Professorship.

I rehearsed some of the arguments that appear in the book in prior work. In addition to *Speech Out of Doors*, my other publications concerning the law of public protest include "Arming Public Protests," 104 *Iowa L. Rev.* 233 (2018); "Managing Dissent," 95 *Wash. U. L. Rev.* 1423 (2018); and "The Costs of Dissent: Protest and Civil Liabilities," 89 *Geo. Wash. L. Rev.* 233 (2021).

I would like to thank participants at the 2020 Yale Law School Free Expression Scholars Conference for their engagement with early draft chapters. I am grateful to a wonderful and accomplished group of readers, including Tabatha Abu El-Haj, Ash Bhagwat, Joshua Braver, John Inazu, Greg Magarian, Nick Robinson, and Nadine Strossen, all of whom provided invaluable feedback on chapters or, in certain cases, the entire manuscript. I also want to thank the anonymous reviewers of my book proposal for their insightful comments and suggestions.

I am grateful for the work of my research assistants, Mikaela Phillips and Sarah Bradley. Special thanks to Mikaela Phillips, who produced detailed research memoranda concerning several public protest-related topics.

Last, but certainly not least, I want to express my gratitude to those who continue to organize, participate in, and support public protests despite the challenges examined in this book. More than anything I can propose, or the law can accomplish, your actions will help preserve our long tradition of public protest and speech out of doors.

Introduction

Historically, American authorities have reacted to public protest movements not by seeking to accommodate or facilitate them, but rather by relying on laws, regulations, and often brute force to control and deter speech and assembly in the public square. Among other actions, officials have infiltrated and surveilled protest groups, tightly controlled access to public properties, punished protesters under a wide range of broadly worded public disorder laws, and used aggressive police tactics against even peaceful protesters. To be sure, as the Supreme Court observed long ago, no one has a right to meet in the middle of Times Square at rush hour, block access to buildings, or ignore all traffic laws.[1] Nor does the First Amendment protect violent conduct or destructive behavior. Clearly, governments must enforce some rules to maintain public order and keep the public peace. But as this book will show, the law of public protest manages public contention and dissent far beyond such rudimentary requirements. The law imposes limits and obstacles that generally favor order and tranquility over disruptive, noisy, and untidy forms of direct public action.

THE LAW OF PUBLIC PROTEST

In the U.S., public protest and dissent are actively managed through judicial precedents, laws, regulations, common law actions, policing practices, and embedded norms that collectively comprise what the book refers to as the "law of public protest." In general, scholars have not identified or analyzed these subjects as a coherent body or area of law.[2] The book maintains that we can and should do so. Indeed, *only* by adopting this approach can we appreciate the serious challenges public protest currently faces.

Although "protest" is a complex concept, for now let us generally conceive of a public protest as a gathering of individuals, in a public place, for the purpose of communicating some thought or idea to a public audience. Protest in that sense usually takes familiar forms such as demonstrations, rallies, and pickets.

1

Constitutional, statutory, and regulatory provisions affect everything from whether, where, how, and when a protest can occur. Protest organizers, participants, and supporters are subject to common law actions for personal injuries, damages to reputation, and infliction of emotional distress. Federal and state laws affect the remedies protesters may be entitled to in the event their constitutional rights are violated. Customs, practices, and norms relating to policing protest also affect the ability and willingness to organize and participate in public protests. The sources of the law of public protest range from local ordinances to state and federal statutes and constitutional provisions. The body of law is defined, administered, amended, enforced, and interpreted by a variety of officials – lawmakers, courts, local officials, administrators, campus officials, police officers, and in extraordinary cases even members of the National Guard and U.S. Armed Forces.[3]

As large and diverse as this body of protest law is, the commonality is the act of public contention at the center of it all – assembling with others to engage in a public demonstration that communicates viewpoints to various audiences, bands people together in common causes, and contributes to self-worth. This is such a familiar ritual that most Americans probably take it for granted. However, beneath the surface, there is a very real and identifiable *body of law* that affects everything from a public protest's inception to its culmination – and even matters beyond the event itself, including the criminal and civil liabilities of organizers and participants.[4]

The law of public protest, which is described in more detail in Chapter 2, includes lengthy and detailed administrative codes that govern the permitting of protest events, the time, place, and manner of their occurrence, and the imposition of costs. Detailed statutory and administrative codes dictate the number of protesters who can assemble, the places where they are allowed to march and speak, and the types of activities in which they can lawfully engage. The codes often impose significant upfront costs on protest organizers, including the posting of security bonds and charges relating to cleanup.

Under the First Amendment's "public forum" and "time, place, and manner" doctrines, protest is only allowed in limited categories or types of places. Laws and regulations exclude protest and other expressive activities from highly symbolic places, including areas near courthouses and national monuments. "Free speech zones" cabin and trap public protest. Targeted protest regulations (TPRs) strictly limit protest in specific locations including near medical facilities, vaccination sites, funerals, and polling places.

Law enforcement has broad discretion to enforce laws and regulations affecting public protest wherever it occurs. Some of that discretion is built into permitting schemes.[5] Law enforcement authority also includes enforcement of a variety of offenses relating to public safety and order: for example, "breach of peace," "disorderly conduct," "unlawful assembly," and "incitement to riot."[6] Under these laws, officers can arrest protesters for a wide range of offenses, including minor breaches of the peace.[7] Using their broad discretion under these laws, police can quickly declare and remove "unlawful assemblies," charge protesters with "disorderly conduct" and "conspiracy to riot," and issue orders for even peaceful protesters to disperse from a public area they otherwise have a legal right to occupy.[8]

Enforcement of these public order laws is a critically important aspect of the law of public protest.[9] As much – perhaps even more – than any First Amendment doctrines, law enforcement's exercise of broad discretionary power determines the scope of protesters' rights on the ground.[10] For example, while the First Amendment may grant protesters a formal right to speak in a particular place, officers can effectively countermand or undermine that right with a discretionary order to disperse. The protester's choice is then to refuse to comply and risk arrest or to compliantly move along. Moreover, as will see, the law of public protest offers little prospect of recovering damages from officials who violate the First Amendment or other constitutional rights.

As the 2020 BLM protests showed, aggressive protest policing remains one of the most significant threats to the exercise of public protest rights.[11] The norms and practices of law enforcement, including its reliance on surveillance and militarized policing methods, have a significant impact on the exercise of public protest rights.

As noted, the law of public protest also includes common law and statutory causes of action that apply generally, or sometimes in specific terms, to protesters. Protest organizers can be liable for damages for committing civil offenses such as trespass to property, defamation, infliction of emotional distress, and damage to business relations. In recent years, litigants have pursued increasingly novel civil liability theories against protesters, arguing that they "negligently organized" a demonstration or "aided and abetted" riots.[12]

As if this were not enough to contend with, protesters must now consider the possibility that some counter-protesters and other attendees will carry firearms. The Supreme Court's recognition of public carry rights and state laws authorizing open and concealed carry may have a profound effect on the exercise of First Amendment speech and assembly rights. For that reason, these rights and legal protections have now become part of the law of public protest.

As the recent pandemic and widespread civil unrest have shown, the law of public protest must also account for emergency circumstances. Special state and federal laws apply to public protests that take place during both declared and undeclared emergencies. As we saw during the COVID-19 lockdowns, state laws and executive orders can significantly affect the right to assemble in public places. Indeed, in some states public protest was deemed a "non-essential" activity.[13] During periods of civil unrest, the law of public protest provides broad discretion to state and national officials to maintain public order.

Finally, the law of public protest includes potential remedies that apply when protesters' First Amendment or other constitutional rights are violated. Suits for damages are severely limited by federal and state civil rights statutes, which generally grant broad legal immunity to law enforcement and other officials. Under current remedial law, protesters may find it difficult, if not impossible, to obtain monetary damages against state or federal officers.

The law of public protest is always changing and growing. Lawmakers have responded to mass and other protest actions by adopting additional restrictions on public protest. This backlash legislation includes additional limits on where protest can occur, authorization of protest-specific civil actions, an increase in criminal and civil penalties for even minor acts of civil disobedience, and even loss of public benefits for protest-related offenses.[14]

Each of the foregoing aspects of the law of public protest is subject to or influenced by federal constitutional rights provisions. These provisions are, of course, part of the law of public protest.

The most important is the First Amendment, which limits the scope of official authority to restrict protest activities. First Amendment precedents and doctrines govern place regulations, application of permit schemes and regulations, imposition of protest-related costs, common law and statutory liabilities of protesters, and enforcement of laws that restrict speech, assembly, and press activities. Among other things, First Amendment doctrines determine which public properties are available to protesters ("public forum"), how, when and where protest can occur ("time, place, and manner"), and the extent to which counter-protesters can interfere with protest speech ("hostile audiences"). As we will discover, although the First Amendment contains rights of speech, assembly, *and* petition – each of which would support a constitutional right to organize and participate in public protest – the Supreme Court has not developed any distinct doctrines or standards concerning assembly and petition. It has treated assembly and petition rights as essentially subsumed by the First Amendment's free speech right.[15]

Two other provisions round out the constitutional dimension of the law of public protest. As noted, the Second Amendment and state laws recognizing the right to bear arms in public places can affect protesters' exercise of speech and assembly rights.[16] The right to bear arms in public places also affects the policing of public protests, including law enforcement's ability to keep protest participants safe.[17] The Fourth Amendment also imposes some limits on whether and how police can surveil, arrest, and detain protesters.[18] Although the bulk of the book's discussion will focus on the First Amendment, to the extent they affect public protest these other constitutional rights will also be considered.

In 1965, when the civil rights protests were still in the news, Harry Kalven, Jr. observed, "what is required is in effect a set of Robert's Rules of Order for the new uses of the public forum, albeit the designing of such rules poses a problem of formidable practical difficulty."[19] Kalven was correct on both scores. His comments foreshadowed a system or body of law that today consists of a wide array of administrative, common law, and criminal law standards. That system affects everything about public protests, including where, how, and when they may occur, how protest activities are policed (during ordinary times and in "emergencies"), whether one may come armed to a public protest, the costs and liabilities imposed on protest organizers and participants, and the remedies available to protest organizers and participants.

MANAGED DISSENT

Greg Magarian has criticized the Supreme Court's recent free speech decisions for adopting a "managed speech" perspective. He has argued the Court's decisions generally favor social order and established institutions over a culture of disruptive expression.[20] This book borrows Magarian's managerial nomenclature and critique, but applies it to the system of law that limits public protest activity. The Court's decisions and the laws, regulations, and norms that have sprouted from them generally favor the status quo over socially disruptive protest and dissent. The law of public protest imposes a system of "managed dissent" that makes collective contention more dangerous, more expensive, less effective, and ultimately less likely to occur. In short, managed dissent overburdens protest in the service of societal and other forms of order.

Under the managerial system, which has been in force for at least half a century, public protest is obviously allowed to occur; however, it is subject to severe limitations. Managed dissent is rooted in the perspective that even peaceful protests are worrisome acts of public contention that must be strictly regulated in the name of order, safety, tranquility, and other government interests. The primary concern is the maintenance of public order. Under managed dissent, even minor disruptions of ordinary commerce and social life are valid justifications for the exercise of regulatory authority.

It has not always been so. The First Amendment's text protects the freedom of speech and the right to "peaceably" assemble with others. As Tabatha Abu El-Haj has shown, notions of "peaceably" have changed dramatically over the course of American history.[21] Her work has demonstrated that up until the nineteenth century, officials and courts were relatively tolerant of disruptive forms of public protest – even when they interfered with commerce or posed a potential threat to public order. As Abu El-Haj has written, "Nineteenth-century Americans had a much higher social and legal threshold for the irritations that come with democracy."[22]

Over time, however, this tolerance gradually eroded and was replaced by a more restrictive law of public protest. Today that law is predisposed to favor passive, polite, and "respectable" forms of demonstration. Managed dissent is manifested in doctrines that restrict access to public forums and allow government to limit the time, place, and manner of protest. It favors regulatory devices such as "free speech zones" and targeted place restrictions (TPRs) over freedom of movement and access to broad swaths of the public protest topography. As one commentator has noted, "It seems that, in general, acceptable or protected forms of protest are planned, scheduled, organized, and choreographed – they are set in locations and scheduled at times that do not disturb the smooth flow of traffic, of predictable consumer activity."[23]

In orientation and practice, managed dissent is antithetical to, or at least in considerable tension with, a supposed national commitment to robust and unreserved
public discourse.[24] The popular narrative is that the First Amendment operates as a
broad license for dissenters to engage in expression that agitates audiences, stirs people to anger, and disrupts daily life. But as discussed in greater detail in Chapter 2,
from a very early point in time, the Supreme Court has been most likely to protect
speech and assembly when these activities did *not* create unrest or threaten to disrupt the status quo.[25] Most significantly, the Court has never been disposed to treat
public protest as a fully legitimate and protected form of expression.

The Warren Court's rights revolution was, of course, the notable exception.
During the Civil Rights Movement, public protesters achieved some storied First
Amendment victories – even though their message was unwelcome, upsetting, and
purposefully disruptive to defenders of racial segregation. (So, by the way, did Ku
Klux Klansmen, who "won" the right to hurl racially derogatory invective so long as
it did not incite imminent unlawful action.)[26] Although the Civil Rights Movement
of the 1950s and 1960s publicly and expressly committed itself to peaceful and
orderly forms of public protest, direct actions including marches and sit-ins were
messy and disruptive of the then-prevailing social and political order.[27]

As discussed in Chapter 2, the Warren Court's decisions established important
First Amendment breathing space for public contention. Although they set what
would become a high-water mark for the protection of public protest, Supreme
Court precedents from this era also frequently emphasized that public demonstrations were "passive."[28] Further, even the Warren Court expressed ambivalence
regarding whether public protests and demonstrations were worthy of *full* First
Amendment protection. Robust protection was reserved for what the Court referred
to as "pure speech," in contrast to less-than-pure forms of expression such as demonstrating, marching, and picketing – speech, as one opinion described it, "brigaded
with action."[29] As Kalven observed at the time, the Court's opinions "bristled with
cautions and with a lack of sympathy for such forms of protest."[30]

Although modern First Amendment doctrines broadly protect contentious and
offensive messages and ideas, they create less physical and conceptual breathing
space for collective forms of dissent. Insofar as public protests are concerned, the
First Amendment's most robust protections have long been reserved for those who
curb their behavior or conform it to societal norms and expectations. Further, protest
policing has been infected by managerial biases and related abuses. As the nation
witnessed during the summer of 2020, even the most peaceful public assemblies
are frequently met with tear gas, non-lethal projectiles, and command-and-control
policing tactics.

Judicial skepticism of direct action, including street protests and pickets, has
profoundly influenced the law of public protest, which allows officials to manage
dissent by restricting movement, controlling time and place, and curbing disruption. Administrative codes, criminal laws, civil actions, protest policing, and other

forces all conspire against forms of protest that are not polite, compliant, orderly, and socially conformist.

Protesters generally have no First Amendment right to be seen or heard by their intended audiences, and no right to dissent in the place, at the time, or in the manner that they deem most effective.[31] As Occupy Wall Street demonstrated, they have no First Amendment right to calmly commandeer public places for extended periods. Indeed, those who fail to comply with a multitude of administrative and other prerequisites and conditions may be prevented from assembling at all. To ensure they do not step or march out of line, protesters are subject to a host of criminal and civil liabilities. Meanwhile, law enforcement officers who violate law-abiding protesters' First Amendment or other rights are very likely to escape accountability for their actions, owing to legal and constitutional doctrines that favor their discretionary use of force or immunize their unconstitutional behavior altogether.

Even before the tear gas dissipated in Minneapolis, Portland, Kenosha, and other cities where mass BLM protests occurred, there were already calls for more and broader public protest management. As noted earlier, Republican-controlled legislatures quickly churned out measures that increased the criminal penalties for protest-related offenses such as "riot" and "obstruction of passage," shifted the costs of cleanup and security to protest organizers, recognized new civil causes of action against protesters, declared offenders of broad new "riot" and other protest-specific laws ineligible for benefits including housing assistance, student loans, and state employment, and even immunized drivers who negligently ran over protesters in the streets.[32]

In the aftermath of recent mass protests, increasing managerial authority is precisely the wrong lesson to learn and direction to take. The First Amendment does not protect acts of violence and vandalism, which are already unlawful. There is no absolute right to protest in public. Some degree of public order is necessary. But the law of public protest ought to allow and even facilitate peaceful public protests – even if, perhaps *especially* if, they disrupt everyday routines, offend public audiences, and compel people to take notice. Public protest deserves full First Amendment recognition and protection, even when it is not passive and polite. As Jeremy Waldron has observed, "disorder and disruption are not pathological versions of demonstrating, as though a civically virtuous protest would be self-effacing."[33] Unfortunately, the system of managed dissent is based precisely on these conceptions of pathology and virtue.

PUBLIC ATTITUDES AND PUBLIC PROTEST

The law of public protest and the system of managed dissent are, at least in part, reactions to public concerns about the potential dangers associated with large public displays of contention and dissent. Many of the most restrictive aspects of this body of law developed in response to concerns about maintaining "law and order."

As we unpack and consider the laws regulating public protest activity, it is important to situate them in a broader narrative about public protest and public disorder in the United States.

Notwithstanding the nation's venerable tradition of public protest, Americans have a complicated relationship with this form of democratic activism. Many recognize the need to create and preserve public breathing space for people to communicate their grievances and celebrate both their differences and the traditions that bind them together. However, in general, Americans do not have a favorable view of public protests.

A recent aggregate review of polls regarding public protests concluded that "the public's overall attitude toward mass demonstrations seems to range from skepticism to outright condemnation. Historically, even the most popular protest events have support levels that hover below fifty percent, and positive responses to protest movements are rarely higher than negative ones."[34] Americans might support robust protest rights in the abstract, even if they do not tend to support specific movements. But other polling reveals a general and growing hostility to dissent and disruption. For instance, in one recent poll, more than half of the respondents agreed that individuals who publicly burn the U.S. flag should lose their citizenship and that controversial speakers should be banned from university campuses if students are likely to engage in violent protests in response to the speakers' visits.[35]

Although they may have strong views on protests, few Americans have traditionally participated in them. One recent survey put the number at approximately 15 percent of the adult population.[36] Although millions of Americans may participate, only a small percentage are actively engaged in this form of dissent and are shouldering most of the burden. The news is not all bad though. There have been recent upticks in both protest support and participation numbers. Data show that Americans' general support for public protests increased during Donald Trump's presidency.[37] Recent protests including the March for Life, Women's March, and BLM demonstrations have attracted large groups of participants. So have those focused on gun control, climate change, immigration restrictions, and healthcare. Finally, the largest share of protesters at the 2020 BLM protests consisted of those under 35 years of age, and many reported this was their first time getting involved in any form of public activism or demonstration.[38]

Americans' apparent ambivalence toward public protest likely has many causes and explanations. Part of what may be affecting the polling is media coverage of protests, which skews heavily toward conflict and violent episodes while ignoring mostly peaceful demonstrators. As Magarian has observed, "Whenever violence erupts in or around a protest, the dominant narrative portrays the protest as pervasively violent."[39] As he noted, that is a "dangerous fallacy to indulge if we care about sustaining a vibrant democracy."[40] Moreover, as Magarian points out, to the extent the narrative reinforces racist stereotypes, it is particularly harmful to people of color who participate disproportionately in public protests.[41]

When assessing the public's generally negative attitudes concerning public protest, we should not discount the influence of politicians and other opinion leaders. In recent years, high-level federal officeholders including Senator Mitch McConnell and former President Trump have denigrated both protests and protesters. They have referred to public protests as a form of "mob rule" and derided them as "embarrassing." Members of the Trump Administration, including the president himself, encouraged law enforcement and state militias to "dominate" the streets as a "battlespace" during protests and to charge protesters with "sedition." (The former president's attitude toward the Capitol insurrectionists has been notably different.)[42] Right-wing media outlets have echoed and amplified many of these sentiments, characterizing even peaceful protests as lawless and violent and protesters as domestic terrorists.

Public protests do impose actual costs in the form of noise, disruption, and individual acts of vandalism and violence. These costs are likely to be fueling some of the negative public attitudes concerning protest. Some Americans cannot (or simply refuse to) distinguish between lawful forms of "protest" and unlawful "riot" and hence are prone to characterize all collective forms of dissent as threats to public order. Like much else in modern American politics and culture, public protest has become sharply politicized. In broad terms, the ideological right has come to see public protest as "mob rule" rather than a form of legitimate democratic dissent (at least when engaged in by ideological opponents), while the left generally continues to support public protest as a legitimate means of public discourse. At the same time, some who supported (or did not publicly object to) protests near the homes of abortion providers adamantly oppose that same activity near the homes of Supreme Court Justices – and vice versa. In sum, to some degree, public attitudes about public protest are ideologically contingent.

As Magarian has observed, "protests are a *fluid, contestable, radically democratic* phenomenon."[43] For protesters and their supporters, these may all be positive attributes. For others, however, these same characteristics may be viewed as threats to social order. The tension between the core democratic need to engage in sometimes disruptive public contention and concerns about maintaining public order is a central concern of this book. How does a society that recognizes the value of public protest but prefers that it generally be orderly and peaceful balance these competing concerns? How do we preserve a robust culture of protest and dissent when so many forces are aligned against public displays of contention?

IN DEFENSE OF PUBLIC PROTEST

This book critically analyzes the law of public protest and the system of managed dissent this body of law models and sustains. It assumes that a robust culture of public protest and dissent is necessary to preserve democratic self-government and furthers other critically important First Amendment values.[44] Judging by opinion polling concerning public protest, a significant percentage of Americans do not share this assessment. Part of my burden, then, is to convince those who view public protest as unworthy of preservation that they are wrong – or at least suggest reasons why they should be more open to supporting it.

As noted, today's protesters can trace a lineage of dissent back to their colonial forbears, who frequently assembled, protested, and petitioned in public places – often disruptively and disrespectfully.[45] Indeed, early American protests sometimes included acts of vandalism, destruction of property, and even physical assault. Demonstrators tore down statues of King George, set fire to officials' homes, and destroyed private property.

Today many celebrate these protest pioneers not for their violent actions, which the First Amendment does not shield, but rather for their courage to dissent and the legacy of their contention. Large, disruptive demonstrations are not a new phenomenon in the U.S. America's founders well understood the potency of disruptive dissent, as have subsequent generations.

The acts of prior generations suggest that the law governing public protests ought to facilitate a culture of dissent rather than manage it into submission. Many of the reasons are rooted in the principal and well-known justifications for freedom of speech, assembly, and other expressive rights – the need to foster self-government, facilitate the search for political and other truths, and protect the speaker's autonomy in choosing how to communicate.[46]

Although protests are many things, they are fundamentally a means of expression. To be sure, as noted earlier the Supreme Court has expressed ambivalence about granting protest activity full First Amendment protection. In a decision since overturned, the Court indicated "such united and joint action involves even greater danger to the public peace and security than the isolated utterances and acts of individuals."[47] However, during the Civil Rights Era, the Court once described political demonstrations as the exercise of expressive rights "in their most pristine form."[48]

When they assemble in public places, protesters engage in a kind of augmented expression. The Court has recognized that "effective advocacy of both public and private points of view, particularly controversial ones, is undeniably enhanced by group association" and collective forms of expression.[49] Through collective expression, many protests seek to convey a message to governments, fellow citizens, or both.

One could simply rest a defense of public protest on the fact that some "speech" is involved, and the First Amendment protects the right of collective expression (at least to some degree). However, that would do public protest a disservice; its political and social values are much broader and deeper.

Some consider protest and dissent to be aspects of civic virtue. In this view, participation in such activities is a necessary predicate for self-government. Justice Louis Brandeis defended protection for group dissent in a famous concurring opinion in *Whitney v. California* (1927) – the same decision, incidentally, in which the Court's majority described political assemblies as dangerous.[50] In *Whitney*, Brandeis claimed "the greatest menace to freedom is an inert people" and that "public discussion is a political duty."[51] He relied on principles of civic republicanism, which hold that raising one's voice in protest is not merely a *right* one possesses but a *duty* one owes to the political community.

Leading justifications for freedom of speech, including the principle that public discourse facilitates self-governance and the search for truth, are based on the collective *democratic* benefits of expression. Public protest facilitates interaction among diverse groups of citizens in the public square. This is a necessary predicate for exercising democratic agency and engaging in public discourse on matters of public concern.[52] Public protest represents the politics of the people out of doors. It contributes to local, state, and national public discourses. By moving these conversations outside or beyond committee rooms and office suites and into public streets and other venues where the public gathers, protest democratizes political and other forms of dissent.

Public protest also increases the responsiveness and transparency of the government. Demonstrations and rallies communicate, in part, through their numbers and the physical presence of those in attendance. One of the unique things about protests is that they make bodies visible to both the public at large and public officials. Through their presence in public places, protesters demand recognition and notice from government officials and other intended audiences. In these and other ways, public protests amplify political and social identity claims that may not otherwise receive any – or at least not as much – public attention and sympathy.

Public protest also serves as a critically important safety valve for collective grievance and dissent. Environmental, immigration, abortion, firearms, and a variety of other groups have all gathered in public places to blow off political steam and make their voices heard. Public protests act as important outlets for grievance and dissent.

In addition to these collective benefits and interests, public protests support individual interests. Demonstrations allow people who feel oppressed or disregarded to physically demonstrate their presence on a public stage. For many, protest is a cathartic act of self-fulfillment. As one commentator noted, public protests are "often as much about increasing the individual's sense of power and self-actualization as they are about the actual content of the words spoken at such events."[53] Further, for many organizers and participants, protest has *dignitary* value separate and apart from any specific message the group seeks to convey or any collective enterprise.[54] In sum, for the individual, public protest is the performance of identity and solidarity, a public act of resistance to authority, and a rejection of the status quo.

Public protest also has strategic advantages relative to other forms of expression. Unlike emails, newspaper op-eds, and social media posts, public protests disrupt ordinary routines in public places. They can require drivers to change their routes, pedestrians to walk around or through certain areas, and some businesses to close their doors for a time. Because of these effects, protests are much more difficult to ignore than other kinds of expression. As the Supreme Court observed in a case involving restrictions on "sidewalk counselors" located outside abortion clinics:

> It is no accident that public streets and sidewalks have developed as venues for the exchange of ideas. Even today, they remain one of the few places where a speaker can be confident that he is not simply preaching to the choir. With respect to other means of communication, an individual confronted with an uncomfortable message can always turn the page, change the channel, or leave the Web site. Not so on public streets and sidewalks. There, a listener often encounters speech he might otherwise tune out.[55]

Notably, the Court described the difficulty in avoiding public expression as "a virtue, not a vice."[56]

As Magarian has written, "without *noise* democracy dies."[57] Public protest is part of the soundtrack – the "noise" – of democracy. A self-governing and civic-minded people must be both willing and able to present their grievances in public places, including in collective form, to representatives and others in a way that makes them difficult to disregard. A society that boasts of its robust cultures of liberty and dissent must not only tolerate protest and dissent, but indeed *embrace* them as legitimate forms of democratic politics.

The COVID-19 pandemic provided a brief glimpse of what life might look like without the "noise" of public protest and dissent. If democracy dies without noise, government edicts that characterize public protest as "non-essential" and the prospect of empty public streets represent an acute crisis. Thankfully, as activists showed, not even a pandemic could fully suppress public protest. Given the constitutional, political, and social values related to public protest, we ought to make it easier, not harder, for individuals – whatever their political affiliation or point of view – to participate in collective expression. In light of recent events, many Americans may be experiencing a degree of "protest fatigue."[58] But a political community that values liberty, recognizes the values of robust public discourse, and believes in self-government must preserve ample breathing space for public protest and dissent.

PUBLIC PROTEST IN A MANAGERIAL SYSTEM

This book describes the law of public protest so that we may critically examine its effects and consider possible reforms. To the extent the law of public protest produces a system of managed dissent, it threatens an important aspect of democratic exchange and a peaceful channel of political change. Understanding how the managerial system works, in a holistic sense, can lead to reforms that provide more secure constitutional, legal, and political foundations for public protest and dissent.

Chapter 1 briefly discusses the scope of the concepts of "protest" and "dissent" at the heart of the book's analysis. It then elaborates on free speech and other values associated with public protest. The chapter closely examines how and what protests communicate, to whom, for whose benefit, and to what end(s). It also analyzes the complicated dynamics concerning the potential for protest violence and the government's frequent use of force against even peaceful protesters. It asks why the state generally views protests as threatening, and why we continue to witness aggressive forms of protest policing in the U.S.

Chapter 2 provides an overview of the basic rules of engagement for public protest – the legal, constitutional, and other sources of authority that together constitute the law of public protest. It begins with a discussion of the roots of managed dissent in Supreme Court precedents. The chapter then discusses the law of public protest, much of which arises from First Amendment doctrines. It offers a basic taxonomy of protests, which distinguishes among peaceful and lawful, peaceful but unlawful, and violent and unlawful protest activities. Working from this conceptual framework, the chapter summarizes the legal and other restrictions on where, what, and how protesters can lawfully assemble and communicate. It gives special attention to law enforcement's broad discretionary power to enforce public order laws in ways that disperse even peaceful protests and the use of aggressive protest policing tactics. The chapter also describes several additional aspects of the law of public protest: the presence of firearms at public demonstrations, civil causes of action that expose organizers and participants to significant monetary damages, a "campus management system" that limits protest on university campuses, the invocation and exercise of governmental "emergency" powers during public health emergencies and periods of civil unrest, and severe restrictions on protesters' remedies for constitutional violations. Individual aspects of this body of law are discussed in subsequent chapters.

Chapter 3 examines legal and other restrictions on the place or location of public protests. It emphasizes the strategic and expressive dimensions of protest placement and criticizes First Amendment doctrines that allow governments to displace protesters. In addition to criticizing the public forum doctrine for shrinking the protest topography, the chapter discusses spatial management tactics including restrictive "free speech zones" and the militarization of public forums during protest events. It also addresses laws that limit or ban protest activity in specific places including abortion clinics, government plazas, the residences of public officials and judges, and areas of "critical infrastructure" such as oil and gas pipelines. The chapter closes with a consideration of the relationship between what the Supreme Court has called the "modern public square" of social media and more traditional public forums. It emphasizes that the "old" and "new" public squares are both critically important to facilitating and preserving public protest.

Chapter 4 focuses on the rising costs of participating in public protest. It examines the various costs and liabilities that may be imposed on protest organizers, participants, and supporters. Monetary costs include permit fees, cleanup costs, policing charges, and insurance liability mandates. These can add up to many thousands of dollars, and in some cases substantially more. On top of these "traditional" costs of dissent, protest organizers and participants sometimes face civil penalty enhancements and punitive damages. They may also be liable for damages under a wide variety of civil causes of action. These include increasingly novel theories of liability, including "negligent protest organizing," "riot boosting," "wrongful petitioning," and "aiding and abetting defamation." These lawsuits can result in the imposition of crushing civil damages awards, as well as attorney's fees and court costs. The rising costs of dissent may deter or chill individuals from organizing, participating in, or supporting protests or demonstrations. After considering various forms of protester self-help to contain these costs, the chapter addresses Supreme Court precedents and First Amendment principles that impose strict limits on protesters' costs and flatly prohibit some of the civil causes of action. It encourages courts and policymakers to take action to contain the rising costs of dissent.

Chapter 5 examines the application of the law of public protest to university campuses. Historically hotbeds of political and social contention, campuses have been transformed by the law of public protest. Officials have borrowed permitting requirements, forum distinctions, time, place and manner regulations, and other parts of the law of public protest to manage public demonstrations that occur inside campus gates. University administrators have exhibited some of the same pathologies as government officials regulating protest elsewhere, including resorting to strict and detailed limits on how, when, and where protests can occur. Like their off-campus counterparts, university administrators are facing increased tension concerning the scope of free speech rights in their communities, the presence of provocative speakers, and the management of hostile students and other audiences. Americans are having a robust national debate regarding the extent to which universities can or should restrict speech and assembly on campus. Relying in part on my experience as the co-chair of an ad hoc committee on First Amendment rights on the William & Mary campus, the chapter identifies and assesses obstacles to organizing, participating in, and regulating campus protests. Places of higher learning have special managerial authorities and must consider communal interests in belonging and inclusion along with expressive rights. However, they have traditionally served as incubators of active and engaged citizens. We must ensure that the nation's campuses remain places where communities not only tolerate the exchange of ideas but also, to the full extent possible, welcome and facilitate that exchange.

Chapter 6 examines the bearing of firearms at public protests, which has recently become a more frequent phenomenon. The Supreme Court has now held that the Second Amendment applies outside the home. However, gun-related fatalities during recent demonstrations confirm that firearms and free speech cannot safely coexist at public protests. New evidence shows that the presence of firearms intimidates protesters and interferes with their peaceful assembly and protest rights. Arming public protests is, moreover, inconsistent with democratic commitments to peaceful means of democratic change. The chapter focuses on the actions state and local authorities can take to ensure the safety of protesters as they exercise First

Amendment rights. It concludes that neither the Second Amendment nor the First Amendment prohibits the enactment of bans or restrictions on the public carrying of firearms at permitted events. At the very least, it concludes states can likely ban the two most intimidating forms of confrontation in the public forum: armed groups and the open display of firearms.

Chapter 7 addresses public protest rights during periods of instability, specifically during public health emergencies and civil unrest. Recent experience with pandemic-inspired "stay-at-home" orders has highlighted the surprising contingency of First Amendment rights. Governments declared public protest a "nonessential activity," making even peaceful public protest unlawful. The COVID-19 pandemic raised fundamental questions about the government's power to limit or even ban public protests during health emergencies. Similar questions arose during the civil unrest that followed the murder of George Floyd. In addition to closing public forums and dispersing peaceful protesters with tear gas and other aggressive tactics, officials invoked seldom-used federal laws prohibiting insurrection and riots and authorizing the deployment of the U.S. military to protest venues. The chapter addresses the delicate balance between the government's interests in health, public order, and safety and the protection of First Amendment rights to protest government policies even – perhaps especially – during public emergencies. It argues courts should be wary of government edicts declaring peaceable assembly and speech "non-essential activities" and equally skeptical of broad restrictions on protest activities during declared or undeclared emergencies. When it comes to the federal government's role in policing domestic political protests, the chapter urges officials and courts to interpret existing grants of authority narrowly and avoid escalating tensions through deployments and rhetoric.

Chapter 8 addresses the remedies protest organizers, participants, and supporters can pursue in the event their constitutional rights are violated. The principal legal remedy for unlawful actions against public protesters is a federal civil rights lawsuit. However, such actions are notoriously difficult to win. Immunity doctrines often protect federal, state, and local authorities from paying monetary damages. The doctrine of "qualified immunity" broadly immunizes state and local officials who violate First Amendment and other constitutional rights when no "clearly established law" indicates their actions were unlawful. As the Supreme Court has stated, qualified immunity "provides ample protection to all but the plainly incompetent or those who knowingly violate the law."[59] The Court has also hamstrung protesters and others who claim law enforcement retaliated against them for engaging in protected speech and assembly. Finally, the Court's precedents strongly suggest protesters cannot bring *any* First Amendment claims against federal officials. The chapter takes a critical look at these remedial limitations. It presents original data concerning how these obstacles have affected public protest organizers and participants, and identifies "clearly established" law concerning protesters' First Amendment rights. The chapter joins many others in calling on the Court or Congress to eliminate or significantly reform qualified immunity, restore civil rights remedies for retaliatory actions, and recognize federal officials' liability for First Amendment violations. In the event federal institutions are unwilling or unable to act, states and localities should continue to reform their qualified immunity laws.

Chapter 9 concludes by identifying a variety of measures and proposals that can help preserve public protest. Some aspects of the managed dissent system, including the "public forum" doctrine, are so deeply embedded that the Supreme Court is not likely to reconsider them. However, several specific reforms and changes are within reach. The chapter offers ten general proposals: (1) judicial recognition and elaboration of independent First Amendment "assembly" and "petition" rights; (2) review and overhaul of administrative codes and permitting schemes to ensure First Amendment compliance; (3) more skeptical judicial review of protest displacement tactics; (4) protest policing reform, with a focus on training and supervision; (5) amendment and more limited enforcement of public disorder offenses that restrict public protest; (6) reduction of the costs of dissent, including limits on civil protest liability; (7) reform or abolition of qualified and other immunities for state and federal officials who violate protesters' constitutional rights; (8) holistic review of campus policies on free speech and assembly to ensure protection for protest and dissent; (9) banning or significantly restricting the bearing of arms at public protests; and (10) more careful definition and narrowing of state and federal powers to suppress public protest during public health and civil unrest emergencies.

To summarize, the book offers a comprehensive and critical examination of the law of public protest. It affirmatively supports and defends public protest activities and the American tradition of public contention. The book argues in favor of reducing several burdens on public protest and dissent. It presents an honest, if often unflattering, picture of the extent to which the First Amendment protects speech, assembly, and petition rights in connection with public protests. Finally, the book offers various solutions and strategies, both within the bounds of current law and in connection with proposed reforms, for preserving public protest.

1

Protest, Dissent, and Democracy

This is a book about the laws that apply to public protest. As discussed in the Introduction, it is premised on the notion that preserving a robust culture of public protest and dissent is necessary for the functioning of our constitutional democracy. Before turning to the law of public protest, this chapter first describes the acts and concepts of "protest" and "dissent" at the center of the book's arguments. It then considers the purposes and values of public protest. What democratic or other values are associated with public protests? Why do people demonstrate and dissent in public assemblies? To whom are they communicating? What benefits do protesters and the political community at large derive from such activities? Laws and judicial precedents have strikingly little to say about such matters. However, to understand what is at stake in the adoption, enforcement, and potential reform of the law of public protest, it is necessary to have some understanding of the values associated with public protest and the motives, purposes, and aspirations of those who organize and participate in them.

"PROTEST" AND "DISSENT"

The law of public protest regulates certain types of acts and activities, namely "protest" and "dissent." There is no legal or theoretical consensus regarding the definition of either term.[1] But I want to be clear about the types of activities the book is primarily concerned with defending and preserving. Chapter 2 will describe several different protest "types" and where these might be situated in terms of the First Amendment and other legal frameworks. The book does not propose an "ideal type" of protest.[2] As an introduction to the arguments and claims in the book, however, it is helpful to have a general sense of the activities governed by the law of public protest.

In the broadest sense, a protest is a declaration of dissent or disapproval. According to one of several dictionary definitions, protest is "a solemn declaration of opinion and usually of dissent."[3] Hence, we can generally think of protest as a statement or action expressing disapproval of or objection to something – a government policy, for example, or the actions of the police.

Protests can take many different forms. They can be formally lodged against an official for performing an allegedly unlawful act or abusing their power. In a broad sense, a whistleblower report made to a government agency is a "protest." So is the leaking of classified information.

However, the protests I am concerned with generally take more public and collective forms – for example, demonstrations, marches, rallies, pickets, and parades. In general, the book conceives of a "public protest" as an assembly of individuals gathered in a public place for the purpose of communicating about a matter of public concern to a public audience. This conception of "protest" excludes actions such as whistleblowing and leaking of classified or secret documents. That is not to say these are not important acts of protest. But because they lack critical "public" attributes or characteristics, they are not the primary focus of the law of public protest or this book. As we will see, the law of public protest is concerned primarily with "managing" protests of a more public and collective kind.

The objects and audiences for this kind of protest are typically – though, as we will see, not always – governments or public officials. These institutions and individuals represent the status quo or some action that has given rise to public disapproval. Of course, public protest actions do not *always* or invariably target public officials or governments. A protest can be aimed at private parties, such as when activists engage in economic boycotts or picket private residences.

While the book is principally concerned with collective actions in public venues such as streets and parks, not every "public protest" neatly fits this mold. Not all protests boast large crowds. Indeed, a single individual speaking on a street corner is engaged in a type of "public protest." And this kind of activity surely would be governed by the law of public protest.

At the margins of concern in terms of the book's scope, a constituent who reaches out to public officials to object to some government project or policy may also be engaged in an act of "public protest" – even though the communication occurs through more private channels and does not involve a public audience (at least initially). Some aspects of the "law of public protest" may apply to this kind of activity, which is "public" in the sense that the speaker is communicating with a *public* official about a matter of *public* concern. Again, although I am principally concerned with more traditional forms of public protest, there is some room in my conception for "protests" that do not share all their characteristics.

In substance, as the dictionary definition indicates, the kinds of protest the book addresses typically oppose something: the BLM protests opposed police brutality and systemic racism, the Tea Party protests opposed government-run healthcare, the March for Life opposed access to abortion, and so on. However, the expression of opinion need not be negative in either substance or tone to fall within the domain of the law of protest. Protests may also communicate opinions *in support of* some right, policy, or idea. Indeed, the BLM and Tea Party protests may be recast as protests *for* racial justice and limited government, respectively. A gay pride parade supporting equal rights, while also decrying unequal treatment, protests in both positive and negative registers. In general, protests are often animated by the rejection of status-quo conditions that demonstrators believe fail to sufficiently value the right, policy, or idea they support. For example, the March for Our Lives protests criticized lax gun regulations, climate change rallies objected to the slow pace of climate-focused policymaking, and right-to-life protests decry recognition of a right to abortion.

The book is centrally concerned with identifying and analyzing the rights, liabilities, and remedies of "protesters." Although participants' rights are of central concern, the law of public protest also extends to those who help organize, facilitate, encourage, or support public protests. Thus, the book discusses the free speech and assembly rights of organizers and supporters of protest movements, as well as their potential civil liabilities for damages related to demonstrations and other protest events.

Protests typically communicate or are acts of *dissent*. Protest and dissent are thus closely related concepts. As noted, public protests often involve dissent in the general sense of *disagreeing with* some policy or objecting to some prejudice or condition. Thus, protests may be a manifestation or type of dissent. Both protest and dissent are intentional, critical, and *public* – in the broad sense that they occur in or are connected in some way to the public realm.[4]

However, protest and dissent can also be meaningfully distinguished. According to some scholars, because of its deep historical, social, and normative foundations, dissent is protest's "nobler cousin."[5] It is perhaps "nobler" because it is a more deeply rooted legal and theoretical concept than "protest." For these reasons, perhaps, dissent seems to enjoy a higher degree of social tolerance and normative acceptance in American society than does protest. As a form of "protest-plus," dissent can help flesh out the core values associated with expressing one's public opposition or disagreement through acts of speech and assembly.[6]

Dissent is about speaking truth to power. According to Steve Shiffrin, dissent is "speech that criticizes existing customs, habits, traditions, institutions, or authorities."[7] Sometimes dissent is communicated through mass protests and demonstrations. However, like protest, dissent is not limited to this form. The concept extends to the communication, through whatever form, of "popularly disdained views."[8] On this view, dissent is part of the broader liberty of self and a manifestation of self-realization, self-expression, and identity.[9] Such "elevated values" may be less often associated with the idea of "protest."[10] Unlike a messy or disruptive public protest, linguistic, intellectual, and societal conceptions of "dissent" are sometimes linked to deeply held beliefs and intellectual ideals. To note the distinction is not necessarily to embrace it; protest *could* also be associated with these "elevated values." In any event, as noted, thinking in terms of "dissent" can help clarify what is at stake when public protest is subject to regulation.

Dissent has a deeply rooted tradition in America and a special hold on the American imagination. As Ralph Young's important study of dissent's history in the U.S. shows, "Americans have instinctively understood, even if unconsciously, the interrelatedness of dissent and what it means to be an American. Dissent created this nation, and it played, indeed still plays, a fundamental role in fomenting change and pushing the nation in sometimes-unexpected directions."[11] There is a strong historical link between dissent and "patriotism." As Young observes, dissent is "one of the consummate expressions of 'Americanness.' It *is* patriotic in the deepest sense."[12]

Dissent is an expression of non-conformance, a statement of opposition by outsiders directed at those in power. Like protest, dissent does not play ideological favorites. Tea Party members, environmentalists, anti-lockdown activists, pro-life protesters, pro-gun rights demonstrators, Occupy Wall Street protesters, and BLM demonstrators have all challenged the status quo or contested some form of group orthodoxy. Individuals in these groups have conveyed public opposition to power structures by speaking their truth to power.

In their detailed study of dissent, Ron Collins and David Skover suggest dissent is revered in part because it entails some form of risk of adverse consequences – "from public condemnation and social ostracism to personal injury and imprisonment."[13] Part of what contributes to dissent's normative power is the fact that dissenters expose themselves to such personal risks. Speaking truth to power can have significant economic, physical, and other consequences. As we will see, these consequences have deeply affected those who engage in what might be characterized as less "cerebral" forms of dissent. Like dissenters, many protesters commit to their beliefs and hold firm to them whatever the consequences.[14]

Like protest, dissent serves a variety of instrumental purposes. As Steve Shiffrin notes, because they "seek coverts and colleagues," dissenters foster "engaged association" rather than atomistic individualism.[15] Cass Sunstein likewise posits that dissent encourages "independence of mind" and "imparts a willingness to challenge prevailing opinion through both words and deeds."[16] He argues dissent helps counteract the detrimental effects of group polarization, an acute problem, especially in our digital era.[17] Sunstein notes that when not confronted with dissenting views, homogenous groups end up taking more extreme positions.[18] Dissenters, he argues, reduce the effects of polarization. Sunstein encourages not just granting constitutional protection for dissent, but the need to preserve a *culture* of dissent that "encourages independence of mind" and "a certain set of attitudes in listeners, one that gives a respectful hearing to those who do not embrace the conventional wisdom."[19]

Many of these instrumental reasons for protecting dissent extend to protest more generally. As discussed, protesters participate in a form of engaged association, seek converts, and contribute to a diverse culture of dissent.

Both protest and dissent share conceptual space with the concept of "civil disobedience" – conscientious breaches of law for which actors take full responsibility.[20] Individuals and groups can register dissent through purposeful breaches of law, such as trespass, obstruction of passage, or disorderly conduct. Though often expressive or related to expression, these forms of dissent are not generally protected by the First Amendment. Those who participate in a sit-in or street blockade are subject to legal punishment for breaking applicable laws. More violent forms of civil – or even *uncivil* –[21] disobedience such as arson, violent rioting, or assault are also outside the domain of the First Amendment's protection. Conceptually, civil disobedience qualifies as a form of protest and dissent. However, given its lawbreaking character, many dismiss it as a form of legitimate dissent.

Although they are acts of dissent, violent actions such as the January 6, 2021, Capitol riot or the burning of public buildings are not considered legitimate forms of dissent and are not protected by the First Amendment.[22] However, we ought not to be too quick to rule out the possibility that *non-violent* lawbreaking should be entitled to at least some First Amendment consideration.[23] Dissent comes in many forms. In seeking to preserve a venerable tradition of dissent, we should not view every minor law infraction – every street blockage or other act of disruption – as fully or inexorably beyond the First Amendment's concern. As some have suggested, perhaps courts should reject felony penalties for minor acts of expressive civil disobedience and limit the liability of protest organizers when these sorts of infractions occur.[24] As Collins and Skover observe, "the notion of dissent stands to expand the domain of the First Amendment, properly interpreted."[25] Providing at least some measure of protection for minor infractions committed during acts of civil disobedience is consistent with that goal.

In considering what is and is not "legitimate" dissent, we must also be aware of the racial implications of how one defines "disruptive" or "uncivil" dissent. As Juliet Hooker argues, "Black anger is hardly ever accepted as a legitimate response to political, social, and economic grievances."[26] Hooker observes that "Black politics has been uniquely constrained by expectations of democratic civility in the face of deadly racial injustice."[27] Moreover, Black dissenters may *want* to be viewed as radical and provocative rather than "civil." We should recognize that as a means of persuading the powerful to act justly, some dissenters may choose moral outrage and certain forms of incivility, disruption, and civil disobedience over reasoned discourse.[28]

This perspective argues against idealizing and romanticizing the tactics of the Civil Rights Movement of the 1950s and 1960s. We ought not to automatically view more offensive or confrontational forms of dissent as illegitimate or threatening. As Hooker observes, dissent is not, for everyone, "a project of democratic repair."[29] She notes that "African American political thought has long recognized that the value of dissent exceeds its communicative potential, i.e., its effect on spectators."[30] In sum, as we consider *why* people engage in acts of protest and dissent and how these acts are managed pursuant to the law of public protest, it is important to appreciate how and why different people participate in public acts of contention and how they experience the exercise of managerial authority.

WHAT PROTEST AND DISSENT COMMUNICATE – AND TO WHOM

What is the actual *point* of a protest or demonstration? What does it signify and what functions does it serve – for its participants, its audiences, and perhaps society at large? The answers to these fundamental questions are important both to defending the American legacy of protest and dissent and analyzing the effects of the law of public protest on its subjects. While some legal scholars, myself included, have addressed these matters, I will also draw on the work of political theorists to unpack the "what" and "to whom" of protest.[31]

Protests, demonstrations, pickets, and rallies typically express an opinion about a political or other issue, either in opposition to or in support of something. The physical presence of protesters, particularly in large assemblies, manifests or shows that opposition or support to the public.[32] As the political theorist Jeremy Waldron observes, in this way a protest makes something – an idea, grievance, or cause – manifest and undeniable to its audiences.[33] Showing up and showing out are important characteristics of events intended, as he writes, "to rivet the audience's attention in real time on the propositions being put forward."[34]

Even during the heyday of public protest, the Civil Rights Era, the Supreme Court waffled on the question of whether collective protest is a form of *conduct* or *speech* for First Amendment purposes.[35] But anyone who recently watched millions gathered in the public streets to protest police brutality understood this display as a means of communicating or delivering a pointed message. The demonstrators communicated a demand to hold police accountable and urged changes in public discourse on racial equality.[36]

As Waldron writes, during a protest event "a form of public courage becomes shared and publicly so."[37] Visibility in *public* places is a key component or function of a demonstration or rally. Protest in these forms "makes a grievance or a demand visible through defiant human presence in a place where the public have access."[38] The "grievance" and "defiance" of protest are sometimes one and the same. For example, "anti-lockdown" public protests opposed COVID-19 policies by openly and visibly defying them.

The meaning of protest is inseparable from its public character. According to John Rawls, political protest is "a mode of address taking place in the public forum."[39] As discussed in Chapter 3, protest is deeply impacted by restrictions on access to public places such as streets, parks, and government plazas. Part of the message of the public protest or demonstration is communicated through "the public presence of a group or class of citizens for all to see – associating a set of political demands with their being there, standing there, walking there."[40] Meaning is conveyed through a form of embodied presence. As Waldron notes, "Sometimes the presence of the protesters is itself the message, or it conveys a powerful message implicitly."[41] A protest, he claims, "puts numbers on display; *here we are* in our thousands or hundreds of thousands."[42]

Analyzing the civil rights protests, John Berger once observed that protesting in public is a way of rehearsing revolutionary awareness.[43] He also noted that the choice and effect of location are critical to this rehearsal. Thus, it is no coincidence that public protests typically target highly symbolic civic and national places including official residences, police stations, state capitols, and the National Mall.

Nor should it come as a surprise that public protests often occur in urban areas. As one scholar has observed, "Protests disrupt territories of power and interject uncertainty, introduce explicit precariousness into the scheduled ongoingness of everyday life."[44] In urban locations, participants can significantly interrupt commerce and other "ordinary" daily activities. Although these activities occur in rural areas too, the nature and degree of disruption in urban centers are greater.

The protests that followed former President Donald Trump's initial "Muslim ban" at airports across the nation exemplify this "state of exception, where the normal flow of daily events is called into question through the contestation of a law or practice that is seen by the protesters to be unjust."[45] Civil Rights Era protesters who marched across bridges, BLM protesters who blocked streets, and Occupy Wall Street members who camped out in public parks and plazas all did so, in part, to disrupt the status quo. As Waldron observes, "A demonstration disrupts ordinary, quotidian uses of the public space – for promenading, sightseeing, picnicking, moving from one place to another."[46]

Disruptive protest activity helps assure people are seen and heard. Unlike a tweet or social media post, a public protest generally cannot be tuned out or avoided – or, worse, screened out in advance. The disruption is, as Waldron writes, "troublesome," by which he means "disruptive of ordinary routines like traffic on the street or peace in the park."[47] However, this does not mean protest disorder and disruption are "pathological versions of demonstrating, as though a civically virtuous protest would be self-effacing."[48] Rather, we ought to understand disruption as a *virtue*, rather than a vice, of protest.[49] It is a central part of the message being delivered by public protesters.

Physical occupation of public places is one type of disruption. But disrupting commerce and other aspects of daily life is not the only point. Sometimes protesters take steps to alter the meaning of the public places they occupy. For example, in Richmond, Virginia, BLM protesters altered the physical appearance and symbolism of Lee Circle, formerly home to a looming statue honoring Confederate General Robert E. Lee. What had been a mostly defunct public space dominated by a monument to the Confederacy was transformed during the summer of 2020 into a new, more diverse communal space by protesters no longer willing to accept the monument's presence in their community. BLM protesters repurposed and reimagined the space in a way that not only disrupted its ordinary usage but ultimately changed its meaning. During the protests, groups constructed memorials to victims of police violence, planted flowers, and engaged in recreational activities in Lee Circle. They also tagged the Lee monument in ways that repurposed and reimagined it as a symbol of oppression.

As important as these communicative functions are, public protest is not just a means of collective expression. Protests and demonstrations are also *self-affirming* events. As Nick Suplina has observed, "Demonstrations are often as much about increasing the individual's sense of power and self-actualization as they are about the actual content of the words spoken at such events."[50] Gathering in the public square, with others, expresses not just political ideas but also emotions, feelings, and a sense of solidarity.[51] Protest, in this sense, is about self-actualization.

Another function of protest is to encourage those assembled to view themselves as part of a class of individuals with collective strength. Amna Akhbar has described protest as "an expression of feeling, a tool of constituting a political community alternative to the mainstream and communicating to other similarly situated people."[52] One measure of success, she argues, is whether the protests grow this base.[53]

Finally, Mari Matsuda has observed that protests and demonstrations also have a "dignitarian element."[54] She has written about the way civil rights protests dignified their participants by forcing recognition of their rights to equal access to accommodations and equal treatment under the law. The protests communicated a message of equality, but also a demand for recognition of the fundamental dignity and humanity of those who organized and participated in them. As Matsuda's work confirms, the communicative and dignitarian elements of protest are often inseparable or, as Waldron puts it, "tangled together."[55]

As these protest functions confirm, the message or communication of a protest may have multiple target audiences – some external and others internal to the event or cause. Some demonstrators appeal to the government in a direct sense. Judging at least by their outward manifestations, public protests often aim to influence policies and directives by showing mass support for change or reform.[56]

However, protesters may also communicate with non-state audiences. As John Berger observed, "It would seem that the true function of demonstrations is not to convince the existing State authorities to any significant degree."[57] Berger surmised the state may lack the democratic conscience demonstrators might be appealing to anyway. Rather, he suggested, the real aim of a public protest is to demonstrate to participants and those witnessing the event an opportunity for a revolution in thought or awareness of some public issue.[58] Thus, in some sense, "protest can also be thought of as addressing *itself*. Those who gather, assemble to solemnly object, can have the experience of recognition, of belonging to a whole."[59] Civil rights protests, including recent BLM demonstrations, clearly meet this description – as do a host of others.

DEMONSTRATING AS/AND DEMOCRACY

Demonstrating in public with others is a physical and vocal manifestation of democratic citizenship and other First Amendment values. Public protests and demonstrations are proof of democracy in action and tangible evidence of citizen self-government.[60] Demonstrations, rallies, and the like are also physical and tangible marketplaces of ideas.[61] They contribute to a culture of robust public discourse. Certainly, they are not always venues for what many would consider "polite" discourse and conversation. But while public protests tend to be more "uninhibited, robust, and wide-open" in form and character, they are acts of self-governance that contribute something important to discourse on matters of public concern.[62]

Organizing or participating in a public protest is an exercise of civic duty. In one of the Supreme Court's earliest cases testing the boundaries of political dissent through association, Justice Louis Brandeis posited that "the greatest menace to freedom is an inert people; that public discussion is a political duty; and that this should be a fundamental principle of American government."[63] Brandeis went on to observe, "Those who won our independence were not cowards. They did not fear political change. They did not exalt order at the expense of liberty."[64]

As Greg Magarian has noted, "without *noise*, democracy dies."[65] Public protest is a central aspect of the "noise" that has thus far sustained American democracy. As discussed, it forces officials and fellow citizens to take notice of grievances and concerns shared by many in their communities. A public place where protest occurs is, or at least can be, "a place of political truth."[66] Protests contribute to marketplaces in public discourse – in part, as noted, by seeking to alter the course or direction of conversations in those marketplaces.[67] However, managerial interventions can alter or even suppress protest messages. These interventions are justified in the minds of lawmakers, courts, and a sizable portion of the public by overriding interests in peace, order, tranquility, repose, and even aesthetics. However, at a certain point, managerial control turns an event with democratic potential into a spectacle of state control.

As subsequent chapters will show, the system of managed dissent interrupts the search for truth in the public square and seeks to quiet the "noise" of public protest. Managing dissent is a response to the disruptions – both real and imagined – associated with public protest. Governments respond to protesters by forcing them, whenever possible, to comply with permits, provide advance notice of their activities, respect spatial limitations including "free speech zones," and accept other mechanisms of control. The system of managed dissent neutralizes radical action by forcing participants to do things like file into pens and zones – structures which are, of course, built by the same officials that protesters often oppose.[68] These limits are backed up by discretionary law enforcement authority to arrest protesters for even minor infractions. As we will see, the tools and tactics of managed dissent significantly limit opportunities for public speech and assembly and reduce the public space available for public protest activities.

As these restrictions indicate, the relationship between government and public demonstrations is deeply problematic. Although protests and demonstrations are critical means of self-governance and self-actualization, governments fear them. So, they discount the number of participants and, far more concerning, react aggressively toward even peaceful protests.[69] Waldron surmises that government officials may "fear and denounce demonstrations ... because of an implicit worry about being coerced."[70] They may fear the prospect of small-scale or large-scale insurrection. That fear often translates into efforts to standardize, neutralize, and control protest events through managerial tools and force.

Governments may also react negatively to protests owing to their general message. Officials may view demonstrating as a means of undermining their own legitimacy – "the most important pillar of power."[71] Demonstrations communicate that governments do not have complete control of what happens in public places they own and manage. Relatedly, governments may not like the act of demonstrating because it "interrupts the government's narrative. It is the opposite of public acclamation; it's a display of the government's unpopularity (on some issue), an undeniable manifestation of dissent. It shows that some brave portion of the public is fed up."[72]

The negative official response to protest may also relate, in part, to a simple economic calculus. Legislators may be pricing protest "out of the market" to reduce its disruptive costs.[73] If governments prefer economic stability, "[t]he protester as such becomes a public enemy, a burden to the taxpayers."[74] Measures that shift the costs of protest to those exercising speech and assembly rights, increase penalties for even peaceful protesting, and provide a form of limited legal immunity to those who drive into a public assembly blocking the street all suggest there may be an economic calculus at play.[75] Placing a "right to drive" above concerns for the safety or life of disruptive protesters speaks volumes about the state's cost-benefit calculus.[76]

Official reactions like these seem to be based on the notion that protest is deeply destabilizing. However, as one commentator observed:

> Far from destabilising democracy, protest has been instrumental in forcing the introduction of most of the freedoms that now exist in liberal democracies. Direct action, mostly nonviolent, played a major role in the ending of slavery, extension of the franchise, curtailing ruthless aspects of the exploitation of labour and extending rights to women and minorities.[77]

These changes did not come about "in calm contemplation but in the aftermath of social revolution or turmoil."[78] They occurred because debate on public matters was, at least some of the time, "uninhibited, robust, and wide-open" and disruptive of the status quo.[79]

In U.S. history, public protests, though often disruptive and sometimes even violent, have been an important aspect of democratic discourse and contention. Tabatha Abu El-Haj has shown that American protests have traditionally been disruptive affairs, and that for most of U.S. history the public and public officials were tolerant of what she refers to as "the irritations that come with democracy."[80] She writes:

> The notion that public dissent – given its implicit threat of violence – poses a threat to legitimate political processes and thus to liberal democracy

fundamentally misconstrues both the history and practice of popular sovereignty in the United States. Discordant protest has been a central tactic of our
democratic politics since the Founding – one that was explicitly protected by the
First Amendment.[81]

In many respects, today's orientation toward public protest is fundamentally at
odds with early American tradition. Abu El-Haj concludes that "Nineteenth-
century Americans had a much higher social and legal threshold for the irritations
that come with democracy."[82] Today, by contrast, many Americans seem far less
tolerant and supportive of democratic disruption and far more apprehensive of
public protest.

One reason for the discomfort may be that protest challenges the status quo.
Protest activity is engaged in disproportionately by marginalized groups seeking to
disrupt the way things are. These groups turn to public protest and other forms of
direct action to effectuate democratic change. Although the "normal channels" are
inherently biased in favor of powerful economic and other interests, scholars have
noted that reliance on protest activities by minority and marginalized groups tends
to be treated as problematic. Meanwhile, maneuvers by dominant groups, including
some direct action, largely escape scrutiny. As Brian Martin has suggested, "Direct
action by outsider groups is seen differently because it is a threat to the usual acqui-
escence on which the political system is based."[83] That "threat" is precisely why
protest by the most marginalized groups is not a threat to self-government but strong
evidence of it.

Public protest democratizes politics by creating a space for groups to assemble
and communicate pressing grievances to the government and other audiences. It
provides a critical outlet for political and social grievances and checks governmental
abuses of power.[84] Further, when it is protected and facilitated, protest contributes
to a culture of tolerance in which diverse views can be freely communicated.[85]
Public protest is evidence that an engaged, self-governing people is unafraid to contest power and register its discontent with the status quo.

PROTEST, VIOLENCE, AND FORCE

Despite their many virtues, we cannot ignore or completely discount the possibility
that some public protests will be, or will become, violent events. The relationship
among public protest, private violence, and state-sponsored force is complex. But it
is crucial to address the violent dimension of public protest up front.

When Parliament passed the Stamp Act, "colonists took to the streets in protest:
effigies of tax collectors were burned, royal officials were tarred and feathered, and
in Boston, mobs destroyed government offices and even demolished and plundered
the lieutenant governor's residence."[86] Today many would describe these as the acts
of "anarchists" and "rioters." But if pressed, they might just as likely express some
admiration for those who participated in the Stamp Act protests, the Boston Tea

Party, and other notable early protests as American patriots. It can be difficult to separate the form of protest from its causes and to answer the question of when, if ever, violent protest is justified.

The book does not attempt to answer that question. As a matter of law, violence is not protected expression. But recognizing that direct action can indeed become violent has implications in terms of the law of public protest and the system of managed dissent. There is no shortage of examples of America's streets becoming sites of violent – even deadly – confrontation. The January 6, 2021, storming of the U.S. Capitol is only the most recent reminder that public assemblies can pose a danger to public order and safety.

Protest participants sometimes engage in the destruction of property and other unlawful activities. As noted, the First Amendment does not protect this activity. Under the law of public protest, governments have the power to punish this type of activity.

Protesters are not the only source of violence. Counter-protesters and other third parties sometimes also engage in violence at demonstrations. These individuals and groups take advantage of the protest environment to encourage anarchy or push some other agenda. Thus, public protests can attract agitators who do not share the movement's goals or indeed purposefully act in ways that undermine those goals and public protest more generally.[87] When assessing the relationship between protest and violence, it is important to understand protest organizers do not control who attends or participates in a public demonstration. At least some of the violence the public witnesses cannot be charged to protest organizers or participants.

More generally, it is important that we not falsely equate lawful demonstration and unlawful riot. A riot involves violence or property destruction by individuals as part of a group.[88] Protests and demonstrations in the U.S. typically lack these aspects; they are overwhelmingly peaceable and lawful events. Where, then, does the perception that protest is an inherently dangerous activity come from?

In part, this misunderstanding is related to how the media covers demonstrations. Media coverage tends to focus on violence and conflict to the exclusion of other aspects of public protest.[89] As Magarian has observed, "law enforcement and the media drastically overstate the prevalence of violence in public protests, ... and misleadingly blur the distinction between violent and non-violent protesters.[90] Whenever there is any violence at or near a public protest, the media's tendency is to report that the protest was pervasively violent.[91] Any violence "on the streets," even if it is not part of a demonstration, is falsely attributed to "protesting." This leaves the impression that only "fringe" elements of society participate in public protests. As Magarian observes, that is a "dangerous fallacy to indulge if we care about sustaining a vibrant democracy."[92]

The false impression that protests are actual riots or riots-in-waiting also has deep and troubling racial implications. As Magarian notes, given their over-representation at social justice and other public protests, "[t]he fallacy of the violent protest narrative is especially harmful to communities of color."[93] Exaggerations of protest violence, he observes, "in addition to undermining democracy, often reinforce racist stereotypes of people of color as violent criminals."[94]

Anarchists and rioters challenge the status quo through unprotected violence rather than lawful speech and peaceable assembly. By contrast, as Berger observed, "The aims of a demonstration … are symbolic: it *demonstrates* a force that is scarcely used."[95] The government can and must prepare for and defend against the potential for violence and unlawful activity at public assemblies. However, that does not mean it can or ought to treat every public assembly as an incipient riot or step toward the violent overthrow of the government. The law of public protest can – indeed must – recognize and maintain critical distinctions between illegitimate acts of violence and legitimate acts of protest. And it must also ensure that responsibility and legal liability for violence rest with those who engage in violence or property destruction, rather than with protest organizers or movements that may have nothing to do with such activities.

Governments also bear some responsibility for the perception that protests are violent events. When faced with a public protest, particularly a spontaneous as opposed to a permitted event, governments face an admittedly unattractive choice. If they do nothing, governments demonstrate their weakness. They risk losing control, not just of the public narrative but of the public square itself. However, if they react with force to what is otherwise a peaceful but perhaps somewhat disruptive protest, governments display the undemocratic nature of their authority.[96]

Berger's observation, offered decades ago, rings true today: "Almost invariably, authority chooses to use force."[97] That choice is not generally driven by the scale or nature of the threat of public protest, which in most instances is largely symbolic. The possibility of losing control, of the potential for violence, is used to justify militarized displays and the use of aggressive tactics. The unlawful use of force often backfires. Municipalities can end up paying significant damages for law enforcement excesses. Further, as Berger claimed, "by attacking the demonstration authority ensures that the symbolic event becomes an historical one: an event to be remembered, to be learnt from, to be avenged."[98]

Violent protest policing during the 1968 Democratic National Convention in Chicago, the killings at Kent State University, and the aggressive response to even orderly and peaceful BLM protests in 2020 demonstrate an unfortunate and disturbing government predilection to respond to protest with force. When it cannot be managed through bureaucratic means, dissent on American streets has been "managed" through law enforcement escalation, aggression, and violence. And far too often, these managerial tactics have disparately harmed people of color and marginalized groups. Hence one of the principal reforms identified in the book: ending the tradition of aggressive law enforcement responses to peaceful public assemblies.

WHAT DOES PUBLIC PROTEST PRODUCE?

I have discussed what protest might mean to those who organize and participate in this sort of activity, what it might communicate to those inside as well as those outside a protest movement, and the democratizing nature of public protest. However, many have questioned the efficacy of public protest. Some have argued its costs outweigh any benefits to protesters or the public. Indeed, some commentators view protests as affirmatively *harmful* to the very political and social causes they support.

Like the risk of violence, these concerns cannot be ignored or brushed aside. At the same time, protest efficacy is difficult to measure. Do we focus on the short term and ask whether a specific protest altered public discourse or public policy? Or do we instead question whether a protest movement led to longer-term structural reforms – for example, policing reforms or changes to qualified immunity in the wake of recent BLM protests?

The book focuses on the laws that govern public protest and the means governments use to control and manage dissent, rather than the social or political efficacy of protest activity. However, the two are not unrelated. Legal limits that constrain protest may impose a "cap" on its putative benefits. How governments manage protests may affect how efficacious these events can be. At the same time, protesters who rely on controversial tactics, for example demonstrating in front of the homes of judges, may reap fewer benefits from this tactic even if it is constitutionally protected.

Complaints and concerns regarding the efficacy of public protest as a means of democratic change are hardly new. During the height of the civil rights and Vietnam War eras, scholars expressed concerns about the "impotence" of public protest as a means of political change.[99] Critics have viewed the disruption associated with protests not as a virtue, as some commentators have characterized it, but as a form of violence that did not convince anyone or lead to substantive change.[100]

Whether protests produce "real" and substantive results in terms of discourse and policy reform is certainly open to debate. As mentioned, that kind of efficacy is difficult to measure. Did the protests of the Civil Rights Era play a role in changing discriminatory laws and policies? To what extent have anti-war protests affected public opinion about armed conflicts or, more concretely, changed national defense policies? Did the BLM protests following the murder of George Floyd change public discourse about race? Did they lead to legislative proposals or actual laws concerning policing?

In each instance, and many others, the answer is likely to be affirmative but guardedly so. However, in each case, it is also difficult, if not impossible, for protest opponents or skeptics to establish protest made *no* difference at all or was simply redundant or impotent. Moreover, while some protests may be described this way, so too can more "conventional" forms of communication. We do not typically demand that a speaker demonstrate the utility of an idea or expressive act, even when their speech imposes significant costs on society. On what basis, then, can we demand protests "earn their way"?

Even if protest does bear the burden some assign to it, there is evidence the burden can at least be partially satisfied. Some protest movements, including the Civil Rights Movement, have changed the public discourse and ultimately played a role in producing legal reforms. Recent BLM protests, perhaps the largest in American history, at the very least changed the national discourse about police violence against Black people and, more tangibly, led to legislative proposals for law enforcement reforms and even "defunding" the police. It is still too soon to tell whether these historic protests will change policing itself, much less the laws governing law enforcement misconduct. But in terms of putting these issues on the table, the historic BLM protests certainly deserve some credit.

More generally, public protests have been associated with important democratic values. As Abu El-Haj notes, protest is linked to increased participation in the electoral process.[101] From this perspective, public protest is "efficacious" or "worthwhile" in part because it leads to broader political engagement including voting and running for political office. Similarly, Susan Stokes argues that public protests "improve on electoral democracy, by correcting for inequalities in political resources, offering a voice to those who are kept from the polls, and strengthening mechanisms of accountability."[102]

To be sure, as Stokes observes, some protests can also be viewed as "democracy-detracting."[103] Among other things, protests can promote repugnant ideas and goals such as white supremacy, provoke authoritarian backlashes, and facilitate "anti-deliberative" discourse that simplifies issues and demonizes political opponents.[104] Again, however, that is true of all forms of expression. Protests, like other kinds of expression, can be used in ways that undermine democracy or generate backlash. But we do not generally treat these as reasons to view even offensive or anti-deliberative speech as not "worthwhile."

Daniel Gillion has claimed protests produce tangible and positive electoral effects.[105] He argues that "protests are part of the social learning process, and act as an avenue of social communication between activists and nonactivists."[106] Gillion contends that protests put issues on political agendas and communicate their salience to the public and officials. Through this process, protests have "the potential to shift voters' evaluations of political candidates."[107] Thus, not only does protest increase the likelihood that participants and others will turn out on election day, but over time protests can influence electoral outcomes.[108]

Gillion argues that protests provide information to voters about policies and candidates and create overarching narratives about what is happening in society.[109] They distribute information, attempt to persuade non-activists, and translate passion into electoral outcomes. In addition to increased participation in voting and political organizing, studies have also found that public protests are associated with changes in public opinion.[110] That, again, is a partial answer to the criticism that public protests have zero effect on deep-seated public attitudes about controversial topics.

Nevertheless, some commentators have offered a broadly negative view of public protests. In a recent book chapter entitled "Protest Fatigue," Richard Thompson Ford attacks the legitimacy and efficacy of public protest on several grounds. Since my book defends public protest as a necessary and worthwhile activity, I should highlight the nature and extent of our disagreement.

Ford claims protest has become "safe, predictable – and frequent," and as a result less effective.[111] Even if descriptively accurate, that claim elides *why* protest may have become so "safe" and "predictable." One of this book's central arguments is that the law of public protest is an obstacle to robust forms of public contention. The variety of laws and regulations that govern protest and manage dissent have contributed significantly to the standardization and neutralization of protest. The answer is not to condemn protest as stale or predictable, but rather to address the underlying reasons why it has become so.

Ford also points to the existence of counter-protesters as a reason to dismiss protest events. He argues, "If any protest can be met with an equal and opposite counter-protest, perhaps everyone would have been better off staying home."[112] That argument dismisses a fundamental First Amendment principle: that in a democracy it is critically important that speech and counter-speech contend with one another in the public square. Counter-protest is a form of counter-speech, and counter-speech is one of the foundations upon which the First Amendment's "marketplace of ideas" metaphor is built. That metaphor has many critics, to be sure. But condemning protest on the grounds that it gives rise to counter-protest is like arguing that if speech can be met with counter-speech, what is the point of communicating in the first place? The point is that the First Amendment values and protects precisely this sort of exchange because it contributes to the search for political and other truths.

Ford argues that protests are "overused and often misused."[113] He claims that in assessing the wisdom or civic-mindedness of protest, we must "distinguish legitimate and potentially useful protests from those that are needlessly irritating or downright counter-productive."[114] Ford suggests a distinction between "ideal" protests, which he claims are characterized by legitimacy, efficacy, and self-sacrifice, and "problematic" protests which lack one or more of these characteristics.[115]

The obvious problem with this proposed dichotomy is that it is shot through with subjective impressions. The problem of ideological bias is acute. Whether one views a public protest as "needlessly irritating" or "counter-productive" is likely to depend on the person's (or official's) sense of the worthiness of the protest cause. This objection to public protest echoes the general attitude and approach of managed dissent. Governments, as noted, may believe most or even all protests are misguided. But we do not allow the state to suppress speech or assembly when it finds the expression "illegitimate," "irritating," or just plain "counter-productive." Just as there is no "ideal" book, poem, or political address, there is no achievable consensus on what constitutes an "ideal" protest.

Ford is doubtless correct that many Americans feel a degree of weariness or cynicism about protest and that some may even be experiencing what he calls "protest fatigue."[116] Protests can be disruptive and expensive, and some portion of the public may indeed not see them as "worth" these costs. Like Ford, many Americans might agree that the "Critical Mass" bicycle protests, which jammed the streets in many cities, are annoying and ill-conceived. At the same time, many others might be more than willing to tolerate the annoyance of these events to raise awareness of alternative forms of transportation and cycling safety. Some might even be influenced to pay more attention to the protests' cause.

In any event, as discussed earlier, protests are not directed exclusively to external public audiences. Thus, we cannot judge their efficacy solely from the perspective of those who might be wary of or fed up with public protests. Yet Ford suggests that protests organized for the benefit of participants are of the "problematic" type.[117] He even characterizes the desire to experience protest as an illegitimate form of "Selma envy."[118] However, as other commentators have observed, the constitution of communities, dignitary values, and other internal efficacies have genuine value – even if external audiences are turned off or tuned out.[119] Ford's argument that protest is essentially a form of "psychotherapy" is dismissive of its internal benefits.[120] Protests by Black people, in a Black community, largely for the benefit of that community, should not be labeled "problematic" or dismissed as a manifestation of "Selma envy." The same goes for any other inwardly-focused protests.

Finally, like other protest critics, Ford does not consider public protests to be part of institutional politics. He claims they are a distraction from the hard work of political change that occurs *within* institutions. Protests are indeed generally "outsider" events. In that respect they are not meant to be, nor should they be, considered part of the ordinary political process. Dissenters speak out against these power structures. Even Ford acknowledges the need for and legitimacy of protests that respond to political processes that are closed off to certain groups.[121] Many public protests meet this benchmark of "legitimacy." As suggested earlier, public protests are politics by other means. They are most frequently relied upon by "others" who lack or have been denied institutional political access.

Public protests are no panacea for what ails American democracy – far from it. In a democracy that still operates through traditional power structures, over-reliance on public protest and dissent is perilous. As one cynic of protest movements opined, "Protesting, acting up, and acting out will not do it. The age of movement politics is over, at least for now. We need more than marchers. We need more mayors. And governors and state legislators and members of Congress."[122] All true. It is worth noting, however, that these words were published three years prior to the largest mass public protests in American history. It turns out we still need public protests, which can be catalysts for the kind of change critics say is needed to change democratic outcomes.

Minority and marginalized persons cannot rely solely on public protests to advance their rights and claims. But preserving protest as an avenue or channel of change is essential to democracy. We should not judge the efficacy of protest by any single measure. As Gillion observes, "Success through protesting is not one single thing: it is not just electing new officials; it is not just convincing elected officials to consider a new perspective on an issue; it is not just enlisting a greater portion of the public to cast their vote in elections. Success can take a variety of forms."[123]

2

The Managerial System

Americans pride themselves on having a permissive speech culture. However, when it comes to public protest, U.S. laws impose a multi-layered and complex system of restrictions. In addition, law enforcement policies and actions often sharply limit protest activities and expose protest participants to physical harm. When protesters and others sue for damages, First Amendment and other doctrines sharply limit or even eliminate remedies. As noted in the Introduction, I refer to the rules of engagement applicable to public protest in the U.S. as a system or framework of managed dissent.[1] The managed dissent system covers and circumscribes every aspect of protest – from the content of communications to the time, place, and manner of its occurrence. As far as the exercise of protest rights is concerned, the framework of managed dissent operates as a highly restrictive floor. As subsequent chapters will discuss, additional aspects of the framework – the presence of firearms at protests, rising civil costs and liabilities, and broad emergency governmental powers – raise the ceiling of burdens managed dissent imposes on protesters. As the name suggests, under the managerial system, dissent is allowed to occur but is subject to a host of regulations and other obstacles. By the measure of a society that boasts of its "uninhibited, wide-open, and robust" expressive freedoms, protest in the U.S. is over-managed.

THE DEEP ROOTS OF MANAGED DISSENT

America owes its founding, in part, to disruptive and even sometimes violent public protest. However, our public and institutional commitments to collective displays of contention have been more tepid than the Supreme Court's standard narrative of "robust, wide-open, and uninhibited" expression suggests. In fact, public protest has never received the full respect it deserves – including from the Court. Viewed as a potential threat to overriding interests such as public order, safety, and tranquility, protest has been managed and curtailed through precedents, doctrines, practices, and norms.

In a critique of the current Supreme Court's First Amendment precedents, Greg Magarian claims that the Roberts Court "has authorized established, powerful institutions ... to exercise managerial control over public discussion, with the apparent goal and typical result of pushing public discussion away from destabilizing, noisy margins and toward a stable, settled center."[2] Because the central insights of Magarian's critique also apply to the law of public protest, I have borrowed his managerial terminology.

Before discussing specific aspects of the managerial system, let us look first at the roots of the law of public protest and the system of managed dissent. The foundation is set in Supreme Court decisions, which have long exhibited ambivalence toward public protest and collective expression. The modern bureaucracy of control described below is a manifestation of that ambivalence.

American judicial and other officials have not always viewed public protests and demonstrations with suspicion and skepticism. Until the mid-nineteenth century, the public and local officialdom – including state courts – not only tolerated but seemed generally comfortable with noisy and disruptive public parades, rallies, and demonstrations.[3] Groups regularly used public streets and squares to socialize, celebrate, and communicate. Absent some imminent threat of violence or other emergency, courts tended to invalidate legal and other restrictions on these activities. Tolerance for crowds and the disruption of daily commercial and other activities was relatively high.

By the end of the nineteenth century, officials and courts began to view public protest as disruptive and potentially dangerous. There was indeed some cause for concern. Labor activists and radicals engaged in violent, sometimes deadly, bombings and attacks.[4] This would lead to the first of many historical backlashes against public protest. Lawmakers and officials moved to exert greater control over public activities. With the widespread adoption of municipal permitting systems and the rise of organized police forces – factors, as we will see, that continue to pose obstacles for modern-day protesters – the seeds of the modern system of managed dissent were planted.[5]

Although officials sometimes tolerated protests and other forms of collective expression, for most of American history individuals and groups had no First Amendment *right* to assemble and speak in public places.[6] Prior to the 1940s, the Supreme Court's view was that governments, like private property owners, could exclude speakers from any property they owned.[7] Although protesters and other speakers today can assert a First Amendment right to access certain public places, as explained in Chapter 3, these claims are governed by First Amendment doctrines rooted in managerial principles.

During the 1930s and 1940s, the Hughes Court handed down several early decisions on the law of public protest that established the foundation for the managerial system. The Court recognized the rights to leaflet and solicit door-to-door, but it also made clear that authorities had ample discretion to maintain public order in the streets. Thus, the Court upheld permitting schemes, imposition of fees to defray protest costs, and public disorder prosecutions – all part of the backbone of today's law of public protest.[8]

In early decisions, the Court was most likely to extend protection to public expression if it did not offend public audiences or threaten disruption of the prevailing social order. For example, in one case, the Court overturned a breach of peace conviction against a Jehovah's Witness because he was "upon a public street, where he had a right to be, and where he had a right peacefully to impart his views to others."[9] There was no evidence, the Court observed, that the speaker's "deportment was noisy, truculent, overbearing or offensive," or that he had demonstrated any "intentional discourtesy," or had any intent to "insult or affront" the public audience.[10] By contrast, in another decision involving similar facts, the Court concluded that certain impolite epithets and swear words, directed to a person "without a disarming smile," were not entitled to any First Amendment protection at all.[11]

The Court would eventually extend broad First Amendment protection to caustic and profane language.[12] However, its decisions involving hostile reactions to public addresses have always been inconsistent and ambivalent about the First Amendment value of public protest. In *Terminiello v. City of Chicago* (1949), the Court held the trial court erred when it instructed the jury that a speaker, whose address led to hostile and violent reactions, could be arrested merely for provoking an angry response.[13] The Court reasoned that speech "may indeed best serve its high purpose when it induces a condition of *unrest*, creates *dissatisfaction* with conditions as they are, or even *stirs people to anger*."[14] But not all Justices shared this welcoming attitude with respect to provocative street protests. In a dissent, Justice Robert Jackson decried the "battle for the streets" represented by assembled fascistic "mobs," and the Court's refusal to defer to local officials who had the authority to control the streets.[15] Justice Jackson wrote:

> But we must bear in mind also that no serious outbreak of mob violence, race rioting, lynching or public disorder is likely to get going without help of some speechmaking to some mass of people. A street may be filled with men and women, and the crowd still not be a mob. Unity of purpose, passion and hatred, which merges the many minds of a crowd into the mindlessness of a mob, almost invariably is supplied by speeches. It is naive, or worse, to teach that oratory with this object or effect is a service to liberty. No mob has ever protected any liberty, even its own, but, if not put down, it always winds up in an orgy of lawlessness which respects no liberties.[16]

The very next term, in *Feiner v. New York*, the Court upheld the criminal conviction of a speaker who had done far less to rile up a public crowd than the speaker in *Terminiello*. In *Feiner*, when two attendees told an officer they would shut down the speaker – by force, they implied – if he did not desist, the officers arrested the *speaker* rather than the threatening onlookers. Echoing Justice Jackson, the Court emphasized the need to uphold "peace and order on the streets."[17]

Although subsequent decisions distinguished *Feiner*, it has never been overruled. Indeed, even today there is significant uncertainty regarding whether or to what

extent law enforcement and other officials have a duty to protect provocative speakers from hostile audiences that may harm them.[18] What Fred Schauer has referred
to as the "law of interference with demonstrations" does not provide clear protection
for speakers when confronted with a "hostile" audience.[19] As we will see, that uncertainty continues to affect the rights of modern-day protesters when faced not just
with hostile counter-protesters, but also with government officials seeking to avoid
contentious encounters on public streets and university campuses.

When, in 1958, the Supreme Court finally recognized a First Amendment right
of "expressive association" that protected groups, including the National Association
for the Advancement of Colored People (NAACP), it acknowledged that "effective
advocacy of both public and private points of view, particularly controversial ones, is
undeniably enhanced by group association."[20] Associations engage in many types of
activities, including lobbying, litigating, petition-writing, and protesting. Only with
respect to the last has the Court expressed significant reservations about allowing
full First Amendment protection.

Distinguishing *Feiner*, the Warren Court extended some First Amendment protection to disruptive civil rights protests in two decisions, *Edwards v. South Carolina*
(1963) and *Cox v. Louisiana* (1965), notwithstanding the presence of apparently hostile onlookers.[21] Perfectly conveying the Court's ambivalence, in *Edwards* the Court
described the civil rights march as "an exercise of … basic constitutional rights in
their most pristine and classic sense," while in *Cox* the majority darkly warned of the
potential that protests would descend into "mob" dominance.[22]

In *Cox*, the Court "emphatically reject[ed] the notion … that the First and
Fourteenth Amendments afford the same kind of freedom to those who would communicate ideas by conduct such as patrolling, marching, and picketing on streets
and highways as these amendments afford to those who communicate by pure
speech."[23] Justice Black, who opined that picketing "is not speech" and therefore
could not claim First Amendment protection, had more pointed words for protest
organizers and activists.[24] He wrote, "Those who encourage minority groups to
believe that the United States Constitution and federal laws give them a right to
patrol and picket in the streets whenever they choose, in order to advance what they
think to be a just and noble end, do no service to those minority groups, their cause,
or their country."[25]

The majorities in *Edwards* and *Cox* distinguished passive forms of protest such
as chanting, singing, and praying, which should have upset no one, from more
disruptive forms like protesting and picketing. Thus, as the First Amendment
scholar Harry Kalven, Jr. observed, even during the iconic civil rights marches
and demonstrations of the 1950s and 1960s the Court's opinions "bristled with
cautions and with a lack of sympathy for such forms of protest."[26] Despite the
ambiguities, the Court was clear about one thing: in both cases, law enforcement
had things under control and hence there was no danger, as in *Feiner*, of mob
violence in the streets.

Other Civil Rights Era decisions extolled the contributions of different forms of expression to self-government, the search for truth, and individual liberty – all central First Amendment values. In 1964, the Court's decision in *New York Times Co. v. Sullivan* altered state libel laws to protect "uninhibited, robust, and wide-open" discourse about public officials.[27] As Kalven presciently warned, the Court was likely to "find its exuberant formula put to hard tests when speech is in public places."[28] In *Brandenburg v. Ohio* (1969), the Court held that a group of Klansmen could not be punished for racially derogatory public speeches unless they intended to incite imminent lawless action that was likely to occur.[29] *Brandenburg* paved the way for contentious civil rights advocacy, including forms of direct action like boycotts. In *NAACP v. Claiborne Hardware* (1982), the Court held that civil rights activists engaged in a contentious boycott of local white businesses could not be held liable for substantial business damages even though some used harsh and intimidating rhetoric to keep fellow boycotters in line.[30]

As we will see in subsequent chapters, these were significant victories for free speech and assembly – and for civil rights more generally. The Court's decisions created critical breathing space for civil rights protests, which were socially disruptive and often chaotic. However, without in any way diminishing the importance of these decisions, they never went so far as to express full-throated support for collective forms of dissent. Even the Warren Court's record exhibits judicial ambivalence concerning at least some forms of public contention.

Indeed, one of the most consistent themes of the Court's First Amendment jurisprudence has been its wariness of public protest and other forms of collective expression. Part of that skepticism is rooted in a longstanding distinction the Court has tried to draw between speech and conduct or, as Kalven described it, between "speech pure" and "speech-plus."[31] Protests, demonstrations, and rallies all combine elements of speech and conduct, a fact that has engendered doubts on the Court about extending full First Amendment protection to these forms of collective expression.[32] Thus, for example, the Court has long treated labor pickets as a form of intimidation rather than a means of protected collective expression.[33] In *Claiborne Hardware*, which recognized economic boycotts were entitled to some First Amendment protection, the majority likened the civil rights action in that case to a "chameleon-like" conspiracy that "included elements of criminality and elements of majesty" and warned of the "special dangers" associated with concerted activity.[34]

Other Civil Rights Era decisions protected disruptive, but primarily silent and orderly, forms of protest. For example, the Court upheld the First Amendment rights of young Black male civil rights protesters to sit *silently* in a public library reading room.[35] As the Court noted, "They said nothing; there was no noise or boisterous talking."[36] As well, "Petitioners did nothing and said nothing even remotely provocative."[37] Later, the Court held that public elementary and junior high school students had a First Amendment right to wear black armbands, as part of a *silent and non-disruptive* protest of the Vietnam War.[38] By contrast, when protesters got too close for comfort to public jails where fellow activists were held or courthouses, First Amendment claims faltered.[39] Nor, although it reversed some breach-of-peace convictions on due process grounds, was the Court willing to treat civil rights lunch counter sit-ins as a form of protected expression.[40] The Court also ruled against political protesters who publicly burned their draft cards to protest the Vietnam War and, later, homeless advocates who sought to sleep outdoors on the National Mall.[41]

The Roberts Court has continued to look askance at public protest. In *McCullen v. Coakley* (2014), the Court invalidated a 35-foot buffer zone that banned speech outside reproductive health care centers providing abortion services.[42] The Court emphasized that the plaintiffs challenging the zone were "sidewalk counselors" – individuals the Court was careful to note wished to engage in peaceful, orderly, and reserved conversations with those visiting the facilities – rather than "protesters."[43] The implication of the Court's distinction seemed to be that speakers wishing to engage in what the Court described as "personal, caring, consensual conversations" were entitled to full or even special First Amendment protection, while "protesters" could or might be treated differently.[44] In another decision involving restrictions on abortion clinic protests, the Court emphasized that governments could enforce speech restrictions to protect audiences from "the cacophony of political protests."[45]

Even when "protesters" have prevailed, the Court has emphasized their success hinges in part on their good and orderly behavior. For example, in *Snyder v. Phelps* (2011), the Court invalidated a significant civil judgment against a group of protesters who assembled near the funeral of a soldier who had been killed in action in Afghanistan. It emphasized the protesters were in a place they had a right to be, "did not yell or use profanity," did not engage in any disruptive activity, and in fact were neither seen nor heard by anyone attending the funeral.[46] While the Court proclaimed that offensive protest (undetected by its target audience) was protected by the First Amendment, it approved and invited measures – now adopted in federal, state, and local jurisdictions across the nation – designed to zone such protests out of eyesight and earshot of their intended audiences. Although frequently cited as examples of the extension of First Amendment protection to deeply offensive forms of political dissent, on closer inspection, the Court's decisions are consistent with its longstanding predilection to support subdued, polite, and "non-truculent" protest.[47]

Despite the Supreme Court's ambivalence, in some infamous cases the First Amendment has been interpreted as protecting protests that threaten significant unrest and may stir people to anger. In the late 1970s, a federal court of appeals invalidated several regulations intended to prevent Nazis from marching in Skokie, Illinois, a town where many Holocaust survivors lived.[48] The Supreme Court declined to review the case and thus did not address the merits.[49] The permit-seekers never actually marched in Skokie, but the precedent is often cited, positively or negatively depending on who is citing it, as evidence of the First Amendment's protection for "uninhibited" public protest. On closer inspection, the court's decision shows that blatant or thinly disguised viewpoint-based restrictions on protest activities violate the First Amendment. It does not purport to address whether restrictions designed to displace a march, or otherwise protect survivors from the "cacophony of political protest," might have fared better.

The Court's ambivalence toward public protest is also evident in its treatment of the First Amendment's text. The text refers not only to freedom of speech but also to separate rights "peaceably to assemble" and to "petition the government for a redress of grievances." Although it is centrally important to public protest, the Court has not decided a case based on the Assembly Clause in four decades.[50] The Petition Clause likewise might just as well have been written in invisible ink.[51]

The narrative of a First Amendment bending always toward expansive public protest rights is misleading. To be sure, Court decisions during the latter half of the twentieth century recognized First Amendment rights to engage in public protest activity that disrupted social order and to caustically criticize government officials. As we will see, those precedents continue to benefit public protest organizers, participants, and supporters. However, even the Warren Court was ambivalent about speech "brigaded with action" – public protests, marches, demonstrations, and pickets. The modern law of public protest and system of managed dissent reflect and codify this ambivalence. "Protesters" continue to confront laws, biases, and tactics not applied to those engaged in "pure" speech.

Commenting on the Roberts Court's First Amendment decisions, Magarian has argued that the Court has "disregarded the expressive interests and First Amendment claims of outside speakers" and demonstrated "a consistent preference for modes of public discussion that promote social and political stability, while disfavoring modes of public discussion that threaten to destabilize existing arrangements of social and political power."[52] Likewise, the Court's protest decisions have often treated dissenting protesters as threatening, truculent, and noisy "mobs." As currently interpreted, the First Amendment extends full recognition and protection to more passive and orderly forms of expression.

MANAGING PUBLIC PROTEST

The law of public protest reflects managerial biases against protest and in favor of the maintenance of public order. The remainder of this chapter provides a general overview of the "rules of engagement" applicable to organizing and participating in public protest activities. Subsequent chapters analyze specific elements and attributes of the system of managed dissent.

A Basic Protest Typology

Public protests come in many different forms and sizes. They may involve different types of protest-related activities – marches, rallies, sit-ins, die-ins, etc. For purposes of understanding the basic components of the managerial system, it is helpful to

	Lawful	Unlawful
Peaceable	**1** Marches Demonstrations Parades Rallies Pickets	**2** Trespassing Blocking streets Failing to disperse violating curfews "Shouting down" (?)
Non-Peaceable	**3** Flag burning Destruction of private property	**4** Riot Arson Tagging Destruction of property

FIGURE 2.1 Protest typology

distinguish among a few general protest types. The law of public protests applies to each type somewhat differently. Imagine four general types of public protest events (Figure 2.1).

In the *first* type of protest, participants and supporters engage in peaceable (non-violent and non-destructive) and lawful demonstrations, protests, rallies, pickets, and other activities. They secure the necessary permits, stay within the time and place limits afforded to them under the law, and otherwise follow the protest protocol. This type of protest enjoys the maximum constitutional and legal protection. Even so, note that protest organizers, participants, and supporters must still comply with a variety of regulations to come within this lawful protest zone. They will likely not be allowed to engage in all the protest activities they desire, in the place or manner they prefer. Finally, organizers and participants may be subject to arrest and other penalties should the event at any point involve unlawful conduct or unprotected speech.

In the *second* type of protest event, organizers and participants also plan and engage in peaceable activities such as marches or demonstrations or participate in counter-protests. However, assume some participants also commit technical or minor violations of law. For example, participants may trespass on private property, block a public sidewalk or street, fail to disperse after being ordered by law enforcement to do so, or violate a curfew. Even though these activities are all non-violent in nature, the First Amendment does not protect them.[53] This is so despite the fact that peaceful acts of civil disobedience "can promote democratic values, including the ability to dissent and the possibility for marginalized populations to be hard."[54] Protesters may engage in these and other violations as forms of "civil disobedience" – public, non-violent, and conscientious breaches of law undertaken with the aim of bringing about changes in laws or policies. However, when doing so they are presumably willing to accept the legal consequences of their actions. Whether or not the civil disobedience is *morally* justified, it can and often does lead to *legal* sanctions. The nature and extent of these sanctions may raise serious First Amendment and other concerns.[55] Similarly, protesters who "shout down" a speaker who has advance permission to hold an event may be engaged in non-violent but still sanctionable expression. Members of a student group on a public university campus who engage in this type of protest activity may face sanctions.

The *third* type of protest consists of a very narrow category of non-peaceable but potentially still lawful activity. For example, the destructive act of burning a flag can be either unlawful arson or a lawful expressive act. Assuming it is done in a lawful place and in compliance with permitting and public safety laws, burning an object may be protected expression. The act may still be made a criminal offense, pursuant to a content-neutral law or regulation.[56] In addition, a protester could perform even violent acts (destruction of personal property, for example) on private property, so long as these acts do not implicate any interests in public order and safety. Only in these very limited respects does the First Amendment protect destructive – but otherwise lawful – conduct.

Finally, consider the *fourth* protest type, characterized primarily by non-peaceable and unlawful activity. This type includes riots or conspiracies to destroy property or cause injury to persons. It may also include individual acts of violence by protest participants – physical assault, arson, and other violent or destructive conduct. The First Amendment does not protect violent unlawful conduct, even if it is meant to express some message or point of view.[57] The act of burning down a police headquarters building to express opposition to police brutality is clearly not protected by the First Amendment. Assembling on the National Mall is generally protected, but storming the Capitol building, vandalizing it, and assaulting Capitol Police officers are clearly not. As discussed in Chapter 4, whether the First Amendment allows protest organizers, participants, or supporters to be held legally responsible for the violent acts of *others* at a protest event remains unclear. Individual protesters can be criminally and civilly liable for their own unlawful actions, as can those who intentionally conspire with them to engage in violence. However, their liability cannot rest solely on actions protected by the First Amendment.

Although useful for thinking about the diversity of protest activities, the typology is admittedly over-simplified. Public protests may blend different elements, requiring officials and courts to sort protected from unprotected activities. Further, as noted, there are lingering uncertainties concerning the boundaries of First Amendment protections as they pertain to various protest actions. The scope of protesters' liabilities for the acts of others, the scope of First Amendment protection for acts of civil disobedience, and the First Amendment status of some disruptive forms of protest such as "shouting down" a speaker are examples. These permutations are examined in subsequent chapters.

Classifying the different protest types in this way is still a useful starting point for understanding the system of managed dissent and the law of public protest. One thing the typology makes clear is that protesters occupy a relatively narrow First Amendment "safe zone" consisting primarily of the first type of peaceable and lawful protest. As noted, under the requirements and principles of managed dissent, even in this space protest is heavily constrained.

Conduct and Content Limits

As the typology suggests, the scope of First Amendment protection is an important aspect of the system of managed dissent. There are some basic substantive limits on protected activities (conduct) and protest messages (content).

As noted, the First Amendment protects a wide variety of lawful and peaceable (non-violent and non-destructive) activities. Protesters can make speeches, hand out leaflets, carry posters, sing, chant, and march. These activities are generally within the protected protest zone – although as we will see, governments can still broadly regulate where, when, and how they occur.

Protesters can also engage in acts that communicate a message or viewpoint. For example, they can wear costumes, dance, burn flags, sleep in parks, and participate in "die-ins." However, the First Amendment treats only *some* of this conduct as expressive. In general, it only applies to conduct when a protester intends to convey a message an audience is likely to understand.[58] Burning a flag as part of a political protest is speech potentially protected under the First Amendment. But publicly carrying a firearm, for example, is probably not an expressive act.[59] The Court has recognized certain protest-related activities, such as parades and marches, as inherently expressive. Restrictions on these forms of conduct are subject to First Amendment limits even if they do not communicate a coherent message.[60]

These "expressive conduct" rules leave out a range of protest conduct that might have some "expressive" element, but whose message might be inaccessible or unclear to public audiences. And as already discussed, First Amendment protection does not extend to violent criminal activity including physical assault and destruction of public property – regardless of any claim that the act was intended to communicate some message or viewpoint.

Even if conduct is considered "expressive," that does not necessarily mean it is *protected* under the First Amendment. Governments cannot punish a protester who burns a U.S. flag at a political protest because of the negative reaction some have to this potent act of dissent.[61] However, they can place strict limits on where or how a person can set fire to a flag or engage in other expressive acts.[62] More traditional expressive activities, such as leafletting, are also subject to restrictions. For instance, laws and regulations can dictate precisely where protesters can hand out flyers or pamphlets. While protesters can approach audiences with leaflets, petitions, and requests for donations, if asked to do so they must generally leave members of the public alone. Protesters or groups of demonstrators who "dog" or physically harass audiences or targets by engaging in a pattern of unwanted conduct can be arrested or sued.

With respect to public properties where governments allow protest (which, as we shall see, constitutes a rather limited category), states and localities impose a wide variety of restrictions on protesters' conduct. These restrictions typically consist of detailed lists of "don'ts" for users of public spaces.

For example, in Richmond, Virginia, there once was a large statue of Confederate General Robert E. Lee. The statue, a focal point of BLM protests during the summer of 2020, was in the middle of a small traffic circle, Lee Circle. In addition to a general warning that any "unlawful activity" is prohibited in Lee Circle, regulations prohibit driving or parking vehicles there, climbing on the statue or its steps, and placing or affixing banners, flags, or posters to the statue.[63] Lee Circle is closed from sunset each night until sunrise the next morning. Its maximum capacity is 500 people. Events expected to draw ten or more people there require the issuance of a city permit, which triggers a separate set of requirements. Violation of any of these rules is a misdemeanor criminal offense.

These types of restrictions on the "time, place, and manner" of protest are common; they apply in nearly every corner of public space potentially available to protesters. In addition to place-specific regulations, law enforcement also has extensive authority to arrest protesters for even minor offenses and to order them to disperse. Federal, state, and local laws are full of "public order" offenses that frequently limit public protesters' activities. Protesters who block streets or sidewalks, interfere with others' access to buildings or businesses, violate noise ordinances, refuse to disperse when given a lawful order to do so, or disregard regulations pertaining to the use of public property are subject to "breach of peace," "disorderly conduct," "trespass," "conspiracy to riot," "unlawful assembly," and other criminal charges. In addition, as discussed in Chapter 4, protest-related activities including minor acts of vandalism, trespass, or blocking passageways may also lead to significant civil damage liabilities for protest organizers.

As mentioned, public disorder laws may broadly restrict protest activities. "Disorderly conduct" laws cover everything from merely "offensive" conduct to acting (or speaking) in a "tumultuous" manner.[64] In cases where they determine event participants *intend* to commit imminent violations such as property destruction or personal harm, officers can arrest protesters for criminal offenses such as "unlawful assembly" and "conspiracy to riot."[65] They can also issue dispersal orders based on these and a host of other potential offenses, including those already mentioned. Failure to obey such orders constitutes a separate offense. Thus, an officer can order a "disorderly" group to leave an area, even a place where they otherwise have a permit or other right to be, if the officer reasonably expects the group's presence will result in substantial harm or serious inconvenience. This is the sort of broad discretion the law of public protest vests in law enforcement to maintain public order.

As I discuss later, protest policing is a critically important component of managing dissent. Law enforcement officers have wide enforcement discretion with respect to the rules applicable in public places. Any technical violation is sufficient to warrant a citation or arrest. Police can interpret a provision broadly or narrowly – or may decide not to enforce a regulation at all. Evidence suggests law enforcement sometimes declines to arrest demonstrators engaged in peaceful, but technically unlawful conduct.[66] However, other evidence shows this discretion has been exercised unevenly, sometimes with disparate racial effects. Tabatha Abu El-Haj has observed that "a citizen's right to come out to protest ... depends significantly on local officials' tolerance for inconvenience and disorder."[67]

Studies have found that police acted more aggressively, in terms of arrests and use of force, against left-wing protests, anti-police brutality protests, and protests involving predominantly Black participants.[68] In addition to raising concerns about disparate and discriminatory enforcement of protest rules, the sheer breadth of discretion makes it difficult for protesters to anticipate the likely consequences of their actions. Protest organizers who believe in good faith that what they are doing falls into the First Amendment's limited zone of protection may end up on the wrong side of law enforcement discretionary enforcement actions.

One important potential check on aggressive protest policing and other law enforcement abuses is the right of protesters to record interactions with police. Federal courts of appeals have concluded the First Amendment generally protects the right of individuals to record police activity in public places, including during public protests, so long as the person recording does not physically interfere with law enforcement.[69] Some states are pushing back against this important transparency mechanism. Arizona recently enacted a law that bans individuals from recording within eight feet of what they know or have reason to know is law enforcement activity.[70] Among other issues with the law, it is not clear how it would apply in the context of fluid protests, where officers often advance toward individuals who gather in places where they otherwise have a right to be.

So far, the discussion has focused generally on restrictions on protesters' *conduct*. But there are also general limits on the *content* of protesters' communications. The First Amendment protects a wide range of offensive and derogatory speech and generally prohibits the government from restricting speech based on its subject matter or viewpoint. These protections offer protesters critical latitude to try to provoke public crowds, invite disputes, and arouse emotions.

Profanity, strong rhetoric, and communication of views derogatory of others are protected speech. However, protesters do not have a First Amendment right to say *anything* they wish. In some narrow circumstances, protesters may be arrested and punished for the words they use.

For example, speakers may be charged with "incitement" if they expressly encourage others to commit specific illegal acts and those acts are likely to occur imminently (i.e., right now or within a very short time).[71] Thus, assuming the group is imminently likely to heed and act on the speaker's charge, a protester cannot expressly advocate that a nearby group burn a police station to the ground. White supremacist tiki torch carriers in Charlottesville, Virginia who urged imminent violence against counterdemonstrators ran afoul of the "incitement" limitation when they expressly advocated that counter-protesters be assaulted.[72] However, protesters can advocate violence in general ("Kill the police!").

Protest organizers and participants cannot intentionally direct serious threats to inflict bodily harm or death on a person or group.[73] Laws criminalizing such communications typically refer to them as "threats" or sometimes "terroristic threats." Again, however, there is still some protection for violent rhetoric, satire, and other content not likely to be experienced by a reasonable person as a threat to inflict bodily harm or death. In one notable case, the Supreme Court held that a civil rights leader, Charles Evers, who threatened to "break the necks" of activists who refused to participate in a boycott of white businesses could not be held liable for making threats.[74] As discussed in Chapter 4, the Court also held that Evers and other protest participants could not be held liable for the violent acts of other boycott participants.

Protesters who use racial and other epithets in face-to-face encounters with counter-protesters or police can be arrested for communicating what is known as "fighting words" – epithets or profanity likely to induce the reasonable person to act violently toward the speaker.[75] Although the Supreme Court has recognized so-called fighting words as an unprotected category of speech, it has not upheld a conviction for communicating such words since the 1940s. Still, protesters need to be aware that this speech can provide the predicate for arrest under "disorderly conduct" and other statutory offenses mentioned earlier.

Protest organizers, participants, and supporters can also be civilly liable for making false statements that harm the reputations of government officials, private businesses, and other targets of dissent. Under defamation law, communications about public officials and public figures (for example, celebrities and well-known sports figures) give rise to civil damages only if made with the knowledge they were false or "reckless disregard" of their falsity.[76] These limits only apply to statements of fact about an individual, including statements about things that person has done. They do not generally apply to statements of *opinion*, for example that a government official or police officer is "corrupt" or is a "racist."[77]

Incitement, threats, fighting words, and certain kinds of defamation are narrow, but nevertheless important, categorical limits on protesters' speech. If they violate these standards, speakers can lose the broad protection the First Amendment typically provides – even in the "safe zone" of an otherwise peaceful and lawful protest. Moreover, protesters may be arrested *even if* they do not run afoul of these narrow exclusions from First Amendment protection. Protesters have been unlawfully arrested for communicating protected profanity, advocating violence in the abstract, displaying gruesome images, and communicating other protected speech.

In the context of public protest, conduct and content concerns sometimes intersect with one another. Imagine that a hostile audience of counter-protesters and hecklers appears at a scheduled protest event. As events in Charlottesville during the "Unite the Right" demonstrations showed, this situation can turn violent and even deadly. The First Amendment should not permit an offended or angry audience to exercise a "heckler's veto" over the speaker, for instance by having law enforcement suppress speech based on the audience's hostile reaction to it. However, the extent to which speakers in this circumstance are entitled to continue communicating, even if what they are communicating is protected speech, is not clear.

The "law of hostile audiences," which requires that courts and officials balance protesters' rights with public safety concerns, remains indeterminate.[78] As noted earlier, in cases decided during the 1950s and 1960s, the Supreme Court upheld the conviction of a provocative speaker who refused to be silent in the face of hostility but also sided with civil rights protesters engaged in peaceful and non-provocative demonstrations. This aspect of the law of public protest affects the rights not only of the protester in the public square, but also of the university student who shouts down or otherwise responds to a campus speaker. Under the law as it currently stands, whether a speaker can continue communicating when faced with a hostile public audience depends on a rough balancing of interests that may result in the suppression of otherwise lawful expression. A counter-protester who shouts down an invited speaker on campus may be subject to code-of-conduct or other penalties.

In sum, as the basic protest typology suggests, a substantial amount of protest-related conduct and speech content may reside outside the scope of the First Amendment. Violence, vandalism, blocking streets and sidewalks, and physically occupying public places are not protected in any respect. In terms of content, the First Amendment provides protesters and supporters robust, but not absolute, rights to express their views. The First Amendment covers and protects strong rhetoric, derogatory speech, profanity, and negative opinions about public officials and others. It does not provide protection for certain narrow categories of speech including incitement, threats, harassment, and some false statements of fact. Finally, when a hostile audience of counter-protesters arrives at an event, the scope of protesters' First Amendment rights remains uncertain. A scheduled protest might be shut down or limited based on the prospect that a hostile audience is likely to engage in imminent violence against the protesters.

Place and Permit Restrictions

As we have seen, the basic substantive rules of engagement for protest-related conduct and communications, and the nature of their enforcement, follow managed dissent principles. They focus on preventing social and political disruption and provide officials broad discretion to purse those ends. Other parts of the managed dissent framework perform similar functions. The discussion so far has generally assumed protesters have a First Amendment right to demonstrate in a public place. However, under First Amendment doctrine, most public properties are not open "forums" for protest and dissent.[79] Even in such places, governments can typically impose managerial conditions and restrictions on public protest. As discussed further in Chapter 3, place restrictions are a key component of the law of public protest and managed dissent.

The "Public Forum"

Among the very first things protest organizers or activists must do is to choose an appropriate location for their protest event. The Supreme Court has held there is no First Amendment right to protest on *private* property.[80] As a result, protesters who want to engage in a boycott of a business where it operates or reach large public audiences that patronize private venues have no constitutional right to do so.

With respect to *public* properties, governments exercise significant control over where protest activities may occur. The authority over public places stems primarily from what is known as the "public forum" doctrine. A "public forum" is a location generally open to the public for the purposes of assembly and communicating views on political, social, and other issues. Prior to the 1940s, officials possessed the plenary authority to exclude speakers from properties that the government owned or operated.[81] This included the public parks and streets, where many protests commonly occur.

As labor picketers, pamphleteers, and others discovered, speech and assembly rights could only be "robust" if there was some opportunity to exercise them in public places where audiences could be reached. Since the government could exclude speakers for any reason based on its possession of the title to the property in question, the First Amendment was effectively a dead letter in public places.

The modern "public forum" doctrine breaks with this history, but not as sharply as some might assume. The doctrine, which the Court developed over the course of nearly five decades, determines the scope of public protest rights by categorizing public properties or places owned or operated by the government.[82] The category of place dictates the right of protesters and other speakers to assemble and communicate there.

The First Amendment applies most robustly in "traditional public forums." This category of property consists of public streets, (most) public sidewalks, and public parks – all properties critically important to public protest. The rationale for recognizing this category is that "time out of mind," people have used such places for expressive activities.[83] In such places, governments cannot restrict expression based on the speaker's subject matter or viewpoint but otherwise retain broad authority to determine how, when, and where protest activities occur. Thus, for example, protesters can march down a public street (assuming they have a permit, or that one is not required), but the government can enforce regulations to ensure that the marchers do not block traffic, interfere with access to businesses, or disturb residential tranquility.

Governments can also allow speech activity to take place in other public locations. If the government *intentionally* opens a public place under its control to expressive activities, it creates a "designated public forum."[84] Lee Circle in Richmond is an example of this kind of "forum." The Commonwealth of Virginia has historically allowed the public at large to use this property for expressive purposes, subject to various rules and conditions. Other common examples of "designated public forums" might be plazas in front of government buildings, public auditoriums, and state fairgrounds. As discussed in Chapter 5, on public university campuses some places may qualify as "designated" public forums although most will be open on a more limited basis.

The existence of a "designated public forum" depends on the government's intent with respect to the property or place. A forum is "designated" only where clear and convincing evidence shows authorities intended to allow public expression to occur there.[85] Thus, no speech "forum" exists merely because the government owns a property, or if speakers happen to express themselves there without the government's knowledge or consent. If a property does qualify as a "designated public forum," the same First Amendment rules apply to protest activities there as in a "traditional" public forum: government can regulate the time, place, and manner of protests but not the content of their messages.

Protesters occupying public places that are not a "traditional" or "designated" public forum may still enjoy some First Amendment rights, but these are far more limited than in other types of forums. In these places, sometimes called "limited" and other times referred to as "non-public" forums, officials can preserve the property for what they view as its primary function. They can limit these properties to only certain speakers or subject matters. For example, Congress has not intentionally opened the Capitol Rotunda in the U.S. House of Representatives for the public to assemble and speak there, so it is a "non-public" or "limited" public forum. In the Rotunda, the forum is open to legislators' expression and official legislative business. Many campus places may likewise be lawfully "limited" to students, faculty, and other members of the university community.

The Supreme Court has reasoned that because these kinds of properties serve primarily non-expressive functions, governments, like private property owners, can limit access according to those functions. So long as speech and assembly regulations are reasonable and do not discriminate based on the viewpoint of the speaker, officials can restrict or even entirely cut off access to "non-public" forums. Pursuant to this broad authority, lawmakers have banned speech near public places including courthouses, jails, and other government buildings. Congress bans public protests in places including the plaza outside the Supreme Court building and iconic national monuments such as the Jefferson Memorial.[86]

As discussed further in Chapter 3, the "public forum doctrine" is a powerful managerial tool. It grants officials broad authority to determine where protest and other speech activities can take place. Under this framework, other than public streets, parks, and sidewalks protesters have relatively weak or in many cases no viable First Amendment access claim. In terms of expression and assembly, the government's managerial power allows it to open and close most places at its discretion, limit properties to only certain content or speakers, and heavily regulate expression in forums otherwise open to public expression.

Permitting Protest

Assume organizers are planning one of the lawful and protected protests described in the basic protest typology discussed earlier. Assume further they want to hold their protest event in a public park – a "traditional" public forum. In most jurisdictions, provision is made for holding smaller, spontaneous events in such places without advance permission. Courts have also invalidated permit requirements that apply to only one or two individuals.[87] However, in general, protest organizers and participants must navigate a complex maze of bureaucratic and administrative requirements.[88] These requirements include obtaining a permit for the event, paying for (or posting a bond covering) certain costs, and complying with a variety of "time, place, and manner" regulations. (As discussed in Chapter 5, similar requirements apply on most public university campuses.)

To highlight the nature of these requirements, let us return one last time to Lee Circle. According to the regulations governing this parcel, any event expected to draw more than ten participants requires a "special event permit." To obtain such a permit, the organizer must submit a permit application, on a form provided by the city, at least 45 days prior to the event (in the case of more spontaneous protest events, the regulations allow for a six-day notice period so long as organizers meet all other permit requirements). The application must state, "at a minimum":

- Type and purpose of event, meeting, or function.
- Name, address, telephone numbers, and email address of the applicant.
- Name of the organization, date of origin, status (corporation, unincorporated association, partnership, non-profit corporation, etc.), address, and telephone numbers. If applicable, the federal tax ID number, registered agent's address, telephone numbers, and email address.
- Organization's primary point of contact, to include name, title, permanent address, telephone numbers, and email addresses.
- Organization's primary and alternative point of contact who will be on-site at the Lee Monument for the event, to include name, address, telephone numbers, and email addresses. The organization's on-site primary point of contact shall be responsible for the conduct of participants at the event.
- If the event is designed to be held by, on behalf of, or for any person other than the applicant, the applicant shall file with the director written documentation from the person or organization seeking to host the event, authorizing the applicant to apply for the permit on behalf of the person or organization.

- The estimated number of participants for the event. The maximum occupancy for the Lee Monument is 500 persons.
- Requested date and start and end times.
- Whether the event is being advertised, to include advertising on social media platforms.
- Proof that all needed permit applications have been submitted to the City of Richmond, to include a road closure permit if necessary. The applicant understands that if the City of Richmond will require road closure, authorized events will be permitted to last one hour, with an additional 30 minutes to set up and 30 minutes to break down the event. All events will begin at the agreed-upon time and must fall within the allowable time periods addressed in this section.
- List of requested items or equipment to be used during the event.
- Waste management plan and a point of contact for the plan, including name and telephone number.[89]

In addition, there are specified time limits for permitted protest events at Lee Circle, with regulations allowing for protests only during certain hours of the day. Moreover, permitted events can last only two hours – unless road closures are required, in which case the event may last only one hour. Lee Circle's regulations also limit the *manner* of protest in various respects. The regulations ban the following:

- Weapons: any pistol, rifle, shotgun, or other firearm of any kind, whether loaded or unloaded, air rifle, air pistol, paintball gun, paintball rifle, explosive, blasting cap, knife, hatchet, ax, slingshot, blackjack, metal knuckles, mace, iron buckle, ax handle, chains, crowbar, hammer, or any club, bludgeon, or any other instrumentality used, or intended to be used, as a dangerous weapon.
- Bricks, stones, rocks, or pieces of asphalt or concrete.
- Glass bottles, glass jars, or glass containers of any kind.
- Tents, tables, scaffolding, or staging.
- Penetration of the ground by any object.
- Stick-holding placards.
- Solicitations, sales, collections, or fundraising activities.
- Food or beverages of any type.
- Auxiliary and portable lights.
- Open air burning (hand-held candles with drip guards are acceptable).
- The use of unmanned aircraft systems (drones).
- Hazardous, flammable, or combustible liquids or materials.
- Animals, except service animals that are individually trained to do work or perform tasks for people with disabilities.
- Fossil-fuel powered generators.[90]

Under the Lee Circle regulations, permit applicants must also agree to *indemnify or reimburse* the Commonwealth of Virginia for any loss or damage to the monument that may occur in connection with the applicant or event organizer's use of the property. They must agree to leave the premises clean and orderly, and notify law enforcement if any unlawful activities occur during the permitted event. Failure to abide by any one of these conditions or the previously listed requirements will result in the immediate revocation of the permit. Failure to leave Lee Circle upon such revocation will result in a state law charge of trespassing.

Even if all these requirements and conditions are met, the city's director of the Department of General Services may still deny the permit application. The decision must be made within ten days of receipt of the permit application. The director can deny the permit because another application has already been submitted for the same date and time, approving the permit "would pose a significant threat to public safety," the applicant has not agreed to the necessary conditions, the director concludes the event "could not possibly conform" to the prescribed conditions, or any of the information in the application is found to be false or inaccurate.[91]

This granular level of regulatory detail is common, even in small public areas like Lee Circle. Sociologists have referred to this bureaucratic maze as part of the "public order management system" that applies to all or nearly all protests and demonstrations.[92] In much larger cities than Richmond, including New York City and Washington, D.C., the regulations are far more detailed and complex. In D.C., a common protest location, permitting and other regulations cover many pages in the Federal Register, Code of Federal Regulations, and D.C. Code.[93] Protesters must generally obtain permission and notify various government agencies prior to an event: the sidewalks in D.C. are under local jurisdiction, the national park lands are under the purview of the National Park Service, and certain areas near the U.S. Capitol are governed by the U.S. Capitol Police. Protesters are sometimes required to deal with all three agencies.

These are just the *basic* requirements for organizing and participating in a regulated protest event. During any event, law enforcement and other authorities can impose additional restrictions. For example, they can alter the route of a march, the time of a demonstration, sound levels, and crowd sizes. They can and often do limit protesters to designated "free speech zones."[94] As noted earlier, law enforcement can declare an assembly "unlawful" – even before any violent or unlawful activity occurs and even though the gathering otherwise complies with all applicable permitting requirements.

From the government's perspective, these detailed requirements and restrictions serve two general purposes. First, they provide notice of who is planning to protest and what type of event they are planning. This allows law enforcement and other agencies to prepare in advance for things like traffic control and parade routes. It also facilitates the negotiation of protest specifics (routes, arrests, etc.) with designated protest permit applicants. Second, by connecting the event to specific individuals or groups, the application process allows authorities to hold individuals and entities responsible for any violations of permit regulations and costs.

But these requirements impose significant burdens and costs on protest organizers and participants. In addition to the time and resources required to comply with burdensome permit application procedures, the regulations can negatively affect protest spontaneity and lead to protests that seem stale or canned. They also create an expressive anomaly, as protesters are required to comply with laws promulgated and enforced by governments that may be the central targets or objects of dissent.

As noted, permit schemes often require that protest organizers pay certain costs including permit fee applications, provide security deposits for cleanup and law enforcement overtime, and secure insurance policies.[95] These costs, which are addressed further in Chapter 4, impose significant and sometimes censorious financial burdens on organizers.

In recent years, municipalities have sought to shift more and more of these costs, which in the case of mass protests can run to hundreds of thousands of dollars, onto protest groups. Concerned about limited budgets, university administrators have also had to grapple with cost considerations. Courts have generally upheld charges that cover the actual administrative costs of protest events, although officials cannot increase or vary these costs based on a prediction an event will be controversial or a hostile crowd might materialize.[96] For large "million-person" marches and other events, protesters must be prepared to raise and spend significant sums and provide any necessary protest infrastructure (tents, restrooms, medical care, etc.).

Formal permitting requirements are not always strictly enforced. For example, had Richmond police enforced every detailed regulation applicable at Lee Circle, few, if any, public protests would have occurred there. As discussed in Chapter 4, protesters who engage in spontaneous mass protests can avoid some of the permit requirements and monetary costs in permit schemes. Many BLM protests during the summer of 2020, including those at Lee Circle, skirted local regulations by relying on spontaneous demonstrating. That did not mean protesters were allowed to peaceably assemble. Law enforcement in many jurisdictions used tear gas and other non-lethal weapons to disperse even the most peaceful assemblies.

In general, however, to comply with local laws protest organizers are responsible for knowing what ordinances and regulations require in terms of time, place, manner, and other restrictions. Law enforcement has broad discretion to impose additional content-neutral conditions on protest events. While such restrictions may violate the First Amendment if they are unnecessary for traffic control or public safety, or if they interfere significantly with effective communication with the intended audience, courts tend to apply a very deferential standard of review to protest regulations. Although they do occasionally invalidate permit requirements, when reviewing protest regulations courts generally defer to official explanations concerning the government's need to preserve order and protect public safety. Thus, even in places where protesters have a First Amendment right to be, they may be denied access for failing to comply with permit requirements or subjected to burdensome time, place, and manner restrictions.

Protest Policing

Formal ordinances, laws, and regulations are important components of the law of public protest and the system of managed dissent. But just as important, if not more so, is how law enforcement polices public demonstrations. Protest policing raises two primary, related concerns: the extraordinary discretion granted to officers on the ground, and the use of escalated force and militarized policing tactics. Both can have a chilling effect on public protest.

Focusing on the Charlottesville "Unite the Right" rallies in 2017, Rachel Harmon has explained the central role policing plays during protest events.[97] As she observed, in Charlottesville, police rather than prosecutors or permit administrators were squarely in charge of preparing for and handling the dueling rallies. As for the applicable law of public protest, she wrote:

> [T]he First Amendment is only one piece of the law that governs encounters between the police and the public. Even as it bars certain law enforcement options, the First Amendment permits many others, leaving police substantial discretion to determine who gets to speak and what consequences exist for those who gather with something to say.[98]

Harmon pointed to traditional law enforcement means of controlling crowds, including orders to move along and arrests to enforce these orders. She noted that police can arrest protesters for a wide variety of offenses, "from criminal assault to jaywalking."[99] As discussed earlier, police officers arrive at protests armed with a thick codebook that includes public order offenses such as "disorderly conduct," "failure to disperse," "breach of peace," "unlawful assembly," and "conspiracy to riot." In addition, Harmon observed that officers can arrest protesters for "crossing roads outside of marked crosswalks; walking in roadways when sidewalks are available; and willfully standing, sitting, or lying in a street in a manner that impedes the flow of traffic – all activities that protesters are wont to do."[100]

Further, under the Fourth Amendment, which prohibits "unreasonable searches and seizures," Harmon observed that officers can arrest protesters even for very minor or technical offenses,[101] make pretextual arrests,[102] and use force as necessary to compel compliance.[103] The First Amendment prohibits purposefully using these offenses to silence a speaker. However, proving purposeful content discrimination is quite difficult. Moreover, as discussed in Chapter 8, a recent Supreme Court decision makes it nearly impossible for protesters to sue police under federal civil rights laws for retaliating against them based on their speech.[104] As a result of loose public disorder laws, the absence of meaningful Fourth Amendment limits on their enforcement, and the general unavailability of civil rights remedies, police can impose public order and stability by engaging in what are effectively pretextual arrests for minor crimes.

As Harmon has argued, law enforcement's discretionary exercise of power can be vastly more important than the constitutional and regulatory constraints that apply during public protests. Even if a permitting scheme like the one applicable at Lee Circle *appears* to authorize protesters' presence and activities, officers can break up or shut down a protest based on any number of "public order" offenses. In this way, law enforcement operates to some degree outside the boundaries of the formal First Amendment. As Harmon has noted, "whatever policing strategy a department chooses, it is largely the police department rather than the law that determines what constitutes permissible protest and what instead represents a sufficient threat to public order to justify a forceful response."[105] In sum, both the formal law of public protest and norms of policing, which are part of that law, combine to severely restrict protest activity.

More generally, protest policing methods and tactics have long been a central means of managing dissent – particularly during large-scale and mass protests. Before and during these events, law enforcement conducts a variety of enforcement activities. Agencies and police departments engage in extensive surveillance, including the monitoring of protesters' internet postings and attending protest planning meetings. When they attend public protests, police often record and photograph demonstrators. In some cities, during recent BLM protests, local law enforcement worked with private security outfits that used advanced technology tools that collected data on protesters and journalists.[106] The data and other information were shared with law enforcement. While some local police departments have internal policies forbidding in-person infiltration of activist groups, not all have such policies and, in any event, they do not bind state and other law enforcement officials.

Some activists have objected to this surveillance as an invasion of privacy or complained that it chills lawful protest activity. In *Laird v. Tatum* (1972),[107] the Supreme Court held that surveillance of protest groups does not generally cause a cognizable injury for purposes of bringing a federal lawsuit based on the First Amendment. In *Laird*, the Court rejected protesters' claims that U.S. Army monitoring of anti-Vietnam War protest groups chilled members' exercise of First Amendment rights.[108] While the surveillance claim failed in *Laird*, some have argued that police *dissemination* of protest surveillance videos causes cognizable harms to protesters' rights to associate and engage in public expression.[109] Whether these sorts of claims will be successful depends, in part, on whether courts will be receptive to "chill" and privacy-related claims based on mass dissemination of videos and live streams of public protest activity. The use of private security companies to police protests raises its own concerns, not least of which is the lack of public accountability of such outfits.

Protest policing has frequently involved significant demonstrations of force, spatial restrictions on protesters' movements, the use of aggressive policing tactics, and mass arrests. Policies regarding the use of force have varied over time.[110] Prior to and during the 1960s, police departments relied on "escalated force" methods to control public protests. Under that approach, officers would typically order crowds to disperse from public places. If they refused, police would immediately resort to the use of physical force and violence to control and manage the situation. These practices resulted in mass arrests, police brutality, and the deaths of protesters including those on the Kent State University campus.

Over time, policing practices generally shifted to a model of "negotiated management," which relies on the sort of advance planning and cooperation exhibited in the Lee Circle regulations.[111] Under this approach, protest organizers and police discuss the details of protest events in advance – including the location or route of the planned demonstration or march, the number of expected participants, the nature of visual displays, and even arrest logistics. In some jurisdictions, negotiated management is the primary protest policing model.

However, during the past few decades, many police forces have reverted to more militarized and aggressive protest policing methods.[112] Many departments have relied on a "command-and-control" approach, which in many respects resembles the "escalated force" model.[113] Command-and-control emphasizes "the micromanagement of all aspects of demonstrations," including efforts to control public space using barricades, police lines, and other means of surrounding, subdividing, and directing the flow of protesters.[114] Police exhibit "a willingness to use force against even minor violations of law."[115] Police often use military vehicles and weapons such as flash grenades, tear gas, and semi-automatic rifles. The avatar of the command-and-control model is the "warrior" officer, decked out in riot gear and armed to the teeth. There are many explanations for this law enforcement shift, including the terrorist attacks that occurred in 2001 and the flow of federal money to state and local police forces, many of which used the funds to purchase surplus military equipment and riot gear.[116]

This policing model has had profoundly negative effects on public protest. The policing of racial justice protests that followed the deaths of George Floyd, Breonna Taylor, and other Black Americans exhibited the very worst elements of "command-and-control." Police fired tear gas and flash grenades at peaceful protesters, assaulted public demonstrators and members of the press, made mass arrests, targeted journalists, and used force in many situations where negotiation or de-escalation were clear options. Judging from these and other recent mass protests, police departments either still lack the necessary training to police public demonstrations in ways that preserve First Amendment rights or "warrior" officers are simply being ordered to clear the streets at all costs. Whatever the reason, law enforcement continues to manage dissent through sometimes brutal policing methods.

The trend toward command-and-control protest policing raises questions about how law enforcement handled the January 6, 2021, Capitol riot. When Trump supporters stormed the U.S. Capitol building on January 6, 2021, to disrupt the counting of electoral votes for the 2020 presidential election, law enforcement seemed uncharacteristically unprepared or unwilling to use force to defend the Capitol. While some officers fought valiantly, groups of rioters appeared to have free rein as they breached the perimeter and moved about inside congressional buildings. Similarly, in Michigan and other states, heavily armed protesters were permitted to enter legislative chambers without serious pushback from law enforcement. While in these instances they may have had cause to resort to at least non-lethal force, officers stood down. The difference in responses has once again raised significant questions about the disparate application of policing force to Black and other marginalized protesters.

Protest organizers and participants must contend with not only complex and detailed permitting regimes, but also the prospect that police officers will respond to even peaceful and lawful protests with barely disguised pretextual arrests and aggressive policing. Protesters caught up in policing dragnets are required to spend significant time, money, and other resources fighting unlawful charges, while those subject to escalated force suffer physical and other harms. Protest policing continues to be one of the most concerning aspects of the law of public protest.

ADDITIONAL MANAGERIAL CHALLENGES

The limits and conditions described so far impose substantial burdens on protest organizers and participants. Several other aspects of the law of public protest pose additional challenges. These include lawsuits and statutes that expose protesters and their supporters to significant civil liabilities, severe limits on remedies available to protesters whose constitutional rights have been violated, the presence of armed protesters and counter-protesters, and governmental powers to restrict public protest during public health emergencies and periods of civil unrest.

Protesters' Civil Liabilities and Remedies

Protest organizers, participants, and supporters may face significant legal liability for their actions. They can be sued for damages for actions they take leading up to and during public demonstrations. However, when their constitutional rights are violated, protesters discover that they have little or no legal recourse against police officers, municipalities, and others who have harmed them. As discussed in Chapters 4 and 8, the laws governing protester liabilities and remedies manage dissent by exposing participants to substantial damages awards while at the same time eliminating paths to recovery for constitutional violations.

The law of public protest includes general "tort" or personal injury causes of action, as well as statutory causes of action applicable to protest organizers, supporters, and participants. Demonstrators and counterdemonstrators may be held liable for assault, battery, false imprisonment, interference with business relations, trespass to property, negligence, and other civil wrongs. State laws have also increased the civil penalties for trespassing on public and private lands. In some jurisdictions, legislatures have extended civil racketeering laws to protest organizations.[117]

Protesters' potential civil liability exposure has been increasing. In response to recent mass protests, policymakers have proposed or adopted measures increasing the civil liabilities of protesters. States have significantly increased civil fines for obstructing traffic, trespassing, and "mass picketing"; allowed businesses to sue protesters who target them; authorized civil suits against those who support protests that result in property or other damage; enacted new civil penalties for protests that take place near "critical infrastructure" ranging from gas pipelines to telephone poles; and applied asset forfeiture provisions to protest groups.[118] Protest activity is managed through these legal actions and statutes, which raise the financial stakes of organizing and participating.

In recent years, civil actions have been morphing and multiplying in ways that pose serious threats to dissent. Protest organizers, supporters, and participants have been sued for "negligent protest organizing," "riot boosting," and other alleged civil wrongs. The combination of these statutory and common law causes of action threatens protesters' First Amendment rights and can result in severe restrictions on public protest.

At the same time that these laws have increased the potential exposure of protesters to civil damages, others have closed off opportunities for protesters to recover damages for constitutional violations. The law of "qualified immunity" shields state and local public officials – including law enforcement officers – from civil liability unless they have violated "clearly established" First Amendment or other rights. As interpreted, this immunity precludes civil liability for police and other officials except in cases of egregious violations. Meanwhile, the Supreme Court has all but slammed shut the door to recovery against federal officials who violate First Amendment rights.

This stingy remedial regime facilitates the management of dissent by letting officials – and their employers – off the hook for all but the most obvious First Amendment violations. Officers and officials who act secure in the knowledge they are unlikely to be held personally liable, and municipalities that likewise enjoy this shield except in rare circumstances, are less likely to uphold and preserve protesters' rights and more likely to engage in aggressive forms of managed dissent.

Armed Protests

State laws and a recent Supreme Court decision recognize a broad right to carry firearms in public places.[119] In recent years, people have increasingly been appearing at public protests openly carrying firearms. As the Kyle Rittenhouse prosecution and other protest-related incidents have shown, the confluence of protest and carriage of firearms can be dangerous and even fatal. Individuals and groups that carry firearms during protests pose a unique challenge to peaceful protest. To the extent laws and decisions authorizing public carry intersect with and affect public protest, they become part of the law of public protest and the system of managed dissent.

As discussed further in Chapter 6, the presence of armed individuals and groups, including self-styled "militias," at public protests threatens to chill peaceful speech and assembly.[120] Protesters who are intimidated by armed individuals or groups may lower their voices, literally and figuratively, or change their messages so as not to provoke armed audiences. They may decide it is too dangerous to participate in public protests where counter-protesters or others have access to a means of lethal response. Protesters may be reluctant to "stir people to anger," as the Supreme Court has put it, for fear of being shot.

The right to public carry can "manage" dissent by limiting its occurrence, place, and manner. The presence of firearms also adds to the challenge of policing demonstrations, including protecting First Amendment speech and assembly rights and keeping protesters and bystanders safe.

As it becomes increasingly armed, the public square may take on the character of an arms race in which protesters and police feel it is necessary to carry more and more lethal weapons to public demonstrations. Law enforcement has already leveraged informal "militias" and others to assist it in maintaining order. When that happens, protesters are forced to contend with an intimidating and potentially lethal combination of aggressive policing, armed and dangerous counter-protesters, and informally deputized "citizen-militias."

How public officials and courts react to the presence of firearms at protests will significantly affect the exercise of public protest rights. More than that, what is at stake is the peaceful resolution of cultural and political differences through speech and counter-speech rather than armed conflict.

Emergency Powers and Protest Rights

As the nation recently experienced, governments exercise broad powers during public health emergencies and periods of civil unrest. At such times, state and federal officials exercise significant managerial control over public activities including demonstrations.

During the COVID-19 pandemic, some states declared that public demonstrations were "non-essential" activities and effectively banned them.[121] They also imposed social distancing, curfews, limits on public gatherings, and other restrictions that targeted or affected public protest. Similarly, state and federal officials reacted to the civil unrest that followed George Floyd's murder by calling out the National Guard, enacting curfews, and threatening to impose order through the deployment of U.S. military forces.

The balance between governmental authority and individual liberty (including the exercise of First Amendment rights) has not been clearly drawn for such extraordinary situations. Courts have sent mixed signals regarding the extent to which they will defer to medical or scientific judgments when constitutional rights are at stake.[122] That deference could pose serious concerns when it comes to the right to protest government policies and other matters in public. Civil unrest triggers its own unique set of legal authorities, including the federal Anti-Riot Act and the Insurrection Act of 1807.[123] Public unrest in response to George Floyd's murder once again raised largely unanswered questions about the scope of executive authority to quell civil unrest.

As recent events have clarified, exigent powers are an important component of the law of public protest. Although such authorities are more temporally and otherwise limited than permit codes and other restrictions, they are nevertheless tools for managing dissent. Those tools apply at crucial moments of public contention, and their application can have devastating effects on public protest rights.

* * * * *

Public protest and dissent are thoroughly managed and constrained through the First Amendment's conduct and content limitations; the authority granted to government officials to categorize and designate which properties are open to expression; detailed permit schemes; time, place, and manner regulations; and aggressive protest policing. Although the First Amendment does not protect violence or other unlawful conduct, dissent in the U.S. is managed far beyond the boundaries suggested by these narrow limitations. Under the system of managed dissent, officials over-regulate non-violent assemblies, over-punish civil disobedience, impose burdensome costs and liabilities on protesters, respond to even the most peaceful protest with violence and aggression, and far too often escape liability for their actions. This system is inconsistent with, if not directly contrary to, the nation's history of public contention, its civic traditions, and its commitment to robust and wide-open public discourse as a central means of social and political change.

3

Displacing Dissent

Place or location is critically important to effective public protest and dissent. As discussed in Chapter 1, *public* protest serves a variety of communicative and democratic functions. It is critically important that this activity takes place in public. Having adequate public space is a prerequisite for collective displays of contention and dissent. Access to public places also facilitates collective enterprises such as self-government and the search for truth in the marketplaces of ideas – indeed, public places are a special kind of "marketplace." Further, as I have explained in prior work, *where* individuals and groups engage in speech and assembly is often closely related to their message.[1] The law of public protest grants governments broad and, I will argue, in many cases unwarranted authority to manage dissent by denying or restricting access to place. It does so first by generally restricting the places where protest can occur, and then imposing a variety of "time, place, and manner" restrictions even in places open to expression. Spatial management of dissent includes permit requirements, the use of "free speech zones," and the "militarization" of the public square during protest events. It also relies on targeted protest regulations (TPRs), which limit protest in specific locations – usually in response to controversial protest activity in these places. Managing dissent by and through place is part of a deeply rooted tradition of zoning, concentrating, confining, dispersing, and displacing public assembly and contention.

PLACE AND PUBLIC PROTEST

Place is critically important to effective public protest. Americans have traditionally relied on access to public places to communicate dissent and present collective grievances. In fact, the inclination of the American people to gather in public places and express themselves is older than the Republic.[2] Colonial Americans assembled in public committees, conventions, and even "mobs" to petition public officials, make their collective grievances known, and realize social and political goals.

American conceptions of "popular sovereignty" originated in this fashion – out of doors, on the ground, in the public square. In *Democracy in America*, Alexis de Tocqueville wrote:

> When one allows a political association to place centers of action at certain important points of the country, its activity becomes greater and its influence more extended. There men see each other, means of execution are combined and opinions are deployed with the force and heat that written thought can never attain.[3]

A century and a half later, Justice Anthony Kennedy wrote, "At the heart of our jurisprudence lies the principle that in a free nation citizens must have the right to gather and speak with other persons in public places."[4] Assembling and protesting in public squares, streets, and other locations is a venerable American tradition. As the Supreme Court has recognized in its public forum doctrine, people have engaged in these activities "immemorially" and "time out of mind."[5]

Protesters' access to and use of public places support a variety of First Amendment values. The leading justifications for having freedom of speech and assembly are that these activities facilitate self-government and propel the search for truth in the "marketplace of ideas."[6] Public places have historically been, and remain, instrumental to citizen self-governance and the search for truth. They have created "breathing space" for democratic participation and provided a stage for speech and counter-speech in the marketplace of ideas.

As John Inazu has observed, "The ideal of the public forum represents one of the most important aspects of a healthy democracy. It signifies a willingness to tolerate dissent, discomfort, and even instability."[7] Providing public places where peaceable assemblies can gather is a necessary predicate to realizing important democratic goals. As the Supreme Court has observed, "First Amendment freedoms need breathing space to survive."[8] Collective forms of dissent such as protests, rallies, and demonstrations are *only* possible in public places that can accommodate assemblies of various sizes.

Public places, including the nation's streets and parks, have traditionally functioned as sites of public discourse and contention on matters of public importance. They have enabled public citizenship and the "search for truth" by facilitating interactions among diverse groups of citizens and among citizens and their representatives in government. As the legal scholar Cass Sunstein has argued, democratic participation requires at least some exposure to speakers and messages that audiences do not wish to encounter or engage with.[9] The special characteristics of public places make it more likely audiences will be aware of protesters' messages. In public places, proximity to others and the basic physicality of protest make it difficult for audiences to ignore protesters and other speakers. As the Supreme Court has recognized, that is a singular virtue of preserving access to public forums like streets and parks.[10] For some protest audiences, proximity annoys, offends, or even breeds contempt. But in theory, at least, the First Amendment recognizes protesters' right to elicit precisely such reactions.[11] Disruption of the status quo purposefully inconveniences, nudges, and even annoys.

Public presence matters to full democratic citizenship. In public places, people are visible, accounted for, and reckoned with. Indeed, presence in a public place can itself be an expressive claim to political identity and representation. During the 1930s and 1940s, Jehovah's Witnesses made these sorts of identity and representation claims by confronting audiences on the public streets.[12] During the 1950s and 1960s, civil rights activists communicated similar messages by demonstrating in the streets and occupying public places.[13] More recent movements, including the Tea Party, Occupy Wall Street, the March for Life, March for Our Lives, and BLM, have continued these representational and political uses of place. Public presence has historically communicated claims to full legal and constitutional personhood. Access to public places makes such claims possible. Even if such claims are not always or fully recognized, public activities spark national political conversations about religion, race, income inequality, immigration, and other issues.

Public places also lend invaluable transparency to the democratic process and help check governmental abuses of power. Public contention challenges governmental authority in ways that are direct and transparent to the rest of the political community. Public places also render the exercise of sovereign power more visible. People bear witness to official reactions to citizen grievances, in venues that are more difficult to "script" in the manner of town hall meetings or legislative sessions. The aggressive response of law enforcement to a multitude of BLM protests during the summer of 2020 helped expose the very grievance that animated the demonstrations in the first place.

Finally, in terms of democratic functions, public places provide a safety valve for potentially violent movements and expose those movements to public and official scrutiny. Peaceful protesters are not the only ones that access public places. The white supremacists in Charlottesville, Virginia and the insurrectionists who stormed the Capitol on January 6 communicated hateful, violent, anti-democratic messages. The public forum provided a space for extremist views so they could be seen and heard, subjected to scrutiny, and widely debunked and rejected. These protests exposed, in a tangible and public way, continuing threats to order, equality, and democracy itself. The public nature of these events also helped authorities hold many lawbreakers accountable.

Freedom of speech has also been justified by reference to autonomy values, including individual self-fulfillment. Public places have furthered these individualistic values, providing sites for the self-actualization of individual speakers and group members. Preserving access to public places helps individuals and groups realize all the benefits of collective expression discussed in Chapter 1 – including communicating with internal and external audiences and experiencing the solidarity and dignity of protest.[14] Public places are stages for the expression and amplification of collective grievances. Participation in a public protest or demonstration is a form of acting out in public. In this sense, public places are "theatrical" venues "in which one is seen and shows oneself to others."[15]

Media coverage can be critical to the amplification of protest messages. Assemblies in the public square present attractive visuals and compelling footage. In this way, too, demonstrating in an open public venue facilitates the distribution of protesters' messages. News media are typically attracted to conflict, including clashes with authorities and other forms of disruption of daily routines. As I have noted, this bias can prejudice some protesters and even protest itself. However, media coverage can also sometimes be leveraged to help individuals and groups reach and even expand their audiences.[16] Sharing protest images on social media bypasses the institutional media and ensures an even larger audience.

For protesters, public places can be uniquely communicative. As I have argued elsewhere, the concept of "place" is more central to expression than lawyerly notions of "property," which form the basis for First Amendment place doctrines, recognize.[17]

Places often have uniquely symbolic importance. Protesters may assemble at a state capitol where controversial bills are being debated, a jail holding people they earnestly believe are political prisoners, a public monument at the center of a conversation about racism, a health care clinic that provides abortion services, or a police station where officers accused of brutality work. These spatial choices are intentional and themselves communicative – or intended to be so. Protesting in or near *these* places, as opposed to elsewhere, focuses attention on an object of contention and controversy. It helps audiences orient disputes and understand protesters' complaints.

The *vocality* of place is generally overlooked or downplayed in First Amendment doctrines.[18] "Public forum" and "time, place, and manner" standards give broad control over access to public properties to government proprietors. These standards also assume places are fungible: so long as speakers and groups can communicate someplace, courts often reason, their First Amendment rights are not violated. The false premise underlying these doctrines is that displacement constitutes only a minor inconvenience or is an insignificant impediment to expression. The Supreme Court used to state, "one is not to have the exercise of his liberty of expression in appropriate places abridged on the plea that it may be exercised in some other place."[19] But it has since narrowed which places are "appropriate" venues for expression and made clear that speakers are entitled only to *some* place and not their preferred locations.

Of course, protesters do not possess an absolute right to protest in any location they desire. They have no right to commandeer legislators' offices, university classrooms being used for instruction, or the corridors of hospitals. As these examples show, venue or location can implicate an array of countervailing interests including efficient operation of workplaces and the tranquility required for patient care. While recognition and some accommodation of these and other interests are certainly in order, First Amendment place doctrines have tilted in the direction of minimal access rights and a presumption against protesters' choice of place.

Finally, there are important distributive advantages associated with access to public places. Providing adequate public space for speech and assembly is especially
critical to what the Supreme Court once referred to as "the poorly financed causes
of little people."[20] Across generations, employees, racial minorities, and dissident
speakers have benefited immensely from access to public streets and other properties. Throughout American history, they have relied on such access to organize
and propel social and constitutional movements that faced a variety of financial
and structural disadvantages. Today, speakers and groups continue to face similar
disadvantages. Ensuring access to public places helps a variety of "poorly financed
causes" reach their audiences.

Some may be skeptical of the continued value or necessity of access to tangible
places. After all, we live in an era of "cheap" and seemingly far more democratic
expression.[21] Digital platforms help facilitate communication of the "causes of little
people." During the late 1990s, the Supreme Court gushed about the ability of a
lone speaker to communicate from a "virtual soapbox" to a worldwide audience.[22]
Of course, that is not exactly how things have worked out online – at least for most
speakers. However, it is certainly true that today's speakers have plenty of virtual
outlets for protest and dissent (as well as other subjects).

As I emphasize later, virtual places are a critical part of our expressive culture and
media environment. People cannot engage in effective political and social contention in
the streets and parks alone. However, neither can they self-govern from their keyboards
and laptops. To preserve public protest, we will need both tangible and virtual spaces.
Each has advantages and disadvantages in terms of facilitating public contention.

THE PROTEST TOPOGRAPHY

Given the obvious and close connection between public places and expressive values, one would think Americans have access to a wide variety of public venues for
the purpose of exercising First Amendment speech, assembly, and petition rights.
Harry Kalven, Jr. once observed that the extent to which a nation provides this space
constitutes an "index of freedom."[23] But judging by that measure, the U.S. "score"
is far lower than one would expect – particularly for a nation that regularly boasts of
its robust free speech culture. The "expressive topography," or places where speech
and assembly rights are robustly protected under the First Amendment, has many
gaps and is not broadly welcoming of public protest.[24]

The reality facing protesters in the U.S. has long been that they are entitled – in
the sense of having an enforceable constitutional right – to access relatively few
public properties for the purpose of engaging in speech or assembly. As explained
in Chapter 2, protesters and other speakers have relatively robust access rights to
public streets, parks, and sidewalks (at least those that function as ordinary sidewalks and do not serve some other purpose).[25] But outside these "traditional public
forums," protesters have access rights only to the places where the government has

clearly demonstrated an intent to allow expressive activities. And in all places where speakers can claim *any* First Amendment right to demonstrate, governments can impose significant restrictions on when, where, and how they do so. Putting things bluntly, one legal scholar described these access rules as "a declaration of deference to forum administrators."[26]

As I explained in my book *Speech Out of Doors*, to appreciate the nature and scope of this limitation on public protest, imagine a map of all the places in and around a single large metropolitan area somewhere in the U.S. On the map, there are public thoroughfares such as streets, sidewalks, medians, and rights of way. There are also public parks, plazas, squares, and monuments. There are a variety of public buildings, gardens, and transit hubs. There are public and private university campuses, shopping malls and districts, housing developments, auditoriums, museums, and a stadium. On the outskirts of town there is a municipal airport, and beyond that highways and travel plazas.

Now imagine that the same map is divided into zones represented by three colors. Green spaces on the map represent places where speakers and groups have an enforceable First Amendment right to engage in expressive activities. They have a right to be in these places to assemble and protest, subject to regulations on the time, place, and manner of their activities. Yellow spaces on the map represent areas where the government has allowed expressive activity to occur but has limited the types of speakers that can use the place, allowable subject matters of discourse, or both. In yellow areas, governmental proprietors can generally dictate what kinds of expressive activities are allowed so long as regulations are minimally reasonable and do not discriminate against speakers based on their point of view. Finally, in red spaces, speakers enjoy no access or First Amendment expressive protections at all. In those spaces, governments – or private property owners – can exclude all expression from the premises. In these places, speakers cannot rely on either a longstanding tradition of access or a demonstrable government intent to provide access for speech and assembly.

This mapping is the result of the Supreme Court's public forum doctrine, which has been the subject of extensive scholarly criticism. One commentator summed things up by characterizing the doctrine as "crude, historically ossified, and seemingly unconnected to any thematic view of the free expression guarantee."[27] As a result of this doctrine, yellow and red areas on the expressive topography far outnumber those colored green. An observer would quickly notice that not all public parks, streets, and sidewalks are "green" spaces. For instance, as one court observed, under forum doctrine, whether an area *within* a national park is open to expressive activity depends on its traditional functions and uses.[28] As explained below, many laws and regulations impose special restrictions on protesters' access to streets and sidewalks in specific locations.

Under the public forum doctrine, ossification is a significant problem. No "traditional" public forum has *ever* been added to the list of streets, parks, and sidewalks.

That is so despite massive social, demographic, technological, and a great many other changes over the past half-century that have affected where and how potential audiences can be found. Other forces, including the privatization of once-public areas and security measures put in place after the September 11, 2001, terrorist attacks on U.S. soil, have further restricted protesters' access to public places. Private properties, to which speakers have no First Amendment access claim, are not part of the expressive topography.

Harry Kalven, Jr. once praised the Supreme Court's recognition of the "public forum" for recognizing speakers' right to "commandeer" certain public places.[29] But as the Occupy Wall Street movement plainly demonstrated, protesters' ability to "commandeer" public places to communicate their messages is limited. Protesters sought to literally occupy public places to bring attention to income inequality and other matters of public concern. Consistent with principles of managed dissent, law enforcement responded to the Occupy movement with aggressive tactics and courts largely upheld bans or significant limits on their presence in public parks and plazas.[30]

Owing to a variety of legal and non-legal influences, the topography's green spaces are shrinking while the yellow and red spaces are expanding.[31] Further, even within the "green" spaces challenges and obstacles continue to mount for protest organizers and participants. They include a rise in costs associated with public protest, increased penalties for even minor unlawful acts, endemic and continuing problems with aggressive protest policing, and the presence of armed counter-protesters. The steady erosion of expressive space has obvious and significant implications for the preservation of public protest as a means of democratic discourse. As already discussed, without adequate "breathing space," collective forms of public expression are not possible and public protest cannot serve its many democratic and expressive functions.

There are two potential solutions to this problem. The Supreme Court could refashion its "public forum" doctrine wholesale, or at least reconsider it in ways that recognize more public properties and places as "traditional" forums generally open for expressive activity. Although this would be a welcome development, the prospects for that kind of doctrinal change seem very remote.[32] If we cannot bring additional "green" spaces into being, then courts ought to be more critical and skeptical of the variety of spatial laws, regulations, and norms that restrict protest activities in places where they should be allowed. These laws, regulations, and norms will be the focus of the remainder of this chapter.

MANAGING PROTEST PLACES

When it comes to public protest, public forums raise a central contradiction. On the one hand, to function as democratic spaces these places require a certain level of disorder and unpredictability. On the other hand, democratic discourse requires a certain level of order and public security.[33] The First Amendment is not a license to engage in violence, destroy property, or incite riots.[34] At the same time, however, the system currently grants governments overly broad deference to use spatial regulations and tactics to constrain, control, and even displace public dissent.

Permits and Time, Place, and Manner Regulations

Chapter 2 explained the burdensome nature and expressive effects of protest-permitting schemes. The days when officials tolerated a significant degree of disorder during public rallies, demonstrations, and parades appear to be behind us.[35] Supreme Court jurisprudence has signaled a strong preference for public expression that does not threaten to disrupt daily routines, challenge official authority over public places, or upset audiences. The rules and standards the Court has adopted heavily favor order and other government interests over messy, unpredictable, and disruptive public contention.

Although demonstrations sometimes spill into the streets spontaneously, for example in response to the Supreme Court's decision overturning *Roe v. Wade,* most protest activities are planned. These plans are subject to detailed permitting requirements. Permitting requirements are an aspect of what political sociologists have called the "public order management system."[36] Officials rely on permit schemes to maintain order during public protests. But for protesters, these licensing schemes can have devastating effects on massing and messaging.

Officials from the smallest town to iconic federal enclaves have adopted permitting requirements that apply to public protests and demonstrations in "green" areas on the expressive topography. Permits are a longstanding feature of the law of public protest. The Supreme Court first upheld a permit requirement (along with a permitting fee) in 1941.[37] In most circumstances, conditioning speech or assembly on prior governmental permission would amount to a presumptively unconstitutional prior restraint. However, the Supreme Court has held that so long as they are based on objective considerations like traffic control and other matters not having to do with the content of expression, permit schemes are not equivalent to prior restraints.[38]

Permit regulations impose various conditions on the time, place, and manner of demonstrating in a place. From the perspective of officials, permitting helps law enforcement maintain order and provides notice of potential safety and security concerns relating to public protests. From the perspective of the protester, permits and other time, place, and manner regulations are problematic because they can significantly interfere with the exercise of First Amendment rights and significantly alter or suppress the content of dissent.[39] Despite the obvious expressive effects of these regulations, courts have generally upheld permit requirements so long as they are "reasonable."[40]

As discussed in Chapter 2, permit regulations apply in nearly every place on the expressive topography in which a group wants to peaceably assemble and communicate. In most jurisdictions, very small assemblies can gather without a permit. However, in some localities, even a *single person* wishing to demonstrate must obtain a permit.[41] In most public venues otherwise available for speech and assembly activities, subject to exceptions for small and spontaneous assemblies, protesting or demonstrating without a permit is unlawful.

Consider New York City's permit requirements, which vest extraordinary discretion in officials to deny permission to demonstrate in the City. New York's code provides, "It shall be unlawful for the police commissioner to grant a permit where the commissioner has *good reason to believe that the proposed procession, parade or race will be disorderly in character* or *tend to disturb the public peace.*"[42] Permits are also not to be issued for parades or processions on streets or public places, or portions thereof, "ordinarily subject to great congestion or traffic."[43] They must specify the exact route of processions and the "width of the roadway to be used."[44] Read and applied literally, the New York City code would allow – perhaps even *require* – the police commissioner to deny applications to march or process on nearly any street in the city.

Municipalities are constantly amending their permitting restrictions. In recent years, New York City officials sought to further restrict protests and demonstrations. The city instituted a ban on all parades down congested city streets, including Fifth Avenue, which had not been allowed prior to 2001.[45] Officials defended the ban on the ground that Fifth Avenue and other streets had become "over-saturated" with events. However, the ban allowed the mayor to grant "special permits" relating to "occasions of extraordinary public interest," defined as "celebrations organized by the city honoring the armed forces; sports achievements or championships; world leaders and extraordinary achievements of historic significance." A federal district court upheld the ban on "new" parades and processions but struck down the provision granting the mayor special permit discretion.[46] The current New York City administrative code allows the New York City police commissioner to authorize a "procession or parade" if it has marched annually over the past decade.[47] The Code also allows for the issuance of special permits for events of "extraordinary public interest," without providing any definition of that phrase.[48]

New York City has also limited the *size* of permitted assemblies in some traditional public forums. In 2004, city officials refused to allow anti-war protesters access to the Great Lawn in Central Park during the Republican National Convention.[49] The city argued that since it had spent considerable sums to restore the park and the lawn it should be allowed to restrict protests to 50,000 participants to protect its investment. A federal court upheld the restriction.[50] As a result of a settlement with protesters, the city ultimately agreed to increase the size of permissible assemblies to 75,000 participants – pending a study (funded by the city) to determine the optimal and sustainable use of the Great Lawn. By way of comparison, a February 3, 2003, anti-war protest in Rome, Italy was reported to have involved approximately *three million* participants.[51]

Permit and other time, place, and manner requirements can also alter or prohibit march and parade routes in response to safety, traffic, security, or other governmental concerns. These decisions can significantly affect protesters' ability to
access special sites of contention where target audiences are gathered. For example,
demonstrators hoping to march past a political convention site can be re-routed to
distant streets well beyond "sight and sound" of the gathering or, as discussed later,
penned into "free speech zones." Some courts have rejected the argument that protesters have a First Amendment right to be within "sight and sound" of intended
audiences.[52] As one federal district court proclaimed, "there is no constitutional
entitlement to see the whites of the eyes of one's intended audience."[53] These decisions are rooted in a managerial bias that devalues face-to-face or proximate protest
or considers it inherently dangerous.

Although permitting requirements can displace or suppress protest anywhere in
the U.S., their application in iconic places disparately affects public protest activity. Mass demonstrations, especially, tend to occur on the streets of larger metropolitan areas and in places with historically symbolic value. Nowhere are the rules
more complex than in the District of Columbia.[54] An entire section of the Code
of Federal Regulations sets forth detailed and elaborate rules for holding protests,
demonstrations, parades, or rallies on Pennsylvania Avenue, the National Mall, and
other historically significant protest sites. Multiple governmental agencies, including the National Park Service, the Secret Service, and the District of Columbia
Police exercise jurisdiction over every space in D.C. Permit requirements are strict,
and, as discussed in Chapter 4, protesting in D.C. is becoming prohibitively expensive for some. Demonstrations of certain sizes are exempt from permit requirements.
However, "million-person" marches and other large events must obtain permits well
in advance of an event and negotiate their terms with agency and police officials.

Permitting requirements and time, place, and manner regulations make it
increasingly difficult to gather near symbolic places including the White House,
Congress, and the Supreme Court. The National Park Service recently proposed
adding to these restrictions near Congress and the White House, and on other portions of the National Mall.[55] One of the agency's proposals would have reduced the
protest area on sidewalks near the White House by 80 *percent*. The Park Service
later withdrew its proposed rule. However, as the District of Columbia continues to
be the site of a new era of public contention – including the January 6, 2021, riot –
such proposals are likely to resurface. Indeed, after the January 6 riot, new security
measures including fencing and location restrictions were implemented to protect
the Capitol from further riots and attacks. Whether those measures will become
permanent features remains to be seen. However, it seems likely that protesting
near the Capitol and other iconic venues in D.C. is likely to become more, not less,
difficult in the future.

As mentioned, some jurisdictions allow for unpermitted "spontaneous" demonstrations. These provisions may provide relief from permitting requirements, at least for

certain kinds of demonstrations. However, the backlash against the 2020 BLM protests may cause some states to cut back on or even try to ban spontaneous demonstrations. It is not clear whether the First Amendment *requires* officials to allow spontaneous protests. The Supreme Court has never addressed the issue. Some lower courts have held that the First Amendment requires governments to provide at least some opportunity for protests responding to fast-developing events.[56] That ought to be the constitutional rule. It is not clear what government interest outweighs the right of at least small groups to spontaneously assemble. After all, many municipalities exempt funeral processions and other small gatherings from permit requirements. Imposing a license requirement on assemblies formed on short notice in response to events of public concern implicates First Amendment concerns of the highest order.[57]

Requiring a permit for spontaneous events also puts protesters in an unacceptable bind. Groups that have been allowed to demonstrate in response to breaking news may find that permission has been revoked by authorities without notice. As Judge Richard Posner observed in a case involving the arrest of protesters who had been allowed to demonstrate, but then arrested for doing so: "The underlying problem is the basic idiocy of a permit system that does not allow a permit for a march to be granted if the date of the march can't be fixed in advance but does allow the police to waive the permit requirement just by not prohibiting the demonstration."[58]

Permitting schemes implicate a delicate balance between the Robert's Rules of Order civil society requires and the disruption protest and dissent often thrive on. It is obviously necessary, for example, to ensure that two parades or marches do not occur on the same thoroughfare at the same time.[59] The chaos and violence associated with the "Unite the Right" rallies in Charlottesville are evidence of what might happen without such control. However, the complexity and burden of most modern permit schemes are out of all reasonable proportion to the government's basic interests in traffic control and public safety. They are part of a legal system that lodges extraordinarily broad discretion in officials to ban, minimize, or displace public parades, marches, rallies, and demonstrations on the grounds that they might cause disorder, disturb the peace, or harm precious park lawns.

Zoning, Penning, and Caging Protest

One of the most troubling kinds of spatial restriction, often imposed through permitting schemes, is the so-called "free speech zone." As the name implies, zoning speech involves designating officially sanctioned areas or places (zones) in which speech and assembly are confined and permitted.[60] Zoning separates speakers from audiences, distorts dissent, and eliminates many of the symbolic and other benefits associated with protesters' choice of location.

Free speech zoning has been a response to public contention in the U.S. since at least the beginning of the twentieth century. The first "zones" were enforced against labor agitators – members of the International Workers of the World, or "Wobblies" –

who assembled in public places to press for changes to labor laws.[61] Officials relied on zoning restrictions to suppress the Wobblies' public agitation. Although the First Amendment did not yet apply to state and local speech regulations, the Wobblies nevertheless raised "free speech" objections to these restrictive zones.

Since then, free speech zones have cropped up across the expressive topography. Zoning has been used at or near political campaign events and conventions, abortion clinics, funerals, public auditoriums, national parks, university campuses, and presidential inaugurals.[62] Free speech zones can be disturbingly minimalist. For example, in California's Muir Woods, a 500-acre parkland, officials designed a small "First Amendment Area," marked by a posted sign, where speech is allowed. As discussed in Chapter 5, on some large university campuses, administrators have designated minuscule "zones" where students and others can communicate without advance permission.

Zoning has generated its own lexicon. Protesters and other speakers now must navigate a gauntlet of "free speech zones," "speech-free zones," "demonstration zones," "buffers," and "bubbles." Whatever the label, the concept is the same – speech and assembly are restricted to officially approved locations. According to current First Amendment doctrine, these zones do not violate the First Amendment so long as they are content-neutral, serve important governmental interests, do not burden more speech than necessary to further the government's interests, and leave open alternative channels of communication.[63]

Proponents have sometimes defended free speech zones as *facilitative* of free expression. After all, officials are setting aside a special place for speech and assembly. But the defense is misleading or cynical. Rather than preserving robust expressive rights in a public forum or one of the "green" areas on the protest topography, free speech zones effectively downsize public forums by limiting expression to cramped and confined areas. Courts have sometimes taken issue with the tailoring of free speech zones – particularly if they effectively suppress *all* opportunity for protest.[64] However, under the First Amendment's time, place, and manner doctrine, officials retain broad authority to rely on zoning to manage dissent.

The most egregious example of free speech zoning occurred in Boston, Massachusetts near the Fleet Center, the site of the 2004 Democratic National Convention. Authorities set up a "Demonstration Zone" (DZ) within a "hard" security zone, which was itself located within a "soft" security zone extending beyond the Fleet Center (the site of the convention). The DZ was an oppressive architecture. Barricades and fences marked its perimeters. Two layers of thick mesh were added to the zone's shell, ostensibly to prevent protesters from throwing or spitting objects at the delegates. To prevent anyone from climbing out of the "pen" or "cage," as prospective protesters referred to it, officials placed coiled razor wire at the top. Once positioned inside, protesters would have no access to convention delegates and would not be within sight or sound of the Fleet Center. They could not pass leaflets or other materials to convention attendees or anyone else. Officials also restricted the types of signs allowed in the DZ.

The district judge who heard a First Amendment challenge to the DZ described it as "a space redolent of the sensibility conveyed in Piranesi's etchings published in *Fanciful Images of Prisons*."[65] This "internment camp," the judge continued, was "a symbolic affront to the First Amendment."[66] Nevertheless, citing "security" concerns, the district court judge and later the Court of Appeals for the First Circuit upheld the use of the DZ.[67] Neither court was moved by protesters' argument that they at least had a First Amendment right to be seen and heard by convention attendees. Under the First Amendment time, place, and manner standard, the courts held that protesters did not have any such right. Further, so long as their protest message might be covered by the media or discussed on the internet, the First Amendment's requirement that a regulation leave open "alternative channels of communication" was satisfied. Not surprisingly, not a single protester used the DZ during the convention. Ultimately, it was the perfect mechanism of control.

While most are not as egregious as the DZ, free speech zones are generally designed to neutralize protest and dissent by confining it to designated spaces approved by the government. The zones disparately affect expressive forms such as protests, parades, and processions, which are naturally fluid events intended to disrupt everyday routines. Since courts have generally tolerated the practice under First Amendment place doctrines, officials have increasingly turned to protest zoning.

The characteristics of free speech zones significantly burden expression. As noted, the area designated for freedom of speech and assembly is often very small relative to the available forum space. Sometimes fences, gates, barriers, and other objects separate speakers from audiences. These prevent speakers from communicating, distributing materials, and reacting to audience movements at protest events. Further, as the Boston DZ demonstrated, free speech zones can have a significant chilling effect on public protest. Again, not a single protester used the DZ. If speakers know that stepping into a "free speech zone" will effectively prevent them from reaching their intended audiences and stepping outside the zone will subject them to discipline or punishment, they may simply decide not to enter at all.

By forcing protesters to file into pens, cages, and other architectures of control, zoning distorts attacks on the status quo and neutralizes the disruption of protest activities. Further, compliance with speech zones signifies capitulation to authority, which is directly contrary to the message of dissent. As Keith Whittington has observed, "It is stifling to dissent to insist that the dissenters 'present their concerns in a way that is most palatable to those who are responsible for addressing their grievances.'"[68] Marginalized speakers, sensing that they are being pressed to submit to power they oppose as systematically aligned against them, may be particularly sensitive to such concerns. Finally, the zones communicate that those penned and caged are worthy of confinement because they are dangerous. They suggest to the public that protest is a perilous activity or confirm the biases of those who already view it as such.

The district court judge who reviewed the Boston DZ observed that the DZ was "a symbolic affront to the First Amendment." Indeed, "free speech zones" are an *actual* affront to freedom of expression. As John Inazu has noted, "In many cases involving curfews, zones, or buffers, a city council can come up with some rationale to regulate expressive activity that is unrelated to expression. But the First Amendment requires more than just some reason to overcome its presumptive constraint against government action."[69] The fact that courts have often upheld zoning structures and strictures as "content-neutral" regulations is another demonstration of the deep managerial bias in First Amendment place doctrines.[70]

Militarizing Public Protest Venues

Free speech zoning is one component of what I have elsewhere referred to as the "militarization" of public places.[71] Zoning is one of several tactics that have been used to displace and suppress protest and dissent in public forums where protesters have a First Amendment right to assemble and speak.

Militarization involves the use of a range of technologies and tactics that "secure" public places by essentially preventing any meaningful public expression from occurring there. In addition to expressive zoning, militarization involves the surveillance and infiltration of protest groups, the establishment of "security zones" that limit access and presence, the display of military resources and equipment, the "kettling" or rounding up of protesters (which typically leads to mass arrests), and the use of aggressive protest policing methods including flash grenades, tear gas and other non-lethal weapons.[72]

The idea behind militarizing public places is to impose a distinct kind of order there. As the use of the DZ in Boston showed, these tactics have been especially prominent during critical democratic moments such as mass protests, political conventions, presidential inaugurals, and summits or world leaders. In such moments, officials and law enforcement personnel have militarized venues to maintain public order. Militarization of place transforms a "traditional public forum" from a place open "time out of mind" to a "battlespace" that is physically dangerous for protesters to use. The purpose of militarization was expressed by former President Trump's Secretary of Defense, who maintained during the BLM protests in 2020 that officers and U.S. military forces needed to "mass and dominate the battlespace."[73]

After the terrorist attacks of September 11, 2001, but even prior to those events, when policing public demonstrations and marches authorities have turned to tactics often used to fight foreign terrorists. They have amassed and displayed military equipment and dressed in military gear. Authorities have prohibited expression in "hard zones" close to the target event or activity. In "soft" zones, typically located some distance from the event, authorities have confined speakers to "free speech zones" or otherwise strictly limited their movements with physical barricades or military equipment.

As discussed in Chapter 2, political sociologists have documented the steady rise of "escalated force" and "command-and-control" protest policing.[74] Both methods rely on force as a first, rather than a last, resort. They are manifestations of the "battlespace" mentality adopted by law enforcement.

Militarizing place might seem likely to reduce reliance on physically aggressive protest policing methods. However, aggressive protest policing methods have become part of the militarization of place. As demonstrated during the BLM protests during the summer of 2020, in at least some contexts protest policing remains extremely aggressive and violent. ProPublica examined nearly 400 social media posts showing police responses to BLM protesters during the public unrest of the summer of 2020.[75] Reporters found troubling conduct by officers in at least 184 of the videos. In 87 of the videos, officers punched, pushed, and kicked retreating protesters. Officers used pepper spray, tear gas, and batons against non-combative demonstrators. The authors of the report concluded that police tactics frequently *escalated* confrontations with peaceful demonstrators.[76] These findings were consistent with other studies of protest policing during the summer of 2020.[77]

When the police perceive a protest to be threatening to law enforcement or public order, they resort to escalated force.[78] Unfortunately, that perception appears to apply to many if not most public protests. Across a wide range of protest issues and environments, reporters, activists, scholars, and officials have documented countless examples of law enforcement engaging in repressive forms of physical confrontation including the use of tear gas, assaults, and forcible arrests. As currently interpreted, the Fourth Amendment does not clearly apply to militarization tactics such as the mass dispersal of protesters.[79] As discussed, the First Amendment has not posed a significant barrier to protest surveillance, expressive zoning, and other militarization tactics.

The primary goal of militarizing public forums is to neutralize agitation, disruption, and dissent. Militarization manages dissent through architectures and tactics that facilitate surveillance, inhibit movement, suppress contention, and deter disruption.[80] The special order imposed, again in public forums that "time out of mind" have been used for assembly and speech, broadly restricts and sometimes (as in the case of the DZ's architecture) suppresses public protest. Further, militarization escalates violence and disruption, undermining the government's stated goals of maintaining order and protecting the public. It also undermines public trust and confidence, which makes protest groups reluctant to negotiate and cooperate with authorities.

The practices and norms of militarized place facilitate the management of dissent. Neither First Amendment place doctrines nor Fourth Amendment limits on searches and seizures currently impose sufficient restrictions on the militarization of public forums.

Targeted Place Regulations

One lesser-noted but critically important phenomenon with respect to the displacement of public protest relates to the adoption of targeted place regulations (TPRs). Some TPRs explicitly provide that a designated place is *not* a public forum open to expression. Others apply *within* places that are "traditional" or "designated" public forums, restricting or banning speech and assembly in specific locations. These latter TPRs are considered a type of content-neutral "time, place, and manner" regulation. Examples include laws that restrict protest near "reproductive health care facilities," polling places, churches, residences, and "critical infrastructure" such as oil and gas pipelines. TPRs contribute to, and in some ways exacerbate, the problems associated with the shrinking protest topography.

As noted earlier, whether a particular place belongs on the protest topography depends almost entirely on the government's *intent* with respect to that place. Certain public places one might expect to be open to at least some assembly and speech have been entirely closed off to such activities. For example, under federal regulations, iconic places on the National Mall including the Lincoln Memorial are off-limits to protesters.[81] Upholding a ban on protest activity inside the Jefferson Memorial, a federal appeals court observed, "[n]ational memorials are places of public commemoration, not freewheeling forums for open expression, and thus the government may reserve them for purposes that preclude expressive activity."[82] States have also banned protests near courthouses, a restriction the Supreme Court has upheld.[83] Congress has similarly declared that protests and other expressive activities are prohibited on the plaza directly in front of the Supreme Court.[84]

This type of TPR is an exercise of the government's authority to determine whether or to what extent specific public properties will be open to *any* expressive activities, including public protest. They manifest one pathology of the "public forum" doctrine. Governments have been able to wipe iconic and highly symbolic places off the expressive topography. Courthouses, municipal plazas, jailhouses, and other places where public protests are likely to occur can either not take place in these locations, or can be heavily regulated so long as any restrictions are "reasonable" and neutral as to the speaker's viewpoint.

Governments also impose targeted place restrictions that affect protest and other expressive activities *within* "traditional public forums" like public streets, parks, and sidewalks. The Supreme Court has upheld a wide variety of these TPRs, including restrictions on speech at state fairs, on sidewalks near "reproductive health care facilities" and outside private residences, near polling places, and in Lafayette Park in Washington, D.C.[85] In one case, the Court overturned a jury award for intentional infliction of emotional distress to the parents of a soldier killed in action against protesters who targeted their son's funeral.[86] But the Court assured legislators that they could adopt content-neutral restrictions on "funeral protests."[87] Indeed, at the time of the Court's decision, nearly all states and the federal government had already expressly limited protest activities on public sidewalks and in other public areas near funerals.[88]

TPRs have been a common response to disruptive forms of protest. For example, federal and state laws have long banned protests outside the residences of judges.[89] In just the past few years, governments have proposed or enacted place-specific regulations after controversial protests outside the residences of public officials,[90] in or near public statues,[91] outside vaccination sites,[92] and in the vicinity of "critical infrastructure" such as oil and gas pipelines.[93] Some of these regulations cover relatively small areas, measured in feet, while others, like the infrastructure laws, could potentially affect protesters' access to areas measured in the many thousands of miles.[94]

Courts are likely to uphold TPRs on the grounds they are "content-neutral" regulations that serve governmental interests in public order, audience privacy and repose, suburban tranquility, the right to vote, national security, or even aesthetics. The laws are treated as content-neutral even though they target known protest venues and were enacted owing to recent controversial protest activities. Courts have not, at least not for these reasons alone, treated the targeted regulations as presumptively invalid "content-based" speech regulations. They are treated as such only if the TPR singles out certain subjects or viewpoints on its face.

As the Supreme Court explained in a decision reviewing a Massachusetts law that imposed a 35-foot buffer zone *only* on public streets and sidewalks in the state outside "reproductive health care facilities," the fact that a facially neutral law may "disproportionately affect speech on certain topics" does not render it content-based.[95] Nor, the Court concluded, does the fact that officials enact a place-specific speech regulation prove an intent or purpose to single out certain subjects or viewpoints. The Court relied on a prior decision in which it upheld speech restrictions outside polling places, which noted "States adopt laws to address the problems that confront them."[96]

In a concurrence, Justice Antonin Scalia criticized the Court for upholding what he called the "peculiar targeting" of the Massachusetts law:

> It blinks reality to say, as the majority does, that a blanket prohibition on the use of streets and sidewalks where speech on only one politically controversial topic is likely to occur—and where that speech can most effectively be communicated—is not content based. Would the Court exempt from strict scrutiny a law banning access to the streets and sidewalks surrounding the site of the Republican National Convention? Or those used annually to commemorate the 1965 Selma–to–Montgomery civil rights marches? Or those outside the Internal Revenue Service? Surely not.[97]

In answer to Justice Scalia's question, courts have indeed sometimes upheld restrictions of the kind he suggests. Consider the DZ, which applied only during the Democratic National Convention in Boston. At least based on its decisions to date, there is little reason to suspect the Court would treat a TPR that prohibited all protest near the IRS building as one based on content.

Because of the Court's blinkered approach to TPRs, mayors, town planners, municipal boards, sheriffs, and other authorities have the legal authority to impose targeted place regulations that affect demonstrations large and small – including on "public forum" streets and sidewalks. Courts have generally accepted the government's "content-neutral" justifications for such laws and held that so long as there are opportunities to protest and demonstrate in some other place, the targeted restriction is valid. On rare occasions, as in the Massachusetts abortion speech case, a court will invalidate the targeted regulation even under the lower-level scrutiny applied to content-neutral speech regulations.[98]

This approach generally fails to reckon with both the purpose and effects of TPRs on public protest. As to purpose, as Justice Scalia noted in his concurrence in the Massachusetts case, there may be reasons to doubt that the problems the legislature purports to be addressing are unique to the targeted place.[99] Lawmakers should at least bear the burden of demonstrating that protests in specific places are uniquely dangerous or threatening to government interests. Further, and more centrally, it does "blink reality" for regulators to deny that targeted regulations of speech near military funerals (following a national controversy over protests there) or vaccination sites (during a pandemic that raised concerns about "disinformation") have nothing whatever to do with the controversial nature of the protests or the content of their messages.

Consider *Hill v. Colorado*, in which the Court concluded that a state law banning unconsented-to approaches near healthcare facilities for the purpose of "oral protest, education, or counseling" was a valid content-neutral regulation of speech.[100] As Justice Scalia observed, this time in dissent, the law, which was enacted directly in response to disruptive protests outside facilities providing abortion services, explicitly singled out as a concern the "right to protest or counsel *against* certain medical procedures" in the targeted places.[101]

The Supreme Court has held that laws targeting certain *speakers* can be content-based.[102] Similarly, a restriction imposed solely on a particular *location*, in response to protest activity in that place, should be considered content-based. While the Court has sometimes expressed concerns about examining legislative "motive" when reviewing speech regulations, treating TPRs as content-based does not require such inquiries.[103] As *Hill* demonstrates, the face of the law itself may provide evidence of an intent to burden certain speech in a location. But even if the law does not reveal itself in that way, targeted protest restrictions should still be considered a form of content-based regulation. The absence of any evidence that a location-specific regulation addresses "unique" safety or other concerns, as well as the overall context in which a targeted speech regulation is adopted, are types of non-motive evidence courts can and should review.

The effects of TPRs on public protest also render them suspect. Like other time, place, and manner regulations, TPRs can have devastating effects on the content of protest messages.[104] Most TPRs appear to impose minor or minimal restrictions on public protest activity. But as noted, some apply in highly symbolic places while others extend across vast geographic areas. Moreover, viewed in proper context, TPRs operate as an *additional* layer of topographic limitation that rests on top of existing public forum limitations. Thus, even if protesters are in "public forum" streets or sidewalks, where they are supposed to have robust expressive rights, they may still find themselves subject to location-specific speech restrictions or bans. TPRs are not pins on the topographic map. They are part of a broader system of protest displacement. Protesters seeking to engage with target audiences may find that their options for doing so are cut off not just at a single location, but in multiple areas across the protest topography.

Consider the recent controversy over protests at the homes of Supreme Court Justices, including Justice Brett Kavanaugh, after a draft opinion overturning *Roe* was leaked.[105] Those seeking to communicate their thoughts to the authors of the leaked opinion could do so on the public sidewalks at the edge of the Court's grounds (so long as law enforcement does not disband or disperse them).[106] At this writing, a large fence has been erected around the Court, which further limits protest activities, ostensibly as a reaction to violent protests by those opposed to the Court's anticipated decision. As noted earlier, protesters are banned by federal law from demonstrating or speaking on the Court's plaza.

Some protesters sought to communicate with the Justices in a more proximate and direct manner, near their residences. A federal TPR prohibits protesting near judges' residences with the intent to intimidate judges or affect the outcome of pending cases.[107] Some state laws also have TPRs that ban residential protests near judges' homes. Some of the state laws contain content-based exceptions, for example allowing protests involving labor disputes.[108] Because they are content-based, those laws plainly violate the First Amendment.[109]

The Supreme Court has treated residential protest bans that are neutral on their face as time, place, and manner regulations. Under that standard, the Court upheld a ban on "targeted" picketing, a protest or demonstration that focuses on a particular residence.[110] The Court has also invalidated expansive (300-foot) buffer zones around the residences of health clinic employees.[111] The upshot of these decisions is that officials can ban "focused" picketing at a particular residence but cannot ban protests throughout entire residential neighborhoods.

Federal authorities allowed peaceful protests near the home of Justice Kavanaugh, apparently so long as they did not target or focus on his residence. So did local officials. Indeed, an ordinance in effect in Montgomery County, Maryland, where Justice Kavanaugh lives, allows "marching in a residential area without stopping at any particular private residence."[112] What many seem to want is a total ban on *neighborhood*, as opposed to *residential*, protests. But the Supreme Court has correctly invalidated TPRs of that sort. They would immediately exclude vast areas, including public streets and sidewalks in neighborhoods, from the protest topography.

Many on the political right were outraged at the idea of protests near the Justices' homes. However, as the Court's own decisions show, residential protests are not a new phenomenon. Abortion opponents have long been allowed to protest in the neighborhoods of abortion providers and clinic staff. The Court has properly concluded, in this case by insisting that residential protest limits be narrowly tailored, that under the First Amendment the privacy interests of targeted residents do not justify bans on protest in entire residential neighborhoods.

There is also a telling postscript to the story of recent Supreme Court residential protests. When a lone, heavily armed, and apparently suicidal man appeared near Justice Kavanaugh's home (where he promptly turned himself in to authorities), there were immediate calls to limit neighborhood protests on the ground that they pose a threat to the justice's lives.[113] This was the case even though the would-be murderer was not part of any "protest" group and did not participate in any of the assemblies that preceded his appearance. Because the media did not report this fact, they left the impression that neighborhood protests are generally dangerous events. Limiting neighborhood protests on the ground that a dangerous person appears in a neighborhood for criminal ends would justify banning protests in nearly any public place. Based on this faulty logic, because we had an actual riot and attempted insurrection at the Capitol on January 6, 2021, we should limit or ban all public protests near that iconic place.

Some may believe legislators and officials need broad authority to respond to the safety and other challenges of residential protests. There may be unique concerns regarding residential protesters intimidating judges, abortion providers, or elections officials. Unlawful intimidation, threats, and harassment are not protected by the First Amendment. Law enforcement can provide necessary security for judges and officials. Cities and towns can also enforce noise ordinances and limit the time of day and number of protesters on residential streets and sidewalks. These alternatives are far narrower than a ban on neighborhood protesting.

Neighborhood protests may be an ineffective means of persuading anyone of the justness of a cause. The same might be said of sidewalk counseling, die-ins, and handbilling. My concern is not whether any specific type of protest is persuasive or effective. Rather, the question is whether the law of public protest ought to protect neighborhood and other protests that occur in traditional public forums – however impolite or disrespectful some may find them.

Although it has not properly considered the content discrimination inherent in some TPRs, the Court has balanced rights to residential privacy and protest in a way that permits protesters to access residential neighborhoods subject to time, volume, and other limits. Had the Court done otherwise, entire swaths of residential streets and sidewalks would have been transformed from public forums into additional "red" areas on the protest topography. Again, if there are compelling reasons to limit speech and assembly in or near specific venues, the government should be required to demonstrate as much and show that any special place restrictions are necessary. They should also have to show that any burdens on protest are tailored, such that they do not suppress more expression than necessary to achieve those goals.

As the Court seems to partially recognize, TPRs can significantly interfere with protest activities in public forums. Protesters often choose places for their communicative and symbolic values. Regulations that single out specific places raise the danger that the laws seek to suppress criticism of judges or officials. Given that danger, the law of public protest ought not generally to allow lawmakers free rein to target known protest venues for the purpose of imposing special burdens on speech in those places.

THE "PUBLIC SQUARE"

Public places have long served as locations or "forums" for the exercise of speech, assembly, and petition rights. Together the nation's streets, parks, and sidewalks have comprised a public square where demonstrations and other kinds of less conventional discourse occur. Although as noted the "public forum" doctrine has many limitations, the Supreme Court has observed, "A fundamental principle of the First Amendment is that all persons have access to places where they can speak and listen, and then, after reflection, speak and listen once more. The Court has sought to protect the right to speak in this spatial context."[114] "Even in the modern era," the Court has noted, public venues such as streets and parks "are still essential venues for public gatherings to celebrate some views, to protest others, or simply to learn and inquire."[115]

That, indeed, is a central contention of the book. At the same time, however, the Court has recently proclaimed that because of the digital revolution the traditional public square is being replaced by a "modern public square."[116] It observed, "While in the past there may have been difficulty in identifying the most important places (in a spatial sense) for the exchange of views, today the answer is clear. It is cyberspace – the 'vast democratic forums of the Internet' in general …, and social media in particular."[117]

The focus of this book is the tangible places that serve as forums for more traditional public protests and demonstrations. Those are the places subject to the law of public protest and what the book refers to as the system of managed dissent. Just now, cyberplaces remain largely immune from these laws and systems. However, as the Court observed, one cannot completely ignore the significance of cyber places as locations where views are exchanged and dissent communicated.

There is of course no clear or definitive metric by which to measure which places are "most important" in terms of these functions. The Court's rough calculation was based on the sheer number of social media users and the economies of digital speech mentioned earlier.[118] Many millions have participated in public demonstrations too. In any event, the Court's calculation does not account for the fact that the "most important" place for speech is not simply a quantitative question of the number of users and functions. It is also a qualitative issue.

As the Court has suggested, "On Facebook, for example, users can debate religion and politics with their friends and neighbors or share vacation photos."[119] But as discussed in Chapter 1, tangible protests in real spaces serve similar values. And they have the advantage of being far more difficult to ignore than social media posts.

The BLM, March for Our Lives, abortion rights, and other mass protest events, as well as countless smaller public protests that have occurred in the U.S. just in the past decade, strongly confirm the Supreme Court's conclusion that tangible public places remain "essential venues for public gatherings."

Ultimately, determining which public places are "most important" to speech and assembly presents a false choice. A healthy culture of dissent needs *both* physical and virtual public spaces to function properly. Insofar as the future of collective expression is concerned, traditional means of participation and speech technologies are not generally at odds with one another. Indeed, they are largely complementary. For example, social media have enabled individuals to form new online associations or "virtual assemblies."[120] In addition to having independent value, these virtual associations help support and sustain the kind of bonds that are critical to physical forms of collective expression.

Moreover, in physical forums, technology has facilitated the organization and execution of public protests and demonstrations.[121] Access to social media and other associational software has helped protesters form swarms and "smart mobs," and counteract regulations and policing methods that limit the effectiveness of public contention.[122] Digitization facilitates spontaneous assemblies and can help protesters navigate restrictions on their movements and activities.

Finally, individual cell phone recordings, widely shared on social media, have exposed aggressive protest policing, informed investigations, and led to some reforms of protest policing methods.[123] The use of technology can lead to more effective, transparent, and widely publicized protest activity. In all these respects, too, the "old" public square and the "new" public square are and should be viewed as complementary resources.

This is not to deny that the relationship between public street protests and social media communications is always positive or mutually beneficial. Online communications can escalate tensions, facilitate the distribution of disinformation about protests and protesters, and lead to violent confrontations in the streets. In these ways, communication in the "new" public square can make the "old" public square a more dangerous place to communicate and demonstrate. However, on balance, as activists have demonstrated, the two public squares often operate together to advance protest causes.[124]

4

The Rising Costs of Dissent

As discussed in Chapter 2 and elsewhere, protest organizers and participants face an array of potential *criminal* penalties. These include arrests under breach of peace, disorderly conduct, unlawful assembly, and other public order laws. But when it comes to protesters' liabilities, criminal exposure tells only part of the story. Protest organizers, participants, and supporters also face a variety of potential *civil* costs and liabilities. These "costs of dissent," which include administrative fees, security bonds, damages awards resulting from personal injury lawsuits, and loss of benefits, are rising. Congress, federal agencies, state legislatures, local officials, and campus administrators have all proposed or adopted measures that would shift substantial financial costs onto protesters, enhance civil penalties for even minor offenses, and even deny protesters convicted of "riot" and other public disorder offenses access to state employment, housing assistance, and student loans. Plaintiffs have also sought to expand the civil liability of protesters, under new theories such as "negligent protest organizing," "riot boosting," "wrongful petitioning," and "aiding and abetting defamation." The costs of dissent, which can chill or suppress protest, are an important aspect of the law of public protest and the system of managed dissent. This chapter argues courts and policymakers have special obligations, rooted in the First Amendment, to contain these rising costs.

A PAGE OF HISTORY – THE CIVIL RIGHTS ERA

Using civil costs to suppress protest is not a novel tactic. During the Civil Rights Era, the prospect of large civil damages awards was a grave threat to public protest and civil rights activism. Public officials and private plaintiffs used civil actions and other measures to financially burden the press, individual protesters, and civil rights organizations.

Among other strategies, state and local public officials used civil defamation lawsuits, which claim damages for harm to reputation from publication of false statements of fact, to prevent reporting on events taking place across the segregated south. Defamation awards posed a serious threat to local press outlets that lacked the resources to pay and to the Civil Rights Movement.

Through defamation lawsuits, Southern officials used the courts and the common law of defamation to stifle criticism and dissent aimed directly at their own brutal tactics and segregationist policies.[1] Defamation actions were intended to intimidate journalists and others from publishing reports critical of state and local efforts to preserve racial segregation and suppress the Civil Rights Movement. Many state defamation laws provided for strict forms of civil liability, placing the burden of proving the truth of all statements of fact on the publisher or speaker and presuming damages to reputation from any published false statement. Moreover, plaintiffs could file a defamation lawsuit each time a newspaper or other outlet published an allegedly false statement.[2]

As scholars have demonstrated, civil damage awards had the cumulative effect of silencing thousands of journalists and others seeking to report on the Civil Rights Movement.[3] In 1964, the Supreme Court, recognizing this pernicious effect, placed demanding First Amendment-based limits on defamation actions. The limits have played an important role in countering the weaponization of civil defamation lawsuits.[4]

Private individuals and companies also used civil actions to deter civil rights activism. In *NAACP v. Claiborne Hardware*, a precedent we will return to later, civil rights activists demanded that local officials and businesses change a variety of practices they claimed harmed Black residents in the community.[5] When these changes predictably did not materialize, the protesters mounted an economic boycott of white businesses in the area. Owners subject to the civil rights boycott sued for damages to their businesses. The trial court concluded that the boycott itself was an unlawful restraint of trade and held all organizers and participants jointly liable for $1.2 million in damages for maliciously interfering with the boycotted businesses.[6] The Mississippi Supreme Court upheld the finding of liability but rejected some of the damage claims.[7] As discussed in more detail later, the U.S. Supreme Court reversed the state court judgment because the damages award applied to activities fully protected by the First Amendment.

Private litigants also sought to rely on other forms of civil liability to attack direct action protests. In one case, a jury imposed a $45,000 negligence judgment on a civil rights organization for injuries sustained when a protest bystander fired a weapon during a boycott event at a local supermarket.[8] A federal appeals court rejected the civil rights organization's claim that holding it liable in tort for the bystander's injuries would jeopardize all civil rights protests. Indeed, the court concluded, "The First Amendment is simply not involved in this case."[9] The court opined that where "emotions were charged, there were recent incidents with racial overtones, and there was a potentially if not probably unmanageable number of participants … [i]t may indeed be negligent to foster a 'peaceful' demonstration … or at least to do so without proper safeguards, when it is reasonably foreseeable that harm to persons or property might result."[10]

Since these so-called risk factors were present at many (if not most) civil rights protests, the court's reasoning posed a significant threat to protest organizers.[11]

It suggested organizers could be held liable for personal injuries or economic damages if they failed to exercise "reasonable care" when planning protest events. The appeals court ultimately dismissed the case – not because the First Amendment required that result, it emphasized, but rather because the court concluded (under common law tort principles) that the organizer could not have foreseen that a motorist would fire a shot and injure a bystander when protesters converged on his car in the supermarket parking lot.[12] As we will see, this "negligent protest organizing" claim has recently been resurrected in connection with a BLM protest.

The economic consequences of civil rights activism extended beyond court judgments. State and local governments also invoked a variety of civil and administrative laws that imposed financial costs and burdens on activists. For example, civil rights lawyers were harassed in administrative bar association disciplinary proceedings. Based on their membership and protest activities, NAACP members were routinely denied jobs, credit, and access to goods and services.[13] These "ancillary" costs threatened activists' livelihoods.

As an organization, the NAACP was subjected to special costs and administrative burdens. States invoked foreign corporation laws as a pretext for obtaining access to the NAACP's membership lists and shutting down the organization.[14] The southern anti-NAACP crusade also included the use of lobbyist-registration laws, state income tax laws, and corporate franchise tax ordinances.[15] As a result of these tactics, the NAACP, the only civil rights organization then operating in the south, was forced to shut down from 1956–1964. Legislatures also demanded NAACP branch membership records and held civil rights leaders in civil contempt when they refused to produce them.[16] As in the case of defamation verdicts, monetary fines stemming from these actions could be devastating to cash-strapped NAACP officials and branches. Again, for the target of the investigation, the potential consequences included loss of employment. The Supreme Court would eventually impose First Amendment limits on these suppressive tactics as well – but not before they had a significant negative effect on civil rights activism across the nation.

Burdening protest organizers and participants financially is a historically rooted, though thoroughly discredited, means of managing dissent. The imposition of civil costs and liabilities was part of a widespread and coordinated campaign to suppress and punish civil rights activism. The First Amendment ultimately played a critical role in terms of narrowing or eliminating various forms of civil liability and costs visited upon political protesters. As we will see, these threats have not disappeared.

THE COSTS OF DISSENT

By "costs of dissent," I mean the variety of non-criminal monetary burdens that apply to protest organizers, participants, and supporters. Of course, unlawful forms of protest can be associated with other "costs" – for example, expenses relating to vandalism, riots, and insurrections. My focus here, however, is on generally law-abiding protest organizers, participants, and supporters who engage in protected speech and assembly but are nevertheless subject to permitting and other financial burdens, common law and statutory civil causes of action, and statutory civil damage enhancements. This section provides an overview of the variety of civil costs and liabilities that affect protesters. The remainder of the chapter critically analyzes these costs under the applicable law of public protest.

Administrative Costs

Protest organizers are responsible for paying fees and costs associated with a planned demonstration or other event. These costs include permitting fees, charges for cleanup and protest policing, and indemnification of local governments for any damages that occur during a demonstration.[17]

As explained in Chapter 2, permitting systems control everything from access to public properties to the terms and conditions under which protests can take place. Under these permitting schemes, those who want to organize a public protest involving more than a few participants can be charged various administrative costs. The costs of dissent begin to accrue from the planning stages. Unless it is waived owing to the indigency of the applicant, protest organizers are typically required to pay a permit fee.[18]

The costs of dissent only start there. Municipalities also charge fees for cleanup costs, security, and traffic control.[19] After the 2020 BLM protests, several states adopted laws charging protest organizers for cleanup, law enforcement expenses, and other administrative costs.[20] In some jurisdictions, protest organizers must obtain liability insurance, post significant bonds in advance of an event to cover any costs and damages relating to a protest event, or sign indemnification agreements holding state and local officials "harmless" for any damages or injuries arising from the protest event.[21] Some state laws require permit applicants to obtain as much as $1,000,000 of liability coverage per occurrence and $2,000,000 in aggregate insurance coverage just to procure a permit.[22]

The federal government has likewise considered shifting many costs onto protest organizers. A few years ago, the National Park Service, which oversees protest venues in the District of Columbia, proposed regulations that would have required protest organizers to repay the federal government for some security costs.[23] Federal lawmakers have proposed bills that would require protesters who are arrested during unpermitted demonstrations to pay for police overtime.[24]

Further, in some jurisdictions, including the District of Columbia (an obvious center of protest activity), protest organizers must provide various services and amenities for demonstrators – including toilets, medical tents, and cooling stations.[25] Protest organizers in these jurisdictions must also provide setup and teardown crews for any structures and take steps to protect grassy areas. All these requirements impose considerable costs on protest organizers.[26] Although they do not apply in every jurisdiction, these financial burdens are becoming more routine – especially in urban areas where protests are a more frequent occurrence.

The costs associated with protest security can be staggeringly high. As discussed in Chapter 5, the University of California at Berkeley estimates that it cost approximately $4 million to provide law enforcement and related services for actual or planned speeches by just three individuals – Ann Coulter, Ben Shapiro, and Milo Yiannopoulos. The Univesity of Florida incurred security costs of $500,000 in connection with a planned speech by the white nationalist Richard Spencer. The City of Charlottesville spent nearly $70,000 on the August 12, 2017, "Unite the Right" rally. When a small number of the white supremacists who initiated the 2017 "Unite the Right" demonstrations in Charlottesville gathered in the District of Columbia a year later to celebrate the anniversary of the earlier event, they were greeted by thousands of counter-protesters. The estimated security expenses incurred by D.C. for this single event exceeded $2 million.[27] The 2020 racial justice protests similarly resulted in extraordinary security costs.

As cleanup and security costs have increased, government officials have explored ways to recoup or recover them. As noted, states have required organizers to shoulder the financial costs of cleanup and security. After mass protests connected to the Dakota Access Pipeline, Keystone Pipeline, and former President Trump's inaugural, legislatures in several states considered or adopted bills shifting various costs onto protest organizers and participants.[28] Some localities have also sought restitution for property and business damages they claim were caused by protests.[29]

For many large demonstrations and protest events, security costs can reach tens or even hundreds of thousands of dollars.[30] Shifting these costs onto protest organizers and participants can chill or prevent dissent by making it prohibitively expensive.

Civil Lawsuits and Damage Awards

As noted earlier, during the Civil Rights Era civil damage actions were a prominent threat to protest and activism. Although today's lawsuits do not appear to be part of a coordinated strategy, damages claims remain a potent means of managing protest and dissent. Protest organizers, participants, and supporters may be liable for damages under a wide range of civil actions. These include traditional causes of action as well as some theories of liability that seek to expand protesters' civil liability exposure.

Traditional Tort Actions

Protest organizers and participants may be civilly liable for damages under actions concerning personal injuries and business harms. This "tort" liability, which involves damages awarded for civil wrongs or injuries, can result in significant liability judgments as well as lawyers' fees, court costs, and other expenses. In the context of public protests, plaintiffs can bring a wide variety of potential tort actions.

For example, if a protester or group walks onto private or public land without consent or authorization, they may be liable for civil "trespass." Should they block access to a building or facility, for example a healthcare facility, business, construction site, or residence, they may be liable for damages for creating a "public nuisance" or a "private nuisance."[31] Plaintiffs can also sue protesters for damages relating to their privacy or emotional well-being, although, as will be discussed later, the First Amendment strictly limits these kinds of actions. Many of the damage awards in such cases would likely be relatively small. However, states have been adopting penalty enhancements for these actions when they occur as part of a "riot" or other unlawful assembly.

Counter-protesters can likewise be liable for tort damages. If a university student seeks to prevent a controversial speaker invited to campus from speaking or a counter-protester blocks passage of a march or parade, they may be liable for "assault" and "battery" (actions relating to touching without consent), "false imprisonment" (for detaining the speaker or audience members), creating a "public nuisance," or "interference with advantageous relations."[32] A protester may also incur civil liability under local ordinances, for example rules prohibiting blockage of free passage.[33] Whether or not these or other actions are successful, protesters and counter-protesters may incur significant costs defending against them.

Businesses can also sue protesters for damages caused by their activities. For example, logging and construction companies have sued environmental protesters for damages relating to "trespass to chattels" (for climbing onto construction equipment) and "interference with prospective economic advantage" (for damages relating to construction delays).[34] Protesters who cause economic losses may be held liable under other business tort actions, including interference with contractual relations.

Protest organizers, participants, and supporters can be sued for defamation – as discussed earlier, publication of false statements of fact that damage a person's reputation. The First Amendment requires that public officials and public figures (celebrities and others who have achieved fame or notoriety) prove that a speaker communicated false statements of fact with "actual malice" – knowledge that the statements were false or reckless disregard for their truth or falsity.[35] That standard offers a broad degree of protection to protesters who publicly criticize policymakers and policies, even if they use sharp and caustic terms.[36] However, the "actual malice" standard does not apply to false statements about a *private* individual. In that context, protesters and their allies may be liable under a lesser defamation standard, for example "negligently" (i.e., failing to exercise reasonable care) communicating false statements of fact.

"Negligent Protest Organizing"
Plaintiffs have been pursuing expansive theories of protest liability based on these traditional causes of action. For example, ordinarily a person is liable for breaching a duty of reasonable care owed to others if that breach of duty causes foreseeable

harm. "Negligence," as this form of liability is called, is a traditional tort cause of action. It applies to shop owners who fail to keep their premises safe, drivers who negligently operate cars, and construction companies that fail to secure construction equipment. It also applies to a protester who fails to exercise reasonable care and runs into a fellow protester or bystander at a public demonstration.

Suppose, however, the person accused of "negligence" is the organizer of a BLM protest. The organizer plans a demonstration in a public street, and as part of the protest activity the street is to be blocked (an unlawful act). During the ensuing protest, an anonymous bystander, without any encouragement from the organizer or even his knowledge, throws an object at a police officer, badly injuring him. The officer sues the protest organizer for negligence, claiming that the injury he sustained was a foreseeable consequence of planning a protest in an unauthorized location.

These are the facts of *Doe v. Mckesson,* a case in which a divided federal appeals court ultimately refused to dismiss the officer's "negligent protest organizing" claim.[37] The Supreme Court agreed to review the case, but did not address the merits of the negligent protest organizing claim. Instead, the Court remanded the case to lower courts to determine whether the police officer could sue under state law on the facts presented.[38] The Louisiana Supreme Court revived the lawsuit, concluding that a protest organizer owes a police officer a duty of care not to precipitate a crime by a third party.[39]

This claim has potentially enormous consequences for protest organizers' civil liability. In *Mckesson,* the officer did not sue the protest organizer for damages resulting directly from the organizer's *own* actions. Nor did he allege Mckesson directed, authorized, or ratified the violent conduct of the still-anonymous rock-thrower. Rather, the officer sued Mckesson for all "foreseeable" damages caused by his "negligently planned" protest event. The federal appeals court reasoned that a confrontation between police and protesters was a "foreseeable" result of planning a protest in a location where there was no legal right to assemble and that the organizer's "unlawful" act of encouraging assembly in this location was a breach of his duty of care.[40] The extensive damages that occurred during some 2020 BLM protests highlight the financial implications of such claims. Protest organizers could be sued for "negligently planning a protest" – not just by police officers, but by anyone in attendance who is injured by the "foreseeable" act of a third party.

"Riot Boosting"

The same expansive theory of third-party liability that underlies "negligent protest organizing" claims is also the basis for a new civil cause of action known as "riot boosting."[41] South Dakota enacted this civil action in response to the Keystone Pipeline protests. Indigenous tribes objected to the construction of the pipeline because it traversed tribal lands. Concerned about a repeat of protests that had focused on the Dakota Access Pipeline project in North Dakota, the South Dakota legislature created a new civil cause of action for damages against anyone who engaged in speech or activities that support a protest at which unlawful activity later occurred.[42] Under the law, any person or entity harmed by such conduct could sue the "riot booster" for civil damages. (The state could also sue the "riot booster," and any damages it recovers are placed in a fund used to pay for protest-related damages.)

As enacted, the "riot boosting" law was broad enough to apply to a wide range of protest-related expression. Potentially covered communications included social media posts encouraging environmental activists to join a protest to stop a natural gas pipeline from being constructed and providing protest training to activists. Groups potentially liable under the law included:

- Any organization that plans or assists in planning a protest concerning an issue as to which individuals have engaged in past civil disobedience;
- Any group that knows or should know that civil disobedience might occur at a demonstration and trains protesters how to be peacefully arrested at such an event;
- Any group that provides material assistance, including water or medical aid, to protesters who commit acts of civil disobedience; and
- Any individual who attends a planning meeting for a protest at which acts of civil disobedience later occur.[43]

Like the plaintiff in a "negligent protest organizing" action, the plaintiff in a "riot boosting" case does not have to prove that the "booster" themselves engaged in any unlawful activity or even intended that it occur. Rather, it is enough that the "riot booster" supported or encouraged a protest that subsequently became a riot.

"Inciting a Riot"

Incitement to riot is a criminal offense. In addition, state statutes and judicial decisions have recognized civil causes of action for "inciting" tortious conduct, including riots. Under this theory of liability, a defendant who incites others to engage in violent actions may be liable for civil damages, including personal injuries, stemming from such encouragement or advocacy. Like "riot boosting," incitement to riot actions raise serious First Amendment concerns. As discussed in Chapter 2, the First Amendment narrowly defines the sort of "encouragement" or "incitement" that qualifies as unprotected speech.[44] Incitement to riot claims may extend beyond these speech limitations and affect protected speech and assembly.

The Trump campaign and presidency have pushed the civil incitement action to the fore, in cases that demonstrate the First Amendment implications of such claims. As a candidate, Donald Trump was sued for inciting a riot at one of his campaign rallies in Louisville, Kentucky. Plaintiffs injured by the crowd when Trump repeatedly yelled "Get 'em out of here!" sued the candidate for inciting a riot. A federal court of appeals concluded that Trump had not incited a riot under Kentucky law and that, in any event, his speech was protected by the First Amendment.[45]

After the January 6 riot at the U.S. Capitol, several Congressmembers and two Capitol Police officers sued Trump for inciting, directing, and ratifying the attacks on the Capitol building and the officers during his rally speech on the Ellipse.[46] In these lawsuits, plaintiffs claim that the speaker, who again did not himself physically participate in the riots or attacks, is nevertheless responsible for those attacks because he incited them.

Actions for "incitement to riot" or other misconduct can be applied in ways that imperil the First Amendment rights of protesters, who sometimes rely on provocative and incendiary rhetoric. As discussed later, current First Amendment precedents and doctrines narrow, but do not eliminate, liability for the wrongful acts of third parties.

Civil "Conspiracy"

Conspiring to break the law is both a criminal and civil offense. In conspiracy actions, there must be proof of a conspiracy and of some action taken in furtherance of the agreement. Protesters can be sued civilly for conspiracies to engage in riotous or other unlawful activities. Under the First Amendment, conspiring to engage in a riot is unlawful but conspiring or agreeing to engage in lawful protest is not.

Several individuals injured at the "Unite the Right" protests in Charlottesville, Virginia during the summer of 2017 sued the organizers of the rallies for conspiring to violate protesters' civil rights and commit violence.[47] After a weeks-long trial in *Sines v. Kessler*, all defendants were held liable under that state law claim. But before the jury's verdict, the district court had to address plaintiffs' allegations that anyone who helped organize or publicly supported the protests was liable as a "co-conspirator." The court also had to analyze the substantial communications between and among defendants and their supporters. Although the district court found sufficient evidence of a conspiracy in those communications, many related to organizing, publicizing, and encouraging the rallies themselves rather than violent actions. The jury also held the defendants liable for their individual acts of violence.

As *Sines* shows, one of the central difficulties in civil conspiracy cases involving protest activity is proving that the conspirators agreed or attempted to agree to do something unlawful. This burden will complicate efforts to hold those who participated in the Capitol riot civilly liable under conspiracy theories. For example, several lawmakers have sued former President Trump for conspiring with the Proud Boys, Oath Keepers, and other white supremacist groups to violate the Civil Rights Act of 1871 (also known as the Ku Klux Klan Act), which prohibits conspiring to interfere with the execution of federal laws.

Civil conspiracy claims can be an effective means of holding violent groups responsible for their actions and statements. But as *Sines* and the Capitol riot cases show, courts must still be careful to distinguish support for protected protest from conspiring to engage in unlawful acts.

"Wrongful Petitioning"

Not all "protest" activity occurs at events like demonstrations, marches, and rallies. As noted in the Introduction, protests can take different forms. They can include smaller gatherings and sometimes even individual or small group expressions of public dissent.

The First Amendment protects not only speech and assembly, but also the right to "petition government for redress of grievances." Although the Supreme Court has not developed specific doctrines relating to petition rights, communications directed to public officials in the course of their official duties would seem to fall within the ambit of the right.

In some recent cases, plaintiffs have placed the petition right in jeopardy by suing under tort theories relating to business harms. In one case, a city brought an ultimately unsuccessful action against protesters who shadowed or followed parking enforcement officers hired by the city as they performed their duties. The protesters rebuked the officers for writing traffic citations, encouraged them to walk off the job, and filled expired meters with coins.[48]

In another case, business entities successfully sued a private citizen who petitioned local officials to abandon a stormwater project she believed would harm the environment.[49] The defendant in that case was ordered to pay $4 million to the parties involved in the project for "lost business opportunities." This set of facts lies at the outer boundaries of "protest" as I have described it. However, the upshot is that a citizen who sought to convey dissent or disagreement directly to a public official was ordered to pay a $4 million penalty. Assuming this sort of retail "petitioning" constitutes public protest, we need to be concerned with the First Amendment implications of "wrongful petitioning" actions.

The "wrongful petitioning" claim resembles some of the other expansive civil liability theories described in this section. Under this theory, activists and concerned citizens may be liable for significant damages if their dissent causes business harms, including the rescission of public contracts or discontinuation of public projects.

"Aiding and Abetting Defamation"

As noted earlier, protesters and their supporters can be sued for defamation – publishing false statements of fact that harm reputation. Ordinarily, a private person who alleges they have been defamed must prove that the defendant failed to exercise reasonable care in publishing a false statement of fact that harmed their reputation. The plaintiff can obtain punitive damages – amounts in addition to any reputation harms – only if they prove by clear and convincing proof the defendant made the statement with actual malice (knowledge of, or reckless disregard for, its falsity).[50]

Protest supporters may also be sued for "aiding and abetting defamation." In June 2019, a jury awarded a $44 million verdict (later reduced to $25 million) against Oberlin College, a small private college located in Ohio, in connection with the college's alleged support for students picketing and protesting a local bakery for what activists claimed was racial profiling of its customers.[51] The bakery owners argued, and the jury agreed, that the college was liable because one of its officials, whom the college alleged was required to be present, had joined student protesters in condemning the bakery operators as racists. Some students had also used college resources to print flyers condemning the bakery. An appellate court affirmed the jury's verdict.[52]

The verdict in the Oberlin College case rests on an unusual and expansive theory of defamation liability with important implications regarding the civil liability of protest supporters. The college was held liable for extensive damages not based on its *own* defamatory statements, but rather based on its "aiding and abetting" the allegedly defamatory statements of third-party student protesters. Under that theory, anyone who supports, endorses, or even facilitates protesters' defamatory statements could be liable for resulting reputational or other damages caused by the statements.

Statutory Causes of Action

Legislatures have enacted new civil causes of action applicable specifically to protest activities. In addition to "riot boosting" and civil incitement laws, which have been discussed, other federal and state laws prohibit certain communications and activities that relate to protest. Two laws of special note are those imposing civil liability for threatening communications and "racketeering" provisions.

Threatening communications are not entitled to any First Amendment protection.[53] In one noteworthy case, a federal court of appeals upheld a multi-million dollar judgment against pro-life activists under the Freedom of Access to Clinic Entrances Act (FACE), a federal law that protects the rights of women and health-care workers to access healthcare facilities.[54] An organization of pro-life activists distributed "Wanted" posters that identified certain abortion providers by name and other information and accused them of committing "crimes against humanity." The court held that the posters and other communications violated a provision of FACE that prohibits making threats against clinic employees.

FACE applies specifically to threats interfering with access to health care services. Protesters and activists can also be civilly (and criminally) liable for communicating threats, including terroristic threats, in other contexts. They may also face liability under state laws providing damages for stalking, harassment, and intentional or negligent infliction of emotional distress.

Federal law and more than thirty state laws also prohibit "racketeering," which consists of the commission by "enterprises" of a variety of "predicate acts", including extortion, violent acts, and terrorism.[55] Although protest groups may constitute "enterprises" under these laws, peaceful protest organizations are not likely to violate them. However, plaintiffs may seek to characterize civil rights and other protest organizations as racketeering enterprises. For instance, until the Supreme Court provided a narrowing interpretation of the federal racketeering law, abortion clinic operators had some success invoking it against pro-life protesters.[56]

Some states have recently considered extending the definition of "racketeering" under state law to cover protest organizations. As the "riot boosting" example shows, federal and state lawmakers can enact additional statutory causes of action and civil penalties that apply to protest organizers, participants, and supporters.

Damage Enhancements

Finally, in terms of the costs of dissent, protest organizers and participants may face statutory penalties and damage enhancements for engaging in certain protest activities. The FACE and Racketeer Influenced and Corrupt Organizations (RICO) statutes, discussed earlier, both contain enhanced penalty provisions. Under RICO, violators are liable for treble civil damages in certain cases.[57] Under FACE and federal civil rights laws, violators also face enhanced civil penalties.[58]

The same is true under many state laws.[59] For example, environmental protesters who trespass or interfere with logging or construction operations may be liable for punitive damages – non-compensatory damages intended to be significant enough to punish and deter the activity in question.[60] Even relatively minor acts of civil disobedience can trigger these substantial damages awards. Owing to their focus on repetitive behaviors or patterns of conduct, some penalty enhancement provisions may disparately affect protest activity like long-term demonstrations.

Following high-profile public protests, including at the inauguration of Donald Trump and in connection with the construction of oil and gas pipelines, many states proposed civil liabilities and penalties focused on protest activity. After the summer 2020 BLM protests, more states increased financial and other penalties for protest-related conduct. Among other measures, the laws:

- Significantly increase civil fines for obstructing traffic or trespassing;
- Allow businesses to sue individuals who engage in targeted pickets or protests;
- Increase fines for "mass picketing;"
- Create significant new civil penalties for protests that take place near "critical infrastructure," ranging from gas pipelines to telephone poles;
- Apply racketeering laws to protest groups; and
- Provide that persons convicted of "riot" and other protest-related offenses are ineligible for benefits including student loans and state employment.[61]

These civil costs and penalties add to the rising costs of dissent. They enact another layer of financial burdens and penalties for protest-related misconduct and jeopardize not only protesters' expression but also their pocketbooks and access to public benefits.

THE CHILLING EFFECT OF MONETARY COSTS

The various costs and liabilities I have described raise serious and abiding concerns about the management of dissent through the imposition of civil costs and damages. The costs of dissent chill First Amendment activities in two distinct, but related, ways.

The first concern is that significant financial burdens will directly chill or even suppress expressive activities. The Supreme Court has recognized that fees, civil damage awards, and other costs can have this effect. Indeed, as the Court has observed, "The fear of damage awards … may be markedly more inhibiting than the fear of prosecution under a criminal statute."[62]

Security bonds, cleanup charges, substantial monetary judgments, liability insurance requirements, and lawyers' fees can represent staggering or insurmountable financial burdens. These costs are all *in addition to* the other aspects of the "managed dissent" system described in Chapter 2 – including fines and penalties associated with arrests and convictions under criminal laws.[63] Even for those who have some ability to pay, the prospect of such costs may inhibit organizers, participants, and supporters from engaging in public protest activities.

During the Civil Rights Era, concerns about chilling publications, protests, and dissent were central to the Supreme Court's intervention in defamation and other civil liability areas. As the Court has more recently recognized, "Excessive fines can be used … [to] chill the speech of political enemies."[64] The threat of loss of ancillary public benefits under some state laws, including student loans and employment opportunities, may further chill speech and associational rights.

The second concern, which was also a prevalent factor during the Civil Rights Era, is the indeterminacy of civil liability standards.[65] Chapter 2 discussed this concern with respect to criminal offenses such as "breach of peace" and "unlawful assembly." In the civil context, the adoption and application of ambiguous, overbroad, and indeterminate liability standards can similarly chill expressive activity. Conversely, clear speech-protective standards can facilitate protest and other forms of expression. For example, in the context of defamation claims, rigorous standards of proof embolden speakers and publishers, who may face liability claims based on their communications, to communicate about public officials and matters of public concern.[66]

By contrast, claims such as "aiding and abetting defamation," "negligent protest organizing" and "riot boosting" may chill protest by virtue of their ambiguous and overbroad liability standards. The Supreme Court recognized the chilling effect of unclear liability standards when it held, in *Snyder v. Phelps*, that public protesters could not be held liable for intentional infliction of emotional distress, a tort action that imposes civil liability for "outrageous" speech or conduct.[67] As the Court recognized, imposing liability for "outrageous" protest activity invited courts and juries to base awards on the content of expression or their own subjective biases.

CONTAINING THE COSTS OF DISSENT

Imposition of costs and other financial burdens on protest organizers, participants, or supporters is not a *per se* violation of the First Amendment. The Supreme Court has accepted that, to some degree, protesters can be made to pay their own way. And they are subject to certain forms of civil liability, assuming civil actions and statutory penalties satisfy First Amendment and other constitutional limits. However, administrative costs, enhanced monetary penalties, and civil actions can have a devastating effect on public protest. Protesters can engage in self-help to limit the costs of dissent. But given First Amendment concerns, courts and policymakers should review the costs of dissent with special care and endeavor to reduce and contain them.

Protester Self-Help

Before addressing ways in which courts and policymakers either should or must contain the costs of dissent, let us first consider how protest organizers and participants can exercise self-help toward that end. There are a few ways protesters can protect themselves from the imposition of substantial costs.

It may seem obvious, but the surest way to avoid many of the costs and liabilities of dissent is to understand and comply with federal, state, and (especially) local laws concerning protest activities. This entails accessing and complying with basic permitting requirements, seeking waivers of protest-related costs where this is an option, and complying with legal and administrative requirements.

These forms of self-help will not always be viable. Protest organizers may lack access to information or work under severe time and financial constraints. In some instances, protesters may make a conscious choice to ignore protest restrictions to engage in civil disobedience or challenge them in court. However, to the extent they are willing and able, protesters can reduce some of the costs of dissent through their own actions.

As discussed in Chapter 3, the law of public protest significantly limits the places where protest activity is allowed. Knowing *where* one can lawfully protest limits protesters' potential liability for actions such as civil trespass. Being mindful not to block access to streets, sidewalks, and rights of way can limit protesters' common law and statutory civil liability. Further, a basic understanding of the substantive limits on communicating threats, inciting unlawful acts, and making false statements of fact about protest targets can also help protesters avoid civil liability. The Supreme Court has made clear that "[t]he First Amendment does not protect violence."[68] Thus, to state the obvious, protesters have no right to vandalize or destroy public or private property. These actions can give rise to various civil actions and penalties.

The First Amendment protects the right to coordinate and publicize protest events. But as discussed later, it does not protect conspiracy to commit riots and other violent acts.[69] Further, to avoid liability for the violent acts of other protesters or third parties, an issue that is also discussed in greater detail later, protest organizers and supporters may want to distance themselves publicly and vocally from any known violent protest contingent. They can do so by publicly disavowing and otherwise objecting to violent or destructive acts before, during, and after their commission.

Protest organizers and participants should also understand that their civil costs are highest when they plan a demonstration in advance. Organizers of such events may be responsible for permitting fees, security, and other costs relating to policing and managing a protest event (I will address later whether imposing these costs violates the First Amendment). By contrast, *spontaneous* demonstrations – those that occur in response to a particular event, for example the announcement of President Trump's Muslim travel ban or the murder of George Floyd – are much more difficult to "tax" in this way. Whether or not it is permissible for local governments to assess these costs, as Mark Tushnet has suggested, during spontaneous protests "this will be almost impossible in practice."[70] As the 2020 racial justice protests showed, when a protest event is truly spontaneous, officials may not be able to identify organizers or leaders to tax.

For similar reasons, the spontaneous form of protest may also limit protesters' civil liability exposure under theories such as "negligent protest organizing" and "riot boosting." In the case of spontaneous protests, it may not be possible to identify a responsible organizer, leader, or facilitator. As Tushnet has observed, "when messages go viral, there may not be *any* individual distinctively responsible for the event."[71] Thus, putting aside for the moment whether "negligent protest organizing" and similar causes of action violate the First Amendment, protesters may at least be able to avoid some liability exposure during spontaneous events.

Of course, these limits will not assist protest organizers who need to plan a "million-person" march, an anniversary demonstration, or some other large, coordinated event. But regarding spontaneous events, including recent racial justice, immigration, and pandemic-related protests, administrative costs may not operate as strong access barriers. Most jurisdictions provide for spontaneous protests in permitting schemes, and there is a plausible First Amendment argument they must do so.[72] Assuming they do, it will be more difficult to price this form of protest out of the marketplace.

Organizers and activists can also invoke state law protections against harassing, intimidating, and baseless civil actions including defamation. These actions are sometimes referred to as strategic lawsuits against public participation (SLAPP).[73] Like the defamation claims filed during the Civil Rights Era, the purpose of SLAPP suits is to silence protest and dissent. Thirty-three states and D.C. have anti-SLAPP laws, which protect protesters and others against the financial threat of baseless lawsuits.[74] The laws authorize civil actions to dismiss claims against protesters, the press, and others exercising their First Amendment rights.

Some state laws limit the contexts in which anti-SLAPP actions can be filed, but many of the laws are broad enough to cover actions against public protesters.[75]

For example, a non-profit company supporting environmental protesters challenging the Dakota Access Pipeline successfully sued a natural gas company under an Arkansas anti-SLAPP law.[76] The court rejected the energy company's civil racketeering claim, allowing the protesters to obtain an early dismissal and avoid costly litigation. Courts disagree regarding whether anti-SLAPP laws apply to claims filed in federal court.[77] The Supreme Court has not addressed that issue.

Self-protection and pragmatic limits will not relieve protesters of all costs and civil liability exposure. And despite their best efforts, protesters may still be charged or sued for monetary damages. However, protester self-help can help reduce the costs of dissent.

First Amendment Limits on Fees and Costs

As discussed earlier, permit and rental fees, cleanup deposits, security bonds, liability insurance requirements, and hold-harmless indemnification agreements are all becoming more common costs of dissent. These costs place considerable financial burdens on those organizing, planning, and participating in protest activities.

The Supreme Court has said little about the constitutionality of permit fees and administrative costs. The Court has upheld flat fees for event permits.[78] The reasoning seems to be that governments are entitled to recoup at least some of the costs associated with public protests.[79]

However, the Court has held that governments cannot vest broad discretion in officials to decide whether and how much to charge.[80] Rather, fees must be based on objective appraisals of the costs associated with protests and demonstrations. They cannot vary based on official predictions regarding how much disruption, litter, or violence a specific protest event will cause. These are important limitations, especially for provocative and disruptive protest movements. They disallow the exercise of unbridled discretion and discrimination against protesters based on the content of their message, both of which are forbidden under the First Amendment.[81] Thus, officials cannot charge fees aimed at recouping the costs of policing potential "hostile audiences" or simply deny "controversial" speakers access to the public forum because of cost concerns.[82]

However, this is the extent of the Supreme Court's guidance on whether protest fees and costs implicate or violate the First Amendment. Some legal scholars have argued that administrative fees and costs raise serious concerns regarding differential taxation, imposition of unconstitutional prior restraints, and suppression of minority and other dissident speakers and associations.[83] Although these are serious concerns, they have not resulted in court precedents striking down flat fees. Thus, along with the Supreme Court, lower courts have generally accepted that protesters can, to at least some extent, be required to pay their own way.

The principal scholarship criticizing fees and costs was published long ago, in the early 1980s. During the four decades since, protest fees and costs have exploded. It is

time for courts and policymakers to take another look at the First Amendment implications of imposing these fees and costs. Even assuming governments can charge
some amount as a condition of protest, three issues require immediate attention
from courts and policymakers.

The first issue relates to protester indigency. The Supreme Court has never
decided whether a permit scheme *must* contain a waiver for protesters unable to
afford permit fees and related costs. Lower courts have offered conflicting answers to
the question.[84] Courts that have rejected an indigency requirement have generally
reasoned that protesters priced out of their preferred forum can still assemble and
speak elsewhere. Thus, while not able to afford a public plaza where speech and
assembly are otherwise allowed, indigent protesters can still access the sidewalks or
streets in the surrounding area.[85]

Chapter 3 discussed the principle that under current First Amendment doctrine protesters are not entitled to their preferred place of protest. But courts that
have rejected mandatory indigency exceptions have been almost cavalier about the
importance of access to public forum properties. So long as a parade contingent
has access to sidewalks or other distant venues, some courts have reasoned, there is
no need to exempt them from permit fees that price them out of more central locations.[86] This "alternative channels" principle is problematic enough as applied to
ordinary restrictions on protest. As applied to fees and costs, it violates a fundamental
principle of open access for traditional public forums.

As the Supreme Court has observed, "[f]reedom of speech … [must be] available to all, not merely to those who can afford to pay their own way."[87] It should
not be the case that only financially privileged organizations or those able to
raise significant funds can access iconic venues such as Lafayette Park in D.C.
Like other expressive activities, public protest should not be an activity reserved
only for those with financial means.[88] Given the rising costs of security, cleanup,
and other fees, the lack of an indigency exception threatens to suppress minority, dissident, and other under-represented voices who often cannot afford to pay
to protest.

Further, while the Court has allowed officials to charge fees of $300 to $500 to
"defray the expenses of policing the activities in question," that rationale does not
withstand scrutiny under present-day circumstances. It fails to account for the explosion of cleanup, law enforcement, and other security costs.[89] Permit fees and costs
set at levels that would meaningfully defray such expenses would be cost-prohibitive
for even some well-to-do speakers. The fees and costs are out of range for the average
protester. Even if they are not willing to revisit the flat fee itself, courts should conclude the First Amendment requires an indigency exemption. Whether or not such
an exception is constitutionally required, policymakers should at least have to reduce
fee and bond amounts that exceed an individual or organization's ability to pay.[90] In
any event, under no circumstances should officials be *increasing* such public forum
access fees.

Second, the variety and amount of protest-related expenses raise their own independent First Amendment concerns. Aside from upholding a modest flat fee to defray expenses and invalidating variable fees, the Supreme Court has not decided whether the First Amendment limits specific types of costs or their amounts. Some courts have invalidated costs owing to a lack of specificity or demonstrated relationship to governmental interests.[91] Others have upheld what they consider modest fees intended to defray the costs of traffic control and other expenses associated with protests.[92] Courts should review specific costs just as they would any other speech and assembly regulation – by insisting that they be adequately tailored to important governmental interests.

Further, courts and policymakers should consider the effect these costs, in the aggregate, may have on the ability of protesters to exercise First Amendment rights. Whether protest-related costs can reach an *aggregate amount* that violates the First Amendment is an open question. Government up-charging and cost-shifting measures call for an answer. Here, too, courts have a special obligation to ensure that the amount charged does not effectively result in a "heckler's veto," by which predicted reactions to protest events serve as a basis for excluding speakers or groups from public places otherwise open to expression.

Some have suggested there might be a "compelling" governmental interest in shifting exorbitant costs onto protest organizers.[93] However, for the reasons stated, protest participation generally ought not to be limited solely to those who can post substantial bonds or pay significant cleanup costs out of pocket. If the aggregate amount of fees, costs, indemnification requirements, and other expenses would effectively act as a prior restraint on the expression of all but the wealthiest protesters, it should be treated as presumptively unconstitutional.

Third, certain financial burdens, including proof of liability insurance and indemnification requirements, are directly at odds with First Amendment precedents that limit protester liabilities for the acts of third parties.[94] Insurance mandates and broadly worded indemnification requirements transfer the costs of wrongdoing from third-party (including *intentional*) wrongdoers to protest sponsors and organizers.[95] The Supreme Court has held that protesters cannot be held liable for the misconduct of third parties if they did not incite, approve, or ratify the activity.[96] Insurance and indemnification requirements violate this protester liability principle.

Moreover, requiring liability insurance and indemnification for intentional or negligent conduct by protest participants raises concerns about differential treatment. Considering the many types of public activities, why are *only* protests and demonstrations subject to these coverage and liability requirements?[97] As one commentator observed, "Mandatory liability insurance for special events thus creates a regulatory distinction based precisely on a particular form of constitutionally protected activity – public association – typical of those with dissident perspectives."[98]

There are additional grounds for invalidating insurance and indemnification requirements. In many cases, the requirements are not tailored to serve governmental interests in recovering expenses or reducing costs. They have no effect on direct expenses incurred in hosting protests on government properties. Rather, they are intended to shield the government from liability for injuries associated with the use of its properties. Courts should at least insist governments demonstrate how requiring, for example, $1,000,000 in liability coverage is narrowly tailored to concerns about potential injuries or property losses.[99] Similarly, they should require governments to show how mandating that protesters hold harmless governmental entities generally immune from most tort actions and capable of filing their own actions is narrowly tailored to any important governmental interest.[100] In other words, courts should require that the costs of dissent borne by protesters be narrowly tailored to the actual expenses associated with their dissent.

The *values* associated with free expression support a system in which taxpayers continue to bear most of the costs of public protest.[101] As one critic of user fees and other protest-related costs argued, "If the first amendment is to assure a safety valve for dissatisfaction, genuine discussion of public policy, ascertainment of new scientific truths or cultural forms, and individual self-development, the public system of expression must, at a minimum, avoid replicating the private market's price structure and thereby reinforcing its inequities."[102]

If governments want to avoid the costs and damages associated with certain kinds of protests, they have means at their disposal for doing so without shifting the costs of dissent onto protest organizers and sponsors. Alternatives include objective permitting regulations, more targeted and efficient security policies, and decreased reliance on aggressive and costly methods of protest policing. The First Amendment requires that policymakers consider these less protest-restrictive means before they shift the costs of dissent onto protesters.

Challenging Protest Penalty Enhancements

Enhanced and punitive damages for protest-related activities are also a threat to public protest. The First Amendment does not shield protesters from liability for trespass and other civil wrongs. However, courts and policymakers should ensure enhanced and special damage awards do not have the effect of chilling or suppressing public protest.

As mentioned, some states have proposed or adopted increased civil penalties for trespass and other minor civil offenses. Others have proposed applying civil forfeiture laws to protesters' assets. Recent penalty enhancements for protest-related conduct were proposed or adopted in response to high-profile protest events, including minimum wage demonstrations, indigenous protests of the Standing Rock pipeline, BLM protests in Ferguson, Missouri, and protests during the 2016 presidential inaugural.[103] The measures include increased fines for blocking public streets and denying protesters convicted of public order offenses access to public benefits. The timing suggests some of these measures were directed at specific protests. More broadly, they are part of a recent backlash that aims to make public protest more expensive.

The First Amendment does not generally prohibit penalty enhancements. However, courts and policymakers should ensure the penalties narrowly compensate for actual harms and do not broadly suppress protest activities.[104] For instance, protesters sometimes engage in minor acts of civil disobedience, including trespassing on property or disabling equipment.[105] Environmental and other protests also rely on the concept of "expressive lawbreaking," which involves engaging in minor infractions to make a point.[106]

Increasing civil fines and penalties may suppress these and other peaceful, though technically unlawful, protest activities. Some of the measures impose liability far disproportionate to any actual public or private harm. The award of punitive damages for protest activities raises similar concerns. While protesters are liable for engaging in tortious and other wrongful conduct, courts should be mindful of the close connection between speech and many forms of non-violent activity. For example, in the context of an environmental protest, the communicative aspect of climbing on logging equipment or occupying an access road is hardly negligible. As Leslie Jacobs has noted, in such cases an award of punitive damages punishes the protesters at least *in part* for their communication.[107]

Some commentators have argued in favor of a form of First Amendment "penalty sensitivity" when it comes to non-violent civil disobedience.[108] Under this approach, protesters who engage in tortious conduct would not escape liability altogether, but courts would limit the penalties or damages awarded based on the actual harm done. If adopted, this approach could limit large fines, punitive damages, and denial of public benefits when the sole basis is minor trespass or other acts of civil disobedience.

Penalty enhancements significantly increase the costs of dissent. The First Amendment may not bar these costs, but free expression concerns should lead courts and policymakers to limit and constraint them.

First Amendment Limits on Civil Actions

Political protest is "speech in its most direct form."[109] The First Amendment strictly limits protesters' civil liabilities.[110] The Supreme Court has held that where peaceful and lawful forms of protest form even *part* of the basis for civil liability, courts must carefully consider whether liability comports with the First Amendment.[111] It has emphasized the First Amendment "imposes a special obligation" on courts to "examine critically the basis on which [civil] liability was imposed" and to insist on "precision of regulation."[112] Indeed, it has stated that "precision" is the "touchstone" of protesters' civil liabilities.[113] Thus, the imposition of civil liability is appropriate only "in certain narrowly defined instances."[114] To preserve public protest and dissent, the civil actions described earlier must be tested against, and satisfy, these First Amendment limits.[115]

"Negligent Protest Organizing" Claims

As discussed earlier, the "negligent protest organizing" claim is based on the assertion that a protest organizer failed to exercise reasonable care in planning a protest event. It involves suing an organizer for damages based on any "foreseeable" harm or misconduct that occurs during a public demonstration – even if the organizer did not participate in, advocate, support, or ratify it. This claim directly conflicts with First Amendment standards applicable to protester liability and poses a substantial threat to public protest. Accordingly, courts should explicitly reject it.

As discussed earlier, in *Doe v. Mckesson*, a federal appeals court concluded that a police officer injured at a protest by an unknown assailant had adequately alleged in a complaint that Mckesson, the protest organizer, "was negligent for organizing and leading the Baton Rouge demonstration because he 'knew or should have known' that the demonstration would turn violent."[116] The court held Mckesson owed a duty of reasonable care to protesters, bystanders, and police officers responding to the protest.[117] It reasoned that since it was foreseeable that the protest would involve some protesters being unlawfully present in a public street, which would in turn entail interactions between protesters and police, it was also foreseeable that a participant would "pick[] up a piece of concrete or rock-like object" and throw it at one of the officers.[118] As noted earlier, the Supreme Court remanded the case to the lower courts to determine whether state negligence law allows such a suit, and the Louisiana Supreme Court answered in the affirmative.

Under the theory of liability in *Mckesson*, protest organizers are liable for any foreseeable harms that occur at a public protest. When a protest organizer leads demonstrators who engage in civil disobedience or any other legal infraction, however minor, it may be foreseeable that police will be "required to respond to the demonstration" by clearing the obstruction "and, when necessary," making arrests."[119] "Given the intentional lawlessness of this aspect of the demonstration," the theory contends, a protest organizer "should have known that leading the demonstrators onto a busy highway was most nearly certain to provoke a confrontation between police and the mass of demonstrators."[120] "By ignoring the foreseeable risk of violence his actions created," the court of appeals reasoned, "Mckesson failed to exercise reasonable care in conducting his demonstration" and "provoke[d] a violent confrontation with the police."[121] The state supreme court adopted essentially the same theory of negligence liability.[122]

The civil action in *Mckesson* is fundamentally at odds with the Court's precedents concerning protester liability. First, the "negligent protest" claim ignores the Supreme Court's clear instruction that protest organizers and participants are liable for damages stemming from the violent or destructive acts of others *only* when the organizer "authorized, directed, or ratified" those acts.[123] Thus, if Mckesson had thrown the heavy object at the officer, directed someone to do so, or perhaps even ratified the violence after the fact, the First Amendment would not provide a defense. However, not only did Mckesson commit no violent acts, but the officer did not allege Mckesson uttered a single word encouraging violence by participants or bystanders before, during, or after the protest. Mckesson may have foreseen some protesters would unlawfully occupy a public street based on his instructions. But imposing liability on a protest organizer for a violent act of a third party (assaulting an officer), where the organizer does not commit, authorize, encourage, or ratify that or any other act of violence, ignores the precision of regulation and narrow scope of protesters' liability the Supreme Court has insisted on in its precedents.

Second, and relatedly, imposing liability for "negligent protest organizing" is inconsistent with First Amendment precedents relating to a speaker's liability for the violent conduct of third parties. Holding a protest organizer liable for damages he did not expressly advocate and did not intend to immediately occur – for "negligently causing a third party to commit a crime"[124] – is inconsistent with longstanding speech-protective standards relating to speakers' liability for purposefully inciting violence. As discussed in Chapter 2, those standards require that a speaker *intend* to produce *imminent* unlawful activity that is *likely* to occur.[125] Mckesson's speech did not come close to meeting that standard with respect to the criminal act of an anonymous third party.

Third, the "negligent protest organizing" claim is inconsistent with broad First Amendment protections afforded freedom of assembly and association. As the Supreme Court observed, "The right to associate does not lose all constitutional protection merely because some members of the group may have participated in conduct or advocated doctrine that itself is not protected."[126] As the Court admonished in *NAACP v. Claiborne Hardware*, "[t]he First Amendment ... restricts the ability of the State to impose liability on an individual solely because of his association with another."[127] In *Mckesson*, liability extends even further, since Mckesson was not alleged to have had any connection at all to the anonymous violent actor.

The "negligent protest organizing" action allows juries and courts to impose broad liability on protest organizers and leaders, by virtue of their connection to a protest event that may draw hundreds or thousands of participants, counter-protesters, and bystanders. Under this standard, protest organizers would face liability for merely belonging to groups, "some members of which committed acts of violence."[128] In this sense, the "negligent protest organizing" claim imposes a form of guilt *for* association. As Justice Douglas observed during the Civil Rights Era, "The rights of political association are fragile enough without adding the additional threat of destruction by lawsuit."[129]

Fourth, as a liability standard "negligent protest organizing" lacks the care and precision demanded under *Claiborne Hardware* and other precedents. The negligence alleged against Mckesson related solely to *planning* the protest event.[130] The negligence standard, which relies on concepts such as "duty" and "foreseeability," is far too imprecise to protect assembly and speech relating to matters of public concern.[131] As a state appeals court observed in a case involving targeted picketing of an abortion provider's residence, "the specter of protesters being subjected to unlimited liability for claims of negligent infliction of emotional distress from a contingent of unknown plaintiffs would doubtless have a stifling effect on [expression]."[132] For similar reasons, as discussed earlier, the Supreme Court has rejected protester liability under the amorphous "outrageousness" standard used in *intentional* infliction of emotional distress claims.[133]

In the context of protest planning or organizing, the negligence tort's "reasonable care" and "foreseeability" standards are far too imprecise to offer the requisite protection for speech and assembly rights. The standards invite juries to impose liability on protest organizers and planners based on the content of their protest message or their movement's identity. The First Amendment does not permit substantial civil damages against organizers in *every* case in which they fail to comply with one or more of the countless rules and regulations applicable to public protest events discussed in Chapter 2.[134] As Justice Neil Gorsuch recently acknowledged, in the context of a disruptive public protest "almost anyone can be arrested for something."[135] Protest organizers could face damages awards of hundreds of thousands of dollars, or perhaps more, for merely planning a protest in the wrong place, failing to comply with a single permit condition, or engaging in other minor infractions that may invite law enforcement action. This is not the sort of careful examination, precision, and restraint the Supreme Court has said the First Amendment requires for protester liability.

Fifth, as Justice Gorsuch's comment suggests, the "negligent protest organizing" claim ignores the realities of the contemporary protest environment. Public protests are often fluid and contentious events. They cause disruption, public inconvenience, and offense. It is not uncommon for participants who are not part of the organizing group to attend a protest. The "negligent protest organizing" cause of action would allow juries to hold protest leaders liable for the consequences of any unlawful acts that transpire at public events, so long as they engaged in some act of "negligent planning." Indeed, the claim authorizes holding protest leaders accountable even for the violence of those *opposed* to the protest, on the theory that such violence was a "foreseeable" consequence of protest policing.[136] Where passions run high, as they often do at public protests, is it foreseeable that counter-protesters may engage in unlawful and even violent acts? As discussed in Chapter 6, public protests are increasingly *armed* affairs. Under the "negligent protest organizing" theory, a protest organizer who plans a disruptive protest may even be charged with the "foreseeable" consequence of gun violence.

Finally, and related to this last concern, the "negligent protest organizing" claim allows law enforcement to dictate or at least significantly influence the extent of protesters' civil liability exposure. As the federal appeals court described the scene in *Mckesson*, "The Baton Rouge Police Department prepared *by organizing a front line of officers in riot gear*."[137] Recent protest actions, including those involving BLM, affirm that police departments too frequently respond to even peaceful protests with escalated force – for example, beatings, using chemical agents, and firing rubber bullets. It was arguably the aggressive method of protest policing in *Mckesson*, not the lack of care in protest planning, that made violence and confrontation foreseeable. Yet the decision treats this show of force as a natural and hence "foreseeable" consequence of planning a protest in the wrong place. This essentially makes protest organizers liable for the illegitimate use of escalated force by law enforcement.

For all these reasons, courts should reject "negligent protest organizing" claims on First Amendment grounds. As noted earlier, some plaintiffs filed such claims during the Civil Rights Era. Ironically, the same court that allowed the case against Mckesson to proceed rejected a similar claim of negligence – albeit grudgingly and with little regard for the First Amendment – against a civil rights group.[138] Had "negligent protest organizing" claims been more frequent and successful, the Civil Rights Movement could have been effectively bankrupted. Marches, demonstrations, and pickets frequently turned violent, notwithstanding the protesters' generally non-violent methods. Given the foreseeable unrest, it is hardly unthinkable that courts would have held protest organizers liable for violence and property destruction. Unrest associated with speech and assembly should be a reason to *protect* public protest.[139] As a theory of civil liability, "negligent protest organizing" turns this principle on its head by punishing protest organizers for foreseeable public unrest or disruption.

Rejecting the "negligent protest organizing" action would not immunize protesters from liability for all tortious acts – including some that may be negligent. A protester who engages in intentional, reckless, or even negligent conduct may be liable for resulting damages. For example, a plaintiff could sue a protest participant who wildly swings a protest sign without regard for the safety of others standing nearby. A protester who ignores the health dangers of a pandemic and government stay-at-home orders might be liable for infecting others with a communicable virus (subject, of course, to tort doctrines that account for the plaintiffs' own negligence and assumption of risk).[140] A protester who blocks passage or physically assaults a speaker or audience member who wishes to hear the speaker may be liable for, among other things, false imprisonment, assault, and battery – all forms of harmful *conduct* rather than expression.

The difference between these civil actions and "negligent protest organizing" is that the latter grounds liability on the foreseeability of the actions of *third-party* protest participants, counter-protesters, or bystanders with no connection to the protest. In the case of the protest sign-waver, virus-spreader, and passage obstructer, defendants are accountable only for damages stemming from their *own* intentional, reckless, or negligent acts.

It is the case, as the *Mckesson* court observed, that the First Amendment "does not protect violence."[141] However, that observation is inadequate to justify liability for "negligent protest organizing," a claim in conflict with First Amendment precedents and principles. It is also ultimately beside the point, since under the theory protest organizers are liable not for their own misconduct, but for the unauthorized violent or destructive acts of third parties. As the Supreme Court has made clear, the First Amendment limits protest organizers' liability to damages "directly and proximately caused by *wrongful conduct chargeable to the defendants*."[142] Since it is not so limited, "negligent protest organizing" liability must be rejected.

"Riot Boosting" Actions

As noted, in the wake of high-profile mass protests, states have enacted laws specifically designed to restrict certain public protest activities. One of those laws authorized civil damages for "riot boosting," a variation on the crime of inciting a riot.[143]

In 2019, South Dakota became the pioneer in adopting this new cause of action. Fortunately, a federal district court promptly invalidated the law on First Amendment and vagueness grounds. In *Dakota Rural Action v. Noem*, the court held that the South Dakota law was overbroad and vague insofar as it imposed civil liability on any person who "advises, encourages, or solicits" another to participate in a riot.[144] As the court noted, the covered terms are all protected expression under the First Amendment.[145] Further, the law was inconsistent with the narrow definition of "incitement" to unlawful action.[146] The court asked, "Imagine that if these riot boosting statutes were applied to the protests that took place in Birmingham, Alabama, what might be the result?"[147] Would King's "Letter from Birmingham jail," which questioned the justness of certain laws, subject him to liability for "riot boosting"?

The court's reasons for rejecting "riot boosting" as a theory of civil liability are instructive. The court applied strict scrutiny to the law because its provisions and legislative history indicated it was enacted to address and limit the Dakota Access Pipeline protests.[148] (Chapter 3 argued that "targeted place restrictions" like this merit strict judicial scrutiny.) The court also held that imposing liability for "advising, encouraging, or soliciting" others to engage in unlawful actions was inconsistent with Supreme Court precedents. As discussed, the Court's decisions limit liability for inciting unlawful acts and reject protester liability for the criminal acts of third parties unless the protester incited them.[149] These are the same precedents that should have doomed the "negligent protest organizing" claim.

The South Dakota law shows the lengths to which some states are prepared to go to suppress public protests. It also demonstrates just how critical it is that courts be prepared to skeptically review these efforts, limit the costs of dissent, and preserve public protest.

Civil Conspiracy and Incitement Claims

In a polarized society, political rhetoric has become increasingly caustic, derogatory, and incendiary. Violent gatherings from the "Unite the Right" rallies in Charlottesville to the January 6, 2021, riot at the Capitol in Washington, D.C. were preceded and, some maintain, instigated by conspiracies involving white supremacists, former President Trump, and others. The statements of these parties have formed the basis for civil lawsuits alleging conspiracies to violate federal civil rights, interfere with the execution of federal laws, and incite violence.[150] In the protest context, allegations of civil conspiracy – generally speaking, an agreement between two or more people to do some unlawful act – are popping up all over. For example, the City of Detroit countersued Detroit Will Breathe protesters, who alleged police violated protesters' rights during the racial justice protests, for engaging in a "civil conspiracy" to engage in riots and property destruction.[151] As a result, the city claimed protest organizers were liable for all damages resulting from vandalism at Detroit protest events.

Governments have long used criminal "conspiracy" charges to target protesters.[152] Civil conspiracy claims raise some of the same concerns as these criminal charges, including the prospect that protected First Amendment activities will be chilled or suppressed and speakers will be held liable for their viewpoints. While acts alone can demonstrate a conspiracy, the parties' communications are critically important evidence. Their agreement can be tacit, rather than express, and can be established using their statements to one another and to public audiences.

However, as the Supreme Court admonished in *Claiborne Hardware*, a public protest "cannot be characterized as a violent conspiracy simply by reference to the ephemeral consequences of relatively few violent acts."[153] The Court noted, "A court must be wary of a claim that the true color of a forest is better revealed by reptiles hidden in the weeds than by the foliage of countless freestanding trees."[154] Even when alleged co-conspirators appear mainly to be "reptiles," courts are not relieved of their special obligation to assure First Amendment limits on protester liability are respected.

Speech and conduct can give rise to civil conspiracy liability in the context of public protests. While some of the Ku Klux Klan's activities may have qualified as "protest," that fact alone provides no First Amendment basis for protecting Klan members' conspiracies to engage in violence. But as the Court held in *Brandenburg v. Ohio*, even the vile speech of the Klansman cannot be punished *except* when directed to producing imminent violence that is likely to occur.[155] Further, as *Claiborne Hardware* and other precedents have held, merely "conspiring to protest" or "inciting protest" obviously cannot be the basis for a civil liability claim.[156]

Allegations of unlawful conspiracies and incitement of assaults or other violent acts must not be based on protected speech or associational activities. Under the First Amendment, assertions that defendants organized, promoted, or participated in what was otherwise a lawful public protest, or encouraged others to assemble and protest lawfully, cannot provide the basis for civil liability. By the same token, when protest leaders, participants, or supporters engage in violence or expressly conspire with or incite others to engage in imminent acts of violence that are likely to occur, the First Amendment provides no defense to civil liability.[157] These rules apply whether the protesters are environmental activists or white supremacists.

The central concern in civil conspiracy and incitement cases is the *evidence* supporting such claims. Under the First Amendment standards discussed earlier, if protest leaders enter into an express agreement to engage in assaults and other violent acts, they can be found liable for the harmful consequences of their conspiracy. That was both the judge's and jury's conclusion regarding the lawsuit in *Sines v. Kessler*, which involved white supremacist rallies in Charlottesville under the "Unite the Right" banner.[158] Because *Sines* highlights the difficulties inherent in pursuing civil conspiracy actions against public protesters, I will focus on that case.

The verdict is likely justifiable based on the allegations and evidence adduced at trial. But the presence of "reptiles" masks a difficult evidentiary and legal task. Courts and juries must take care not to impose civil (or criminal) liability based on protected speech and conduct unrelated to the violent conspiracy.[159] Civil liability is appropriate only when the association has unlawful aims *and* the protest leaders or participants intend to further those aims through their own or others' unlawful acts.[160] Thus, as the Court recognized in *Claiborne Hardware*, courts could not impose civil liability for things such as regular attendance at weekly meetings of the NAACP, where illegal conduct had not been "authorized, ratified, or even discussed."[161] The Court noted this would be tantamount to imposing liability based on a principle of "guilt *for* association," which would clearly violate the First Amendment.[162]

Nor, since they are lawful activities, can courts impose civil liability for *non-violent* actions intended to facilitate or enforce a boycott or other protest action.[163] In *Claiborne Hardware*, this included watching the stores to record who violated the boycott or wearing apparel associated with the boycott as a reminder that participants were watching.[164] To be sure, with respect to some protests the line between an unlawful conspiracy and efforts to organize a lawful public protest can be unclear. Indeed, this was true in *Claiborne Hardware* itself, which involved an economic boycott furthered by both lawful *and* unlawful conduct. However, as discussed, *Claiborne Hardware* requires proof of an intent to conspire with others be separated from lawful protest activities.

Based on *Claiborne Hardware* and other precedents, courts and juries cannot rely on lawful organizational activities, communications publicizing a protest, or mere membership in a protest group to support civil liability. The *Sines* case shows how difficult it can be to distinguish these actions. The district court properly held that certain allegations – such as "all rally attendees who disagreed with [plaintiffs] were part of the overarching conspiracy" and all individuals who "posted comments on social media" about the event were "co-conspirators" – simply could not be credited.[165] Similarly, the court easily determined that there is no First Amendment defense relating to defendants' violent acts at the rallies, including throwing torches, participating in personal assaults, and driving a car into a group of protesters.[166] Again, the First Amendment does not protect acts of violence.[167] However, as the Supreme Court has also made clear, the fact that some violence occurs at a rally or demonstration is not a valid basis for condemning the entire collective enterprise as an unlawful conspiracy or imposing liability on all organizers and participants.[168] Instead, plaintiffs must demonstrate that defendants engaged in a conspiracy to violate plaintiffs' civil rights that is *distinct from their agreement to organize a lawful protest.*

This is where matters can become trickier. As noted, the First Amendment protects actions taken to *organize* or *publicize* a protest, so long as the protest itself has a lawful purpose. Such activities include planning and participating in meetings (in person or online), urging members of various groups to attend the events, and discussing protest strategies and tactics – several activities relied on by the district court in *Sines* to establish a civil conspiracy to commit violence.[169] As in the "negligent protest organizing" and "riot boosting" contexts, courts must be careful not to impute unlawful intent to protest organizers and supporters based on membership in the group or acts of violence by others.[170] As discussed in connection with other civil claims, civil liability must be limited to "wrongful conduct *chargeable to the defendants.*"[171]

In conspiracy and incitement cases, courts must also be mindful that caustic, derogatory, and even violent rhetoric is protected speech. In *Claiborne Hardware*, Charles Evers, one of the boycott organizers and Field Secretary of the NAACP, delivered public speeches in which he said that those who did not boycott would be "disciplined." More directly, Evers said, "If we catch any of you going in any of them racist stores, we're gonna break your damn neck."[172] The Supreme Court held that these speeches did not constitute a proper basis for imposing liability on Evers for violent acts later committed by others.[173]

Reviewing the record carefully and demanding the requisite degree of "precision," the Court concluded that Evers' "strong language" did not amount to "fighting words" or speech inciting unlawful action. It was, instead, "an impassioned plea for black citizens to unify, to support and respect each other, and to realize the political and economic power available to them."[174] According to the Court, Evers' speeches "predominantly contained highly charged political rhetoric" that did not pass the bounds of First Amendment protection.[175] Further, there was no evidence aside from the speeches that Evers had "authorized, ratified, or directly threatened acts of violence."[176] Thus, the Court concluded, "The findings are constitutionally inadequate to support the damages judgment against him."[177] The civil judgment "compensated respondents for the direct consequences of nonviolent, constitutionally protected activity."[178]

The record in *Sines* contained some similar communications. White supremacists told supporters to be prepared for "self-defense" considering planned counterprotests, to wear khaki pants and polo shirts because these were a "good fighting uniform," and to be "dressed and ready for action" and prepared to "dominate the streets." These statements, like Evers's, constitute protected speech.[179] Even comments using military and battle jargon – i.e., referring to protesters as "warriors" and "fighters" and urging participants to "bring as much gear and weapons as you can within the confines of the law" – are protected by the First Amendment.[180] So too are statements urging supporters to "fight," "take back the streets," and other forms of pugilistic speech.[181] Can these statements, assuming they are protected speech, nevertheless be considered grounds for concluding an unlawful civil conspiracy existed? Only if there are enough *additional* communications expressing a specific intent or purpose to engage in violence.

To be sure, some of the statements in *Sines* may have been unprotected threats or incitement. Several statements made *at the Charlottesville rally* encouraged others to "charge" at counter-protesters or engage in specific acts of violence. These statements clearly constitute unlawful incitement and can be relied upon to support the civil conspiracy claim.[182]

Courts are facing these difficulties in other civil conspiracy cases. For example, former President Trump is a defendant in a civil suit alleging that he conspired with right-wing groups to interfere with the presidential electoral count. A House Select Committee has investigated the events leading up to and during the riot, and its work has shed additional light on the alleged conspiracy. The former president has raised a free speech defense, arguing his social media communications and speeches regarding the legitimacy of the 2020 election are protected political speech. Many First Amendment scholars reject that claim, arguing Trump's speech prior to January 6 Capitol riot was unprotected incitement to unlawful action.[183]

The federal court handling the conspiracy suit has agreed with that assessment and rejected Trump's argument there is insufficient evidence of a conspiracy to interfere with the House electoral count.[184] The court rejected the plaintiffs' argument that the First Amendment does not protect any statements made in furtherance of a civil conspiracy. Relying on *Claiborne Hardware* and *Brandenburg*, the court concluded, "President Trump's speech cannot be deemed unprotected merely because Plaintiffs have alleged it to be part of a conspiratorial agreement to violate a civil statute. Instead, because his speech is on a matter of public concern, it will lose its First Amendment protection only if it meets the stringent *Brandenburg* 'incitement' standard."[185] Following *Claiborne Hardware*, the court determined that speech was actionable if it is not protected by the First Amendment and caused the alleged harm. Although the district court acknowledged the First Amendment broadly protects political speech and rhetoric, including by presidents, it concluded "in this one-of-a-kind case the First Amendment does not shield the President from liability."[186]

The district court's decision demonstrated the careful, precise, and narrowing characteristics the Court has called for in civil conspiracy cases. The court concluded a speaker, including a president, can be held liable for damages caused by acts or communications that run afoul of recognized limitations on First Amendment protection. But the court refused to treat all statements uttered in the context of the alleged conspiracy as actionable. In former President Trump's case, that approach did not result in the dismissal of the civil conspiracy suit. But it protected Detroit Will Breathe protesters from "civil conspiracy" liability and likely would do the same for activists in other locations, again unless plaintiffs could show their statements constituted unprotected incitement or a threat.[187]

One of the very first actions filed by the Department of Justice during the Trump Administration was a "conspiracy to riot" case brought against hundreds of individuals who protested at the Trump inaugural.[188] Most of those protesters were engaged in lawful and protected speech and assembly, and the government eventually dropped the case after it became clear they could not produce evidence of a conspiracy. *Claiborne Hardware, Brandenburg,* and other precedents instruct courts to tread very carefully when assessing protest-related conspiracy and incitement claims.

"Wrongful Petitioning" Actions

Like "negligent protest organizing," "riot boosting," and some civil conspiracy claims, "wrongful petitioning" claims fall short of First Amendment standards. As discussed earlier, "wrongful petitioning" involves an allegation that a speaker has interfered with business relations or engaged in some other tortious conduct through direct action aimed at government officials. Likely because of obvious First Amendment concerns, so far there have been relatively few such claims. But as discussed earlier, public officials have sued groups of protesters for shadowing parking enforcement agents and for making allegedly false statements about the environmental impacts of public projects. In the latter case, a jury awarded a $4 million judgment against the petitioner.

The "wrongful petition" claim is flatly inconsistent with the First Amendment – specifically the right to petition the government for redress of grievances.[189] Imposing civil liability based on communications between citizens and officials (or their agents) strikes at the heart of the First Amendment. As the Court observed in *New York Times Co. v. Sullivan,* the "central meaning" of the free speech guarantee is that citizens have a First Amendment right to make critical statements *about* government officials concerning the performance of their official duties.[190] It stands to reason they must also be free to communicate those criticisms directly or indirectly *to* officials without fear of ruinous civil liability judgments. Indeed, doing so is arguably the very essence of protest and dissent.

The First Amendment does not provide absolute protection for petitioning or other expression. One argument could be that the First Amendment does not prohibit the government from punishing speakers for making *false* statements that result in financial harms to the government. Under that theory, wrongful or tortious petition liability may lie for false statements that cause business harms such as loss of public contracts.[191] Lying to a public official can sometimes be the basis for criminal or civil liability – for example, when the falsehood leads to obtaining some personal benefit or undermines justice.[192] Further, falsehoods *about* public officials that harm their reputation can sometimes lead to civil damages, even under a heightened standard of liability.[193] Libelous petitioning may be actionable under these standards.

However, the right to communicate specific grievances *to* government officials cannot be limited to the communication of factually accurate or truthful statements. Imposing civil liability for allegedly false statements made while lobbying or petitioning government officials would severely chill speech at the core of the First Amendment. The deterrence could extend to whistleblowing in the context of government contracts, complaints about fraudulent spending, and other matters about which citizens must be free to petition policymakers and representatives. Under the wrongful petitioning claim, a speaker who makes a false statement while presenting a complaint or criticizing a public project at a town hall meeting could face extensive damages for the government's economic harms. For instance, if a false statement involves a proposed stadium or other business project that officials ultimately decline to pursue, the petitioner could be liable for all the economic losses experienced by project participants.

One state appellate court has tried to account for these First Amendment concerns by grafting an "actual malice" limitation onto the interference with business relations tort in the petitioning context.[194] But this does not cure the First Amendment concerns associated with petition-based liability. The "actual malice" standard still allows courts to impose liability for statements made to public officials in the course of their official duties. It would force petitioners, private speakers, to prove they did not engage in false or reckless lobbying. If an affected business can show that petitioner's statements were the product of substandard or reckless research, or misinformation that the petitioner should not have relied on, they may be liable in tort for millions of dollars in damages.

Even with an "actual malice" limitation, petitioning officials would remain a very risky activity. Moreover, the result would be directly contrary to the central purpose underlying the adoption of the "actual malice" standard in other contexts, including in defamation claims – namely, to ensure "that debate on public issues should be uninhibited, robust, and wide-open."[195]

The Supreme Court has recognized precisely this concern in other contexts, including the application of the federal antitrust laws which it has specifically interpreted to *exempt* lobbying activities.[196] Direct action protesters, environmental activists, whistleblowers, and other petitioners should not face civil tort liability for engaging with public officials on matters of public concern. With or without an "actual malice" standard, civil actions based on petitioning activities violate the freedom of speech and the right to petition the government for redress of grievances.

"Aiding and Abetting Defamation" Claims

Finally, with respect to civil liability claims, consider the cause of action based on the allegation public protest *supporters* have "aided and abetted defamation" of a protest target. This was the liability theory relied on by the trial court in the Oberlin College lawsuit, discussed earlier, in which the court ultimately ordered the college to pay $44 million.

Recall that in this case, civil liability was not based on the college's *own* defamatory statements, but rather on its alleged statements and actions facilitating and supporting *students'* allegedly defamatory communications and the participation of students, faculty, and one of the college's administrators in the protest. The college itself did not create or publish the students' allegedly defamatory flyers accusing the bakery of racism, nor did it have a hand in writing or publishing the students' senate resolution that condemned the bakery owners.[197] The college "assisted" students, in the sense that it recognized the student senate and provided it with resources and access to facilities, including a display case that for a time housed the resolution.[198]

An appeals court upheld the jury's (reduced) $25 million verdict against the college on the grounds that there was evidence it "facilitated" or assisted" the publication of the student flyers and the senate resolution.[199] One can reasonably debate whether the students or even the college acted responsibly in making their allegations against the bakery. But the "aiding and abetting defamation" theory, like others discussed in this section, once again raises concerns about the imposition of civil liability based on the harmful actions of third parties. Like those other claims, "aiding and abetting defamation" violates the First Amendment's requirements that protester liability be based on precise legal standards and imposed only in narrow circumstances.

Under basic defamation principles, a speaker is liable for false statements they or their agent or servant publishes, but not generally for statements published by others.[200] To hold speakers liable for merely supporting or even merely "liking" another's defamatory statement would expand the reach of the defamation tort in ways that seriously threaten speech supportive of protest movements and press reporting on such protests.

For example, under this theory, BLM supporters would be liable for "aiding and abetting defamation" if they engage in any acts or statements found to *facilitate* defamatory statements made by others in the protest movement. Those acts may include providing food or water at the defamatory protest or inviting others to participate in a demonstration at which someone else makes defamatory statements. Defamation liability would extend not only to an author of a defamatory statement and the media outlet that published it, but to anyone who thereafter "aided and abetted" its distribution.

In short, the claim is a kind of "defamation boosting," with all the First Amendment baggage that the claim entails. The "aiding and abetting" theory is flatly inconsistent with common law defamation standards and First Amendment limits on civil liability.

MANAGING THE COSTS OF DISSENT

Some might consider civil costs and liabilities less threatening to public protest than, say, criminal arrest and prosecution or even limits on where protesters can assemble. To the contrary, as the history of the Civil Rights Movement demonstrates, civil claims and damage awards can have a devastating effect on public protest activities and movements. That danger remains present today, as plaintiffs pursue new and expansive liability theories against public protest organizers, participants, and supporters.

The civil actions are just one part of a more extensive system of costs and liabilities that manage public protest by means of various financial burdens. Permit fees, security and cleanup costs, insurance requirements, penalty enhancements, loss of public benefits, and other financial assessments all contribute substantially to the rising costs of dissent. The law of public protest has surprisingly little to say about the validity of these costs and cost-shifting measures. In the absence of guidance, policymakers and administrators have been increasing the costs of dissent.

Protesters can engage in various kinds of self-help to limit the scope of their own liability. However, courts and policymakers have a special obligation under the First Amendment to ensure civil costs and liabilities do not chill public protest, are based on precise legal standards, and limit vicarious and collective forms of liability. Containing the costs of dissent does not entail absolving protesters from responsibility for their own violent or unlawful acts. But it does require that courts and policymakers recognize the limits of that responsibility and ensure that the costs of protest are managed and contained.

5

Managing Campus Protest

This chapter addresses how the law of public protest applies to university campuses. While private universities are generally committed to protecting campus expression and in some contexts may be contractually obligated to do so, only public universities are obligated to comply with the First Amendment. While the law discussed in the chapter only formally applies to public universities, the general free speech and assembly principles discussed ideally should apply across the range of colleges and universities. University campuses have traditionally been hotbeds of protest and political activism. Students may first encounter public activism and engage in self-government on campus. Conflicts over free speech and assembly on campus continue to generate heated debate and legal disputes. This chapter focuses on protest-related issues on university campuses: the rights of students and others to access campus places for the purpose of speech and assembly; the standards that apply to student speech; the scope of protest and counter-protest rights on campus; and the problem of rising security costs associated with campus protests. The chapter's analysis is informed, in part, by my service as co-chair of a public university committee charged with examining campus policies affecting expressive rights.[1] Universities differ from other places on what I referred to in Chapter 3 as the "expressive topography." Universities pursue academic missions, and administrators have distinct managerial powers relating to that function. Even taking these interests into account, the law of public protest as applied to universities exhibits many of the pathologies of the managerial system that applies outside campus. The pursuit of an academic mission should not extinguish the "spirit of rebellion" that has traditionally prevailed in these special places.[2]

THE CAMPUS AS A CENTER OF PROTEST

Public protest and dissent, in the form of demonstrations and rallies, have been commonplace on U.S. campuses since the 1960s. Campus activism, more broadly conceived, existed long before this period.[3] However, the Civil Rights Movement and opposition to the Vietnam conflict placed campuses on the protest topography.

During the 1960s, campuses across the U.S. exploded in protest. Public contention on campus initially focused on students' rights to access certain common
areas of campus for the purpose of speech and assembly.[4] The "Free Speech
Movement" originated on the University of California at Berkeley campus in
1964, as a direct result of students' demands that Sproul Plaza and other campus
areas be available for student demonstrations.[5] Students objected to the university's designation of small and out-of-the-way "free speech areas" that displaced
student expression – as discussed later, an issue that continues to affect speech and
assembly on some campuses.[6]

The Free Speech Movement spread to campuses across the nation, creating
vitally important breathing space for student activism. During the 1960s, Students
for a Democratic Society (SDS) and other activist groups organized protests by students, faculty, and others. Protesters on 300 to 500 of the nation's 2,000 campuses
engaged in non-violent pickets, demonstrations, occupations of university buildings, sit-ins, strikes, and other disruptive actions, and confrontations with university
administrators became more frequent.[7]

Not all campus dissent was non-violent. In 1969 and 1970, student radicals bombed
police stations, corporate offices, military facilities, and campus buildings. Some
26,000 students were arrested and 1,000 more were expelled for engaging in violent
protests. The violence and disruption sometimes spilled beyond campus gates, as
entire cities were affected by riots and other destructive acts. The climax of this
period of unrest occurred during the spring of 1970, when four Kent State University
students and two Jackson State students were killed during campus protests.

In a 1972 decision, Justice Lewis Powell, writing for the Court, reflected on the
violence and disruption of this period:

> A climate of unrest prevailed on many college campuses in this country. There
> had been widespread civil disobedience on some campuses, accompanied by
> the seizure of buildings, vandalism, and arson. Some colleges had been shut
> down altogether, while at others files were looted and manuscripts destroyed ...
> Although the causes of campus disruption were many and complex, one of the
> prime consequences of such activities was the denial of the lawful exercise of First
> Amendment rights to the majority of students by the few. Indeed, many of the
> most cherished characteristics long associated with institutions of higher learning
> appeared to be endangered.[8]

The Court's characterization of the era highlights several protest-related controver-
sies still affecting campuses today, including the scope of protesters' rights and how to
balance those rights with the rights of others and universities' educational functions.
These concerns will be considered in turn.

However, campus protests also had salutary effects concerning public protest and
dissent. They established universities as places where this activity could occur – on
public university campuses, under the protection of the First Amendment.[9] More

broadly, the Court observed, "the precedents of this Court leave no room for the view that, because of the acknowledged need for order, First Amendment protections should apply with less force on college campuses than in the community at large."[10] The Court also concluded university administrators could not deny recognition to SDS and other organizations solely because they were "disruptive."[11]

As campuses became centers of public protest, they galvanized public discourse and affected public policies. As John Kenneth Galbraith observed with respect to the anti-war movement on campus:

> It was the universities … which led the opposition to the Vietnam War, which forced the resignation of President Johnson, which are forcing the pace of our present withdrawal from Vietnam, which are leading the battle against the great corporations on the issue of pollution, and a score or more of the more egregious time-servers, military sycophants and hawks.[12]

Despite these benefits, campus protest also raised complex issues concerning the extent to which campuses should be centers of protest, the need for order and discipline on campuses, and the educational and other costs associated with disruptive and sometimes violent dissent. In the wake of the Free Speech Movement and campus unrest, many state legislatures engaged in more aggressive oversight of expression on public college and university campuses.[13] As we will learn, there are again signs of a legislative backlash against campus protest.

Universities serve many purposes. As Keith Whittington has observed, "At heart, the mission of a university is to produce and disseminate knowledge."[14] But universities also serve broader democratic interests, some closely aligned with First Amendment values. For instance, John Inazu has claimed "a central purpose, if not *the* central purpose, of the university is to be a place of facilitating disagreement across differences."[15] Justice William O. Douglas once wrote, "Without ferment of one kind or another, a college or university … becomes a useless appendage to a society which traditionally has reflected a spirit of rebellion."[16] Making room for protest and dissent on campus is vitally important for initiating students into conflict and reasoned disagreement, robust and uninhibited debate, and "enact[ing] the aspirations of democratic governance."[17]

THE FIRST AMENDMENT ON CAMPUS

The Supreme Court has said remarkably little about how the First Amendment applies specifically to speech and assembly on campus, including to protest activities by students and other members of the academic community. When it has spoken, its pronouncements have not been directives concerning the application of First Amendment doctrines, precedents, and principles but instead more aspirational statements about the role of institutions of higher learning in a democratic society. For example, the Court has observed that the university classroom "with its surrounding environs is peculiarly the 'marketplace of ideas.'"[18] As we will see, the Court has had little to say about the actual scope of First Amendment protest rights on campus.

The Court's relative silence has created space for an ongoing debate about whether the First Amendment *applies* at all on public university campuses. Robert Post has argued that, for the most part, it does not.[19] He claims that since universities exist to serve the primary functions of knowledge discovery and dissemination rather than self-government or other First Amendment values, campus administrative authority is generally subject to principles of "academic freedom" rather than free speech standards.[20] Post generally considers the First Amendment an inappropriate lens through which to view and settle campus speech disputes, including student and faculty speech rights and the "disinvitation" of invited speakers who spark controversy.[21]

As far as I can tell, Post's position on the scope of the First Amendment is a decidedly minority one.[22] Nevertheless, given the lack of clear precedent or guidance on the role of the First Amendment on campus, his position cannot be ignored. Post's argument has merit insofar as it concerns the application of First Amendment content-neutrality rules to curricular policies, faculty and committee assessments of research and course assignments, classroom pedagogy, and other aspects of educators' zone of professional conduct. As a general matter, these concerns lie within the realm of "academic freedom," an amorphous but important body of principles that govern academic affairs. As Post argues, that body of authority anticipates and permits content-based standards and assessments on campus that would violate the First Amendment in other settings. For example, professors are *expected* to grade papers and examinations based on the content of the answers. Tenure committees are expected to have the authority to assess the substance and content of an applicant's file.

In these and related professional-academic domains, the First Amendment cannot be strictly applied. However, concerning more "public" and non-professional activities such as student protest and dissent on campus, Post's position goes too far. As noted earlier, the Supreme Court has already concluded that officials' desire for order does not allow them to apply First Amendment standards with "less force" on campus. That statement certainly assumes the First Amendment applies to some degree on campus. As the Court has more directly observed, "state colleges and universities are not enclaves immune from the sweep of the First Amendment."[23] The Court has invalidated university decisions not to recognize student groups based on the content of their expression or perceived "disruptive" character.[24] It has also invalidated, on First Amendment grounds, a university requirement that faculty members disclose their membership in the communist party.[25] More recently, the Court struck down a university policy that refused to fund certain student publications based on the publications' point of view or perspective.[26]

Lower courts have also applied First Amendment standards to campus policies and decisions that implicate free speech, assembly, and student press rights. Among other matters, they have applied free speech and other constitutional standards to "campus speech codes" and penalties for student expression.[27] Further, for what it is worth, my own experience as co-chair of a committee charged with reviewing university speech policies confirms that administrators *understand* policies affecting speech and assembly on campus are subject to First Amendment limits.

Post's argument that the First Amendment is generally – perhaps entirely – inapplicable on campus is based on the premise that the purpose of campus speech is not to contribute to public discourse and self-government but to further the school's educational mission.[28] Here, again, the argument sweeps too broadly – especially as it pertains to protest and dissent on campus. As the Free Speech Movement demonstrated, campus protest contributes significantly to public discourse and self-government. So do other kinds of campus speech, including student and faculty political activism.[29] Even accepting Post's premise that *only* speech necessary to the formation of public opinion implicates the First Amendment, campus protest and dissent readily meet that standard.[30]

Universities pursue academic missions by producing and disseminating knowledge. But as institutions of higher learning, public (and private) universities also prepare future generations of citizens for democratic governance by modeling the free exchange of ideas.[31] If, as the Court recently explained, "America's public schools are the nurseries of democracy," universities are part of a continuing educational process that nurtures democratic principles.[32] The weight of authority, including Supreme Court precedents, shows that the First Amendment and its central values apply within the campus gates. As we will see, determining *how* the First Amendment applies on campus raises more difficult and, in many respects, yet unanswered questions.

CAMPUS ORDER MANAGEMENT

Concerning public protest and dissent, campus administrators and officials have adopted and incorporated a version of the "public order management system" discussed in Chapter 3.[33] On campuses, this system includes a variety of restrictions and limits on protest activity: denying access to certain campus spaces for the purpose of speech and assembly; permit requirements and "facilities use policies"; free speech zoning; codes of conduct; and exclusion of non-university entities from campus. A complex and heavy-handed bureaucratic system limits public protest and dissent on university campuses. The system often imposes constraints beyond legitimate needs for order and the pursuit of educational goals.

Protest Permits and Conditions

Chapters 2 and 3 discussed the onerous permitting schemes that apply in public places including streets and parks. University permit policies, which manage dissent on campus to the same or even greater degrees, often closely resemble these schemes. Students and others who want to organize and participate in campus protests must become familiar with multiple policies, including a "Public Forum Policy," "Advertising, Distribution, and Solicitation Policy," and "Policy on Speakers and Facilities Usage."[34] Penalties for failure to comply with these and other campus policies include denial of a permit, revocation of a group's official registration, and, in extreme cases, expulsion.

On some university campuses, policies require advance notice for expressive events nearly everywhere on campus (except perhaps designated areas or zones, which are discussed below). These policies can restrict or even suppress spontaneous assemblies and demonstrations, which react and respond to breaking news and current events. Policies that require extensive advance notice for demonstrations and other events, in some cases up to two weeks, have a similar effect on spontaneous protest.[35]

Content discrimination, or the threat of it, abounds in some university policies affecting protest. For example, some policies require the advance submission of banners and other materials and ban certain kinds of publicity for non-approved events.[36] One policy granted administrators authority to deny a request for any expressive event or display that did not "serve or benefit the entire University community."[37] Another policy prohibited expressive activities based upon their "potential to disrupt," a standard that falls well short of current definitions of unprotected "incitement" and essentially lodges unbridled discretion in campus officials to define "disruptive" expression."[38] Campus policies sometimes grant administrators authority to exempt events or displays from permitting requirements (although some do provide that such decisions should not be made based on the content of expression). To the extent they vest unbridled discretion in administrators or rely on vague or subjective standards, these policies operate as invalid prior restraints or are unconstitutionally vague.[39]

Some campus permitting policies also ignore important procedural protections for protest organizers and participants.[40] For example, in some cases, administrators are not required to provide written reasons for event permit denials. Policies should, but again do not always, provide for prompt appeals of permit denials.[41]

University policies often limit who in the campus community is eligible to participate in speech activities on campus grounds. The exclusion of campus "outsiders" is discussed later. But even students have sometimes been required to affiliate with a registered student organization as a condition of holding an event. Under one such policy, a student was prohibited from distributing photographs of Iraq's infamous Abu Ghraib prison on campus because he was not affiliated with a registered student group.[42]

These types of conditions disparately affect students with dissident or controversial views. Student groups may be reticent to sponsor messages or speakers that do not comport with the sensibilities of the majority. As in other contexts, administrators with unbridled discretion may disfavor certain messages or messengers.

Other permitting provisions can also negatively affect the ability of students and others in the community to organize and participate in campus protests. For example, some universities have detailed rules concerning the erection of stationary exhibits and structures – some left over from the erection of shantytowns during the 1980s protests over South African apartheid.[43] These restrictions, which are ostensibly enforced to maintain the aesthetics of campus lawns and locations, can significantly affect the content of protests. Policies also limit expressive activity near campus buildings, including administrative offices, and the use of amplified sound – even in some areas far removed from administrative buildings and classrooms. These restrictions are like the variety of "time, place, and manner" regulations discussed in Chapter 3, and they have similarly negative effects on protest.

As discussed in Chapter 4, costs and fees charged to protesters raise significant concerns about chilling and suppressing protest. Some campuses have incorporated this mechanism. They impose permit fees on students and other speakers, require that groups supply their own trash receptacles, and even impose liability insurance and indemnification requirements.[44] As a result, some student speakers and campus organizations must pay to protest on campus.

My experience reviewing the free expression policies of universities suggests many are dated, contain unclear limits, or rely on vague conceptions including whether speech is consistent with "community standards." At a minimum, students, faculty, and other community members are entitled to clear standards to determine where, when, and how they may lawfully engage in campus protest. Administrators also benefit from having clear standards and guidelines they can consult during periods of campus unrest and contention.

Even if they were not adopted to suppress or restrict protest, campus permitting provisions often have precisely that effect. In determining the boundaries of free expression on campus, administrators and officials ought to respect and reaffirm the tradition of democratic engagement on campus. They can start by carefully reviewing campus free speech and facilities use policies. In that review, there ought to be a presumption of spontaneous and open exchange in many outdoor spaces on campus, facilitated by fair notice and precise standards.

Access to Campus Forums

As explained in Chapter 3, access to public places or "forums" is critically important to protest organizers and participants. How the campus "topography" is characterized and regulated is therefore a critical component of the law of public protest on campus. Students, faculty, staff, and non-university entities or speakers all have a stake in how the campus expressive topography is mapped.

The Supreme Court has not addressed the First Amendment status of the variety of places on university campuses. According to Post, the university campus is not a "public forum," and administrators therefore have broad power to regulate or suppress

non-educational expression there.[45] Post has not said how far he thinks campus officials can go in terms of licensing, regulating, and punishing campus speech. However,
he has argued students can be punished for marching through campus while shouting
an offensive slogan "because the relationship – the *entire relationship* – between a
university and its students is governed by the goal of education."[46]

Post is surely correct that classrooms are not Hyde Parks where speakers have
a right to communicate whatever message they wish. Similarly, faculty and
administrative offices, as well as places such as academic medical centers, are not
public forums dedicated to speech and assembly. These places primarily serve
non-expressive, educational, or other functions. Although some of these locations
have been occasional protest targets, they have not been traditional venues for
campus protest.

At the same time, the broad implications of Post's position are contrary to the
Supreme Court's statements about the status of public university campuses. The
Court has recognized that universities "began as voluntary and spontaneous *assemblages* or *concourses* for students to speak and to write and to learn."[47] Further, it
has explained, "This Court has recognized that the campus of a public university,
at least for its students, possesses many of the characteristics of a public forum."[48] As
the Court has also observed, the university classroom *"with its surrounding environs*
is peculiarly the 'marketplace of ideas.'"[49]

These statements invoke important First Amendment values and traditions,
including those concerning access to public forums discussed in Chapter 3.[50] In
any event, they expressly reject the notion that the public university campus is a
First Amendment-free zone. Students and other speakers presumably have First
Amendment rights to and in at least some campus places. The question here, as
elsewhere, is which places.

As John Inazu has observed, "The residential university is a complex physical place, a separate 'town' of sorts, playing host to a variety of campus spaces
with numerous purposes."[51] As noted, student and other protesters presumably
do not have a First Amendment right to access *all* university places for purposes
of speech and assembly. However, campus walkways, quadrangles, plazas, pedestrian malls, and perhaps other common areas have traditionally been used for
these purposes.[52] Especially in the case of large residential university campuses,
public protest by students, faculty, and staff would seem to be compatible with at
least open campus areas.

Recall from Chapter 2 that under the "public forum" doctrine, places are categorized as "traditional," "designated," or "non-public" (sometimes referred to as
"limited") forums, depending on a combination of tradition, governmental intent,
and property characteristics.[53] The Supreme Court has not explicitly *required* lower
courts to apply the public forum doctrine to university campuses. However, when
it has reviewed challenges to university free speech policies, the Court has itself
resorted to the doctrine.[54]

Perhaps for this reason, lower courts have attempted to apply the Court's "public forum doctrine" to campus speech restrictions. This has turned out to be a difficult task. As noted, university campuses vary widely in terms of their physical characteristics and relationships to surrounding communities. That makes broad and sweeping declarations about campus spaces difficult and, indeed, likely unwarranted.

Unfortunately, this complexity has not prevented some courts from painting with a broad brush. As one federal court observed, under public forum doctrine "the great weight of authority ... has rejected the notion that *open areas* on a public university campus are traditional public fora."[55] The category of "open areas" presumably encompasses a wide range of campus locations, from large park-like spaces to smaller quads. Some courts have concluded that entire university campuses, some consisting of more than a thousand acres, should be categorized as "limited public fora" where university administrators can limit speech to only certain subject matters and classes of speakers.[56] The entire campus, according to one court, "is an *enclave* created for the pursuit of higher learning by its admitted and registered students and by its faculty."[57] By contrast, a few courts have categorized the *entire* campus as "more akin to a public street or park than a non-public forum."[58]

The difficulty may lie with the public forum doctrine itself, which as I have observed has been subjected to widespread criticism for, among other things, its wooden focus on categories. If courts are going to apply public forum doctrine to campuses, they should at least adopt a more nuanced and careful approach that analyzes the specific place in question in terms of its everyday functions and compatibility with expression.[59]

For example, the Supreme Court has held that a campus auditorium can be categorized as a "designated" public forum based on the university's intent that it be generally open to expressive activities.[60] Similarly, some lower courts have characterized campus spaces that are "physically indistinguishable from public sidewalks" or otherwise blend into non-campus areas as "traditional" public fora.[61] A campus quad, green space, or sidewalk that has functioned in much the same way as a public park, with access granted to both community members and members of the public, may be characterized as a traditional or designated public forum. Or it may, depending again on its typical use and the restrictions imposed, be a forum limited to members of the university community and perhaps those affiliated with those members. As discussed later, under the forum doctrine campuses are allowed to, but need not, maintain places open exclusively to student, faculty, and staff speech.

Public forum doctrine allows for broad managerial control of expression. As explained in Chapter 3, in many critical respects the doctrine fails to value and facilitate public protest and dissent.[62] We may well be stuck with this doctrine outside campus grounds. However, nothing prevents campus administrators (or courts) from taking a different approach to the campus topography.

Instead of forcing campus spaces into the rigid categories of the public forum doctrine, administrators could treat all open and common spaces on campus grounds as presumptively open for speech and assembly activities, including spontaneous gatherings. To ensure campuses continue to serve their expressive and democratic functions, administrators could adopt a default policy of open access to plazas, quadrangles, pathways, sidewalks, and other campus areas generally compatible with speech and assembly.

Some might worry that jettisoning the public forum doctrine would leave administrators without adequate authority to dictate how facilities are used or maintain a "quiet atmosphere" on campuses.[63] But moving in a more speech-protective direction would not entail ceding all control over the campus topography. If some spaces are in high demand, administrators can institute reasonable permit or other requirements to prevent conflicting events and otherwise manage access. They can also adopt restrictions on protest and other expression that are necessary to prevent disruption or interference with classroom instruction and administrative work.[64] Limits could include content-neutral noise restrictions, limits on crowd size, and provisions ensuring unimpeded access to university buildings. These limits should be narrowly tailored to reduce noise, and ensure the free flow of campus pedestrian traffic and the pursuit of pedagogical goals.

The Supreme Court has made clear the First Amendment does not require "that a university must grant free access to *all* of its grounds or buildings."[65] Thus, we are considering only the types of spaces that are compatible with non-professional and non-pedagogical discourse. Again, there is no First Amendment right to picket or protest in the dean's office, during classes, or on a football field during a scheduled event. Unlike more "public" campus areas, these spaces serve primary functions unrelated to the free exchange of ideas.

A presumption of access to campus common areas would be consistent with the tradition of universities, which the Supreme Court has observed "began as voluntary and spontaneous assemblages or concourses for students to speak and to write and to learn." And it would ensure that at least some of the campus "environs" continue to function as a "marketplace of ideas."[66]

Campus Speech Zoning

Even when they grant a right of access to speak and assemble in open campus spaces, universities sometimes impose significant time, place, and manner restrictions. One method of controlling campus dissent has been to allow students and others to speak and assemble only in campus "free speech zones." Campus policies also sometimes impose "buffer zones" that limit areas around campus buildings where speech can occur and "bubbles" that shield students – such as those visiting campus health care facilities – from unwelcome expression.[67]

As discussed in Chapter 3, speech zoning is a problem across the expressive topography. Zoning has a long tradition on university campuses. The imposition of a "free speech zone" was a major catalyst for the Berkeley Free Speech Movement.

In response to campus activism by SDS and other groups and the unrest associated with that activism, campuses began to impose strict speech zones.

University administrators have long relied on speech zoning to the substantial detriment of various campus speakers, picketers, pamphleteers, and protesters. As on the broader expressive topography, zoning has been used to displace and confine contentious speech and assembly on campuses.[68] Protest activity has been a specific target of campus zoners. As the president of one university stated when his campus's zoning policy was challenged in court, "Free speech can occur anywhere on campus ... But protests or other political activity must stay in the free speech zones."[69]

Some campus speech zones have been absurdly, even comically, small. Texas Tech University, which has a campus of 28,000 students, at one point limited all unapproved expressive activity to a single "free speech area" – a gazebo approximately twenty feet in diameter. Campus speech was "free" only in a space that covered approximately 400 square feet of a 2,000-plus acre campus.[70] Similarly, the University of Houston's speech zoning policy limited free expression and assembly to two free speech zones on its 500-acre campus.[71] West Virginia University at one point designated just two small speech zones on its 22,000-student, 913-acre campus. Each area was the size of a small classroom. At Modesto Junior College in California, students had to seek a permit to use one small cement area on campus. They had to ask five days in advance and each student could only use the zone for eight hours each semester.[72] The Modesto policy strictly limited the times when the "free speech zones" could be accessed and used.[73]

Under these zoning policies, student protesters have been unable to speak and assemble near student centers, campus newspaper offices, administrative buildings, and other symbolic places. In addition to displacing protesters, the containment and dispersal of speech under the zoning policies has made it more difficult to engage in spontaneous and mass protests. The highlighted zoning policies, and others, plainly fail the First Amendment's "narrow tailoring" requirement and often leave students with inadequate alternative channels of communication.

Campus speech zoning seems to be on the decline. Activists, lawyers working at the Foundation for Individual Rights in Education (FIRE), and legislators have all successfully challenged or limited the practice of campus speech zoning. FIRE has successfully litigated several cases against university zoning policies.[74] In 2018, the organization reported that only one in ten surveyed universities were still relying on speech zoning – down from one in six universities in 2016.[75] Many state legislatures have also banned campus speech zoning in "Campus Free Speech Acts."[76] As discussed later, there are problems with these state laws. But one laudable provision denies universities the ability to resort to restrictive free speech zoning.

Although speech zoning has been reduced on campuses, it has not been eradicated. In a recent case that reached the Supreme Court, a university altered its zoning policy in an unsuccessful bid to avoid legal scrutiny.[77] Under the now-repealed policy, student speech activities were limited to areas comprising less than 1 percent of the campus grounds.

Universities frequently highlight their commitment to the free exchange of ideas, while at the same time they adopt restrictive policies that stifle that very activity. Some have even done so on the purported ground that speech zones facilitate students' decisions to avoid being exposed to unwelcome ideas.[78] Campus officials should not require a court decision or state law to convince them that free speech zoning is antithetical to the free exchange of ideas and the democratic functions of college campuses. They can honor the cause of the Free Speech Movement by repealing their speech zoning policies.

Campus Speech Standards

One way to manage contention on campus is to regulate the content of speech and expressive conduct. The Supreme Court has never specifically addressed what substantive standards apply to student speech on college campuses. The U.S. is currently engaged in a robust debate about the extent to which universities can or should prohibit certain language or ideas on the nation's campuses.[79] To the extent that debate focuses on classroom, dormitory, or faculty extramural speech, it is not relevant here. But content control can restrict all manner of campus expression, including protests and demonstrations.

While it has developed several standards applicable to elementary and high school student speech, the Court has said little about the scope of college students' expressive rights.[80] In elementary and secondary schools, administrators can punish speech that causes disruption, is "vulgar and lewd," is part of curricular exercises, or advocates unlawful activity.[81] Most importantly, in terms of campus protest rights, the Court has not addressed whether university administrators can restrict or punish college students' speech when it "materially and substantially disrupts" educational activities or if the content is considered inappropriately lewd, vulgar, or otherwise offensive.[82] These standards would restrict many forms of student activism, including campus protests. Lower courts have considered whether these or other standards ought to apply on public university campuses. Their conclusions have varied and there is currently no consensus on the matter.[83]

Although the Supreme Court has not yet adopted any university speech standards, it has suggested that existing elementary and secondary speech standards are not appropriate in the university context. Some of these standards are justified by the impressionability of young students, for example concerns about their exposure to sexually explicit or other age-inappropriate materials. Some on the Court have emphasized that "the rights of teaching institutions to limit expressive freedom of students ha[s] been confined to high schools, ... whose students and their schools' relation to them are different and at least arguably distinguishable from the counterparts in college education."[84] The Court has recognized that college students are "young adults" and, as such, are "less impressionable than younger students."[85] These statements suggest that universities do not have the authority to broadly suppress protest or other expression on campus because it is distracting, vulgar, or offensive.

The elementary and secondary school "disruption" standard poses a particular danger to campus protest. As it has been interpreted in elementary and secondary schools, the disruption standard should not be applied on university campuses.[86] Lower courts have applied the standard in ways that significantly expand schools' authority.[87] To be sure, universities are not required to tolerate disruptive *violence* of the sort created by some campus protesters during the 1960s and 1970s. However, "disruption" might refer to any form of disturbance, interference, contention, or provocation that might distract students or other members of the campus community from their studies. Student and other campus protesters have no First Amendment right to block passage to classrooms or administrative buildings, occupy these spaces, engage in vandalism or other unlawful activities, or protest in manners that substantially interfere with pedagogy or academic freedom. Outside these limits, universities should preserve ample breathing space on campus for protest and dissent.

Other elementary and secondary school speech standards are even less appropriate for campuses. As the Court has acknowledged, university students are more mature and less impressionable than elementary or high school students. University students should have the right to communicate and protest using "vulgar," "lewd," and other offensive speech.[88] University students must be prepared to live in a disputatious society. That means they need to learn how to encounter, process, and respond to expression that is controversial, offensive, or unwelcome. Contrary to Robert Post's claim, this means a university cannot discipline students for marching across campus shouting a vulgar chant. Post does not think the First Amendment even *applies* to that scenario. As discussed earlier, nothing the Supreme Court has said so far suggests that it agrees. And many lower court decisions have applied the First Amendment to university students' expression.

As for schools' authority to regulate speech that conflicts with its own, including for the purpose of disassociating from certain content, university administrators should likewise enjoy less leeway in that regard than their secondary school counterparts. This authority is to some degree related to the immaturity of the audience and its inability to distinguish between the message of the speaker and that of the institution. In places of higher learning, the Court has assumed mature students – as well as outside audiences – can easily draw such distinctions.[89] Moreover, outside of academic and professional settings where institutional interests generally must prevail, campus administrators should not be allowed to stifle debate because protesters' messages are contrary to or inconsistent with their own. If the campus "marketplace" is to flourish, administrators must tolerate and even encourage student speech that challenges conventional norms and the status quo. In sum, the lesson ought not to be that student speech is limited to communications that agree with university orthodoxy.

Like other officials, university administrators can punish incitement, threats, harassment that is pervasive and interferes with others' educational opportunities, and other narrowly defined categories of unprotected speech.[90] But the absence of Supreme Court authority poses some questions concerning campus officials' authority to regulate content more broadly. Some of those questions pertain to expression that advocates violence or creates apprehension of physical harm. But perhaps the most pressing concern, including with respect to protests, is whether administrators can punish expression that is racially derogatory.

During the 1980s and 1990s, lower courts invalidated campus "speech codes" that sought to penalize offensive student expression.[91] Courts struck the codes on the grounds they were unconstitutionally vague and broadly restricted protected speech. For example, the codes prohibited speech that caused a loss of self-esteem and consisted of inconsiderate jokes, stereotyping, epithets, slurs, sexually suggestive comments, and offensive non-verbal gestures.

Federal court decisions invalidating campus speech codes did not eradicate campus efforts to regulate the content of student speech. A study by FIRE in 2006 – decades after the speech codes had been invalidated – showed that more than 90 percent of the 300 universities studied still had policies that prohibited expression fully protected by the First Amendment.[92] Many restrictions migrated to university codes of conduct or statements of student rights and responsibilities, which banned things such as "offensive communication not in keeping with the community standards" and speech that demonstrates "disrespect for persons."[93]

Like free speech zoning on campus, FIRE has documented a steady decrease in campus content discrimination of this sort. Its 2022 report on speech codes concluded that only 18.5 percent of all universities included in the study retained bans on protected speech, including offensive and provocative expression.[94] However, some universities continue to police the content of expression through other means. For instance, the University of Michigan authorized a "Bias Response Team" to investigate and report "bullying" and "harassment" on campus. A federal appeals court declined to address the merits of the policy but concluded the team's power to investigate and refer cases to administrators potentially chilled speech protected by the First Amendment.[95]

All this expression is protected under the First Amendment, which generally prohibits the government from banning vulgar, offensive, and even racially derogatory expression that does not constitute incitement, a true threat, or some other unprotected utterance.[96] If they apply on campuses, these standards surely disallow punishing students for vulgar chanting or disciplining them for engaging in racially derogatory protests.

But *should* these speech-protective standards apply on campus? Again, we are not concerned with the authority to regulate speech in classrooms or other curricular contexts where administrators have greater authority to control content. Rather, the focus is on the open spaces of campus grounds, where protests and other speech activities can also occur.[97]

Racially derogatory protests undermine the university's commitment to creating an inclusive campus community. They, along with other forms of racist speech, affect the ability of Black and other marginalized students to enjoy their educational experience on an equal basis with others. In 2015, the University of Oklahoma relied on this justification when it expelled fraternity members for engaging in a racist chant on a campus bus.[98] In addition, a racist protest may chill the expressive rights of racial and ethnic minorities.

However, blatant viewpoint discrimination violates the First Amendment and is inconsistent with at least some aspects of the function of the university. As the Supreme Court has observed, "For the University ... to cast disapproval on particular viewpoints of its students risks the suppression of free speech and creative inquiry in one of the vital centers for the Nation's intellectual life, its college and university campuses."[99]

Applied to public university campuses (private universities are generally free to engage in content discrimination), a strict content-neutrality principle would mean the university could not discipline students even for explicitly racist protests and demonstrations – unless, again, they contain unprotected expression. That undoubtedly will strike some as an unwarranted and harmful conclusion. The impulse to condemn the protest and expel the students is understandable. Unfortunately, there may be no clear managerial standard that avoids granting university policymakers broad discretion to shut down or discipline student protesters who express views students or administrators find offensive or harmful. Any protest with an arguably derogatory message, including those amplified online, could become grounds for expulsion. In campus open spaces or forums, that sort of managerial latitude ought to be avoided or at least narrowed to repeated or targeted protests that violate students' rights to equal educational opportunities.

Thankfully, racially derogatory protests of the sort I have described are rare on campuses. Further, as commentators have observed, there are means other than content discrimination for navigating the tension between protest and inclusion. These options include the creation of communal spaces for under-represented minorities, educational programming that highlights the need to balance free speech and inclusivity, and official communications supportive of students or others affected by certain speech on campus grounds.[100] Of course, students and other members of the campus community remain free to condemn the protesters and their message, and will undoubtedly do so.

The Supreme Court has been, and may continue to be, reluctant to engage with the subject of university speech standards. If so, it will be up to lower courts to fashion and apply appropriate standards. When performing this function, courts should consider the distinctive characteristics of both universities and their community members. Protest and dissent on campus should receive a wide berth, again with due consideration of institutional interests in order, safety, and educational functions.[101] The discussion has centered primarily on the speech and assembly rights of *students*. Insofar as faculty and staff also participate in campus protests, their speech rights as public employees may be more circumscribed under the First Amendment.[102] However, as members of the campus community, their ability to protest and dissent regarding matters of public concern should also receive broad protection from administrators and courts.[103]

Excluding "Outsiders"

So far, we have addressed *how* one protests on campus, *where* they can do so, and *what* they can communicate. But *who* is allowed to protest on campus? The Supreme Court has suggested that the campus, "at least for its students," has the characteristics of a public forum and that the classroom and "environs" function as a marketplace of ideas.[104] But campuses are typically part of a broader local community. Conceivably, they could provide forums for the speech and assembly of those who are not enrolled or working there. Issues relating to invitations to outside speakers, by student groups or faculty, are reserved for later discussion. For now, let us focus more generally on access to campus grounds.

Many university "facilities" and other policies draw distinctions between members of the academic community – students, faculty, and staff – and what are typically called "non-university entities" (outside or unaffiliated speakers or groups). While some make room for these outside entities under certain conditions, others substantially restrict or even deny their ability to access campus spaces.[105] These access exclusions have significant implications for campus protest and dissent. Most importantly, from the perspective of student audiences, they create a restrictive enclave in which students and other campus members are denied access to "outside" or "external" voices.

Courts have upheld non-university entity access restrictions challenged on First Amendment grounds. As one federal appeals court reasoned, an outside speaker is "not a member of the class of speakers for whose especial benefit the forum was created" and thus can be "constitutionally restricted from undertaking expressive conduct" in areas available to community members for that purpose.[106] Other courts have upheld special permit requirements for non-university speakers based on safety, space, and other concerns, and requirements that outside speakers be sponsored by student groups or faculty members in order to speak or protest on campus.[107]

Prioritizing student, faculty, and staff access to campus grounds for the purpose of expressive activities makes sense when one considers there is an academic community that resides, teaches, and works there. Students and other community members should have first dibs on the available campus forums, to exchange ideas among themselves and engage in discourse that relates to community concerns.

However, that does not mean universities should broadly exclude members of the "external" community from their grounds. The distinction between "internal" and "external" communities is not as stark as it may seem. Many public university campuses are located near or even within a "non-university" community. The campus may share sidewalks and other common areas with the surrounding communities, and some of these spaces may be difficult to identify as campus or non-campus areas.[108] Further, campus "insiders" like students and faculty often engage and interact with campus "outsiders" including residents and merchants. Itinerant speakers, including evangelists and activist groups, visit campuses. In short, a university may be an integral part of a local "external" community and vice versa.

When crafting speech and assembly policies relating to non-university speakers, universities should consider what granting access to "outsiders" can add to the academic experience. Exposure to locals' messages and ideas may bring campus and surrounding communities closer together. Of course, access may also create a degree of division or discomfort or may conflict with student and faculty expectations about their right to be sheltered from certain messages in spaces they consider "home." But part of preparing students to be participants in democratic discourse entails exposing them to off-campus ideas they disagree with or oppose. A vibrant mix of student groups, street preachers, pro-life and pro-choice activists, anti-war protesters, and canvassers is a closer facsimile of what a robust "marketplace of ideas" looks like than an enclave that excludes all "non-university entities."

Non-university entities can be subject to clear and reasonable permit requirements based on considerations of safety, space availability, and other concerns. And like any speaker or group, they can be excluded for any violent conduct or unprotected speech including threats and incitement to violent action. However, if a space is otherwise available, administrators should not restrict the public's access to it through onerous permit or other restrictions.[109]

Finally, some universities impose conditions that limit access by external speakers or groups to those who are sponsored by an existing student group. Sponsorship conditions facilitate the university's educational mission by limiting access to speakers and groups existing organizations presumably believe offer some educational benefit. They also make it easier to coordinate events and provide the necessary security. But as discussed earlier, universities should consider the possibility that strict sponsorship requirements may have a significant chilling effect on unpopular messages and viewpoints. If registered student groups disagree with the person's message or perspective, the sponsorship requirement may operate as a veto. Even when many students desire to hear the speaker's point of view, existing student organizations may be reluctant to "sponsor" a controversial speaker. Universities should make some space available for external community members to use campus spaces without having to demonstrate an existing relationship with a registered or approved student organization.

Although campus spaces exist primarily to serve the needs and interests of the academic community, "non-university entities" should not be treated as complete strangers. The university campus is not hermetically separated from bordering communities and "non-university entities." Faculty produce research and commentary that is consumed off campus and give talks attended by members of the surrounding community. Students perform community service in cities and towns near campus. Members of the surrounding community ought to be encouraged to participate in the exchange of ideas on campus. If they are not to become, as Justice Douglas's once warned, "useless appendages," whether or not they are obligated to do so universities should try to engage with speakers and groups beyond their gates.[110]

CONTROVERSIAL SPEAKERS AND THE COSTS OF CAMPUS DISSENT

In recent highly publicized instances, university campuses have experienced disruptive and even violent protests in connection with the presence of visiting speakers. Invitations to white nationalists, right-wing provocateurs, and conservative academics have resulted in campus violence and physical attacks on speakers and others. The decision to invite – or *disinvite* – speakers whose views are opposed by some or even many in the community has generated substantial debate.[111] Thus far, I have encouraged universities to make some space for "outsiders" on their campuses. Whether and how to invite certain outside speakers to campus, and how universities and students should respond to such invitations, are complex issues.[112] This section focuses on two aspects of the problem: the speech rights of student protesters and the costs of securing campuses against potentially violent and disruptive audiences.

In 2017, there were violent protests at the University of California-Berkeley in anticipation of an appearance by Milo Yiannopoulos, Ann Coulter, and other right-wing provocateurs.[113] Although the "Free Speech Week" event ultimately did not take place, security cost the university more than $4 million. That same year, students at Middlebury College shut down a talk by Charles Murray, a conservative scholar, and injured a faculty member during protests of his appearance.[114] At my university, also in 2017, William & Mary students prevented a speaker from the American Civil Liberties Union from addressing an audience about freedom of speech in the wake of events during the violent "Unite the Right" demonstrations in Charlottesville, Virginia.[115]

Highly publicized incidents like these, and many others, have raised concerns about a free speech "crisis" on campus.[116] The protests have highlighted concerns about how administrators manage dissent relating to outside speakers.[117] In response to such protests, some universities have cancelled events or "disinvited" speakers. Other universities have revised provisions in their codes of conduct relating to "disruptive" activities and considered shifting rising security costs onto speakers or student groups. Meanwhile, state legislatures have enacted campus "free speech" legislation that may make it more costly and difficult for students to engage in campus protests.

As in other areas relating to campus free speech, it is not clear whether students have a First Amendment *right* to invite outside speakers to campus or whether universities possess the authority to ban all outside speakers.[118] Whether or not there is a First Amendment invitation right, most if not all universities authorize students to invite outside speakers or themselves invite such speakers. Although students have peacefully protested outside speakers, as noted some invitations have resulted in disruptive protests.

As discussed elsewhere in the book, the Supreme Court has not developed clear doctrines relating to what are sometimes called "hostile audiences," including whether speakers are entitled to continue communicating in the face of hostility, universities are obligated to provide security for controversial speakers, or audiences have a First Amendment right to shout down or otherwise interrupt the event.[119] Without clear rules and guidance, universities have been left to manage these concerns on their own.

As Greg Magarian has observed, protests of campus speakers generally "encompass three distinct categories of behavior: violence, preemptive protest, and shouting down."[120] Some means of disruption can be easily taken off the table. Violent conduct is not protected speech; physical attacks on either speakers or their supporters are not protected. Neither are threats communicated to speakers or speech that incites audiences to commit imminent violent acts that are likely to occur.[121]

Still, as Magarian has noted, "[v]iolence in or around a protest does not make the protest a riot."[122] He makes the important point that focusing on violence around campus protests like the one at Berkeley to the near exclusion of non-violent forms of dissent exaggerates the incidence of protest violence, falsely equates protest and riot, and contributes to the panic over a "free speech crisis" on campus.[123] Further, as Magarian has observed, "exaggerations of protest violence, in addition to undermining democracy, often reinforce racist stereotypes of people of color as violent criminals."[124] As coverage of protests shows, this concern exists both off and on campus.[125]

As Magarian has explained, a "preemptive protest" is a non-violent, non-obstructive form of dissent. As such, this activity is protected by the First Amendment. Students and others engaged in preemptive protests urge others not to listen to a speaker, attend an event, or extend an invitation to that speaker. Some have criticized the preemptive protest as part of or contributing to a "culture of censorship" on college campuses.[126] But as Magarian has observed, "preemptive protest works squarely within and honorably serves a system of free expression."[127] Students and other members of the campus community do not betray the principles of free expression by challenging the value or legitimacy of opponents' ideas or even their characters.

Protecting the right to *protest* in this form is a separate issue from the institution's decision to "disinvite" speakers who have been invited. If based on the content of

the speaker's message, that decision likely violates the First Amendment. By contrast, students and other members of the campus community who object to a particular speaker or set of ideas, even if they do so publicly and loudly, lack the power to
"censor" or "silence" speech.[128] Just as they have the right to determine the manner of their own speech, protesters have the right to try to stop the institution from
inviting speakers or allowing speech they disagree with through non-violent and
non-obstructive means. As Magarian has argued, preemptive protest "embodies free
speech values and advances our system of free expression."[129] To be sure, if successful, preemptive protests may produce free speech-related costs in terms of excluding
certain ideas and messages from campus. However, those costs do not constitute a
First Amendment violation of either the speaker's or audience's rights.

"Shouting down" is the most controversial form of campus protest. It "falls
between violence and preemptive protest."[130] Shouting down relies on shouting and
other noise to prevent a speaker from communicating to an audience that wants to
hear what the speaker has come to say. It is different, let us assume, from counter-
speech directed at a speaker or group that does not prevent the speech from reaching an audience but may make the connection between speaker and audience more
strained or difficult – for example, heckling, harsh questioning, or even occasional
booing.[131] It is also different from "staged" disruptions that aim to temporarily disrupt
routines or events to call attention to some cause or issue.[132] These might range from
brief "occupations" of campus spaces to temporary speaker disruptions that are part
of the protest.[133] Last, we ought to distinguish between destroying posters or flyers
and other physical acts of vandalism and shouting down, which consists solely of
verbal activity.

Some First Amendment scholars have characterized shouting down as unprotected *conduct* that is akin to using force to silence a speaker.[134] Insofar as the speech-
conduct distinction in First Amendment doctrine is helpful to the inquiry, as a verbal
rather than physical form of protest shouting down cannot readily be dismissed as
unprotected force (unlike, for example, blocking a speaker's access to a forum or
physically occupying a venue).[135] However, since the assumed intent of those shouting down is to prevent speech from reaching an audience, this form of protest-plus
seemingly offends the free speech marketplace and self-government principles.

One way of looking at "shouting down" is that having failed to preempt the
invitation to speak, campus community members escalate to a form of civil disobedience that they hope and intend will silence the speaker. But as Magarian
has observed, this form of dissent generally "transgresses the boundaries within
which we ordinarily value the contribution civil disobedience makes to the system
of free expression."[136]

Shouting down prevents an audience of community members interested in hearing what the speaker has to say from participating in a scheduled event. It interferes
with the ability of other members of the community to pursue their own goals on
campus. Further, shouting down transforms campus discourse, which should be

based on reason and tolerance, into a shouting match inconsistent with the truth-seeking function. As Keith Whittington has put it, "The best environment for the productive exchange of ideas is not the mosh pit."[137] Thus, some order is necessary for these exchanges. A first-come-first-served or other content-neutral university regulation that aims to ensure scheduled speakers can be heard would be valid under the First Amendment.[138]

In sum, shouting down may sometimes be justified on grounds of civil disobedience but not as an exercise of campus free speech rights.[139] Shouting down or otherwise obstructing the speech of an avowed Nazi who has been invited to campus by a student group may be justified on such terms, even if not as an exercise of free speech. Students and other community members can oppose an invitation. As with other protests, they can engage in counter-protests, which may include heckling and symbolic conduct, that challenges the speakers' ideas. They can organize counter-events to express their own views. Or they can ignore the speaker altogether and urge others to follow suit.

Ultimately, shouting down fails to contribute to public discourse. Indeed, its purpose is to prevent such discourse from occurring. Under the First Amendment, this is not a judgment an audience can or should make. Silencing those with whom one disagrees is inconsistent with both the First Amendment and the mission of the modern university.

Since shouting down is not protected speech, the First Amendment does not prevent a university from disciplining students who engage in this activity. That does not mean they ought to react harshly or severely to such incidents.[140] For one thing, it may be difficult to discern whether a student or group of students have engaged in protected heckling or unprotected "shouting down." For another, given the proximity of shouting down to civil disobedience – which can have expressive value even if it is not protected speech – officials should lean in the direction of lenient discipline.[141] Universities should limit sanctions to extreme cases, such as those in which students combine shouting down with physical acts of obstruction or vandalism.

Some states have adopted versions of a model "Campus Free Speech Act," authored and publicized by the Goldwater Institute. The model Act includes provisions for sanctioning students who engage in "disruptive" protest. Under its terms, "any student who has twice been found responsible for infringing the expressive rights of others will be suspended for a minimum of one year, or expelled."[142]

There are several problems with this legislation. First, it deprives university administrators of the flexibility, discussed earlier, to moderate penalties. Second, the legislation singles out only one form of "disruption." The focus on obstructing speech, which has mostly affected politically conservative speakers, suggests there may be a sanctions bias or a desire to protect conservative, but not other, campus voices. Third, the legislation requires distinguishing between "infringements" of or "interferences" with others' expressive rights and other forms of disruptive protest, a distinction that lacks precision under Supreme Court precedents.[143] As Fred Schauer has explained, "it is hard to imagine a pro-choice speaker not feeling interfered with were a large number of audience members holding up signs portraying aborted fetuses, or even jars containing aborted fetuses in formaldehyde."[144] Yet one hopes universities would not sanction this conduct as "disruptive." If they did, that would suggest a potential for overbroad enforcement. Either way, the "free speech" legislation would chill protected forms of campus protest.

Punishment for student protesters is only one of the issues raised by contentious campus speakers. As discussed in Chapter 2, shouting down occurs in off-campus venues too, where it is sometimes analyzed under First Amendment precedents relating to "hostile audiences." The concept similarly refers to disruptive speech and conduct that prevents, although typically through law enforcement intervention, a speaker from communicating to an intended audience.[145] On campus, the "hostile audience" problem boils down to a few pertinent but complicated questions. We have answered only one of those questions – whether shouting down is protected speech or is subject to discipline. There are two others: Do the invited speakers have a First Amendment right to communicate, even in the face of threats to public order from hostile audiences? Who must or should pay to secure speakers against audiences that may turn on them owing to their messages or ideas, and how expansive is this financial obligation?

What are the obligations of university campus officials and local law enforcement when Milo Yiannopoulos is invited to and arrives on campus? Are universities required to provide security for Mr. Yiannopolous? What if providing security costs millions of dollars that the university does not have, or has but might reasonably want to spend on academic pursuits?

Unfortunately for campus administrators, as Schauer has demonstrated, there are no clear answers under what he has referred to as "the law of interference with protests."[146] As Schauer has observed, the question of "how much" a university must do when confronted with this challenging scenario "involves a complex intersection of financial, logistical, personnel, jurisdictional, and, of course, philosophical considerations."[147]

For example, if policing the demonstration exhausts security resources, campus police could declare the assembly "unlawful" and arrest those who refused to disperse. However, where state, regional, and other local law enforcement resources are available, campus authorities may be required to request their assistance. As Schauer has noted, such requests are hardly unusual where mass protests are concerned and are usually granted by neighboring law enforcement. At some point, of course, even this extra-jurisdictional support may be exhausted, in which case it may be constitutionally permissible for the university to cancel an event because it simply is not possible to secure the speaker's and/or the public's safety. The First Amendment presumably does not require campus authorities to put their communities at actual risk of physical harm and property destruction. Preventing the sort of violence that occurred in Charlottesville in 2017 would presumably constitute a content-neutral justification for prohibiting an event.

However, the mere *potential* for violence is generally not a legitimate basis for suppressing speech and protest.[148] In 2017, a federal district court concluded that Auburn University had not produced evidence that Richard Spencer's planned speech on its campus was likely to incite or produce imminent lawless action. Instead, the court determined Auburn canceled Spencer's talk because listeners and protest groups opposed his ideology and might react violently to his appearance on campus.[149] How to determine when the First Amendment's security tipping point has been reached remains a tricky question for both university officials and judges. Assuming evidence of imminent and likely actual violence is required,[150] as is generally the case where speakers are held liable for advocating unlawful action, universities will need to present it in court to preemptively shut down campus protests.[151]

There are also thorny questions relating to allocating the costs of security. Securing a campus for planned protests or counter-protests can be extremely expensive. As discussed, the University of California-Berkeley estimated it cost approximately $4 million to provide security and related services for actual or planned speeches by just three individuals.[152] The University of Florida spent $500,000 in connection with a single lecture by white supremacist Richard Spencer.[153] How much does the First Amendment *require* universities spend in connection with such events? Can administrators pass these costs on to the speakers themselves, to students, or to the community at large?

Provocative speakers and hostile audiences have forced universities and other institutions to consider how to allocate, or re-allocate, scarce resources to protect speech. There is no First Amendment "balance sheet" that informs the university when or how much it must pay. As discussed in Chapter 4, the Supreme Court has said very little about the cost burdens associated with protests. However, in *Forsyth County v. Nationalist Movement* (1992), the Court invalidated a local ordinance, applied to white supremacist demonstrators, that allowed "a government administrator to vary the fee for assembling or parading to reflect the estimated cost of maintaining public order."[154] According to the Court, "[s]peech cannot be financially burdened, any more than it can be punished or banned, simply because it might offend a hostile mob."[155]

Forsyth County makes clear university officials cannot charge Milo Yiannopolous or the groups that invite him more than other speakers based on concerns about violence. But that still does not tell universities how much they can charge any individual speaker. Nor does it answer whether the university can shift some or all security costs onto a student group wishing to engage with an outside speaker. Shifting the costs of protest onto speakers or student groups would likely disadvantage certain "controversial" speakers. Raising the costs of permitting *all* protests and demonstrations on campus to a level that would cover the sometimes-extraordinary costs of security would threaten campus dissent to an even greater degree. Universities could charge more tuition to cover demonstration security costs, but as Schauer has observed universities "operate in competitive and price-elastic markets" and, moreover, passing costs on to students or faculty (by cutting salaries, for example) requires making other sacrifices.[156]

In sum, preventing the "heckler's veto" from becoming the norm on college campuses may come at a steep price. Provocateurs and hostile audiences impose serious costs and resource allocation decisions on university officials. So does the protection of other rights, including the right to counsel, the right to vote, and the right to access public fora for purposes of speech and assembly. *Forsyth County* may stand for the general proposition that officials cannot charge speakers or protesters for increased security costs, or the narrower principle that they may not do so under a system that allows officials to exercise what is essentially unbridled discretion to determine those costs.[157] As I argued in Chapter 4, it is unjust and contrary to First Amendment doctrines and principles to burden demonstrators and other speakers with the costs of dissent. It is especially repugnant to do so when the reason for the cost burden relates to the controversy, unease, or offense the speech provokes in an audience.[158]

Universities can adopt and enforce content-neutral time, place, and manner regulations, including limits on where and when a speech and any counter-protests can occur. They can and should clarify rules regarding the appropriate response to security concerns in the event of such events, including protocols for campus security and requests for extra-jurisdictional security assistance. However, they ought not to be allowed to shift the costs of otherwise lawful and protected expression onto speakers or groups whose ideas engender dispute.

PRESERVING PROTEST ON CAMPUS

As the Supreme Court has observed, "[t]he vigilant protection of constitutional freedoms is nowhere more vital than in the community of American schools."[159] There is a prevailing narrative that university students want or demand protection from speech they disagree with or that offends them. We should be careful not to blindly accept that narrative. A 2016 Gallup-Knight Foundation survey found that 78 percent of college students say colleges should expose students to all types of speech and viewpoints rather than prohibit biased or offensive speech in furtherance of a positive learning environment.[160] There is at least some evidence campuses are not populated by "coddled" students seeking shelter from what they consider uncivil ideas.[161] Many students understand the value of viewpoint diversity.

Preserving protest and dissent on campus is consistent with the nature of the university. As John Inazu has observed, the university is a kind of political community.[162] A central purpose of this special community is to facilitate disagreement across differences.[163] As Inazu has written, "The democratic university must also strive to protect minority, dissenting, or unpopular views – an aspiration that draws its inspiration from the First Amendment."[164] Protecting protest and dissent on campus helps prepare the next generation of citizens to exchange ideas, argue across differences, and participate in the search for truth.

We must acknowledge universities serve special educational functions that do not affect speech outside campus gates. Those special functions are centrally implicated in places like classrooms and academic pursuits like coursework. However, campuses are also important protest venues. As the Supreme Court has recognized, universities are critically important spaces for teaching tolerance for unpopular ideas, pursuing truth, and engaging in self-government. As Keith Whittington has observed:

> Universities have long offered an arena in which students and visitors engage with and advocate for ideas. Those debates are often boisterous and freewheeling. They reflect the chaos of American democracy rather than the decorum of the seminar room. What holds those two worlds together is a common commitment to taking ideas seriously, to exploring the unconventional and the unexpected, to examining critically what we might otherwise take for granted, and to holding accepted truths up for challenge and reconsideration. If universities are to be a space where ideas are held up to critical scrutiny and our best understanding of the truth is identified and professed, then dissenting voices must be tolerated rather than silenced, and disagreements must be resolved through the exercise of reason rather than the exercise of force.[165]

If a "spirit of rebellion," or anything close to it, is to be preserved on campus then universities will need to create space for campus protest.[166] University administrators, campus police, and others who adopt and enforce campus speech and assembly regulations ought to receive training on basic First Amendment doctrines and principles. This is not a criticism of well-meaning officials. But just as law enforcement must be trained to police protests, campus officials need professional guidance on how to accommodate public dissent on campus. Campuses would also benefit from the work of a standing free speech committee or designated free expression administrator, who would collect information on campus protests and responses and engage in periodic reviews of campus free expression policies.

When campus administrators undertake a holistic review of their facilities and other policies, they ought to adopt a default "maximalist" perspective concerning opportunities for the free exchange of ideas. Onerous permitting requirements should be culled from university policies. Free speech zoning ought to be eliminated on campus grounds. Old speech code holdovers, including content-based definitions of "appropriate" dissent, should be removed. Prior restraints and vague references to "community standards" should all be repealed. The open areas of campus should be treated as presumptively available for speech and assembly, including spontaneous demonstrations, by members of the campus community. To the extent practicable, policies should also provide opportunities for non-university entities to access common spaces on campus.

Universities need to exercise special care when disciplining "disruptive" expression on campus. Violence, destruction of campus property, and other conduct not covered by the First Amendment can clearly be punished. However, disruptive heckling, noise, and other forms of protest are fully protected under the First Amendment. Provisions mandating sanctions for "interference" with others' speech rights should be limited to actual obstructions of scheduled events. But universities may want to approach penalties for this kind of disruption, which often has a civil disobedience component, with sensitivity.

Universities bear the burden of protecting speakers – including provocateurs – from "heckler's vetoes." As recent events show, the price of protecting dissent on campus can be steep. The costs of campus dissent should be borne by the university, not outside speakers, students, or student groups.

6

Arming Public Protests

Over the country's long history, Americans have sometimes mixed guns and politics. Socialists, fascists, the Black Panthers, and the Ku Klux Klan have all used firearms in connection with public contention.[1] As recent protests in the U.S. have shown, the presence of individuals and groups carrying firearms at demonstrations has become a more common phenomenon. Armed demonstrators and counter-demonstrators openly carrying, brandishing, and sometimes discharging firearms challenges the very idea of "peaceable" public speech and assembly. Arming protests creates a tension between exercising First Amendment rights to speak and assemble in public places and the Second Amendment right to carry firearms in public. Many protest participants are likely to be intimidated by the display of firearms or concerned about the risk of bodily harm or death. Thus, they will be reluctant to engage in public protest at all or inclined to moderate their expression. Police officers, who are duty-bound to protect speakers and peaceful assemblies, will find it more difficult to do so or may retreat from such duties fearing they might be outgunned. Arming public protests has ushered in a new brand of violent politics in which firearms threaten to displace peaceful assembly and public discourse as means of democratic change. The law of public carry has become part of the law of public protest. Public carry laws and Second Amendment doctrines are contributing to the management of dissent. This chapter addresses the constitutional and other implications of arming public protests. It concludes that notwithstanding the Supreme Court's recognition of a right to carry arms in public places, governments have a variety of means available to protect public assemblies from the chilling effects of armed protests and preserve the democratic functions of the public square.

THE SECOND AMENDMENT IN THE PUBLIC SQUARE

The book has examined the many rules, regulations, norms, and practices that apply to the exercise of First Amendment rights to speak and assemble in public places. To understand the implications for these rights of the exercise of public carry rights, we need also to understand how the public dimension of the Second Amendment is beginning to take shape.

In *District of Columbia v. Heller* (2008) and *McDonald v. City of Chicago* (2010), the Court recognized an individual right to keep and bear arms – most importantly for the purpose of self-defense in the home but also more generally when needed in cases of "confrontation."[2] *Heller* and *McDonald* did not address whether the Second Amendment right was enforceable outside the home. In *New York State Rifle & Pistol Association v. Bruen* (2022), the Supreme Court answered in the affirmative.[3] Many state laws protect the right to carry firearms in public, either openly or concealed on one's person – or in some states both. However, most states impose some restrictions on public carry. Some may now reconsider those limits or have them challenged in court. After *Bruen*, public carry of firearms will likely become more broadly protected and more common.[4]

The Court has acknowledged the Second Amendment right is not absolute and has identified several limits. *Heller* emphasized that the right to keep and bear arms is not "a right to keep and carry any weapon whatsoever in any manner whatsoever and for whatever purpose."[5] For example, the Court stated, the Second Amendment does not protect keeping or bearing "dangerous or unusual" weapons such as sawed-off shotguns and M-16 automatic rifles.[6] The Court also broadly cautioned:

> Although we do not undertake an exhaustive historical analysis today of the full scope of the Second Amendment, nothing in our opinion should be taken to cast doubt on longstanding prohibitions on the possession of firearms by felons and the mentally ill, or laws forbidding the carrying of firearms in sensitive places such as schools and government buildings, or laws imposing conditions and qualifications on the commercial sale of arms.[7]

Heller also indicated that longstanding bans on armed groups parading or drilling in public places are valid.[8] The Court also noted, "the majority of the nineteenth-century courts to consider the question held that prohibitions on carrying concealed weapons were lawful under the Second Amendment or state analogues."[9] However, the Court suggested, under those decisions a state may not lawfully ban *both* concealed and open carry.[10] Protecting open but not concealed carry was, the Court acknowledged, an "odd reading of the right" – presumably because, in contrast to their forebears, Americans have come to view open carry as the greater threat.[11] In any event, the Court reasoned that banning both forms of public carry would nullify the right.[12]

These are all important limits on the exercise of Second Amendment rights in public. That is true generally, but also specifically, as the restrictions affect and pertain to public protest. The Court's most recent decision, *Bruen*, does not revoke or call into question any of the foregoing limitations. In fact, the Court acknowledged that the history of regulation showed firearms could be banned in certain "sensitive places" such as "legislative assemblies, polling places, and courthouses."[13] *Bruen* invalidated a New York law that limited concealed carry licenses to those who could show "proper cause" as to why they needed a handgun for self-defense. Although the Court concluded that type of law is not "consistent with this Nation's history of firearm regulation," it did not call into question the many state licensing regimes that condition a concealed carry permit on applicants undergoing a background check, fingerprinting, waiting periods, firearms training, and other requirements.[14] Thus, the Court did not embrace a system under which an individual has an *absolute* right to demand a license to carry firearms in public.

Although *Bruen* left several significant limits in place, it substantially altered how governments can justify restricting the right to public carry. Prior to *Bruen*, lower courts had applied a standard that combined historical analysis with scrutiny of the scope and need for regulation.[15] *Bruen* rejected that approach in favor of a standard that focuses on whether a restriction is "consistent with this Nation's history of firearm regulation." That means for governments to defend public carry regulations, they will generally need to find historical analogues from the eighteenth and nineteenth centuries that similarly restricted the right. Although the Court noted that an early law need not be a "dead ringer" to be relevant, it must be "analogous enough to pass constitutional muster."[16] Needless to say, that standard leaves room for significant debate about the historical record and the scope of the Second Amendment as it applies in the public square. The analysis in this chapter will work within the parameters of public carry as they are presently understood.

THE (IN)COMPATIBILITY OF PUBLIC CARRY AND PUBLIC PROTEST

The Supreme Court has now held the Second Amendment applies in at least *some* places outside the home and, further, that it protects a right to carry certain firearms in public for the purpose of self-defense. As noted, states have long provided for public carry rights. Concealed carry is lawful in all states, subject to various regulations. At present, only three states impose outright bans on the open carry of both handguns and rifles in all or most locations although many impose place and type of firearm restrictions.[17] As will be discussed, open carry poses some distinctive threats to public protest. However, even the presence of concealed arms may have detrimental effects on the willingness and ability of individuals to participate in public demonstrations. Unless otherwise indicated, in the remainder of the chapter "public carry" refers to both open and concealed carry.

Although public carry rights have been in place for decades in some states, in recent years the presence of openly displayed firearms at public protest events has become more frequent. In a joint study by Everytown for Gun Safety and the Armed Conflict Location and Event Data Project (ACLED), researchers concluded that in the 18-month period between January 2020 and June 2021, of the 30,000 demonstrations in the U.S., 560 involved demonstrators, counterdemonstrators, or other individuals or groups (openly) carrying or brandishing firearms.[18] Since the study only accounted for openly displayed firearms, it is not clear how many additional protest attendees carried concealed firearms. Similarly, ACLED data shows that from 2021 to 2022 the incidence of openly displayed firearms at abortion rights-related protests doubled.[19] The study also showed a 160 percent increase in the presence of far-right groups such as the Proud Boys at such protests. Anecdotal evidence also supports the conclusion that showing up at a protest event carrying a firearm has become more common.[20]

In some instances, individuals have brandished or even discharged their weapons at public protests. This occurred at the "Unite the Right" rallies in Charlottesville, Virginia during the summer of 2017. It happened again, with fatal consequences, at BLM protest events during the summer of 2020. Although he traveled armed to Kenosha, Wisconsin, a town then gripped by widespread civil unrest, Kyle Rittenhouse was acquitted of murder in the deaths of two unarmed individuals on the ground of self-defense.[21] Self-described armed "militias," some claiming to be present to maintain order and protect expressive rights, have increasingly exercised public carry rights at public protests – with many openly carrying semi-automatic long guns and dressed in bulletproof vests.

Commentators have forcefully argued that displaying firearms at public protests is *inherently* incompatible with the exercise of First Amendment free speech and assembly rights and basic democratic principles.[22] David Frum has argued that "[w]ithin metropolitan areas, there is no reason – zero – that a weapon should ever be carried openly. The purpose is always to intimidate – to frighten others away from their lawful rights, not only free speech and lawful assembly, but voting as well."[23] Other commentators have similarly called for bans on open carry of firearms, in particular at public protests, contending that the display of firearms "chills" the exercise of First Amendment rights.[24] As Mary Anne Franks has argued, "The display of loaded weapons allowed by open-carry laws directly infringes upon the First Amendment freedom of expression. People cannot express themselves freely when they fear grave bodily injury or death."[25] Franks has noted this "chilling effect … is felt most acutely by the least powerful members of society."[26]

Shortly after *Heller* was decided, Darrell Miller asserted the right to keep and bear arms should be interpreted as "home-bound" and thus not enforceable at all in public places.[27] According to Miller, part of the justification for treating Second Amendment rights this way is that in public contexts government has "a monopoly on legitimate violence."[28] Further, he has argued, the public display of firearms "must be tempered by other constitutional values, including the preservation of the social compact and democratic norms."[29] Miller claimed, "the presence of a gun in public has the effect of chilling or distorting the essential channels of a democracy – public deliberation and interchange."[30] As he observed, "Valueless opinions enjoy an inflated currency if accompanied by threats of violence. Even if everyone is equally armed, everyone is deterred from free-flowing democratic delib- eration if each person risks violence from a particularly sensitive fellow citizen who might take offense."[31] As Miller claimed, "[a] right to freely brandish firearms frustrates one of the very purposes of a constitution, which is 'to make politics possible.'"[32]

Other commentators have argued open carry is fundamentally at odds with principles of self-government. Addressing the claim by some gun rights proponents that public carry rights are necessary to resist the government, Greg Magarian has argued that "[e]ven keeping arms to enable insurrection would undermine debate by fostering a climate of mistrust and fear."[33] Simply put, Magarian has asserted, "insurrection short-circuits political debate."[34] According to this view, in our democracy, the First Amendment provides the legitimate vehicle for political revolution. Allowing individuals to openly carry firearms at public protests is repugnant to the premise of peaceful self-government the First Amendment instantiates. Open carry elevates armed conflict over peaceful democratic discourse and substitutes brandishing arms for counter-speech – the First Amendment's long-preferred response to expression one disagrees with.[35]

In sum, the argument that public carry – particularly but not exclusively open carry – is incompatible with public protest rests on two premises. The first premise is that public carry is a form of intimidation that chills public debate by threatening violent suppression of speech, assembly, and petition activities. Again, although that argument has special force with respect to open carry, the knowledge or belief that many in the crowd are carrying concealed arms could also intimidate protesters. The second, and related, premise is that carrying a firearm at a public protest undermines fundamental democratic values, including the commitment to peaceful discourse and constitutional change through reasoned discourse rather than violence. Again, while these effects may be most acute where firearms are openly displayed, they may still be present to some degree even when firearms are present but concealed on the person.

These concerns resonate with many people – including, it should be noted, some gun rights proponents who view the open display of firearms as a means of protest or counter-protest as unhelpful to the cause of gun rights and inconsistent with peaceful protest. The stated concerns apparently influenced the decision of the American Civil Liberties Union, after Charlottesville, not to defend the First Amendment rights of armed militias and hate groups.[36]

However, not all commentators have agreed with the foregoing assessment. Eugene Volokh has observed that New Hampshire, Vermont, and Washington, which have long imposed few restrictions on public carry, appear to enjoy the same level of robust political discourse as more restrictive states like Hawaii, Maryland, and New York.[37] Addressing the "chill" argument, Volokh claimed public carry at protests might actually *facilitate* the exercise of First Amendment rights.[38] He asserted public carry could "support public interchange, by assuring minority speakers that they can protect themselves against violent suppression."[39] Thus, rather than viewing public carry as undermining or chilling public discourse, Volokh suggested it may level the playing field by protecting the communication of dissident and minority viewpoints. If so, the Second Amendment might be said to preserve rather than undermine First Amendment rights. (This is a common refrain among gun rights supporters, emblazoned on t-shirts and other Second Amendment paraphernalia.) Some of the armed militia groups that participated in the Charlottesville "Unite the Right" rallies echoed the claim, asserting they were present to ensure that *all* participants' First Amendment rights were respected.[40]

Assuming Volokh means to do more than play devil's advocate, the defense of armed protest has several flaws. Consider the empirical case, such as it is. Having a legal *right* to publicly carry firearms and the actual *exercise* of the right are not the same thing. It is thus possible, for example, that despite having a legal right to do so, relatively few individuals brought their firearms to protests in New Hampshire, Vermont, or Washington. For all we know, that forbearance may have lessened the potential for chilling public expression.

Until very recently, there was no data concerning the prevalence of public carry at public protests, the relationship between public carry and protest violence, or whether the presence of firearms at public protests might chill expressive activities. We now have data on all three aspects of this debate. They all support the conclusion that public carry and peaceful protest are fundamentally incompatible activities.

As mentioned earlier, a recent joint study by Everytown for Gun Safety and ACLED concluded that armed demonstrations have become more prevalent.[41] The Everytown/ACLED study found that "armed demonstrations are nearly six times as likely to turn violent or destructive compared to unarmed demonstrations."[42] The study also concluded the presence of firearms at demonstrations does not make such events safer; in fact, the study found open carry significantly increased the chance that a demonstration would involve a fatality.[43] One in six armed protests that took place during the study period turned violent or destructive, and one in sixty-two turned deadly. By contrast, one in thirty-seven unarmed protests turned violent or destructive, and only one in 2,963 unarmed gatherings turned fatal. A similar pattern has emerged at recent abortion rights-related protests.[44]

Further, the presence of firearms and the increased risk of violence affects people's willingness to participate in public protest activities. In her research, Diana Palmer studied how the presence of firearms affects people's willingness to protest.[45] Palmer found the presence of firearms has a statistically significant negative impact on individuals' willingness to attend public protests, vocalize their opinions at protest events, carry signs, and bring children to public protests.[46] Palmer's study, which relied on both quantitative data and qualitative assessments, concluded that respondents overwhelmingly viewed the presence of firearms as a means of intimidation, a threat to public safety, and a deterrent to protest participation. The study also showed that concerns about firearms-related violence at public protests were consistent across political ideologies – in other words, there was a widely shared perception that firearms were dangerous in the hands of demonstrators or counterdemonstrators (although the perception of who posed a threat varied depending on political ideology).[47]

These studies confirm that public carry and public protest are fundamentally incompatible. Given the increase in violence and chilling of speech and assembly associated with armed protests, public carry must be limited in ways that preserve First Amendment rights. This is so whether the chill emanates from state laws that allow public carry at protests, or the exercise of those rights by armed individuals or groups.[48] We now know that for some or perhaps many potential protesters, public carry adds to the long list of physical, psychological, financial, and other barriers to participation. That evidence compels an examination of measures to mitigate or eradicate arms-related obstacles.

We have also learned from recent events that the presence of firearms complicates protest policing and undermines law enforcement's ability to protect peaceful assemblies and speakers. Among other issues, officers must quickly separate lawful public carriers from those inflicting or seeking to inflict harm. As discussed throughout the book, law enforcement's relationship to public protest is complex. Law enforcement often plays a negative role in terms of managing dissent through aggression, intimidation, and force. However, law enforcement also "manages" dissent by ensuring that it can be peacefully communicated through public assembly and speech activities. As the Supreme Court has recognized, the First Amendment imposes a duty on law enforcement to protect those engaged in lawful speech and assembly from "hostile audiences."[49] Faced with the proliferation of firearms, law enforcement may be unable to carry out this duty. Or they may align themselves with armed private militias, further endangering protesters.[50] In either event, peaceful protesters would be at the mercy of an armed and hostile crowd.

Arming public protests is part of a broader concern about the effects state and political violence have on public protest. As discussed in Chapter 3, certain protest events already occur in heavily militarized places. Top officials have referred to the streets as a "battlespace" or war zone. Armed individuals have staged protests at seats of government, as happened at the Michigan statehouse during the pandemic.[51] These attitudes and actions perpetuate an impression that in the U.S. social and political conflicts will be resolved by physical force rather than peaceful deliberation and discourse.

If current trends continue, the proliferation of firearms at public protests will fundamentally change the protest environment. An increasing arms race involving protesters, counter-protesters, armed militias, and law enforcement will make engaging in peaceful but robust public protest increasingly difficult if not impossible. Protest venues will become dangerous powder kegs, ready to explode with deadly force at the slightest provocation. Perhaps only a small segment of the population will be willing to risk engaging in protest activities. Alternatively, armed protesters and counter-protesters may drive peaceful assemblies and unarmed persons out of the public forum altogether.

REGULATING FIREARMS AT PUBLIC PROTESTS

Bruen held that one type of licensing scheme for concealed carry violated the Second Amendment. The decision narrowed government authority to regulate public carry but did not invalidate all regulations on who can carry in public, how they can carry, what types of firearms they can carry, or where they can carry them. Public carry can still be banned or restricted in ways that can help preserve First Amendment speech and peaceable assembly rights. Although the scope of public carry rights remains uncertain, most of the remainder of the chapter will focus on regulations that could be upheld under the standards set forth by the Court in *Heller* and *Bruen*.[52]

Banning Public Carry at and During Permitted Events

As discussed, the Supreme Court has indicated that Second Amendment rights are subject to substantial regulation in public places. As one federal appeals court observed, "Our review of more than 700 years of English and American legal history reveals a strong theme: the government has the power to regulate arms in the public square."[53] One possibility is for governments to ban public carry at or during public protests, demonstrations, and rallies that take place on public property. Governments could either adopt a statutory ban or allow officials to condition a permit on the applicant's agreement not to carry firearms at the event.[54]

The Supreme Court has described streets, parks, and other public forums as places where people have gathered "time out of mind" for the purposes of "assembly, communicating thoughts between citizens, and discussing public questions."[55] The Court has never described the public forum as a place where people have "time out of mind" carried handguns, long guns, or other weapons. As Darrell Miller has observed, "[T]he idea of a right to peaceable assembly presumes two things: first, that there is actual space for such an assembly to occur, and second, that such assemblages must be peaceable, as opposed to disorderly."[56] Because it poses the risk that public assemblies will become violent confrontations, public carry undermines one of the fundamental premises of the public forum.

Recognizing this problem, several states and the District of Columbia have enacted laws that prohibit possession of a firearm at or near public events including protests, demonstrations, parades, and pickets.[57] In the District of Columbia and Alabama, for example, non-law enforcement personnel are prohibited from carrying firearms within 1000 feet of a demonstration.[58] North Carolina law makes it a crime for "any person participating in, affiliated with, or present as a spectator at any parade, funeral procession, picket line, or demonstration upon any private health care facility or upon any public place owned or under the control of the State or any of its political subdivisions to willfully or intentionally possess or have immediate access to any dangerous weapon."[59] Some cities and towns have imposed local bans on bearing firearms at permitted events such as protests, demonstrations, or parades.[60] Some of these regulations exempt authorized concealed permit holders, but they all generally ban the open display of firearms at or near protest events.

Prior to *Bruen*, many legal scholars were confident that these limited public carry bans would withstand Second Amendment scrutiny.[61] As noted, *Bruen* requires that restrictions on public carry be "consistent with this Nation's history of firearm regulation." The Court clarified that early historical analogues need not be "dead ringer[s]" to be relevant, but still must be "analogous enough to pass constitutional muster."[62] It did not say precisely what quantum of historical evidence would suffice to uphold public carry restrictions but stressed that "analogical reasoning under the Second Amendment is neither a regulatory straightjacket nor a regulatory blank check."[63] In any event, after *Bruen*, the government bears the burden of demonstrating sufficient historical support for any public carry regulation. To support a ban on public carry at, during, or near public events, the government must produce evidence of a "tradition" of such laws.

Restrictions on public carry at and during public assemblies are rooted in both British and American history. As discussed in more detail later, efforts to preserve the public peace by banning armed *assemblies* in public places date back to the Tudor era.[64] The English Statute of Northampton, enacted in 1328, forbade any individual from riding armed "nor to go nor ride armed by night nor by day, in Fairs, Markets, nor in the presence of the Justices or other Ministers, nor in no part elsewhere, upon pain to forfeit their Armour to the King, and their Bodies to Prison at the King's pleasure."[65] In *Bruen*, the Court cast some doubt on the authority of the Northampton statute by suggesting it may be too old to be relevant to the question of public carry rights circa 1791 or 1868.[66] At the very least, the Court indicated, early English history did not support a flat ban on handguns or "all firearms" in public places.[67] However, the Court left open whether the Northampton law might support more limited restrictions on public carry.

Other historical evidence more directly supports banning public carry at public events including protests and demonstrations. By the time of American independence, there was widespread agreement that armed public assemblies were dangerous to public order and safety.[68] Colonial laws and state restrictions enacted both before and after Reconstruction banned public carry of firearms at public assemblies to preserve civil order.[69] An 1858 Tennessee law banned carrying firearms at any "public assembly of the people."[70] Texas broadly banned public carry "where any portion of the people of this State are collected to vote at any election, *or to any other place where people may be assembled to muster or to perform any other public duty, or any other public assembly*."[71] In 1879, Missouri banned concealed carry in "any ... public assemblage of persons met for any lawful purpose other than for militia drill."[72] An 1890 Oklahoma law banned both concealed and open carry in public assemblies.[73]

As noted, *Bruen* does not make clear *how many* historical analogues would demonstrate a "tradition" of banning public carry at permitted events such as protests and demonstrations. Some scholars argue the foregoing laws violate a broad right to public carry.[74] But they can also be construed as narrow restrictions on public carry, a kind of time and place restriction that applies only at, during, or near public events. Viewed as such, early state laws demonstrate that lawmakers and officials have long understood public carry is incompatible with public assemblies including protests and demonstrations. The historical limits ensured public assemblies and gatherings remained peaceful and orderly. Then as now, there did not appear to be much dispute about the legality or propriety of such bans.

The Court is fond of pointing out that the Second Amendment, like the First Amendment, is a fundamental right and that both rights should be afforded similar weight and subject to similar restrictions.[75] Banning public carry at public events would create just that kind of doctrinal symmetry. Courts have upheld limits on bringing signs and other objects to public protests because they can be "turned into weapons."[76] Similarly, the Second Amendment allows that *actual* weapons be restricted during public demonstrations.

Even if the Northampton law and all the state analogues do not suffice to support a ban on *all* forms of public carry, they still may support bans limited to long guns or the *open* display of any firearm at public gatherings. These more limited bans would be consistent with the Court's interpretation of the Northampton statute and public carry regulations more generally. It would preserve the right to self-defense by allowing the carriage of some firearms, or concealed carry but not open carry, at public protests and demonstrations. Of course, as discussed, public display of *any* weapon and concealed carry can affect the mental and perhaps physical well-being of protest participants. But lawmakers could at least ban the most dangerous and most intimidating aspects of public carry during a demonstration or other public assembly.

Banning Public Carry in "Sensitive Places"

As the Court observed in *Heller*, "nothing in our opinion should be taken to cast doubt on longstanding prohibitions on … laws forbidding the carrying of firearms in sensitive places such as schools and government buildings."[77] A ban on public carry during protests and demonstrations could be viewed as a type of "sensitive place" restriction.[78] Further, public carry can be banned in many "sensitive places" where protests regularly occur.

Whether a public assembly can qualify as a "sensitive place" is unclear. The Court has never defined the concept with any precision. Insofar as "sensitive place" regulations are to be treated like other public carry restrictions, they must be based on historical tradition. The evidence already presented demonstrates that a ban on public carry limited to protest events would be valid under that standard.

Some commentators have argued that the government can treat a place as "sensitive" only if it undertakes to provide security in such a place.[79] As I have emphasized throughout the book, during most protest events police are present in large numbers and heavily armed. Hence, both conceptually and practically speaking, there is no need for individuals or groups to carry arms for self-defense at a public protest.

Even if a ban on public carry, or only open carry, at protests violates the Second Amendment governments can still ban public carry in discrete "sensitive places." Many of these places are vitally important to public protest. For example, *Heller* mentioned "government buildings" and "schools" as representative examples of "sensitive places."[80] In *Bruen*, the Court observed that a historical tradition clearly supported public carry bans in (or presumably near) "legislative assemblies, polling places, and courthouses."[81] Protests that occur in these "sensitive places," which include federal and state capitol buildings and city halls, could be disarmed. Although "government buildings" would also seem to include places such as jails and police stations, *Bruen* may require states to establish a record of relevant historical analogues to support public carry bans in these places. Even so, prohibiting public carry in or near "sensitive places" like legislatures, courthouses, and polling places will help preserve public protest rights in those significant places. Such places are, as Justice Douglas once noted, "obvious center[s] of protest."[82]

As discussed in Chapter 5, university campuses are also important protest venues. *Heller* suggests public carry bans in "schools" are presumptively constitutional. To the extent that *Bruen* now requires a historical demonstration of a long tradition of banning public carry on university campuses, that record arguably exists.[83] As Darrell Miller has observed, campus carry bans date as far back as the seventeenth century and several states enacted nineteenth-century laws banning firearms in educational institutions.[84] Like most of the historical record, this aspect of firearm regulation is contested. Indeed, some insist that there is no historical support for *Heller's* designation of "schools" as "sensitive places."[85] But as noted, there is historical evidence that early state laws banned at least some forms of public carry at universities.

Bruen instructs legislatures to be specific about the places they treat as "sensitive" for purpose of public carry bans. Thus, the Court stated, "there is no historical basis for New York to effectively declare the island of Manhattan a 'sensitive place' simply because it is crowded and protected generally by the New York City Police Department."[86] This admonition may call into question state laws that ban or restrict public carry in populous cities.[87] These restrictions are distant relatives of the Statute of Northampton, which banned carrying firearms in crowded public places. As discussed, the Court has discounted this specific English authority. However, more limited restrictions, for example on the open carry of long guns in populous cities, may be "consistent with this Nation's tradition of firearm regulation." Early American laws restricted public carry, the storage of gunpowder, and other arms-related activities in populous towns and cities.[88] If they are enforceable, public carry restrictions in densely populated areas would help disarm mass and other protests, which tend to be concentrated in urban areas.

If they do their historical homework and legislate carefully, lawmakers can use the "sensitive places" doctrine in ways that help preserve peaceful public protest by banning public carry in locations that are commonly used for public protests and demonstrations. Public carry bans, including those relating to protests, are about maintaining public order and safety. But as the protest example shows, they are concerned with interests beyond safety and order. As Miller has observed, a proper understanding of the "sensitive places" doctrine is that it "is concerned with whether the costs on other margins – the opportunity to participate in public life, to engage others in public spaces with your ideas, to express unpopular opinions – are undermined by the presence of private firearms in that space."[89]

Prohibiting Armed Parades, Marches, and Assemblies

One of the most serious threats to public protest is the presence of self-styled "militias" or other armed groups. The presence of even a lone gunman at a crowded public protest may intimidate and chill protesters. The presence of armed *groups* magnifies these concerns. Self-described armed "militias" make contentious protest events more dangerous. As discussed earlier, there have long been bans on carrying firearms at public assemblies and gatherings. In addition, colonial and early state laws expressly banned armed private groups from marching and parading in public places and from engaging in "paramilitary" exercises.

Twenty-three states prohibit groups from "parading," "marching," or "associating" in public with firearms under laws that have been in force since at least the nineteenth century.[90] For example, a Massachusetts statute provides: "No body of men shall maintain an armory or associate together as a company or organization for drill or parade with firearms, or so drill or parade."[91] Rhode Island's law prohibits any "body of persons, [unless expressly authorized to] ... parade in public with firearms in any city or town of this state."[92] These are precisely the kinds of longstanding firearm regulations *Heller* and *Bruen* indicated are consistent with the Second Amendment.

Indeed, in *Presser v. Illinois*, decided in 1886, the Supreme Court upheld a state law prohibiting armed private assemblies against both Second Amendment and First Amendment challenges.[93] In *Heller*, the Supreme Court expressly cited the law upheld in *Presser* as the type of "longstanding" prohibition on public carry allowed by the Second Amendment.[94] Thus, general restrictions on armed parades and assemblies can be enacted and enforced, including at or during public protests.

In addition, twenty-nine states have enacted laws against training paramilitary forces.[95] These laws, like the one upheld in *Presser*, make it illegal for individuals to assemble to train with firearms, or to train others on the use of firearms, for the purpose of furthering civil disorder. They have been used in the past to prohibit militia units of the Ku Klux Klan from intimidating minority groups.[96] After the violent rallies in Charlottesville, the city sued several "militia" groups for violating Virginia's anti-paramilitary training law. It obtained a consent decree against several of the groups, which bans them from participating in future public protests in Charlottesville.[97]

Some of the paramilitary laws require proof of the group's intent to cause public disorder. For example, Virginia's law makes it a felony to teach or demonstrate the use of a firearm when the individual knows or intends such training will be used in furtherance of civil disorder.[98] Other laws require that the government prove the assembly constitutes a "paramilitary" group. Owing to these requirements, the laws may be more difficult to enforce than a flat ban on armed parades and marches. Nevertheless, they represent another type of longstanding restriction on public carry that officials can enforce to restrict public carry by "militias" and other armed groups.

These and other longstanding restrictions date back to Second Amendment ratification-era concerns about maintaining a "well-regulated" militia. Every state in the U.S. has at least one statutory or constitutional provision restricting paramilitary or private militia activities like those on display at Charlottesville's "Unite the Right" rallies in 2017 and some of the BLM protests during the summer of 2020.[99] Some state laws expressly subordinate the military to civilian power or prohibit the false assumption of military duties.[100] These provisions directly contradict or countermand assertions by armed private "militias" that they are somehow deputized to maintain civil order at public protests. They also counsel against law enforcement and other officials embracing or informally "deputizing" these unlawful armed assemblies at public protests. In sum, laws prohibiting marching or parading with firearms, as well as those barring groups from training others on the use of firearms for the purpose of causing civil disorder, are important restrictions on public carry and effective tools for preserving civic order and peaceful public protest.

Historically, the Second Amendment has not protected a right to parade or march with other armed individuals in the public square. What about the *First Amendment*, which protects a right to "peaceably assemble" with others? Do individuals have a *collective* right under the First Amendment to assemble with others while openly displaying firearms?

Michael Dorf has asserted, "As a simple matter of common sense, a march or rally by people who are heavily armed is not an exercise of what the First Amendment calls the 'right of the people *peaceably* to assemble.'"[101] In addition to this "common sense" interpretation, Dorf has provided persuasive historical evidence that early courts and commentators did not understand armed assemblies to be part of the tradition of peaceable assembly in the U.S.[102]

The Supreme Court has never explicitly defined the meaning of "peaceable" in the context of public gatherings. Thus, it is difficult to know whether it would agree with Dorf's textual and historical arguments. "Peaceable" may mean that the actor is not in violation of any law or regulation or causing any public disturbance. Acting non-peaceably might require more than engaging in merely disruptive or confrontational behavior.[103] If Dorf is correct that history does not support a First Amendment right to assemble in public bearing arms, then so long as authorities evenhandedly ban *all* armed assemblies there would be no First Amendment violation.

Despite its own assertions to the contrary, the Supreme Court has not generally interpreted the First Amendment, including the right to peaceably assemble,
by reference to original public understandings.[104] As I have indicated elsewhere in
the book, the Court has never developed any distinct First Amendment doctrine
of peaceable assembly. Some time ago, it refashioned the assembly right into one
of "expressive association."[105] That right protects a right to assemble with others for
expressive purposes – for example, to hold meetings, litigate for social or political
causes, or inculcate values.

Courts are generally deferential to groups' assertions of communicative intent
and assessments of regulatory burdens on their ability to communicate.[106] But as
discussed later, outside the context of a gun rights protest where public carry arguably communicates a group's support for the right, the expressive association claim
is weak. As self-styled militia groups and others have claimed, they purportedly carry
firearms at public protests for self-defense and the defense of others. Further, when
analyzing this type of First Amendment claim, a court must balance any expressive burden against the government's interest in regulating the activity in question.
Given the risk of protester intimidation and armed conflict at public protests, that
balance would likely be struck in the government's favor. Further, as one federal
appeals court held in rejecting an expressive association claim of this sort, a public
carry restriction does not prevent anyone from joining a gun club or engaging in
other expression in support of the Second Amendment.[107]

In sum, neither the Second Amendment nor the First Amendment – nor the
combination of the two provisions – prevents lawmakers from banning most armed
assemblies in public places. As required under *Bruen*, such bans are "consistent
with this Nation's history of firearm regulation." State and local officials should
enforce these laws as part of their effort to preserve public protest.

"Going Armed to the Terror" and Other Public Carry Crimes

State laws have historically prohibited individuals from "going armed to the terror
of the people" in public places.[108] They have also criminalized brandishing and
other threatening behavior involving firearms. These laws can be enforced against
individuals who commit offenses during a public protest event.

The offense of "going armed to the terror" has deep roots in English common law
and early American law.[109] In *Bruen*, New York state relied on the offense as part
of its historical argument supporting broad regulation of public carry. Although the
Court recognized their historical pedigree, it significantly narrowed the scope of
"armed to the terror" laws.[110]

One interpretation of the "armed to the terror" offense is that it broadly prohibits carrying arms in public places.[111] Under the English common law rule,
because carrying a dangerous weapon (such as a firearm) in populated public places *naturally* terrified the people, it was considered a crime against the

peace – even if unaccompanied by any threat, violence, or additional breach of the peace.[112] A 1701 English court explained "going armed to the terror of the public" in these terms:

> If a number of men assemble with arms, in terrorem populi, though no act is done, it is a riot. If three come out of an ale-house and go armed, it is a riot. Though a man may ride with arms, yet he cannot take two with him to defend himself, even though his life is threatened.[113]

Some English treatise writers and state courts also appeared to adopt this broad view of the offense.[114]

However, as the Court observed in *Bruen*, other authorities interpreted the offense more narrowly – to prohibit only the carrying of certain *types* of weapons (for example, "dangerous and unusual" firearms) or to require the government to prove public carry with the intent to terrorize or threaten.[115] After canvassing the history of the offense, the Court concluded it required "something more than merely carrying a firearm in public" – either carrying an especially dangerous firearm or having the intent to harm others.[116]

After *Bruen*, states can continue to make "going armed to the terror" a criminal offense. For example, North Carolina law allows open carry of firearms in most public places but provides a person is guilty of the offense of "going armed to the terror of the people" if he arms himself with an "unusual or dangerous weapon" and goes upon the public highways with the purpose of terrifying the public.[117] In that form, the law is consistent with the Second Amendment right to public carry as interpreted in *Bruen*. Thus, if armed individuals attend a public protest carrying "unusual or dangerous weapons" such as sawed-off shotguns, or carry firearms with an intent to terrorize, intimidate, or threaten protesters, they can be prosecuted for going "armed to the terror."[118]

Similarly, states can prohibit individuals and groups from using firearms in ways that threaten or intimidate protesters or others who attend a demonstration. Under state laws, criminal actions include pointing, displaying, or brandishing any firearm with the intent to cause fear or alarm in another or committing assault with a deadly weapon.[119] Although *Heller* recognizes an individual right to self-defense, which *Bruen* has extended to certain areas of the public square, these longstanding criminal offenses qualify the right to public carry.[120]

As commentators have observed, brandishing and other firearms offenses can be especially difficult to interpret and enforce. Because it offers neither clear rules of conduct for public carriers nor clear rules of enforcement for law enforcement, criminal law "falls woefully short of effectively regulating gun displays in a society as saturated with firearms as the United States."[121] As with "armed to the terror" laws, enforcement in the context of crowded, contentious public protests may pose distinct difficulties. Moreover, as with many aspects of the law of public protest, broad law enforcement discretion built into firearms display laws can lead to disparate enforcement against Black people and others subject to discriminatory law enforcement scrutiny.[122]

These concerns should not prevent or deter law enforcement from arresting individuals who violate brandishing and other criminal prohibitions on the use of firearms during protests. Bearing arms in a manner intended to intimidate or threaten protesters prevents them from engaging in protected speech and assembly. Moreover, we have witnessed the fatal results that can follow when individuals and groups are allowed to bear arms at public protests with impunity.

Arms-Specific Regulations

In *Heller*, the Supreme Court observed that the Second Amendment does not protect a "right to keep and carry *any weapon whatsoever in any manner whatsoever and for whatever purpose.*"[123] As discussed earlier, the Court stated that keeping and bearing certain "dangerous and unusual" weapons, including the M-16 automatic rifle, are not protected by the Second Amendment. Thus, in addition to giving officials some latitude in terms of regulating *where* firearms are carried and *how* they can be carried or used in public places, including at public protests, precedent and history authorize limits on what *types* of firearms individuals can bear in public places.

Although some protesters may find the presence of any type of firearm intimidating, certain kinds of long guns may be more likely to cause fear and alarm at public protests. For example, some jurisdictions have adopted outright bans on the sale and possession of specific kinds of long guns, including the AR-15, as well as high-capacity ammunition magazines. Prior to *Bruen*, federal appeals courts generally upheld these bans.[124]

However, after *Bruen*, the bans must be defended anew, as being "consistent with this Nation's history of firearm regulation." While there is not sufficient space here to address the historical record, it may be a harbinger that prior to *Bruen* one federal appeals court invalidated a state ban on large-capacity magazines. The decision, which was later overturned by the full appeals court (based on a standard *Bruen* has rejected), observed that "[f]irearms with greater than ten round capacities existed even before our nation's founding, and the common use of LCMs for self-defense is apparent in our shared national history."[125] The case was one of several, including a case involving a ban on AR-15s, the Court remanded for reconsideration after *Bruen*.

Many states and localities also ban non-firearm weapons, including tear gas projectors, Molotov cocktails, and artillery projectiles.[126] Presumably, these and other arms are not weapons typically used by "law-abiding and responsible" citizens or are within the class of "dangerous and unusual weapons" that *Heller* says states can ban. Again, however, whether states can ban these arms will now depend on an analysis based on the presence or absence of historically analogous bans.

Outright bans on these types of arms would be one direct way of ensuring some of the most intimidating and lethal firearms do not impact the First Amendment rights of protesters. As discussed, however, an outright ban on certain types of fire-arms is not the only means of restricting or banning firearms, or at least open carry of firearms, from the protest environment. At the very least, courts should uphold restrictions on tear gas, projectiles, and other dangerous and unusual arms. It would facilitate the exercise of public protest rights if states and localities could also ban the open display of AR-15s and similar intimidating firearms during demonstrations.

* * * * * *

In sum, after *Bruen* states and localities still have a panoply of options – bans on public (or at least open) carry at public protests, enforcement of laws prohibiting armed assemblies and private paramilitary activities, bans on public carry in "sensi-tive places," and criminal laws prohibiting going "armed to the terror," brandishing and other unlawful conduct – for ensuring that the presence of firearms does not chill or suppress public protest. At the very least, the historical record supports bans on armed assemblies and the open display of firearms – two of the most intimidating and chilling forms of confrontation at public protests. The proposals discussed in the chapter are not the only possible means of protecting protesters and the public. For example, some have advocated establishing "open carry zones" that limit the location of arms-bearing at protests or requiring individuals who want to bear arms at a protest to pay a bond or "surety" in advance.[127] In short, lawmakers and policy-makers looking to preserve public protest in the face of an increasingly armed public square do not lack options; however, they will need to muster the political will to generate and defend any public carry restrictions.

THE FIRST AMENDMENT AND ARMED PROTESTS

As the discussion thus far indicates, firearms regulations relating to public protests implicate the Second Amendment. In a more limited respect, these regulations may also implicate the First Amendment. I have already discussed the possibility that an armed group could assert a First Amendment "expressive association" claim. This sec-tion addresses more fundamental First Amendment issues relating to public carry. It concludes the First Amendment is not a barrier to content-neutral firearms regulations.

Content-Neutral Firearms Regulations

The First Amendment generally requires that speech regulations not discriminate based on subject matter, idea, viewpoint, or message.[128] That means public carry regulations, including those discussed earlier, must be content-neutral.

Thus, for example, a public protest carry ban could not distinguish between armed individuals or groups based on whether they conveyed ideas associated with white supremacy or the message of BLM. Regulations would need to apply and be

enforced against *all* firearms carriers, not just individuals or groups authorities suspect or believe might be more dangerous or provocative.

The First Amendment content-neutrality standard is not implicated by the types
of public carry regulations previously proposed and discussed: banning firearms at
protests, prohibiting armed paramilitary and other groups, restricting arms in sensitive places, or prohibiting firearms crimes. On their face, these measures do not
target expression. Rather, they apply to dangerous conduct – public carry – when
exercised in locations where the public gathers, sometimes in large numbers, or in
ways that raise public safety concerns.

Under the First Amendment, these regulations would be valid so long as they
are not substantially broader than necessary to achieve the government's significant
interest in protecting public safety.[129] Even substantial restrictions on public carry at
protests would not restrict substantially more *speech* than necessary; they would not
limit the ability of armed individuals and groups to communicate in other places
or contexts.[130]

Public Carry as Expression

Some public carry proponents have argued that openly carrying firearms, including at public protests, is a form of "speech" protected by the First Amendment.
Free speech doctrine does not generally support that argument. Even if some
forms of carry are intended to express a message the public would understand, First
Amendment standards allow the government to ban or restrict public carry for non-
content-based reasons.

As noted in Chapter 2, some forms of expressive conduct are protected by the First
Amendment. For example, people who burn a draft card or U.S. flag at a political
protest meet the threshold requirement that they intend to communicate a message
their audiences are likely to understand.[131] But the Supreme Court has rejected
"the view that an apparently limitless variety of conduct can be labeled as 'speech'
whenever the person engaging in the conduct intends thereby to express an idea."[132]
The Court has also said that if a putative speaker needs to explain why the act is
expression, this constitutes "strong evidence that the conduct at issue ... is not so
inherently expressive that it warrants protection."[133]

Courts have resoundingly rejected the argument that public carry is expressive
under this standard.[134] They have concluded that openly carrying a firearm is
not an *inherently* expressive act. To be sure, open carriers may intend to communicate their support for firearms rights or open carry, or the view that citizens
should be armed in the event a tyrannical government threatens their liberties.
But the mere fact that a person may intend to communicate some idea does not
suffice to bring an act within the First Amendment.[135] The audience must also
understand the message being communicated. In addition to a lack of intent to
communicate, courts have concluded open carry is not *likely* to be understood

by an audience without some further explanation. Since any speech element associated with public carry is decidedly marginal, as a general matter open carry is not "speech."

A few courts have recognized one possible, but narrow, exception to this First Amendment "symbolic conduct" analysis: the open display of a firearm might be expressive if it occurs as part of a protest about gun control and Second Amendment public carry rights.[136] In that context, a person openly displaying a firearm may intend to communicate support for open carry and the audience might understand this is part of the message. However, even in this specific context, under the First Amendment governments could impose content-neutral "time, place, and manner" restrictions on displaying firearms. As discussed, so long as the limits were based on public safety concerns and not the content of any pro-gun message, they would not violate the First Amendment.[137] Thus, even if public carry is part of the message, the government can regulate the underlying *conduct* under regulations that do not restrict speech more broadly than necessary and leave open alternative channels of communication.

In sum, even if public carry is expressive in some narrow circumstances, the First Amendment is not a barrier to regulating it. Further, the First Amendment does not protect *all* open carry messages. A speaker has no right to communicate threats or engage in intimidating forms of expressive conduct.[138] Brandishing a weapon in a threatening manner or menacing a crowd with firearms constitute criminal acts outside the First Amendment's coverage.

RESTRICTING FIREARMS AND PRESERVING PUBLIC PROTEST

Increasingly, public protests are becoming armed events. This phenomenon could have serious and lasting implications, not just for public safety but also for the preservation of public protest in the U.S.

As we have seen, introducing firearms into the public forum alters an important channel of public discourse. Civil democratic exchange depends on access to public places and "peaceable" discourse. Public carry undermines and threatens the tradition of peaceful public protest. As Joseph Blocher and Reva Siegel have observed, "As gun-brandishing protesters and armed invasions of legislatures demonstrate, guns inflict more than physical injuries – they transform the public sphere on which a constitutional democracy depends."[139]

A new brand of politics increasingly relies on demonstrations of force rather than the strength of ideas. As part of the law of public protest, the law of public carry actively manages dissent. Lawmakers need to turn this dynamic around: to manage arms in ways that protect and facilitate dissent. Regulating public carry is necessary not just to preserve physical safety, but to save the public forum and its democratic functions. As Blocher and Siegel have argued, "Government can regulate weapons to protect the public sphere on which a constitutional democracy depends."[140] They can, indeed must, "promote the sense of security that enables community and the exercise of all citizens' liberties, whether or not they are armed."[141]

Although they have expanded the right to keep and bear arms, *Heller* and *Bruen* allow governments "to preserve public safety by preventing weapons from interfering with equal liberties of all citizens."[142] The chapter has proposed a variety of options. Neither the Second Amendment nor the First Amendment presents an obstacle to significant public carry restrictions affecting protests. Blocher and Siegel have accurately summarized the core dilemma raised by armed protests: "If Americans do not recognize the social dimensions of public safety – the ancient role that weapons laws play in securing peace and public order – the use of guns will come to define America's constitutional democracy, rather than the other way around."[143]

7

Public Protest and Emergency Powers

The COVID-19 pandemic and the public unrest that followed the murder of George Floyd raised substantial concerns about preserving public protest and dissent during public health emergencies and widespread civil unrest. During declared and undeclared emergencies, governments sometimes invoke extraordinary powers to protect public health and restore order. The legitimacy and extent of these powers, which are an important aspect of the law of public protest, remain uncertain. It is vitally important that we appreciate and understand the nature, scope, and division of governmental authority to manage dissent during public health emergencies and periods of civil unrest. This chapter identifies various legal authorities relating to public protest bans, restrictions, and law enforcement during public emergencies. Although it recognizes governments' constitutional and statutory authorities to preserve public health and order, it encourages courts and policymakers to invoke these powers carefully and interpret them narrowly.

PUBLIC PROTESTS DURING PANDEMIC AND CIVIL UNREST

Recent events have highlighted the precarious nature of public protest during times of public health emergencies and civil unrest. The COVID-19 pandemic, which would become the greatest infectious disease threat the world has experienced in a century, led to severe restrictions on public activities. A variety of measures curtailed, and in some instances banned, public protest. During the widespread civil unrest following the murder of George Floyd, some of which overlapped with the height of the pandemic, federal, state, and local governments engaged in aggressive protest policing and invoked emergency powers. Official responses to the pandemic and public unrest highlight important lessons concerning the law of public protest and the management of dissent during public emergencies.

Pandemic-Related Protests

State executive officials have broad powers to respond to public health and other emergencies. For example, Nevada law gives the state's governor the authority, in the event of "a natural, technological or man-made emergency or disaster of major pro-portions," to "perform and exercise such ... functions, powers and duties as are nec-essary to promote and secure the safety and protection of the civilian population."[1] In mid- to late-March 2020, states around the country began enacting stay-at-home orders to combat the spread of COVID-19. Exercising these powers, by the end of March 2020, every state governor had issued emergency or disaster declarations – a first in U.S. history.[2]

State legislatures and executives imposed a vast array of emergency public health measures including quarantines, isolations, closures, curfews, and shelter-in-place or stay-at-home orders.[3] Most "stay-at-home" orders issued under emer-gency declarations limited or banned public gatherings.[4] Some expressly banned "mass assemblies." In other states, stay-at-home orders prohibited gatherings of more than ten people and required that individuals maintain social distancing and wear face coverings. Some state orders exempted outdoor exercise, funerals, and small worship services as "essential activities," but expressly excluded public protests from that category.[5]

Although they likely reduced the number of events and participants, stay-at-home orders and bans on assemblies did not eliminate public protests. Thousands still gathered in public places to protest pandemic policies.[6] Between April and May 2020, there were more than 400 reported "anti-lockdown" protests around the nation.[7] Most had relatively modest numbers, although a few drew thousands of protesters to state capitols.

"Anti-lockdown" protesters, encouraged by then-President Trump's call to "liberate" states from pandemic restrictions, refused to comply with pandemic-related masking, social distancing, and assembly restrictions.[8] As discussed in Chapter 6, one anti-lockdown protest at the Michigan Capitol included armed protesters. Some of the armed participants were later tied to a plot to kidnap Governor Gretchen Whitmer owing to her pandemic-related orders. Although anti-lockdown protesters openly flouted pandemic restrictions there were few reported arrests or instances of police using aggressive tactics to manage the demonstrations.[9]

Some governors reacted to anti-lockdown protests by issuing new restrictions on public protest. For example, in California, Governor Gavin Newsom and the California Highway Patrol banned all public protests at the state capitol after 500 anti-lockdown protesters appeared there.[10] Governor Newsom later issued strict guidelines for public protests in the state, limiting participation to 25 percent of a venue's capacity and capping all events at 100 protesters.[11]

Public demonstrations focused on different aspects of pandemic policymaking. For example, nurses and other healthcare professionals protested hospital conditions and demanded more personal protective equipment (PPE).[12] Other essential work-ers, including grocery store clerks, Amazon workers, and truckers protested working conditions and issued public calls for PPE and hazard pay.[13] Families of inmates and organizations advocating on behalf of prisoners protested their confinement owing to the increased risks of infection.[14] Immigrants' rights advocates and families protested immigrants' detention in federal centers.[15]

In some instances, small groups were able to participate in in-person public protests while still complying with assembly restrictions, mask mandates, and social distancing guidelines. For example, people in several states gathered in person to *support* public health orders.[16] These demonstrations may have been even less frequent because participants were concerned about complying with social distancing and other restrictions. Owing to pandemic-related restrictions, protesters sometimes relied on substitutes for in-person demonstrations. For example, some participated in car and truck rallies, where individuals remained in vehicles rather than gathering face-to-face. Other protesters relied on symbolic actions, including the delivery of body bags to Trump Tower in New York City and "die-ins" meant to draw attention to COVID-19-related fatalities.[17] One immunocompromised protester rented an airplane to fly a banner over a Raleigh, North Carolina "anti-lockdown" protest supporting more deliberate reopening policies.[18]

At the height of the COVID-19 pandemic, state laws and policies gave rise to protests for and against public health policies. When asked how officials were going to balance public protests with public health concerns, New York City's Police Commissioner responded, "So while we greatly, greatly respect the right of the people to protest, there should not be protests taking place in the middle of a pandemic by gathering outside and putting people at risk."[19] New York City Mayor Bill de Blasio agreed, stating "people who want to make their voices heard, there's plenty of ways to do it without gathering in person."[20] These statements, and state bans on public gatherings, suggested officials could prohibit public protests if they believed a ban was necessary to preserve public health.

Racial Justice and Civil Unrest

On May 25, 2020, George Floyd was murdered by Officer Derrick Chauvin in Minneapolis. A video depicting Chauvin kneeling on Floyd's neck for over eight minutes went viral. Public protests of police brutality, many taking the form of mass spontaneous demonstrations, erupted across the U.S.[21] Details later emerged about another killing, this time of a Black woman, by police. In March 2020, police in Louisville, Kentucky shot Breonna Taylor in her home eight times as they executed a no-knock warrant.[22] One after another, stories about other police shootings of Black people followed.

Public protests rapidly spread across the nation from Brooklyn, to Minneapolis, to Seattle. The racial justice protests, many organized by the group BLM, became perhaps the largest protest movement in U.S. history.[23] In just the first few months after Floyd's murder, there were more than 4,700 public demonstrations across the nation.[24] On June 6, 2020, nearly half a million protesters turned out at over 550 demonstrations around the U.S. No corner of the nation was untouched by the police brutality and racial justice protests that occurred during the summer of 2020.[25]

Racial justice protests during the summer of 2020 were predominantly peaceful events. However, by the third night of protests, civil unrest broke out in Minneapolis and several other U.S. cities.[26] That unrest included instances of looting, property damage, and vandalism. In some locations, police cars, buses, and government buildings were set ablaze and Confederate monuments were damaged or destroyed. During demonstrations, several protesters were shot, and officers were assaulted or hit with objects thrown from crowds. Vandals, arsonists, and rioters marred an otherwise peaceful protest movement, causing many millions of dollars in damages to public and private property and threatening public safety. Violent and destructive incidents received a significant amount of media attention. As explained elsewhere in the book, the media often devote disproportionate coverage to violent conduct during public protests.

Nevertheless, the violence and destruction in some cities posed a clear threat to public order. In response to the civil unrest, state governments declared emergencies. During the first several days of public protests, at least thirty-one governors activated National Guard troops under their command.[27] As a result, even peaceful protesters in Minneapolis, Louisville, Philadelphia, Atlanta, and other cities faced a combination of state and local law enforcement and National Guard troops. In addition, nearly eighty cities enacted curfews requiring residents, with few exceptions, to remain in their homes throughout the evening and early morning hours.[28] State and local enforcement of curfew orders would ultimately result in over 1,000 arrests.[29]

As described elsewhere in the book, law enforcement personnel responded to even peaceful protests with aggression and escalated violence. Since the summer of 2020, over a dozen cities have released official reports reviewing how their police departments handled the 2020 racial justice protests.[30] According to these reports, police were poorly trained, unprepared to deal with large crowds, and utilized over-aggressive and militarized approaches that often led to escalated violence and disorder in the streets.

Police dressed in riot gear and used military surplus equipment, beat protesters retreating from demonstrations, and drove patrol cars into crowds of demonstrators.[31] Police departments in at least 100 U.S. cities used tear gas against racial justice protesters, most of them engaged in peaceful forms of protest and demonstration.[32] Safety protocols generally advise firing tear gas canisters at the edge of crowds. However, in many instances, police fired the canisters directly into crowds at short range. Police also fired non-lethal but harmful projectiles into protest crowds. Law enforcement in several cities again violated standard safety protocols relating to rubber projectiles, often shooting them at peaceful protesters' faces within close range.[33] Protesters suffered head injuries, including broken jaws, blindness, and brain trauma. Journalists covering the protests were not spared; indeed, in some instances, they were *targets* of aggressive police targets.[34] By June 4, 2020, police had made at least 10,000 protest-related arrests, for infractions ranging from curfew violations to unlawful assembly.[35]

The rioting and vandalism that occurred during some 2020 racial justice protests quickly became a national political issue. Former President Trump glorified violence against Black protesters, whom he referred to as "thugs," when he tweeted the racially charged phrase, "When the looting starts, the shooting starts."[36] He repeatedly called for "law and order" and urged "weak" state governors to "dominate" and jail racial justice protesters.[37] Trump's Secretary of Defense, Mark Esper, told state governors they needed to "mass and dominate the battle space" (a phrase he would later claim he regretted using) – public streets – and that he was ready to send in troops if needed for that purpose.[38] The former president called for massive law enforcement and National Guard interventions even in cities that were not experiencing significant civil unrest, leading to questions about the political motivation behind the president's statements and actions.[39]

In a Rose Garden speech delivered on June 1, 2020, former President Trump declared himself to be "the president of law and order" (and a "friend" of peaceful protesters) and reiterated Secretary Esper's call for state governors to deploy the National Guard to "dominate" protesters.[40] In the event governors did not take sufficient action to quell violence and restore order, Trump threatened to "deploy the United States military and quickly solve the problem for them."[41] He further claimed to have "dispatched thousands and thousands of heavily armed soldiers, military personnel and law enforcement officers to stop the rioting, looting, vandalism, assaults and the wanton destruction of property" in Washington, D.C.[42] In his speech, Trump also referenced the Insurrection Act of 1807, a federal law that allows the president to deploy federalized National Guard personnel and active-duty U.S. military personnel in certain extraordinary situations. Among other things, the Act provides the president can order the deployment of such personnel when a governor or state legislature requests assistance in response to an "insurrection" or when an "insurrection" is hindering the enforcement of state or federal law.[43]

Prior to the Rose Garden speech, Attorney General William Barr ordered the security perimeter around the White House expanded.[44] Secret Service officers, Park Police, and other law enforcement personnel later cleared a crowd of peaceful protesters from Lafayette Square, a site near the White House, by firing tear gas and flash grenades into the crowd. Trump subsequently walked to St. John's church nearby, for a photo-op with a bible. U.S. Department of Justice Inspector General Michael Horowitz opened a federal investigation into federal agents' use of force against protesters in Washington, D.C. The report, which identified concerns about the use of force against peaceful protesters, ultimately did not find any connection between the clearing of Lafayette Square and the former president's photo-op.[45] However, it did not absolve authorities of allegations that their use of force was unwarranted.

Beginning in mid-July 2020, U.S. Department of Homeland Security (DHS) Customs and Border Patrol (CBP) agents were deployed to Portland, Oregon, where mass protests and some rioting had occurred for approximately two months.[46] Former President Trump ordered the agents to protect federal properties in Portland, including a courthouse used by protesters as a symbolic location.[47] However, the agents, dressed in military gear but bearing no clear law enforcement insignia or credentials, appeared to function beyond the limited scope of protecting federal buildings. Like other law enforcement officers, the federal agents clashed with Portland protesters, used tear gas against those present (including the "Wall of Moms" and the Portland mayor), shot some protesters with rubber bullets, and snatched protest participants off the streets using unmarked vans.[48]

The presence of CBP agents, who appeared to be engaged in local law enforcement activities far from the border, escalated violence and disruption in Portland's streets. The federal presence also led to additional protests focusing on the deployment of federal law enforcement personnel.[49] The state's elected officials did not ask for or want the federal intervention. In fact, Oregon's governor, Kate Brown, asked acting Homeland Security Secretary Chad Wolf to remove federal agents from Portland, but he refused. Oregon's Attorney General filed a lawsuit alleging federal agents were violating Oregonians' civil rights by seizing and detaining protesters without probable cause.[50] As discussed later, the deployment of federal agents, again seemingly to combat local crime and unrest, raised questions about the distribution of state, local, and federal constitutional authority concerning these tasks.[51]

The deployment of DHS agents was not the only federal intervention in the civil unrest that gripped the nation during the summer of 2020. Federal prosecutors pursued charges against protest participants under the federal Anti-Riot Act and the Civil Obedience Act.[52] These federal laws criminalize, respectively, crossing state lines for the purpose of engaging in riots or causing "civil disorder" that disrupts interstate commerce. Ordinarily, local vandalism and other crimes are charged and prosecuted under state and local laws. However, in some instances, U.S. prosecutors pursued federal charges. Finally, in terms of federal laws, Attorney General William Barr at one point suggested prosecutors should pursue charges for "sedition" – conspiring to overthrow the government, wage war against the U.S., or use force to obstruct enforcement of federal law – in protest cases involving vandalism and other unlawful acts.[53]

The racial justice protests produced legislative protest backlash at the state level. As noted in the Introduction and discussed elsewhere in the book, in direct response to BLM protests, Republican-controlled legislatures either proposed or enacted measures aimed at increasing the punishments for protest-related civil disobedience and other offenses. Among other things, the bills and laws increase the criminal and financial penalties for engaging in acts of civil disobedience, shift security and other costs onto protest organizations, reduce or eliminate opportunities for spontaneous protests, deny social welfare and employment-related benefits to those convicted of "riot" and other offenses, and provide legal immunity to drivers who unintentionally run over protesters who are in the street.[54]

As some commentators have observed, the aggressive and in many cases unlawful response to civil unrest during the racial justice protests stands in stark contrast to law enforcement's response to "anti-lockdown" protests, where protest policing was far less aggressive.[55] Although law enforcement did not arrest protesters for violation of pandemic-related restrictions in either context, their general response to the BLM protests exhibited far greater reliance on aggressive and escalating tactics.[56] This was true even with respect to smaller groups of peaceful protesters. The response to BLM's racial justice protests was also notably different from the general lack of preparedness and security in connection with the January 6, 2021, riot at the U.S. Capitol. During these other public emergencies, law enforcement did not respond with violence or other aggressive tactics; indeed, in the case of the January 6 riot, law enforcement seemed not to view the protest that preceded the event as even a potential threat to public safety and order.

The political response to these two protest categories was also notably different. Former President Trump urged protesters to "liberate" (mostly blue or purple) states requiring masking, social distancing, and closures, while he urged law enforcement to "dominate" racial justice protesters and threatened to "send in the feds" to check BLM protesters. Later, Trump encouraged his followers to disrupt the certification of the 2016 election results – which many then attempted to accomplish through rioting. The former president praised "stop the steal" protesters and expressed sympathy with their cause. In general, official responses to protests during public health and civil unrest emergencies highlight a recurring theme of this book, namely the discriminatory assessment and treatment of Black protesters.

EMERGENCIES, CRISES, AND CONSTITUTIONAL RIGHTS

As discussed, public health emergencies and widespread civil unrest give rise to special legislative and executive powers. Federal, state, and local law provide for the issuance of "emergency" declarations, which in turn can activate special legislative and executive authorities. When these special authorities intersect with constitutional rights, including First Amendment rights, questions arise concerning the scope of governmental powers and the preservation of constitutional rights during national emergencies. In the U.S., such issues are complicated by a lack of emergency constitutional provisions and ongoing debates about the distribution of power between the states and the national government. However, one pattern that has emerged is that emergencies often result in diminished protection for First Amendment rights.

National emergencies and crises can stem from a variety of domestic and foreign events – terrorist attacks, wars, economic conditions, natural disasters, etc. This chapter focuses on public health emergencies and widespread civil unrest, and the domestic powers governments exercise when they occur. The scope and distribution of federal and state power during declared and undeclared emergencies is a complex topic. There is a vast academic literature on emergency constitutional powers, which I will not attempt to engage broadly with in this discussion.[57] However, since the analysis that follows touches on some of the complexities of emergency constitutionalism, I briefly discuss certain relevant authorities.

In contrast to other democracies, in the U.S. there is no explicit general power in the Constitution that provides for suspending constitutional rights or invoking special governmental powers during national emergencies or crises. Indeed, there are no agreed-upon definitions of either "emergency" or "crisis."[58] However, some provisions of the U.S. Constitution contemplate the exercise of special powers in response to extraordinary events or circumstances. For instance, the Constitution provides that Congress cannot suspend the Writ of Habeas Corpus, an important right against unlawful detention, "unless when in Cases of Rebellion or Invasion the public Safety may require it."[59] It also requires the federal government to protect the states against "invasion" and, at a state's request, "domestic violence."[60] Congress has the power to call forth the militia "to execute the Laws of the Union, suppress insurrections and repel invasions."[61] It also has the power to "provide for organizing, arming, and disciplining" the state militias, and governing them when called into federal service.[62]

These provisions are the basis for a variety of federal laws, some of which are discussed later, which set forth executive powers necessary to enforce them. Emergency powers are not limited to invasions and rebellions. Federal and state governments have declared "emergencies" in cases of infectious diseases, natural disasters, terrorist attacks, and civil unrest.[63] Emergency declarations invoke special governmental powers. They do not suspend constitutional rights, although they may significantly affect their exercise. Nor do they establish a predicate for martial law, or military control of the nation's streets. Indeed, a long American tradition opposes military control of domestic territories, including urban centers.

Except as mentioned, the Constitution does not establish clear or explicit lines of federal, state, and local authority that apply during emergencies and crises. Governmental responses to the COVID-19 pandemic and civil unrest during the 2020 racial justice protests showed how lingering uncertainty about "federalism," or the distribution of power between nation and states, complicates responses to emergencies and crises. Which unit or institution is responsible for ensuring public health? Which is empowered to respond to civil unrest in cities? As with many "federalism" issues, the answers are not clear. Although some domestic emergencies may be clearly within the federal government's purview, more typically both national and sub-national governments perform important responsive functions.

Emergencies and crises can pose significant challenges for the preservation of First Amendment and other constitutional rights. As Oren Gross has observed, "Emergencies present decisionmakers with a tension of tragic dimensions. Democratic nations faced with serious threats must maintain and protect life and the liberties necessary to a vibrant democracy. Emergencies challenge the most fundamental concepts of constitutional democracy."[64]

During public health and other crises, freedom of speech and assembly can seem like niceties or luxuries reserved for normal or ordinary times. The Constitution, the Court has observed, is "not a suicide pact."[65] On the other hand, it is precisely when governments claim extraordinary powers that preserving First Amendment rights seems most necessary.

One general lesson from U.S. history is that when emergencies and crises arise, protection for civil liberties often diminishes.[66] First Amendment rights have been especially vulnerable during times of real – or perceived – crises. The Supreme Court has upheld the criminalization of speech and political association during World War I, the Cold War, and the war on terrorism.[67] Courts have also allowed state executives, acting pursuant to emergency powers, to restrict or ban public protests and other political activity.[68] John Hart Ely once observed that the history of free speech jurisprudence in times of crisis "mocks our commitment to an open political process."[69] During wartime and other national crises, authorities have suppressed freedom of speech and press and cracked down on freedom of assembly.[70]

However, these rights were not formally *suspended* during national emergencies. Even during national crises, Americans have been able to mass in the streets to protest racial segregation, wartime policies, and other matters. Further, judicial review has led to the correction of governmental excesses once emergencies have faded.[71] However, the question is not simply whether some exercise of public protest rights will be permitted, but when, how, and under what conditions. Managed dissent significantly burdens public protest even in ordinary times. Crises and emergencies have given rise to governmental laws and policies aimed at restricting the disruption associated with constitutionally protected protest activities.

As Gross has observed, "Crises tend to result in the expansion of governmental powers, the concentration of powers in the hands of the executive, and the concomitant contraction of individual freedoms and liberties. Enhanced and newly created powers are asserted by, and given to, the government as necessary to meet the challenge to the community."[72] During the public health and civil unrest emergencies discussed in this chapter, these powers produced additional obstacles to public protest including curfews, bans on public gatherings, and aggressive law enforcement tactics.[73] Emergency- or crisis-based restrictions have also limited the exercise of other civil liberties, including the right to travel and the right to worship.

During ordinary times, judges balance free speech and other constitutional rights against governmental interests such as protecting public health, safety, and order. They require a degree of fit or proportionality between the measures adopted by governments and their asserted interests. For various reasons, during national crises, the balance tilts heavily in the government's favor.[74] During a public health emergency, for example, courts may not feel competent to make judgments based on rapidly developing scientific evidence. During periods of civil unrest, courts may sympathize or identify with the government's interests in maintaining order on public streets and combating crime. Judges may seek to avoid being held responsible for exacerbating a serious health crisis or undermining law and order.

One answer to concerns about judicial under-performance during emergencies and crises is to remove courts from the picture – to acknowledge governments have some "extraconstitutional" powers and rely on executive transparency and political checks to constrain those powers.[75] Some scholars have argued this approach will avoid normalizing interpretations of constitutional powers and rights rendered in exceptional periods.

However, the recent pandemic and civil unrest crises again highlight the danger of relying on the political branches – and the people themselves – to determine the scope of power during declared "emergencies" and "crises."[76] During the COVID-19 pandemic, officials expressed the view that public health and public protest were incompatible. Similarly, law enforcement's response to mass protests associated with civil unrest was aggressive and escalated disruption and violence. Former President Trump's public statements about the protests and protesters showed how lack of clarity concerning the U.S. military's role in preserving domestic order can affect peaceful assembly and expression. Unbridled government power presents a grave threat to First Amendment and other rights. Although they have not always been effective at pushing back against broad executive and other powers during national crises, independent courts are a necessary check against speech-suppressive "emergency" measures.[77]

Assuming the judiciary will be involved, one important question is the degree to which judicial balancing of interests should tilt in the government's favor. Should courts apply an "ordinary" standard of review, adjust that standard based on the nature of the contingency, defer to governmental regulators under a "suspension" of rights model, or come up with some other approach that both accommodates the emergency and preserves constitutional rights?[78]

In answering that question, the nature of the "emergency" is an important variable. This chapter is only concerned with whether, and if so how, First Amendment rights can be preserved during (1) public health emergencies and (2) periods of civil unrest. Whether different responses or First Amendment protections may be warranted in the event of a terrorist attack, natural disaster, or economic crisis is beyond the scope of the present discussion.

There is no binding text, precedent, or principle that fully determines the balance between government power and First Amendment rights during emergencies. Courts responding to claimed violations of free speech and assembly rights must draw on the doctrines and precedents at hand, considering the nature and scope of the emergency. As they perform this critical task, courts' decisions should be influenced by First Amendment values and the need to create space for dissent – even, or perhaps especially – when governments claim and exercise extraordinary powers.

PUBLIC HEALTH, PUBLIC PROTEST, AND FIRST AMENDMENT PATHOLOGY

Prior to the COVID-19 pandemic, Americans did not have a wealth of experience concerning public protests during declared public health emergencies. Confronted with novel stay-at-home orders, masking and social distancing requirements, and other restrictions, many responded by gathering in public to contest the exercise of emergency powers. Pandemic-related restrictions also gave rise to thousands of lawsuits, many including First Amendment free speech, assembly, and petition claims.[79] In many respects, judicial performance during this crisis followed the historical pattern discussed earlier: although some courts invalidated expressive restrictions, authorities were generally allowed to manage dissent by imposing bans and other significant restrictions on public assembly and expression.

"Suspension" of First Amendment Rights

As discussed, in response to the pandemic state and local governments issued stay-at-home orders and other severe restrictions on public gatherings. Some expressly designated public protest and other exercises of First Amendment rights as "non-essential" activities. Especially during the height of the pandemic, it was not clear anyone had a First Amendment *right* to gather in person in public places. Over time, governors and lawmakers eased or lifted some pandemic-related restrictions on public protests and other gatherings. However, for an extended period, Americans' fundamental rights to gather and speak in public were banned altogether or subject to strict limits.[80]

In many First Amendment lawsuits challenging pandemic restrictions on assembly and expressive activities, courts were generally deferential to public officials. Most courts refused to grant protester or other plaintiff requests for immediate relief from pandemic-related bans or restrictions. In one early case, a federal judge upheld California's flat *ban* on in-person protests.[81] The court concluded the state had a legitimate public health interest in limiting person-to-person interactions and reasoned that permitting 500- or 1,000-person protests would undermine that interest. The court refused to recognize any narrower alternative to banning such gatherings. It observed that a blanket ban on public protests "does not intuitively ring of narrow tailoring. But 'narrow' in the context of a public health crisis is necessarily wider than usual."[82] The court also observed that protesters had several alternative channels of communication, including online forums and vehicle rallies.

A federal court applied similar reasoning in upholding New York City's ban on all "non-essential" public gatherings.[83] Given the "extraordinary" pandemic and the scientific community's understanding of the virus, the court concluded a temporary ban on public gatherings was narrowly tailored to further the city's public health interests.[84] It also suggested protesters could rely on alternative channels of communication, including social media and single-person public protests.[85]

These decisions were not anomalies. Consistent with historical patterns, federal courts generally applied a deferential standard of review to public health emergency-related government restrictions on expressive rights.[86] One state court accepted that so long as the governor acted in "good faith" and had some basis in fact for a ban on large gatherings, it would not second-guess a state-wide assembly ban.[87] A federal judge observed that the state's governor was entitled to a "constitutional learning curve" in promulgating pandemic-related protest restrictions.[88]

The breadth of judicial deference in these cases effectively amounted to an indefinite suspension of in-person public protests, or at least gatherings of more than a small number of people. The restrictions affected pandemic-related protests, religious gatherings, gun rights demonstrations, political rallies, and other public assemblies. During the early and middle stages of the COVID-19 pandemic, several courts effectively suspended the First Amendment's protections for public protest. To be sure, those who openly defied stay-at-home and other restrictions were rarely arrested. However, those seeking to comply with state and local emergency measures were either formally barred from assembling and protesting in public forums or able to do so only in very small numbers.

As Lindsay Wiley and Stephen Vladeck have observed, constitutional challenges to COVID-19 restrictions, including in public assembly and speech cases, neatly presented the question raised earlier: whether constitutional constraints on government should be "suspended" during emergencies.[89] Upholding coronavirus bans on abortion, assembly, and other constitutional rights, federal and state courts relied on a type of suspension principle under which they applied a highly deferential standard of review to constitutional claims.[90] That approach would effectively eliminate public protest rights during the declared emergency.

As noted, there is a deficit of binding authority concerning the scope of constitutional powers and rights in emergency situations. Many courts, including in free expression cases, relied heavily on *Jacobson v. Massachusetts*. In *Jacobson*, decided in 1905, the Supreme Court upheld a Massachusetts law mandating that adults be vaccinated against smallpox.[91] *Jacobson* concluded that emergency measures that curtail constitutional rights are valid so long as the measures have at least some "real or substantial relation" to the public health emergency and are not "beyond all question, a plain, palpable invasion of rights secured by the fundamental law."[92]

In First Amendment cases, courts also relied on *Smith v. Avino*, a federal appeals court case that upheld an extended curfew imposed in response to Hurricane Andrew against challenges the curfew order was vague, overbroad, and violated the right to travel.[93] The standard applied in *Avino* requires only that officials act in "good faith" and with "some factual basis for the decision."[94] *Avino* asserted that "[i]n an emergency situation, fundamental rights such as the right to travel and free speech may be temporarily limited or suspended."[95]

Wiley and Vladeck have persuasively argued that the "suspension approach" applied by courts is significantly flawed.[96] As they observed, the suspension principle assumes emergencies are always of finite scope and limited duration – an assumption at odds with open-ended emergencies like the one relating to COVID-19, which persisted for more than two years. Further, the measures taken to combat the novel coronavirus over this extended period, including stay-at-home orders and social distancing requirements, directly restrict civil liberties including speech and assembly. Many of the protests focused specifically on governments' pandemic responses.[97] The suspension approach also assumes protests themselves are transitory events, further limiting the impact on civil liberties.[98] However, movements like Occupy Wall Street and the extended nature of the 2020 BLM protests also undermine that supposition.

Wiley and Vladeck further challenged the suspension principle's presumption that "ordinary" judicial review cannot be applied to government actions during an emergency. They claimed necessary public health emergency measures can still survive judicial review under "ordinary" standards, which require governments to demonstrate the necessity and proportionality of their enactments.[99] (The authors claimed that even broad bans on public gatherings may be constitutional under ordinary standards, something I address later.)[100] Finally, Wiley and Vladeck have pointed to the necessity of an independent judiciary during emergencies and crises. The judiciary, they observed, provides a vitally important check against governmental abuses of emergency powers.[101]

These are compelling arguments against the suspension principle. The precedential basis for the principle is also suspect. As commentators have argued, to the extent courts have relied on *Jacobson* as support, they have likely misread the decision as requiring extraordinary deference to government officials during public health and other emergencies.[102] Whatever else it may have decided, *Jacobson* did not adopt the suspension principle. Rather, it applied an early form of what has become a familiar balancing approach.[103] The Court recognized that governmental emergency regulations could be "so arbitrary and oppressive in particular cases as to justify the interference of the courts to prevent wrong and oppression."[104] In other words, "*Jacobson* never quite said what it's been said to have said."[105] Moreover, as Wiley and Vladeck observed, "*Jacobson* predated the entire modern canonization of constitutional scrutiny," which requires heightened scrutiny of regulations restricting First Amendment and other fundamental rights.[106]

For similar reasons, judicial reliance on *Avino* is also misplaced. In *Avino* the court assumed the natural disaster at issue, a hurricane, was temporary and transient. But as applied to some emergencies, the court's "good faith" and "some factual basis" standards would license months- or even years-long bans on public protest and other constitutionally protected activities. The court's conclusion that free speech and other constitutional rights could be "temporarily limited or suspended" was based in part on the Supreme Court's infamous decision in *Korematsu v. United States (1944)*, which upheld the federal government's internment of Japanese Americans.[107] *Korematsu* is one of the most poignant examples of governmental abuse of emergency powers and judicial failure to uphold constitutional rights in the face of (what turned out to be false) claims of exigency in American history.[108] Far from justifying the suspension of constitutional rights, even for limited periods, *Korematsu* reinforces the need for an engaged and independent judiciary – especially during national emergencies.

Protest and Pathology

Rejecting the suspension principle does not solve the dilemma of how to protect public protest and other civil liberties during a public health emergency. Clearly, the government must act in response to a global pandemic that caused more than a million American deaths and other serious health effects. When its responses are aimed at or severely restrict the exercise of First Amendment rights, what is the proper scope of governmental power during such an extraordinary public health emergency?

Any answer to that question must acknowledge the central dilemma raised by public protest during a pandemic. On the one hand, as the novel coronavirus showed, public protest may exacerbate the crisis and thus extend the emergency. Mass public protests, even ones in which most protesters are masked, could become "super-spreader" events that contribute to the spread of the airborne virus. On the other hand, the notion that public protest is not an "essential" or even appropriate activity during the duration of a public health emergency devalues and undermines the exercise of First Amendment rights.

As noted, many "anti-lockdown" protests focused directly on the government's pandemic policies. Stay-at-home and other restrictions cut off public dissent relating to the exercise of governmental power. Even if the protest was not about the government's pandemic powers, the notion that public assemblies in the form of political campaign rallies, pro-gun rights demonstrations, and racial justice protests could all be put on indefinite hold is anathema to a culture of dissent that includes the public exercise of First Amendment rights.

As I have argued, the "suspension" model vests too much discretionary power in government officials, who may use it for partisan ends or otherwise seek to extend or exploit the emergency. Thus, suspension is not the proper principle for courts to apply during a public health emergency or crisis.

Times of crisis demonstrate why it is necessary for courts to adopt, during *ordinary* times, what Vincent Blasi has called a "pathological perspective" regarding First Amendment doctrines.[109] Blasi called on courts to make "a conscious effort ... to strengthen the central norms of the first amendment against the advent of pathology."[110] Recognizing that governments would overreach and over-regulate during crises and emergencies, he urged that emphasis be put "in adjudication during normal times on the development of procedures and institutional structures that are relatively immune from the pressure of urgency by virtue of their formality, rigidity, built-in delays, or strong internal dynamics."[111]

Blasi advocated a "keep it simple" guideline under which judges use simple First Amendment principles to strengthen the restraining power of the First Amendment including in times of crisis – which Blasi referred to as "the worst of times."[112] He highlighted the danger that the rush to dilute First Amendment protections in times of great peril will not merely end there, but rather will spill over to "normal" First Amendment jurisprudence and doctrine.[113]

Thus, to the extent practicable, even during crises and emergencies courts should apply "normal" First Amendment doctrines – including rules that treat bans on public expression as presumptively unconstitutional. Courts can "accommodate" for "the pressures exerted on the state in times of emergency, while, at the same time, maintaining normal legal principles and rules as much as possible."[114]

This is somewhat like the position Wiley and Vladeck adopted in their critique of early COVID-19 constitutional rights decisions. As they acknowledged, ordinary First Amendment rules, especially those relating to the *proportionality* of governmental responses to public health emergencies, inevitably "tilt in favor of the government."[115] Nevertheless, the broadest crisis measures, including flat bans on public assembly and speech, will – and should – fail to satisfy First Amendment standards. Given judicial accommodation to emergency circumstances, Wiley and Vladeck believe many pandemic-related measures would still survive First Amendment scrutiny under these standards – presumably including narrow curfews and reasonable limits on public gatherings. "And if they can't," the authors observe, "we think that says far more about the challenged governmental action than it does about the role of the courts."[116]

Especially during an emergency or crisis, there is a danger that governments will act pathologically, seeking to expand their power to restrict public protest – including when dissent focuses on government policies. Powers and precedents relating to health-related restrictions must not outlast the public health emergency or be relied upon to manage dissent outside or beyond their specific context. As David Cole has observed, courts often perform poorly at the outset of a crisis but course-correct when the emergency subsides.[117] But the correction will often come too late in the day to preserve protest rights, which rely on proximity to target audiences and an immediacy of communication to be effective.

That is why it is vitally important, from the outset, that judicial precedents and approaches do not normalize overbroad and disproportionate pandemic responses. Specifically, when assessing restrictions on First Amendment protest rights courts should reject "good faith" and "some basis in fact" standards. As they would during ordinary times, judges should review outright bans on public assembly and protest with great skepticism. Tailored responses including brief and geographically limited curfews, masking requirements, reasonable social distancing requirements, and even some limits on crowd size are all less restrictive than broad bans on public protest.

In contrast to the suspension approach, which treats all emergencies the same, courts should recognize public emergencies can vary in duration, character, and scope.[118] They should read *Jacobson* narrowly. Courts should not blindly apply *Avino* and similar precedents, which upheld temporary curfews in response to natural disasters, to public health or other emergencies that may be much longer in duration. Governments can still pursue important public health concerns. But in doing so, they must preserve access to public places and opportunities for public protest and dissent.

Judicial pandemic decisions far too readily assumed that posting on social media, engaging in single-person protests, and talking to reporters are all adequate "alternative channels of communication." As discussed in Chapter 3, this assumption is a flaw in "ordinary" First Amendment doctrine. During a health emergency in which society is "locked down," it is important to recognize and preserve opportunities for collective public expression. Honking horns in cars and trucks is not a substitute for public assembly. As Justice Gorsuch observed in the context of limits on religious free exercise, "Even if the Constitution has taken a holiday during this pandemic, it cannot become a sabbatical."[119]

CIVIL UNREST AND CIVIL LIBERTIES

During periods of civil unrest, federal and state officials can invoke special powers that implicate First Amendment rights.[120] The racial justice protests during the summer of 2020 intersected with both public health and civil unrest authorities. They shared certain similarities with the pandemic protests, including in terms of governmental reliance on curfews and other restrictions on public gatherings. This section focuses specifically on the civil unrest emergency brought about by mass protests and violent conduct associated with some of those events. Government responses to civil unrest exposed pathologies in the law of public protest, uncertainty regarding the distribution of national and state power, and troubling federal interventions in local law enforcement activity.

Mismanaging Mass Protests – Again

One glaring problem during the civil unrest emergency was the poor performance of law enforcement. In contrast to "anti-lockdown" protests, police responded to the racial justice protests with aggression and violence. The book has argued that law enforcement abuses are a generalized threat to public protests. Once again, this time during a declared emergency, the law enforcement response to the racial justice protests highlighted problems associated with protest policing.

As Karen Loor has explained, "Emergency officials view protests as law-enforcement-centric events, which means that before and after a legal emergency is declared, officials give the police free rein to control protesters."[121] This orientation toward public protest contributed to a wide array of First Amendment violations during the racial justice demonstrations. As discussed, several reviews of how law enforcement policed BLM protests identified unlawful responses to peaceful public protests: use of non-lethal chemical agents, physical and vehicular assaults, and indiscriminate arrests. Among other things, reports criticized police reliance on escalated force tactics, targeting of journalists, and lack of training.

New York's Attorney General took the unprecedented step of filing a legal action against the New York City Police Department based on its protest policing methods.[122] An investigation by the Attorney General's office found that police officers beat protesters with batons, rammed them with bicycles, used a dangerous containment strategy called "kettling" (trapping and restraining groups of protesters by force), and arrested legal observers and medics without proper justification. The Attorney General requested a court-appointed monitor to oversee the department's policing tactics at future protests and a court order to declare that the policies and practices the department used during the protests were unlawful.

Anyone familiar with protest policing will recognize these as longstanding law enforcement abuses.[123] After-event reports concerning the 2020 racial justice protests read remarkably, depressingly, like past publications – including official assessments of law enforcement's performance during the World Trade Organization protests in 1999 and Ferguson, Missouri in 2014.[124] Those assessments also criticized law enforcement's use of escalated force tactics, its poor preparation, and deficient training.[125]

During the 2020 racial justice protests, policing methods forced organizers, participants, and others to seek judicial relief. BLM and other protesters challenged a variety of measures taken by officials to manage dissent during national police brutality demonstrations.

In contrast to the early pandemic decisions, in these cases courts did not generally "suspend" the First Amendment. Indeed, protesters were able to obtain judicial relief from at least the most plainly unlawful police conduct – including the unwarranted use of chemical irritants and rubber projectiles against peaceful crowds.[126] Courts also protected press rights, again against plainly unlawful abuses. For example, the American Civil Liberties Union (ACLU) obtained a preliminary injunction on behalf of journalists covering the Portland protests, which enjoined the U.S. Marshals Service, DHS, and other law enforcement entities from using force against, arresting, or threatening journalists and legal observers.[127]

However, in some other protest-related cases, plaintiffs were less successful. Courts rejected some claims challenging broad curfew orders.[128] Courts also upheld protesters' arrests for "unlawful assembly" and other broad public order offenses.[129] As in the pandemic context, in many cases, courts substantially deferred to law enforcement interests in maintaining public order. Although the "suspension" model was not in full force, the First Amendment afforded only limited protection for protest under ordinary rules, which grant officials broad deference to maintain public order.

Further, as discussed in Chapter 8, legal doctrines grant broad immunities to state and federal authorities alleged to have violated protesters' First Amendment and other constitutional rights. These doctrines apply with full force during periods of civil unrest. They limit or prohibit the recovery of civil damages for constitutional violations, which are more prevalent during mass public protests. In some high-profile cases, racial justice protesters were denied recovery based on these limitations.

For example, a federal court dismissed First Amendment, Fourth Amendment, and federal civil rights claims against former President Trump, Attorney General Barr, and other federal officials in connection with law enforcement's clearing of Lafayette Square.[130] The court reasoned that the officials were immune from some of the claims and faulted plaintiffs for failing to adequately plead claims under other federal laws. Plaintiffs suing federal, state, or local officials for First Amendment violations stemming from emergency protest policing violations face the same steep legal hurdles protesters encounter during ordinary times.

That is not to say protesters have been uniformly unsuccessful in recovering damages for constitutional wrongs. Some have already reached settlements limiting law enforcement's resort to non-lethal force during future protests. Others have recovered significant damage awards against state and local law enforcement because of their use of chemical agents and other aggressive tactics.[131]

Winning court cases is an important concern. But there are also lingering questions about the broader impacts on public protest activity from law enforcement's mismanagement of mass demonstrations. As discussed elsewhere in the book, aggressive and unlawful protest policing has long been a cornerstone of managed dissent. During a period of heightened civil unrest, it is not surprising that law enforcement abuses – including resorting to unlawful force – multiplied. What is missing but sorely needed are adequate means of preventing or deterring this sort of behavior, in both ordinary *and* extraordinary times. Once again, the lack of strong "pathological" standards worked to the detriment of protesters who sought to speak and assemble during declared emergencies.

State Emergency Declarations

State emergency declarations compound some of the problems associated with the mismanagement of protest policing. When governments treat public protest itself as a disaster or emergency, civil liberties become casualties. State emergency declarations trigger broad executive constitutional and statutory powers, many of which resemble those used in connection with the pandemic emergency.

Although state officials perform critical functions in terms of responding to civil unrest, it can be somewhat difficult to ascertain how state and local emergency management systems operate.[132] As a general matter, at the state and local level, emergency management during civil unrest includes activation of National Guard forces, imposition of curfews, use of "no protest" zones and other place regulations, mass arrests, and reliance on "unlawful assembly," "failure to disperse" and other public order offenses. Notably, state constitutional and statutory emergency provisions do not mention the preservation of individual rights – except, in some instances, the right to keep and bear arms.[133]

As noted earlier, in response to the BLM-led protests over thirty state governors activated state National Guard forces. Each state and territory in the United States has a National Guard that is under the direct control of a state's governor. National Guard forces have been lawfully deployed to respond to local civil unrest. Under the Constitution, these forces can also be federalized for national missions. However, the federalization of National Guard forces does not mean the deployment of active-duty military personnel. Former President Trump sowed confusion when, in response to vandalism and violence in Minneapolis and other cities, he tweeted that he told Minnesota's governor that "the Military is with him all the way." As the former president should have been aware, National Guard troops are not the same as active-duty military personnel.

As the response to the BLM demonstrations showed, public confusion about the role of the National Guard can raise concerns about peaceful protesters' rights and escalate contention during public protests. During the 2020 racial justice protests, state National Guard troops provided support to local law enforcement. As Minnesota's Guard commander and governor made clear, the forces were there to assist local law enforcement but did not have the authority to arrest protesters for vandalism, unlawful assembly, or other public order offenses.[34] Although the rules of engagement for state National Guard troops are not made public, it is understood they can use force in self-defense or defense of state property. National Guard troops are also deployed during civil unrest to protect the right to peaceably assemble and protest.

Deployment of National Guard troops may be necessary in some circumstances to restore order. But leaders responsible for their deployment and command should remember the lessons of Kent State. In 1970, members of the Ohio National Guard killed four students and wounded nine others at Kent State University when they employed combat techniques to control a civilian crowd.[35] The Kent State shootings led to reforms, including the development of less lethal crowd control tactics and training designed to de-escalate tensions by the National Guard and law enforcement agencies. As discussed earlier, in the case of many local law enforcement agencies the training still has not had its desired effect.

If armed Guardsmen are to be deployed, it should be as a last resort rather than an initial response to unrest. Protesters can find it difficult to differentiate uniformed and armed state guard forces from ordinary law enforcement. During the 2020 demonstrations, protesters were faced with contingents of National Guardsmen, armed with tear gas, rifles, and fixed bayonets, standing guard at protest sites or sometimes advancing on their groups to control crowds. In addition, so-called private "militias," which do not operate under any legitimate governmental authority, were present at public protests dressed in fatigues and carrying weaponry common among National Guard troops. (The phenomenon of "armed protests" was discussed in Chapter 6.) This array of armed personnel ratchets up the potential for violence and escalates tensions.

State emergency declarations implicate protesters' rights in other respects. Invocation and application of broad emergency powers permit state and local officials to broadly manage dissent during a declared emergency.[136] As discussed in connection with the pandemic emergency, the imposition of extended curfews can significantly undermine public protests and restrict First Amendment rights.[137] For the reasons provided earlier, courts should reject the "suspension" model during civil unrest and insist curfews be narrowly drawn. Particularly in the context of civil unrest, there is a significant risk the curfew power is being exercised in part to restrict protest activity itself. Further, curfews can lead to confrontational policing and mass arrests. As mentioned earlier, during the racial justice protests more than 1,000 individuals were arrested for violating local curfews. When law enforcement needs to impose limited curfews, it should communicate their terms clearly to the public and provide ample notice prior to enforcement.

Another important lesson from past civil unrest emergencies involving protests is the need to require narrow tailoring of spatial restrictions.[138] The use of "no protest zones" and other restrictions on where protesters can gather, or march, can effectively shut down a protest movement in the name of "public safety." Applying deferential standards of review, courts have allowed executive officials to effectively zone public protests out of large areas, including in one case a 25-block radius in downtown Seattle.[139] As with pandemic congregation restrictions, zoning and other measures must be narrowly tailored to the actual threat or disorder.

There are also serious concerns about officials' "emergency" reliance on "unlawful assembly," "failure to disperse," and other public order laws, which law enforcement can invoke to clear public places of all demonstrations. These public order offenses may be supplemented by *ad hoc* emergency rules, which may themselves restrict protest and other expressive activities.[140]

As discussed in Chapter 2, even in ordinary times enforcement of such laws is troublingly discretionary and subject to law enforcement abuse. As post-protest reports show, during 2020's summer of civil unrest law enforcement frequently relied on "unlawful assembly," "failure to disperse," and other highly discretionary authorities to dispatch even peaceful assemblies of protesters. The danger that these authorities will be abused is heightened when law enforcement acts under an "emergency" declaration.

In sum, as during public health emergencies, periods of "civil unrest" should not be viewed as occasions for suspending First Amendment rights. To the extent possible, even during times of civil unrest both policymakers and courts should seek to preserve public protest rights.

Deploying Federal Forces to Local Protests

During periods of widespread civil unrest, the federal government can play an important role in maintaining public order. However, the actions of the federal government during the 2020 racial justice protests raised concerns about the authority and function of federal forces deployed to local protests.

As noted earlier, former President Trump made statements suggesting that he would use federal forces, including active-duty U.S. armed forces, to quell civil unrest relating to public protests. There are several historical precedents for deploying federal forces, including U.S. troops, to keep the peace during street protests and demonstrations. For example, federal forces entered major U.S. cities including Los Angeles during the street riots that followed the Rodney King verdict, Washington, Baltimore, and other cities after protests erupted following Dr. King's assassination, and Detroit in response to riots there in 1967.[141]

Although the standards and rules of engagement are murky, there is legal authority for federalizing militia forces and using federal law enforcement and, in narrow circumstances, the U.S. military to quell civil unrest. As noted earlier, the president can federalize the state militias in response to invasions and, at the request of a state legislature, "domestic violence." Congress can authorize the use of the militia "to execute the Laws of the Union, suppress Insurrections, and repel Invasions." Former President Trump pointed to the Insurrection Act of 1807 as a source of presidential power to dispatch federal agents and active-duty military personnel to restore law and order in American cities; Trump reportedly wanted thousands of active-duty troops patrolling the streets in Washington, D.C. and other cities.[142] A federal law, the Posse Comitatus Act, places restrictions on participation by U.S. active-duty military forces in civil functions including domestic law enforcement, unless expressly authorized by the Constitution or an act of Congress (including the Insurrection Act).[143]

This is not the place for an extended discussion of whether former President Trump had the power under the Insurrection Act to deploy federal forces.[144] Some of the predicates for doing so include when a state legislature or governor requests such assistance when faced with an "insurrection"; a president determines that "unlawful obstructions, combinations, or assemblages" make it impracticable to enforce U.S. law; an insurrection hinders the execution of state or federal laws within the state or people are deprived of a constitutional "right, privilege, immunity, or protection" that the state is unable to or refuses to protect; or an insurrection "opposes or obstructs the execution of the laws of the United States or impedes the course of justice under those laws."[145] Under the Act's broad terms, presidents may be able to make a plausible case for federal intervention.[146]

Even so, invocation of the Insurrection Act and federal force intervention raise two related concerns relating to the preservation of protest rights. One concern, demonstrated by former President Trump's statements and actions, is that federal officials will invoke the Insurrection Act and other authorities to commandeer local law enforcement functions. Ordinarily, enforcement of state and local crimes, including during public protests, falls to state and local law enforcement authorities. In some instances, state and local leaders made clear they did not face extraordinary challenges and thus did not want or need federal intervention.

State and local resistance does not negate presidential power under the Insurrection Act. But when local authorities express such resistance, presidents should respect their views and principles of constitutional federalism – as President George W. Bush did when he decided not to send in federal troops, at the Louisiana governor's request, to deal with the aftermath of Hurricane Katrina.[147] Further, federal officials should be ordered to intervene in domestic political protests only when there is a clear federal predicate, such as the enforcement of federal laws or protection of federal properties.

When that predicate seems lacking, as many thought it was during the summer of 2020, questions arise about pretextual uses of federal force to suppress domestic political protests.[148] Former President Trump called for federal intervention even in cities that were not experiencing widespread civil unrest. Further, his deployment of federal border and other agents, rather than a well-trained federalized militia, raised serious questions about his motivations. Many wondered whether Trump was motivated more by campaign promises to crack down on "left-wing mobs" and the optics of federal intervention than a desire to protect federal properties and enforce federal or state law. Tellingly, Trump never expressed any concern in this context for preserving *protesters'* rights under state and federal law.

A related concern is that rather than seek to maintain public order and protect federal interests, military and other federal forces will engage in ordinary protest policing whenever presidents find state and local efforts wanting. As noted earlier, when they serve in a law enforcement capacity, federal forces become another layer of intimidating military force arrayed against peaceful protesters. Here, again, we are likely not talking about any legally enforceable limits on federal protest policing. By its terms, the Posse Comitatus Act limits federal troops' participation in certain kinds of local law enforcement activities. However, the Act is subject to various constitutional and statutory exceptions, including the Insurrection Act, and has rarely been enforced.[149] Some have advocated amendments to the Posse Comitatus Act, including provisions granting local authorities more command control over federal forces and imposing timeline and review requirements.[150] But as of this writing, the limits of federal authority under the Posse Comitatus Act remain somewhat murky.

Federal policymakers should be hesitant to intervene in domestic political protests unless the predicate for doing so is clear. Aggressive and escalatory protest policing may be the single biggest threat to modern peaceful public protest. Adding DHS, U.S. Marshals, and active-duty military personnel to the "battlespace" (as former President Trump's Defense Secretary referred to U.S. public forums) further imperils the tradition of peaceful protest. Although the deployment of federal forces is not unprecedented, states and localities, and in special instances state-deployed National Guard forces, should be relied upon to keep the peace *and* protect peaceful public protest.

Ultimately, the surge of an array of federal agents to places like Portland, which the Trump Administration dubbed "Operation Diligent Valor," was neither diligent nor valorous. According to a report by a DHS watchdog, "not all officers completed required training; had the necessary equipment; and used consistent uniforms, devices, and operational tactics when responding to the events in Portland."[151] One protester reported that unidentified officers in military fatigues loaded him into an unmarked van without explanation and transported him to a holding facility for questioning.[152] That should be a lasting and, again, cautionary image for a nation dedicated to preserving both law and order and the right to engage in public protest.

In the hands of former President Trump, federal emergency powers became a very dangerous set of tools that threatened to place the country on a war footing at home.[153] Trump referred to protesters as "terrorists" and expressed a desire for "an occupying force" he could dispatch to American cities.[154] He surrounded himself with military generals, including General Mark Milley, Chairman of the Joint Chiefs of Staff, who Trump informed the nation's governors would be in charge of the federal government's response to the protests. (General Millie would later apologize for participating in the Lafayette Square incident and emphasize the military's separation from domestic politics.) The Trump administration's "linguistic impression (protesters as terrorists), bureaucratic porousness (an array of law enforcement bodies operating far outside their usual jurisdiction), and ... violation of norms deployed in coordinated manner" raised legitimacy concerns regarding the federal government's interventions in Portland and other cities.[155]

What ultimately saved protesters and other Americans from a federal occupying force was a combination of resistance by state officials, public retreats by General Millie and Secretary Esper, published objections by former national security officials, and judicial decisions rejecting the excesses of militarized federal policing of domestic protests.[156] But the federal response to civil unrest exposed the lack of clarity in federal laws relating to civil unrest, the danger of invoking those authorities for domestic political ends, and the need for independent and prompt judicial review of the acts of a vast federal law enforcement bureaucracy.

Local Protest Activity and Federal Crimes

The federal response to civil unrest during the 2020 racial justice protests also raised concerns regarding the enforcement of federal laws including the Anti-Riot Act, Civil Obedience Act, and Sedition Act against protest organizers and participants. Application of these seldom-invoked laws in the context of public protests can raise significant First Amendment concerns.

The federal Anti-Riot Act and the Civil Obedience Act were enacted in response to civil unrest associated with civil rights protests during the 1960s. Some of the legislative history of these laws suggests a desire to go after civil rights "agitators."[157] Typically, state law enforcement and prosecutors will bring actions against alleged rioters and vandals under state and local criminal laws. However, like the Insurrection Act, the Anti-Riot Act and Civil Obedience Act provide legal bases for the exercise of federal authority in response to conditions of civil unrest.

The Anti-Riot Act criminalizes interstate travel or use of a facility during such travel with the intent to (1) incite a riot, (2) "organize, *promote, encourage*, participate in, or carry on a riot," (3) commit any act in furtherance of a riot, or (4) aid or abet any person in inciting or participating in or carrying on a riot or committing any act of violence in furtherance of a riot.[158] The Act also defines "incite to riot" and "organize, promote, encourage" a riot to include "*urging* and *instigating* others to riot," but excludes advocacy of ideas or expression of belief, not involving advocacy of any act or acts of violence or assertion of the rightness of, or the right to commit, any such act or acts."

The Anti-Riot Act has been relatively dormant for decades. However, owing to a recent rise in political violence, federal prosecutors have invoked the Act against white supremacists, Capitol insurrectionists, and some racial justice demonstrators.[159] The Act's language includes speech – including promoting, encouraging, urging, and instigating violence – that is fully protected by the First Amendment. As discussed in Chapter 2, the Supreme Court has held advocacy of violence is protected unless the speaker intends to cause an imminent unlawful act that is likely to occur.[160] Under this "incitement" standard, merely "promoting" or "encouraging" riotous behavior is protected expression.

On that basis, two federal appeals courts recently invalidated portions of the Anti-Riot Act that criminalize abstract or general advocacy of riot.[161] The courts did not conclude the Anti-Riot Act is unconstitutional on its face or in its entirety. According to the courts, protesters who merely urge others to engage in a riot cannot be prosecuted under the Act. However, protesters who participate in a riot or engage in communications that satisfy the First Amendment's narrow "incitement" standard, set forth earlier, are still subject to prosecution under the federal Anti-Riot Act. The appeals court decisions highlight the danger the Anti-Riot Act poses to the sort of political dissent and "outside agitation" legislators were apparently responding to when the Act was adopted.

As noted, state and local law enforcement authorities have adequate legal authority to charge vandals and others who commit local crimes. A federal response is needed, if at all, when states and localities are unable or unwilling to pursue such cases – and even then, it would seem, only when the federal interest is itself very significant. As federal prosecutors begin to dust off the Anti-Riot Act, courts ought to continue to interpret the law in ways that protect legitimate political dissent. Insofar as federal authorities feel compelled to pursue federal Anti-Riot Act prosecutions, they should do so only in cases where the *actions* of protesters, and not their communications, form the basis for indictments. Under the First Amendment, encouragement, promotion, and other protected forms of advocacy cannot be grounds for prosecution.

Federal prosecutors have also recently pursued criminal actions against protesters under another Civil Rights Era law, the Civil Obedience Act of 1968. That Act makes it a federal crime to interfere with police or firefighters doing their official duties during a civil disorder in a manner that "in any way or degree obstructs, delays, or adversely affects commerce" or the "conduct or performance of any federally protected function."[162] Unlike state civil disturbance laws (for example, inciting a riot or criminal mischief), most of which are misdemeanors, violation of the Civil Obedience Act is a felony that carries a possible prison term of five years.

Since the Nixon Administration, federal prosecutors have charged this offense in approximately a dozen cases. In response to the racial justice protests during the summer of 2020, however, federal prosecutors invoked this charge more than 125 times.[163] Since the January 6, 2021 insurrection, prosecutors have also brought federal civil disorder charges against some who rioted at the U.S. Capitol.

On its face, the Civil Obedience Act applies in cases where riots interfere with federal interests in the free flow of interstate commerce and the performance of federal functions. However, like the Anti-Riot Act, the Civil Obedience Act is partly rooted in historical concerns about civil rights "agitation" and suppressing certain forms of political dissent. That legislative history is not sufficient reason to invalidate the federal law. However, it should encourage prosecutors to proceed with caution in resurrecting the civil disorder law in the context of mass civil rights protests.

The Act's application to those who interfered with counting electoral college votes is plainly within its legitimate sweep. However, the federal interest in prosecuting racial justice protesters for, again, what are essentially local property crimes and violence against state or local police officers is less clear. One can certainly imagine instances in which protesters block interstate highways, an action that technically implicates federal concerns relating to the instrumentalities and flow of interstate commerce. However, the Act has also been applied to instances of vandalism and other criminal activity that seem to lack any close or substantial connection to the flow of commerce or federally protected functions.

For example, Tia Deyon Pugh was convicted of one count of violation of the Civil Obedience Act.[164] The charge stemmed from an incident in which the government charged Pugh broke out the window of a police cruiser after officers fired tear gas into a crowd of protesters blocking an on-ramp to an interstate highway. The trial court rejected Pugh's claims that the civil disorder law exceeds Congress's commerce power and violates the First Amendment. Concerning the First Amendment challenge, the court refused to rely on the legislative history indicating Congress was motivated, at least in part, by negative sentiment toward civil rights protesters.

The decision in Pugh's case may be technically defensible under current commerce clause and free speech doctrines. However, the specter of prosecutorial overreach and the bringing of federal felony cases to "get tough on crime" or for other partisan purposes remains a legitimate concern. Consider that Pugh was initially arrested and charged under state law with inciting a riot and criminal mischief, both misdemeanors in Alabama. Federal prosecutors later moved to charge her with felony federal civil disorder.

At the same time, former President Trump and other public officials were responding to the police brutality demonstrations Pugh participated in with a coordinated political message of "law and order" and protester "domination." Absent evidence states and localities are unable or unwilling to bring criminal charges in such cases (evidence that has not been apparent or produced), it is not clear federal charges serve any purpose other than to increase the potential penalties associated with unlawful protest-related activity. Like the Insurrection Act, the Civil Obedience Act is being used in contexts where state authorities neither need nor desire federal intervention to address local vandalism and violence. In other words, the charges seem less concerned with responding to an "emergency" than making a political point about law and order and getting "tough" on demonstrators.

To again state the obvious, vandalizing a police cruiser is not protected speech. However, like the Anti-Riot Act, the federal civil disorder law's broad terms, which criminalize "any act" which in "any way or degree" obstructs or impedes official functions that have some minimal connection to interstate commerce, could apply to even lawful mass protest activities. In appropriate "as applied" cases, defendants can and should challenge the application of the federal Civil Obedience Act on commerce clause and/or First Amendment grounds. Given its tainted history, prosecutors and courts should remain reluctant to use or validate this federal Act to address "civil unrest" relating to mass political demonstrations.

Finally, consider then-Attorney General Barr's directive to prosecutors to consider "sedition" charges against those accused of vandalism or assaulting law enforcement during the 2020 racial justice protests. As a legal concept, "sedition" does not narrowly refer to conspiring to overthrow the government. The federal sedition law also applies to lesser interferences with federal properties and functions. However, pursuing sedition charges against political protesters and others involved in public demonstrations invokes a checkered past of prosecuting speakers for wartime and other forms of dissent. The Supreme Court's earliest decisions upheld long prison terms for political dissidents on the grounds that their communications incited opposition to war and tended to obstruct federal functions.[165]

We should not travel this dangerous path, particularly when there is no overriding federal interest in doing so. Talk of "sedition" paints political protesters as enemies of the state. Prosecutions for the crime of sedition bear a substantial risk of criminalizing dissent. To be sure, there could be instances when the charge of sedition is appropriate. The January 6 attack on the Capitol may be one of them, assuming federal prosecutors can present evidence of a conspiracy to interfere with the peaceful transfer of presidential power under the Constitution and federal laws. But concerning street vandalism and other lawbreaking at public protests, state and local prosecutors have more than ample authority to charge violators without resorting to the charge of "sedition."

PRESERVING PUBLIC PROTEST DURING EMERGENCIES

Responses to the COVID-19 pandemic and civil unrest associated with mass political protests provide an opportunity to assess how to preserve public protest during periods of crisis and emergency. The working assumption of many policymakers, and some courts, seemed to be that public protest was incompatible with preserving public health and public order.

One contrary lesson is that it is possible for a culture of public dissent to survive even during public emergencies. Despite efforts to severely restrict or ban public gatherings, American streets did not fall silent. Indeed, they hosted perhaps the largest social justice protest movement in the nation's history. The people managed to preserve public protest, despite well-meaning and in some instances perhaps not-so-well-meaning efforts to quash it. They demonstrated that public speech and assembly are indeed "essential" activities.

We may not be as fortunate during the next public emergency. It is important to prepare in advance for government efforts to manage public dissent during crises. Referring to several religious liberty cases that the Supreme Court decided during the pandemic, Justice Alito said in a public speech: "All sorts of things can be called an emergency or disaster of major proportions. Simply slapping on that label cannot provide the ground for abrogating our most fundamental rights. And whenever fundamental rights are restricted, the Supreme Court and other courts cannot close their eyes."[166]

Justice Alito's statement addresses a fundamental tension between governmental responses to emergency conditions and the preservation of fundamental rights. It rejects the "suspension" of ordinary constitutional standards during public emergencies. That is a critical starting point, and not just for courts. Policymakers, who are charged in the first instance with balancing public health and order against First Amendment and other constitutional rights, must either accept or be reminded by courts that there are limits on their powers. They should issue "emergency" declarations reluctantly and responsibly, acknowledge the need to preserve free speech and assembly rights during declared emergencies, and narrowly tailor restrictions on public speech and assembly – by, for example, limiting their time frames and geographies. Officials should also endeavor to tailor restrictions to the character and nature of each emergency.

In the event executive officials adopt bans on public gatherings and other suppressive measures, as Justice Alito suggested, courts must stand ready to act as independent checks to preserve expressive liberties. Among other things, courts must defend against the normalization of broad restrictions or suspensions of public protest activities by applying First Amendment standards even during emergencies and crises. Precedents established during one type of disaster, such as those upholding curfews after a natural disaster, should not be automatically applied to restrictions on protest during more extended emergencies or crises where public protest rights are more centrally implicated.

Rejection of the "suspension" approach or model ought to extend not only to executive public health decrees, but also to the actions of federal, state, and local law enforcement officials who are responsible for policing public protest during civil unrest. A declared "emergency" does not license anyone, including the President of the United States, to "dominate" public protesters or treat them as enemies of the state. Assessments of law enforcement's performance during the mass racial justice protests confirm that law enforcement continues to treat public forums as "battlespaces" necessitating militarization and the use of force.

Government officials who view public protest itself as a form of unlawful agitation and a threat to public safety will likely continue to rely on broad restrictions on protest and the use of unlawful force. Internal and external checks on emergency powers are needed to reign in executive and law enforcement power, or at least inform the exercise of that power. Karen Loor, who has studied emergency management and civil liberties, has proposed a "council" made up of police representatives, local civil rights attorneys, and others who can work in advance to establish protocols for responding to emergencies, with an emphasis on preserving protest and other rights during any declared emergency.[167]

Finally, federal interventions in local protests should be minimized. Constitutional and legal arguments for limiting some of these interventions face some strong headwinds. As former President Trump's statements and actions showed, presidents can generally find a plausible enough reason to deploy federal forces to local protest sites. But they ought to exercise that power sparingly, and with respect for state and local power to enforce criminal laws. Federal interventions ought to be reserved for instances when states and localities truly need, and preferably request, federal aid to restore public order. Federal agents and active-duty military personnel should be found at protest venues only in the most extraordinary circumstances. Further, application of federal laws such as the Anti-Riot Act, Civil Obedience Act, and Sedition Act should likewise be reserved for clear instances in which some federal interest is implicated. When deploying federal forces and invoking federal laws, policymakers must keep in mind that preserving public protest is also in the national interest.

8

Protesters' Remedies

Chapter 4 examined the "costs of dissent," or monetary outlays and costs that can chill public protest. This chapter looks in the opposite direction, to the legal remedies potentially available to protesters when governments violate their First Amendment and other rights. Injunctive relief may be available, under the standards and doctrines discussed so far. But this chapter focuses primarily on civil actions for damages against law enforcement and governments. Like the imposition of costs, access to these remedies significantly affects public protest. Remedies determine whether individuals can be made whole in the event their rights are violated during a public protest. They also help deter unconstitutional conduct by law enforcement, municipal governments, and other actors. The principal (though as we will see not sole) obstacle to remedying protesters' constitutional harms is "qualified immunity," a doctrine that shields all but the least competent officials from monetary liability.[1] The chapter advocates qualified immunity abolition or reform. It also discusses other remedies available to injured protesters, including claims under state civil rights laws and constitutional provisions.

PROTESTER REMEDIES AND GOVERNMENTAL IMMUNITIES

Protesters injured during a demonstration or other event can bring various legal claims against those responsible for their injuries. The focus here will be on claims protesters might bring against government defendants who violate their First Amendment or Fourth Amendment rights. These defendants include state and local officials, local governments, and federal officials involved in protest policing.

Potential Remedies

There are two general types of remedies protesters can pursue: injunctive relief and monetary damages. Protesters can file lawsuits asking courts to enjoin unconstitutional policing methods. For example, BLM protesters sought an injunction against D.C. and federal law enforcement's use of pepper spray and other non-lethal weapons against peaceful protesters. Whether such relief is available depends on the application of the First Amendment doctrines and standards examined in earlier chapters, which determine the scope of speech and assembly rights. Protesters may also allege violations of Fourth Amendment rights, including the use of excessive force and wrongful arrest.

Injunctive relief is an important, mostly forward-looking remedy. However, an injunction does not compensate protesters for physical and other harms sustained because of law enforcement misconduct. The other kind of relief protesters can seek is monetary damages against individual officials (and their government employers) for constitutional violations. Both 42 U.S.C. § 1983 and the Supreme Court's decision in *Bivens v. Six Unknown Named Agents of Federal Bureau of Narcotics* allow individuals to sue government officials for monetary damages for constitutional torts (injuries stemming from violations of constitutional rights).[2] Section 1983 applies to state officials, while *Bivens* applies to federal officials. Section 1983 explicitly authorizes constitutional claims against state officials, while *Bivens* implies such claims from constitutional rights provisions.[3]

Monetary relief compensates injured protesters for physical, economic, and other tangible harms. As in other contexts, damages for constitutional violations are intended to make injured parties whole. These damages include not only monetary and out-of-pocket expenditures, but also recovery for pain and suffering, and for emotional distress. Because damages are often the only available remedy after a constitutional violation has occurred, as the Supreme Court has recognized they are "a vital component of any scheme for vindicating cherished constitutional guarantees."[4] When plaintiffs prevail in federal civil rights lawsuits, they are also entitled to recover attorneys' fees.

Protesters may also sue under state civil rights laws, which in most cases mirror the protection of Section 1983 for federal constitutional violations under analogous state provisions. They can also bring a variety of state common law personal injury claims against law enforcement officers including assault, battery, false arrest, damages to property, and infliction of emotional distress. Protesters can bring all these claims as part of a single federal civil rights lawsuit or file separate actions. Their state constitutional and statutory claims are governed by state-level requirements and judicial precedents.

The remedial menu sounds expansive. However, as will soon become apparent, protesters' federal and state claims for monetary damages brought against government officials and institutions at all levels are substantially constrained by "qualified immunity" and other liability-limiting doctrines. Protesters injured while engaged in lawful and peaceful expressive activities will often find it difficult or even impossible to hold government officials accountable for their actions.

"Qualified Immunity"

Both Section 1983 and *Bivens* liability are significantly limited by immunity and other doctrines. Under certain conditions, government officials sued under these authorities are entitled to what is known as "qualified immunity."

Qualified immunity is a judicially created doctrine that shields government officials from being held personally liable for First Amendment and other constitutional violations, so long as the officials did not violate "clearly established" law (more on that concept later). When government officials are sued, qualified immunity functions as an affirmative defense they can raise, barring damages even if they committed unlawful acts. (Qualified immunity is not, however, a defense to claims for injunctive relief.) As a general matter, qualified immunity grants officials broad legal protection against civil rights claims. In most states, civil rights actions are similarly limited by a qualified immunity doctrine.

Under past Supreme Court precedents, whether a defendant was entitled to qualified immunity turned on the "subjective good faith" of the official who committed the alleged violation.[5] In 1982, the Supreme Court replaced that standard with a new test framed in "objective terms."[6] Under the new test, officials are relieved of monetary liability when their conduct "does not violate clearly established statutory or constitutional rights of which a reasonable person would have known."[7] Thus, according to the Court, "[i]f the law was clearly established, the immunity defense ordinarily should fail, since a reasonably competent public official should know the law governing his conduct."[8] But the Court made clear its new standard was intended to be more protective of government officials than the "good faith" test. As it observed, qualified immunity "provides ample protection to all but the plainly incompetent or those who knowingly violate the law."[9] Although the standard "provides no license to lawless conduct," it shields officials from liability so long as they acted in an objectively reasonable manner.[10]

Since the Court adopted its "objective" test, it has applied the doctrine in several ways that have made it more favorable to government defendants. First, it has required that plaintiffs show "clearly established" law placed the defendants on notice that their actions violated the Constitution. This "law" consists of the Court's precedents and those from the relevant judicial circuit (and perhaps other circuits). As the Court has explained, "For a right to be 'clearly established,' the law must have been sufficiently clear, at the time of the official's conduct, to put every reasonable official on notice that what he was doing violated that right."[11] Existing precedent must place the matter "beyond debate."[12] Moreover, the Court has instructed that courts cannot establish law "at a high level of generality."[13] While the plaintiff need not present earlier cases with "fundamentally similar" facts to defeat qualified immunity, the Court has indicated such authority provides "especially strong support for a conclusion that the law is clearly established."[14] Under this standard, a protester who alleged that resort to a particular protest policing method violated "clearly established" law would need to point to published precedents which, at the time, put law enforcement on notice that use of the method violated the First Amendment.

Second, the Court has altered the way in which lower courts analyze qualified immunity claims. In a 2001 decision, the Court held that when assessing a qualified immunity defense courts must first determine whether there was a violation of a constitutional right and only then consider whether the law in question was clearly established.[15] However, in 2009, the Court decided that lower courts could grant qualified immunity based only on the "clearly established" determination – without ever determining if there was an actual constitutional violation.[16] This change created a "Catch-22" for civil rights plaintiffs. If courts resolve a case based on the lack of "clearly established" authority, there will be fewer precedents finding constitutional violations. That situation, in turn, makes it more likely there will be no "clearly established" law. Some recent studies have shown this is precisely what is happening in lower court litigation.[17]

Third, the Court's conception of the "reasonable officer" has shifted over time, in ways that again favor government officials. As noted earlier, the Court famously stated that qualified immunity protects "all but the plainly incompetent or those who knowingly violate the law."[18] Since that statement, the Court has held that a defendant's conduct is to be judged on the basis of "any reasonable officer"[19] or "every reasonable official."[20] As one scholar has observed, that shift means "that in order for a plaintiff to overcome qualified immunity, the right violated must be so clear that its violation in the plaintiff's case would have been obvious not just to the average 'reasonable officer' but to the *least informed, least reasonable* 'reasonable officer.'"[21]

The Supreme Court has offered several justifications for recognizing qualified immunity. In general, it has asserted qualified immunity achieves a "balance" between allowing victims to hold officials accountable and minimizing "social costs" to "society as a whole."[22] Noting that "claims frequently run against the innocent, as well as the guilty," the "social costs" the Court has stated must be considered include "the expenses of litigation, the diversion of official energy from pressing public issues, and the deterrence of able citizens from acceptance of public office."[23] As the Court has explained, "Where the defendant seeks qualified immunity, a ruling on that issue should be made early in the proceedings so that the costs and expenses of a trial are avoided where the defense is dispositive."[24] Qualified immunity, the Court has explained, is "an immunity from suit rather than a mere defense to liability; and like an absolute immunity, it is effectively lost if a case is erroneously permitted to go to trial."[25] The Court has also cited "the danger that fear of being sued will 'dampen the ardor of all but the most resolute, or the most irresponsible [public officials], in the unflinching discharge of their duties.'"[26]

In addition to consideration of these social costs, the Court has defended qualified immunity on the ground that it would be unfair to hold government officials to constitutional rules they were not aware of at the time of the violation. It first articulated this idea in an early decision stating that "[a] policeman's lot is not so unhappy that he must choose between being charged with dereliction of duty if he does not arrest when he has probable cause, and being mulcted in damages if he does."[27] Later, the Court wrote, "If the law at that time was not clearly established, an official could not reasonably be expected to anticipate subsequent legal developments, nor could he fairly be said to 'know' that the law forbade conduct not previously identified as unlawful."[28] Reflecting these concerns, the Court has described "the focus" of qualified immunity as "whether the officer had fair notice that her conduct was unlawful."[29]

In sum, as the Supreme Court has explained, "the doctrine of qualified immunity gives government officials breathing room to make reasonable but mistaken judgments about open legal questions."[30] However, as discussed later, critics have mounted strong challenges to the Court's justifications for qualified immunity and the doctrine itself.[31]

Municipal Liability

The qualified immunity doctrine, as described, applies to claims against *individual* government officials. Protesters can also sue municipalities, counties, and other government bodies under Section 1983. These institutions have deeper pockets than individual officers. In some cases, they may be the principal source of the alleged constitutional violation.

In *Monell v. Department of Social Services* (1978), the Supreme Court held that a municipal government can be held liable under Section 1983 if a plaintiff can demonstrate that a deprivation of a federal right occurred because of a "policy or custom" of the local government's legislative body (or of local officials whose acts may fairly be said to be those of the municipality).[32] Municipalities can only be held liable if one of their employees has committed a constitutional violation. However, they cannot be held liable under Section 1983 for the actions of their employees simply because of their employment status: again, an employee must be acting pursuant to a municipal policy, custom, or practice.

The municipal liability standard has produced a complex, stringent, and heavily criticized doctrine. As one commentator has observed, "Th[e] doctrine of municipal liability is convoluted and can require difficult inquiries into which city officials are 'policymakers' under state law on local government, into whether a[n] official was acting in a 'local' or 'state' capacity, into the extent of departmental 'custom' authorizing constitutional violations, into individual cities' training and hiring processes, and into demanding questions about causation and fault."[33]

"*Monell* liability" is thus very difficult for civil rights plaintiffs to establish. It is particularly difficult to prevail on one claim relevant to many protesters' injuries – the failure of a municipality to train its officers to police public protests and demonstrations.[34] As mentioned throughout the book, protest policing has been a recurring issue with police forces across the nation. The Supreme Court has noted "the inadequacy of police training may serve as the basis for § 1983 liability," but "only where the failure to train amounts to *deliberate indifference* to the rights of persons with whom the police come into contact."[35] The Court has narrowly defined the types of training relevant to this claim and required that plaintiffs prove nearly identical past misconduct.[36] Lower courts have also rejected municipal liability based on findings of qualified immunity for individual officers, a form of what one scholar has described as "backdoor municipal immunity."[37]

The upshot of qualified and municipal liability doctrines is that it is very difficult for protesters and others who suffer constitutional wrongs to hold officials and municipalities accountable under Section 1983. These legal doctrines establish a kind of "local sovereign immunity."[38]

First Amendment "Retaliation" Claims

Qualified immunity is just one of several judicially implied doctrines that limit or defeat civil rights claims against government officials. The Supreme Court has also recognized some additional defenses and immunities that can affect public protester claims. One of those limits relates to Section 1983 First Amendment "retaliation" claims.

The First Amendment prohibits government officials from subjecting individuals to retaliatory actions for engaging in protected speech.[39] To succeed on a First Amendment retaliation claim, plaintiffs must prove (1) they engaged in a constitutionally protected activity; (2) the defendant's actions would "chill a person or ordinary firmness" from continuing to engage in the protected activity; and (3) the protected activity was a substantial motivating factor in the defendant's conduct – i.e., that there was a nexus between the defendant's actions and the intent to chill speech.[40] Proving a retaliatory motive is not sufficient. The speaker must show that the adverse action would not have been taken absent the official's retaliatory motive.[41]

For example, suppose a participant arrested at a public protest claimed law enforcement restricted or suppressed speech in retaliation for the message conveyed. To prevail, the plaintiff would have to show the officer would not have arrested them or interfered with their protected speech "but for" the retaliatory reason. If the officer could show the protester was obstructing traffic or there was some other nonretaliatory reason for the arrest, the First Amendment claim would fail.

One longstanding issue in retaliation cases was whether the existence of probable cause to arrest the speaker *precluded* a First Amendment retaliation claim. In *Nieves v. Bartlett* (2019), the Supreme Court answered that question in the affirmative. In *Nieves*, the Court upheld the dismissal of a First Amendment retaliation claim brought by an individual arrested at a festival after he exchanged heated words with officers assigned to police the event.[42] The Court held that where speakers allege officers arrested them in retaliation for their exercise of First Amendment activities, probable cause for the arrest is generally a complete defense.[43]

The *Nieves* majority was concerned that officers, who must often make "split-second" decisions when deciding whether to arrest, will sometimes rely on the suspect's protected speech in doing so. The Court also reasoned that determining whether the arrest was in retaliation for the speech in such cases would often be difficult. Thus, it concluded plaintiffs should be required in retaliation cases to plead and prove the arrest was objectively unreasonable before inquiring into the official's subjective mental state.

The *Nieves* rule applies to a variety of free speech contexts. But the majority justified it with a protest-related example. The Court was concerned, it said, that "policing certain events like an unruly protest would pose overwhelming litigation risks" for officers who arrest participants.[44] "Any inartful turn of phrase or perceived slight during a legitimate arrest," the Court worried, "could land an officer in years of litigation."[45] The Court worried officers would be deterred from discharging their duties or "would simply minimize their communications during arrests to avoid having their words scrutinized for hints of improper motive – a result that would leave everyone worse off."[46]

The rule that probable cause to arrest defeats a First Amendment retaliation claim is subject to narrow exceptions. The Court recognized state laws give officers broad discretion to charge speakers for even minor offenses, which could lead to abuses a probable cause requirement might fail to identify. An officer might arrest a vocal protester for jaywalking, for example, but not arrest others for the same conduct. To prevent such abuses, the Court concluded "the no-probable cause rule should not apply when a plaintiff presents objective evidence that he was arrested *when otherwise similarly situated individuals not engaged in the same sort of protected speech had not been*."[47] If a plaintiff produces this comparative evidence the burden shifts to the official to show some non-retaliatory basis for the arrest.

Prior to *Nieves*, the Court had recognized another narrow exception to the probable cause requirement. If a municipality adopts an official policy of retaliation against a speaker or group, the Court has held, it may be held liable even if there is probable cause to arrest the speaker. "[W]hen retaliation against protected speech is elevated to the level of official policy," the Court reasoned, "there is a compelling need for adequate avenues of redress."[48]

Official policies targeting protesters are likely to be rare. Even assuming this exception survives *Nieves*, it will apply only in exceptional situations where a governmental body adopts a policy of retaliating against an individual or group for protected expressive activities.[49] Protesters are far more likely to be subject to arrest by individual officers, as was the case in *Nieves*, than to be subject to such targeted policies.

First Amendment Bivens *Claims*

The Supreme Court has also imposed strict limits on damages claims against *federal* officials. Recall from Chapter 7's discussion that federal agents from various agencies were dispatched to the streets during the 2020 racial justice protests. As noted earlier, in *Bivens* the Court implied a cause of action for damages against federal officials who violate federal constitutional rights.[50] In *Bivens*, the claim was based on a violation of the Fourth Amendment's prohibition on unreasonable searches and seizures. For now, Fourth Amendment claims like the one in *Bivens* would seem to be viable. But there are serious questions concerning the viability of First Amendment *Bivens* claims.

In a series of recent cases, the Court has expressed concerns about *Bivens* liability in general and the expansion of such liability into what it considers new contexts. Regarding the cause of action, according to the Court *Bivens* and its progeny "were the products of an era when the Court routinely inferred causes of action that were not explicit in the text of the provision that was allegedly violated."[51] The Court has criticized this "ancien regime," noting that "[i]n later years, we came to appreciate more fully the tension between this practice and the Constitution's separation of legislative and judicial power."[52] Accordingly, "for almost 40 years," the Court has "consistently rebuffed requests to add to the claims allowed under *Bivens*."[53]

In 2017, the Court outlined a two-step framework intended to limit the expansion of *Bivens* remedies.[54] Under this framework, a court must first consider whether a case "arises in a new context or involves a new category of defendants."[55] The Court's "understanding of a new context is broad."[56] The standard is whether "the case is different in a meaningful way from previous *Bivens* cases" decided by the Court.[57] If so, the court must "ask whether there are any special factors that counsel hesitation about granting the extension."[58] "Special factors" are rooted in concerns about the separation of powers among the branches of the federal government. They include, but are not limited to, the existence of alternative remedies and respect for coordinate branches of government. Thus, a court must "consider the risk of interfering with the authority of the other branches, ... ask whether there are sound reasons to think Congress might doubt the efficacy or necessity of a damages remedy, and whether the Judiciary is well suited, absent congressional action or instruction, to consider and weigh the costs and benefits of allowing a damages action to proceed."[59] If any factor causes a court to hesitate, it should "reject the request" to recognize the *Bivens* claim.[60]

Although it has characterized the inquiry as occurring in two steps, the Court's most recent decision clarified, "those steps often resolve to a single question: whether there is any reason to think that Congress might be better equipped to create a damages remedy."[61] Thus, "[a] court faces only one question: whether there is any rational reason (even one) to think that Congress is better suited to "weigh the costs and benefits of allowing a damages action to proceed."[62]

The Court has described the expansion of *Bivens* as "a disfavored judicial activity."[63] Although it has assumed some First Amendment claims may be brought under *Bivens*, the Court has never expressly held as much and, moreover, has expressed skepticism regarding such claims.[64]

In *Egbert v. Boule*, its most recent *Bivens* decision, the Court rejected a First Amendment retaliation claim against federal border agents.[65] The Court reiterated that it had never held that *Bivens* extends to First Amendment claims. It rejected an "action for First Amendment retaliation." The Court reasoned that such claims were likely to be costly because retaliation is easy to allege but difficult to disprove, and Congress was in a better position to assess those costs and determine whether to authorize the action.[66] As discussed later, lower courts have disagreed about the viability of First Amendment *Bivens* claims. Although *Egbert* does not rule out *all* First Amendment *Bivens* claims, there appears to be a strong presumption against their recognition.

* * * * * *

In sum, protesters seeking monetary remedies against state, local, or federal officials for First Amendment violations face several obstacles. Qualified immunity excuses all but the most egregious and "clearly established" First Amendment violations. Municipal liability claims are very difficult to prove. *Nieves* imposes a separate probable cause defense against claims based on allegations of retaliatory arrest for protected speech. Finally, the Court has consistently rejected *Bivens* claims beyond those it has already recognized and suggested it will not recognize any First Amendment claims against federal officials.

HOW GOVERNMENT IMMUNITIES IMPACT PROTESTER CLAIMS

This section critically analyzes the effects of the foregoing immunities and defenses on protesters' remedies for First Amendment and Fourth Amendment violations. The analysis is based on three sets of data concerning protest-related cases involving immunity claims or defenses:[67] (a) Section 1983 and *Bivens*-related qualified immunity decisions from 1982, when the Supreme Court adopted the objective "clearly established law" standard, to 2022; (b) decisions applying the *Nieves v. Bartlett* probable cause defense; and (c) *Bivens* decisions since 1971. This qualified immunity data tracked both First Amendment and Fourth Amendment claims. My research confirms that qualified immunity does not serve the policy goal of weeding claims out for early dismissal.[68] However, it also confirms that the opportunities for recovery by protesters are quite limited. Substantively, the data identify which First Amendment and Fourth Amendment protest rights have been "clearly established," and which have not been. These findings help clarify an important aspect of the law of public protest. The data further reveal that *Nieves* will likely have a devastating effect on protesters' First Amendment retaliation claims. Finally, although my examination shows lower courts have long entertained First Amendment *Bivens* claims in the protest context, the Supreme Court's most recent decisions likely require the dismissal of such claims.

Qualified Immunity Protest Cases

As discussed, the doctrine of qualified immunity poses a substantial obstacle to protesters' recovery from state and local officials for constitutional injuries. Those injuries include physical and other injuries resulting from aggressive protest policing and wrongful arrest. A review of qualified immunity decisions in protest-related cases shows the defense has not generally served the goal of weeding out cases at the earliest stage of litigation. However, as the doctrine suggests it would be, qualified immunity has been a substantial obstacle to recovery except in the clearest cases of constitutional violation.[69]

The qualified immunity data include 223 final decisions since 1982 by federal district courts and courts of appeals in which protesters pursued First Amendment, Fourth Amendment, and other constitutional claims against individual officials under either Section 1983 or *Bivens*. The study did not specially address claims of municipal liability. In the individual liability cases, plaintiffs pursued 206 First Amendment claims, 136 4th Amendment claims, and four other constitutional claims.

Focusing on the First Amendment cases, defendants brought 69 motions to dismiss claims based on qualified immunity (Table 8.1). Courts denied those motions in 50 cases, or 72 percent of the time. They granted early motions to dismiss in just 19 cases, or 28 percent of the time. The data clearly show that the goal of avoiding the cost of litigating official liability for damages through early dismissal has not been achieved.

Defendants were far more successful at the summary judgment stage, winning 61 percent of their motions (84/137) and losing 39 percent of the time (53/137). Thus, once some evidence had been presented and courts were asked to rule on the qualified immunity defense, defendants frequently prevailed. This was either because the court determined no First Amendment violation had occurred or there was no "clearly established" law on the matter.

Taking both kinds of motions into account, fully half of protesters' First Amendment claims were dismissed on qualified immunity grounds. Again, those

TABLE 8.1 *First Amendment qualified immunity claims*

Posture	QI Denied	QI Granted	Total
MTD	50 (72%)	19 (28%)	69
SJ	53 (39%)	84 (61%)	137

TABLE 8.2 *Fourth Amendment qualified immunity claims*

Posture	QI Denied	QI Granted	Total
MTD	30 (68%)	14 (32%)	44
SJ	40 (43%)	52 (57%)	92

numbers are skewed given the apparent judicial reluctance to grant early dismissal on qualified immunity grounds. My data only speak to the disposition of motions to dismiss and for summary judgment. Of course, just because courts denied qualified immunity motions and allowed First Amendment claims to proceed to trial does not mean protesters ultimately prevailed and received compensation for constitutional injuries. The data only speak to whether courts considered the claims viable enough to defeat a motion to dismiss or for summary judgment.

The data show similar results in terms of protesters' Fourth Amendment claims for wrongful arrest, excessive force, and other violations (Table 8.2). Defendants were successful at the motion to dismiss stage in just 32 percent of cases (14/44) and lost these motions 68 percent of the time (30/44). At summary judgment, however, defendants won 57 percent of their motions (52/92) and lost only 43 percent of the time (40/92). Overall, qualified immunity defeated nearly half of protesters' Fourth Amendment claims.

Since they focus only on final court decisions concerning specific types of claims, my data are far more limited than studies of court dockets including *all* qualified immunity cases filed in specified jurisdictions.[70] My specific and more limited goal is to shed light on the application of qualified immunity to constitutional claims brought by public protesters. Nevertheless, my results are broadly consistent with studies of larger data sets insofar as they indicate qualified immunity (1) does not generally, as the Supreme Court surmised it would, relieve officials of the burdens of constitutional litigation and (2) is a significant although not an absolute bar to recovery.

As discussed earlier, under qualified immunity doctrine, plaintiffs' success depends on demonstrating a constitutional violation occurred and "clearly established" law indicating any reasonable officer would have known their actions violated protesters' First Amendment or Fourth Amendment rights. My study of published decisions indicates that protesters are most likely to succeed in defeating qualified immunity only when government officials engage in the most egregious types of constitutional violations.

The following are examples, drawn from the judicial decisions in the study, of "clearly established" First Amendment and/or Fourth Amendment violations in the public protest context:

- Banning *all* protest activities in a traditional public forum such as a public street or public park, absent evidence of the commission of a crime or unlawful expression;
- Banning *all* distribution of literature in traditional public forums;

- Using non-lethal force such as pepper spray, tear gas, or rubber bullets against non-resisting peaceful protesters;
- Mass arrests of protesters absent evidence the group is engaged in unlawful activity;
- "Herding" or "kettling" protest participants who have not engaged in any unlawful or violent acts;
- Arresting protesters who are in a public place pursuant to a valid permit without first giving them notice of revocation or permission to protest;
- Confiscating protesters' signs or other belongings prior to an event;
- Arresting protesters or press members for recording police activities at a public event;
- Using tear gas and other law enforcement tactics to interfere with reporting on public protests;
- Pointing a red laser from a sniper rifle at a protester engaged in lawful expression;
- Using long-range acoustic devices to disperse peaceful protesters;
- Arresting a protester who burns an American flag to express an opinion;
- Arresting a protester for verbally criticizing or challenging a police officer;
- Arresting or otherwise retaliating against protesters based on the content of their expression;
- Imposing a preclearance requirement (prior restraint) for speakers seeking to address certain audiences; and
- Arresting protesters for demonstrating based on non-existent time, place, and manner regulation.

As the doctrine suggests, qualified immunity does not protect law enforcement when they violate the fundamental or core rights necessary to engage in public protest. Thus, courts have found protesters have "clearly established" First Amendment and Fourth Amendment rights to engage in peaceful, non-violent expression in "traditional" public forums – public streets, parks, and sidewalks. Courts have recognized that simply banning all expression in such places is a patent violation of the First Amendment. Several decisions also condemned aggressive law enforcement tactics used against peaceful, non-violent protesters. Courts have also enforced the cardinal free speech principle of content neutrality, finding that officials who suppress or regulate speech based on its content have violated clearly established First Amendment law. Finally, some courts denied qualified immunity to officers and officials who arrested or used force against protesters or press members recording their protest policing activities. As we will see, however, not all courts agree there is a "clearly established" First Amendment right to record.

While these recognized protest rights are critically important, qualified immunity continues to shield officials from liability when they inflict clear constitutional injuries. Decisions granting qualified immunity show that outside the bare minimum conditions identified, protesters' claims are more likely to be defeated. When the violation is not patently obvious or the First Amendment right in question turns to some degree on context, courts have often granted motions to dismiss or for summary judgment based on qualified immunity.

Courts have concluded the following actions did *not* violate any right and/or did not violate clearly established First Amendment or Fourth Amendment rights:

- Enforcing an unlawful permit ordinance;
- Using non-lethal force, including pepper spray and tear gas, against protesters who refuse to disperse after being ordered to do so;
- Arresting protesters for verbally criticizing police officers;
- Establishing a viewpoint-discriminatory security perimeter;
- Ordering pro-life protesters to relocate signs displaying aborted fetuses under a distracted driving ordinance;
- Arresting a protester for leading the chant, "Two, four, six, eight, fuck the police state;"
- Banning leafletting on a postal sidewalk on income tax day;
- Arresting a protester for projecting messages onto a government building;
- Arresting protesters for demonstrating in public wearing thong underwear;
- Removing a protester from a public park for loudly singing a song with lyrics advocating violence against gay people;
- Imposing a nighttime curfew on protests;
- Arresting a protester for burning the Mexican flag in public;
- Arresting protesters who carried "fake guns" to a protest at the state capitol;
- Issuing a "stand down" order instructing officers not to intervene in the event of violent confrontations between protesters and counter-protesters;
- Interrupting conversations between reporters and protesters during a demonstration; and
- Preventing the video- or audio-recording of police as they interact with protesters (according to one court, there is a lack of "robust consensus" that there is such a First Amendment right).

As these decisions confirm, qualified immunity shields law enforcement and other officials from liability even for plain First Amendment and other constitutional violations so long as their actions are not plainly incompetent or malicious. The qualified immunity determinations accept law enforcement's broad discretion to arrest protesters for public disorder offenses. Note in several cases even content-based speech restrictions were excused, owing to the absence of "clearly established" law prohibiting them under the specific circumstances. The First Amendment plainly protects verbally criticizing police officers, leading chants critical of the police, singing violent lyrics, and demonstrating in one's underwear. Yet protesters lawfully engaged in these activities were denied relief.

As critics of qualified immunity have complained, there are also problems of uncertainty and inconsistency in the application of the doctrine. As the two lists show, courts have adopted both broad and narrow conceptions of the protest rights at issue. Sometimes, though not in all instances, they have demanded plaintiffs identify factually similar or even factually identical precedents to defeat qualified immunity. Thus, whether and to what extent a protester has a "clearly established" right to verbally criticize police, assemble in a public place, or record protest policing activity can vary from jurisdiction to jurisdiction. Protesters thus cannot be certain they possess even these basic First Amendment rights in all locations.

The Fourth Amendment qualified immunity cases similarly confirm that law enforcement has broad discretion to manage dissent through the enforcement of public order laws. Courts relied on allegations or evidence of probable cause to arrest protesters for disorderly conduct, failure to disperse, unlawful assembly, and other public order offenses. One aspect of the Fourth Amendment cases worth noting is that the law remains unsettled regarding whether the use of tear gas and other means to disperse protesters constitutes a "seizure" under the Fourth Amendment.[71] Thus, protesters making that argument will likely find no "clearly established" law on the matter.

Finally, in terms of municipal liability protesters bringing First Amendment and Fourth Amendment claims were rarely successful in efforts to impose liability. Courts found an absence of "official policies" and typically rejected "failure to train" claims. As in other contexts, imposition of *Monell* liability is rare in public protest litigation.

To summarize: The Supreme Court's "objective" qualified immunity standard has not led to law enforcement and other official success in terms of having claims dismissed at early stages of litigation. However, data show the standard operates as a significant obstacle to recovery by protesters once at the summary judgment stage. Thus, for plaintiffs whose claims reach that stage, there is a high probability their constitutional claims will be dismissed. Protesters have been able to pursue remedies for First Amendment and Fourth Amendment injuries only when officials have engaged in egregious and blatant violations: banning protest in public forums, using force against law-abiding and compliant protesters, and engaging in content-based discrimination. In many other contexts, courts found no violation or, more frequently, that even if a violation occurred the law was not "clearly established." Protesters were also generally unable to pursue claims against municipalities.

Protester First Amendment Retaliation Cases

As discussed earlier, in *Nieves v. Bartlett* (2019) the Supreme Court held that probable cause to arrest generally bars a Section 1983 First Amendment "retaliation" claim. To overcome this defense, plaintiffs must present "objective evidence that [they were] arrested when otherwise similarly situated individuals not engaged in the same sort of protected speech had not been."[72] As applied so far, *Nieves* has presented a strong defense to protesters' First Amendment retaliation claims.

My study indicated there have been 32 explicit applications of the probable cause defense in protest-related cases, including *Nieves*, since the Court announced its approach.[73] In 19 of those cases, or 60 percent of the time, the plaintiff's First Amendment retaliation claim was dismissed. In dismissing the First Amendment claims, courts found probable cause to arrest protesters for a variety of minor public disorder offenses, including trespass, obstructing traffic, breach of peace, disorderly conduct, defacing public property, and unlawful assembly.[74]

Courts applied or discussed the disparate treatment exception, which again requires evidence that similarly situated individuals were not arrested, in only seven cases. The Ninth Circuit found in one case that the plaintiff had presented such evidence and was thus entitled to summary judgment on the retaliation claim.[75] Notably, in that case, the plaintiffs demonstrated that *no one* had ever been arrested for the offense specified – chalking public property. This was akin to arresting a protester, but literally no one else, for jaywalking. In three other cases, courts found insufficient evidence of disparate treatment. In two cases, courts concluded in dicta there was either some or no evidence of disparate treatment by law enforcement but did not find it dispositive. In one case, a court opined that the argument would likely have succeeded but the *Nieves* principles itself was not "clearly established" at the time of the arrest.

The data, though preliminary, confirm some of the concerns expressed by the dissenting Justices in *Nieves*. In his partial dissent, Justice Gorsuch observed:

> History shows that governments sometimes seek to regulate our lives finely, acutely, thoroughly, and exhaustively. In our own time and place, criminal laws have grown so exuberantly and come to cover so much previously innocent conduct that almost anyone can be arrested for something. If the state could use these laws not for their intended purposes but to silence those with unpopular ideas, little would be left of our First Amendment liberties, and little would separate us from the tyrannies of the past or the malignant fiefdoms of our own age. The freedom to speak without risking arrest "is one of the principal characteristics by which we distinguish a free nation."[76]

In various protest contexts, plaintiffs' retaliation claims have been stymied by judicial findings of probable cause to arrest. The nature of the charges also substantiates Justice Gorsuch's concern about the expansive scope of criminal laws. Charges that defeated First Amendment retaliation claims under *Nieves* included many of the usual suspects criticized in previous chapters as part of the system of managed dissent. Thus, these "public disorder" offenses affect protest rights both in the moment and after the fact, at the remedial stage.

Post-*Nieves* results also suggest a wooden application of the probable cause defense rather than a more "common sense" application.[77] In her dissent, Justice Sotomayor took aim at the exception to the probable cause rule. She characterized it as unclear and irrational and expressed concern it would lead to perverse results. Which protesters, she wondered, would be "otherwise similarly situated" to the plaintiff? Further, under the Court's approach protesters who have more direct evidence of retaliatory motive, including officers' own statements, cannot rely on it but must instead produce hard-to-come-by comparison-based evidence.[78] Justice Sotomayor also worried that the majority's approach would "breed opportunities for the rare ill-intentioned officer to violate the First Amendment without consequence – and, in some cases, openly and unabashedly."[79] For example, "a particularly brazen officer could arrest on transparently speech-based grounds and check the statute books later for a potential justification."[80]

Justice Sotomayor surmised that plaintiffs who can satisfy the *Nieves* exception "predominantly will be arrestees singled out at protests or other large public gatherings, where a robust pool of potential comparators happens to be within earshot, eyeshot, or camera-shot."[81] But as the cases thus far show, even *those* plaintiffs will usually be hard-pressed to cull the necessary comparative evidence from chaotic mass protest environments. Moreover, the comparative exception incentivizes harmful protest policing activities that are already unfortunately prevalent, including "kettling" all participants regardless of specific offense, using tear gas and other force indiscriminately, and engaging in mass arrests. If *all* protesters are treated this way, the *Nieves* exception will not apply. As the early results suggest it will be the very rare case indeed in which a protester can muster the necessary evidence to proceed with, much less prevail in, a First Amendment retaliatory arrest claim. There will, as Justice Sotomayor warned, be "little daylight between the comparison-based standard the Court adopts and the absolute bar it ostensibly rejects."[82]

None of the separate opinions in *Nieves* brought up the potential for racial or viewpoint disparity in retaliatory arrests. But these possibilities ought not to be discounted. Setting up probable cause as a general bar to First Amendment retaliation claims may disparately affect protesters of color, who as discussed elsewhere in the book are more likely to be arrested for minor offenses such as disorderly conduct and unlawful assembly. Further, as Justice Sotomayor observed, the approach adopted in *Nieves* generally ignores the problem of pretextual arrests.[83]

Justice Gorsuch noted still another general shortcoming of the *Nieves* approach. He asserted that by folding free speech claims into the unreasonable arrest inquiry the Court had made a category error. As Justice Gorsuch explained, "the First Amendment operates independently of the Fourth and provides different protections. It seeks not to ensure lawful authority to arrest but to protect the freedom of speech."[84] By giving so much weight to the existence of probable cause to arrest protesters, the Court elided important free speech claims and interests.

To Justice Gorsuch's point that the First Amendment serves values separate and apart from Fourth Amendment probable cause limits, we ought not to lose sight of the protest activity affected by the dismissal of First Amendment retaliation claims. In post-*Nieves* cases, the activity included petition signature collection, public preaching, singing, recording of protest arrests, and political protests involving LGBTQ rights, Occupy Wall Street, the Dakota Access Pipeline, BLM, Juneteenth, and removal of Confederate monuments. All of this activity implicates fundamental free speech and public assembly rights. Similarly, the *Nieves* rule makes it more difficult for reporters and members of the media who cover public protests to demonstrate they were arrested in retaliation for press activities.[85] *Nieves* encourages lower courts to focus on the legitimacy of the arrest to the near exclusion of free speech, assembly, and press concerns.[86]

Protesters' First Amendment Claims Against Federal Officials

Public protests are commonly policed and managed by state and local officials. These officials and their employers are the most likely defendants in civil rights lawsuits. However, the Secret Service, National Park Service, and other federal agencies and officials may also be involved in policing protest. As discussed in Chapter 7, during the 2020 racial justice protests the Trump Administration dispatched federal agents from multiple agencies to Portland and other cities. Although First Amendment *Bivens* claims against federal officials are relatively rare, the BLM protests showed how they might become more prevalent.

As noted earlier, although the Court has recognized some claims under the Fourth Amendment it has never expressly recognized a First Amendment *Bivens* claim. In several recent decisions, the Court has expressed skepticism about the viability of such claims. As discussed, in *Egbert v. Boule* (2022), the Court expressly rejected a First Amendment retaliation claim against federal agents because Congress was in the best position to determine whether such a claim should exist. That same logic may also doom any First Amendment claims brought by protesters injured at the hands of federal law enforcement or other officials.

Before interring such claims, it is worth considering how the lower courts have treated them. In a variety of contexts, lower courts have disagreed about the viability of First Amendment *Bivens* claims.[87] Given the Court's instruction to assess any "special factors" that might suggest such claims are inappropriate, the disagreement is not surprising.[88] However, in the specific context of public protests, lower courts have almost uniformly held that such claims can proceed.

Since *Bivens* was decided in 1971, lower courts have considered protest-related First Amendment claims against federal officials in 15 cases.[89] They have allowed these claims to proceed in 13 of those cases, or 87 percent of the time. The sample size here is admittedly small, and nearly half the cases emanate from the D.C. Circuit. Nevertheless, the nearly uniform results in protest cases stand out.

A review of two protest-related cases, one very old by *Bivens* standards and one very recent, highlights a change in orientation concerning protesters' First Amendment claims and perhaps public protest itself. In *Dellums v. Powell* (1977), Congressman Dellums and a class of protesters sued federal officials for, among other things, violating their First Amendment rights during an anti-Vietnam War protest at the U.S. Capitol.[90] The D.C. Circuit concluded that the arrested protesters could bring a *Bivens* claim against federal officials involved in the protesters' arrest and detention.[91] The court saw no impediment to judicial recognition and adjudication of such First Amendment claims. It reasoned that courts are generally familiar with First Amendment standards, could readily assess whether federal officials had interfered with the exercise of First Amendment rights "'in their most pristine and classic form,'" and were competent to assess damages in such cases.[92] Consider how the appeals court characterized the protesters' civil rights claim:

> Basically, what is at stake here is loss of an opportunity to express to Congress one's dissatisfaction with the laws and policies of the United States. Staged demonstrations capable of attracting national or regional attention in the press and broadcast media are for better or worse a major vehicle by which those who wish to express dissent can create a forum in which their views may be brought to the attention of a mass audience and, in turn, to the attention of a national legislature. It is facile to suggest that no damage is done when a demonstration is broken up by unlawful arrests simply because one could write an individual letter to a congressman or because the demonstration might be held at another day or time. Few letters to congressmen command a national or regional audience. And often it is the staging and theatrics if you will, the time, place, and manner of the demonstration which express the passion and emotion with which a point of view is held. The demonstration, the picket line, and the myriad other forms of protest which abound in our society each offer peculiarly important opportunities in which speakers may at once persuade, accuse, and seek sympathy or political support, all in a manner likely to be noticed. Loss of such an opportunity is surely not insignificant.[93]

Contrast the result and reasoning in *Dellums* with the much more recent decision in *Black Lives Matter v. Trump*, a 2021 D.C. district court case arising from officials' decision to remove protesters from Lafayette Park during the police brutality protests following George Floyd's murder.[94] BLM protesters alleged that federal and state officials used tear gas and physical force against peaceful groups of protesters without any advance warning. In addition to D.C. and other local police officers, the protesters sued former President Trump, former Attorney General William Barr, and several other federal officials for First Amendment violations under *Bivens*. Some of the plaintiffs alleged very serious physical injuries resulting from the use of physical force to clear Lafayette Square.

The district court dismissed plaintiffs' First, Fourth, and Fifth Amendment claims against the federal defendants. The court brushed aside *Dellums*, reasoning that the Supreme Court has made clear only *its* precedents matter in determining whether a *Bivens* claim arises in a "new context."[95] After acknowledging the Supreme Court's general skepticism toward *Bivens* claims, the district court concluded that protesters' First Amendment and other claims arose in a "new context" because the Supreme Court had never expressly extended *Bivens* to First Amendment claims.[96] The court held the need to preserve the safety and security of the president was a "special factor" counseling against recognition of the protesters' First Amendment claim. It observed, "When it comes to managing crowd activity directly outside of the White

House, decisionmakers must weigh public, presidential, and White House security interests."[97] The district court also pointed to "Congress' activity in the field governing the relationship between the White House and presidential security" as another "special factor."[98] Since Congress had appropriated funds for presidential and White House security and held hearings on these subjects at which it discussed the tradeoffs between national security and protesters' freedoms, the court reasoned, it was inappropriate to recognize a First Amendment remedy. Finally, the district court found as a third "special factor" that protesters had an alternative remedy in the form of their requested injunctive relief.[99]

BLM v. Trump illustrates the difficulties plaintiffs confront in seeking redress for injuries sustained because of federal protest policing. Even in a case where peaceful political protesters in a traditional public forum alleged federal officials had them forcibly removed the claim was rejected. In contrast to the court of appeals in *Dellums*, the district court in *BLM v. Trump* said not a word about the importance of preserving public protest and holding federal officials accountable for constitutional violations.

The Supreme Court, which has expressed skepticism about *Bivens* claims in general, has invited lower courts to discover and apply "special factors" that militate against *Bivens* claims in "new" (to the Court) contexts including public protest. The Court has effectively delegated to Congress the task of establishing redress for federal wrongs. In the *Bivens* context, public protest has thus been transformed from the exercise of constitutional rights "in their pristine and classic form" to the exercise of First Amendment rights in some foreign "new context" where protesters' likely cannot obtain redress for constitutional injuries.

REDUCING REMEDIAL BARRIERS

As my study demonstrates, qualified immunity and related defenses pose significant obstacles to damage claims based on First Amendment and Fourth Amendment violations. Qualified immunity shields officials in all but the most egregious cases; under *Nieves* probable cause to arrest defeats free speech retaliation claims unless protesters can produce evidence of disparate enforcement of public disorder laws; and the Court has essentially held that *Bivens* does not extend to First Amendment claims. These limits on protester remedies are part of the system of managed dissent. To the extent protesters cannot be made whole, they may for this additional reason be deterred from organizing and participating in public dissent. It is unlikely the current Court will reverse its path concerning civil remedies for constitutional harms. But even within existing limitations, protesters still have viable remedial options.

The options include continuing to pursue Section 1983 claims against state and local officials. My study of protest cases indicates these claims are more than likely to survive a motion to dismiss. And in 40 percent of the Section 1983 protest cases I examined, courts rejected summary judgment based on qualified immunity. The study confirms that protest organizers and participants are most likely to defeat qualified immunity claims when they characterize their injuries as violations of bedrock First Amendment doctrines and principles including denial of access to traditional public forums, content discrimination, prior restraint, and unlawful use of force against non-resisting protesters. At least in these contexts, the relevant law has become "clearly established." Protesters should continue to litigate in order to "establish" clear constitutional violations.

Qualified immunity is not an absolute bar to recovery. Indeed, where law enforcement officers have violated fundamental constitutional standards during mass demonstrations, municipalities have settled Section 1983 claims for substantial amounts.[100] For example, in 2004 Los Angeles paid a $1.2 million settlement to ninety-one protesters and bystanders for law enforcement abuses that occurred during the 2000 Democratic National Convention.[101] New York City paid an $18 million settlement stemming from the arrest, detention, and fingerprinting of hundreds of protesters, journalists, legal observers, and bystanders during the 2004 Republican National Convention.[102] Smaller settlements have been entered in response to complaints by Occupy Wall Street protesters who alleged false arrest or use of tear gas during peaceful demonstrations and BLM protesters who were injured by similar misconduct.[103] These settlements show that plaintiffs can obtain substantial monetary awards based on clear violations of civil liberties.

As scholars have suggested, protesters can also pursue claims against municipal employers under "failure to train" or "failure to supervise" theories.[104] Empirical data suggest that while the "failure to supervise" claim has been infrequently litigated, it has been a successful path to recovery in several circuits.[105] My study suggests that plaintiffs are not frequently pursuing *Monell* claims, perhaps owing to the significant burden of proof. However, especially given the long history of law enforcement protest policing abuses, plaintiffs may be able to establish that municipalities are liable for failing to properly train and supervise law enforcement. Civil rights lawyers should carefully consider pursuing such claims in public protest litigation.

Regarding free speech retaliation claims, *Nieves* does not recognize an absolute bar to First Amendment protest lawsuits. But it may require evidence that "similarly situated" speakers have been treated more favorably than arrested protesters. Thus far, litigants have had little success with that claim. But that lack of success could reflect, in part, a lack of experience litigating under the *Nieves* framework.

Nieves is also less than clear about what kinds of objective evidence, including comparison-based evidence, might support a First Amendment retaliation claim. Now that they know such evidence may be necessary, civil rights lawyers can focus on collecting it. Perhaps, as the dissenters in *Nieves* urged, "common sense" will prevail in lower court assessments of this evidence. Police officers should not enjoy a complete defense to significant First Amendment retaliation claims owing to dubious but technically lawful arrests for jaywalking and other discretionary misdemeanor offenses.[106]

In terms of remedial civil rights litigation, the path to recovering against federal officials is the narrowest of all. *Bivens* claims are significant in the protest context, in part owing to the regulatory authority of the Secret Service, National Parks Service, and federal law enforcement agencies. Although the Supreme Court has not expressly ruled out protest-related First Amendment claims against federal officials, it has crept ever closer to doing so and *Egbert* may have slammed the door nearly shut. When the judicial door closes, civil rights advocates need to look elsewhere.

Congress and state legislatures could reverse the most deleterious effects of defenses and immunities that prevent protesters from being made whole in the event of constitutional injuries. After the racial justice protests during the summer of 2020, Congress proposed and considered several proposals for eliminating or scaling back qualified immunity.[107] Numerous scholars have advocated that the Court or Congress abolish or reform qualified immunity doctrine in various ways.[108] Their reasons vary, but focus on arguments that the doctrine is legally suspect, leads to stagnation of constitutional law by deterring courts from grappling with difficult interpretive issues concerning constitutional rights, and fails to serve the policy interests presumably associated with a broad grant of immunity from civil rights suits.

Examination of protest-related cases supports all these objections. Although the focus of the qualified immunity reform or repeal efforts has largely been on Fourth Amendment excessive force injuries, these efforts would also have a significant impact on protesters' First Amendment rights. Reform or repeal of qualified immunity would benefit a variety of speakers, including protest organizers and participants.

The Court appears uninterested, at least so far, in revising qualified immunity doctrine. So, it will likely be up to Congress. Some have also urged Congress to overturn *Nieves* and allow First Amendment retaliation claims to proceed on their own merits, without regard to Fourth Amendment probable cause standards.

As the Court has urged, Congress could codify *Bivens* by creating civil damages claims against federal officials who violate First Amendment rights. However, at the moment the prospects for legislation on this matter seem rather dim.

Whether or not Congress acts to remedy these concerns, state legislatures can act on their own authority. Although the chapter's discussion has focused on remedies for violations of *federal* constitutional rights, states recognize causes of action for violations of state constitutional rights including freedom of speech, assembly, and press. In most states, these lawsuits can be defeated by a qualified immunity defense like the one applicable in federal Section 1983 actions. However, state legislatures can amend or abolish the defense.

For example, Colorado recently enacted a law that *abolishes* the defense of qualified immunity (but caps recovery against individual officers at $25,000) in state court actions for violations of state constitutional rights.[109] Other states, including Connecticut, New Mexico, and Massachusetts have also limited or banned the qualified immunity defense in state courts.[110] The New York City Council enacted a ban on qualified immunity defenses in unlawful arrest and excessive force cases against local law enforcement.[111] Finally, some states have created causes of action against law enforcement officers' employers, but not individual officers, and barred the employer from claiming qualified immunity.

Some states have also brought lawsuits on behalf of protesters injured during demonstrations. If individual protesters are effectively barred in many cases from imposing liability on government officials, states may be able to step in and sue on their citizens' behalf. Attorneys General in New York and Oregon brought these so-called *parens patriae* actions after the BLM protests in 2020.[112]

As commentators have noted, these lawsuits raise tricky and unresolved questions concerning the standing of state officials to assert vicarious constitutional harms on behalf of their citizens and the complexities of suing on behalf of a class of protest claimants.[113] Although there is little caselaw concerning the legal validity of such actions, one commentator has suggested they may be viable where central command decisions to engage in mass arrests are effectuated and individual litigants may not be able to bring their own claims. A specific scenario could involve the disparate impact of protest policing methods on communities of color, members of which might be incapable of successfully asserting their rights to equal treatment under the law.[114]

State lawsuits like these are not ideal vehicles for protecting citizens' First Amendment and Fourth Amendment rights or procuring compensation for constitutional injuries. However, owing to current doctrinal and other impediments to Section 1983 and *Bivens* actions, they are a creative remedial vehicle worth considering.

As discussed in Chapter 4, the costs of engaging in protest activities have steadily risen. Meanwhile, the remedies available to protesters, which have long been limited, have steadily decreased. These trends place First Amendment protest rights in a precarious position. To confidently appear in public places for purposes of speech and assembly requires a certain measure of courage and fortitude. To do so under threat of increased penalties *and* the prospect that officials who abuse their authority will escape personal liability undermines confidence in the safety, security, and fairness of a system that should, but too often does not, protect the right to protest.

9

Preserving Public Protest

This book has catalogued a significant number and variety of obstacles to public protest and dissent. The final chapter considers what can be done to help preserve the American tradition of public protest. As recent events attest, public protest is not about to disappear from the public square. However, there are many things that can be done to ensure that those who want to organize, participate in, and support public protest can continue to do so without fearing over-management, violence, or fiscal calamity. Protesters themselves bear a measure of responsibility for nurturing and maintaining the tradition of public contention. Acts of violence, vandalism, and anarchy are counter-productive. They also run counter to a tradition of peaceable, if disruptive, public assembly. But the focus in this chapter will be on the laws, regulations, policies, and norms that comprise the system of managed dissent. What follows is a general reform roadmap that, I hope, will help ensure Americans can continue to protest, demonstrate, and dissent safely and robustly in the years to come.

THE FIRST AMENDMENT AND PROTEST RIGHTS

When organizers and participants set out to engage in public protest, they should do so with the confidence that First Amendment rights limit governmental authority to restrict or suppress their activities. Unfortunately, as we have seen, that is not the current situation. Although one would not know it from reading Supreme Court decisions or, for that matter, most commentary about protest activity, in addition to a Free Speech Clause the First Amendment also contains an Assembly Clause and a Petition Clause. By virtue of both text and history, assembly and petition rights ought to broadly protect public protest and dissent. However, these rights have not received independent recognition and respect.

The elision means that even when groups gather peaceably to protest in public places, restrictions on their activities are reviewed almost exclusively by the lights of freedom of speech. That is why the discussion in the book has focused primarily on freedom of speech, which dominates the constitutional law of public protest. The

Court has held individuals have a collective right to engage in expressive activity ("expressive association") and can petition governments for "redress of grievances," but in both contexts, it is freedom of speech that is doing the work – often not very effectively, as I have argued – and receiving all the attention.[1]

Scholars have offered grounds for rediscovering and revitalizing assembly and petition rights. John Inazu has commented that "One might think that the most logical safeguard against restrictions on public protest would lie in the First Amendment's right of assembly."[2] However, as he has observed, the assembly right "has long been dormant, owing in large part to a fundamental misreading of the First Amendment suggesting that assembly was limited to the purposes of petitioning government."[3] Inazu has disentangled assembly and protest and explained that freedom of assembly protects gathering with others at the same time and place, as well as the right to control the composition of organized groups.[4] He contends the assembly right is critically important to protecting the right to dissent and agitate for change – both central focuses of this book.

Inazu's account of assembly extends beyond the sorts of activist groups likely to organize and participate in public protest activities. Groups come in all shapes and sizes, and not all of them are focused on political contention. Inazu's core insights are that the right of peaceable assembly "provides a buffer between the individual and the state that facilitates a check against centralized power ... shape[s] and form[s] identity ... [and] facilitates a kind of flourishing."[5] These benefits are directly related to the values associated with protest organization, participation, and support.

Tabatha Abu El-Haj has similarly emphasized the importance of recognizing an independent assembly right. As mentioned at various points in the book, El-Haj has focused on the tradition and significance to democracy of disruptive street protests and other "out of doors" activities.[6] Coupled with the fact that collective displays can be a more effective means of communicating grievances than lonely pamphleteering – something the Supreme Court has at times itself acknowledged – these accounts of the right of assembly clarify what is truly at stake when governments over-manage public protest.

Ronald Krotoszynski has sought to "reclaim" the "right to petition."[7] The fundamental flaw he has identified is that free speech doctrines such as "public forum" and "time, place, and manner" do a poor job of ensuring speakers can reach intended governmental audiences. As emphasized throughout this book and my first book, *Speech Out of Doors*, these doctrines are heavily stacked against speakers and groups that seek to engage in public protest activities.[8] Krotoszynski has proposed to address this problem, at least to a limited extent, not through free speech doctrines and precedents but rather by rethinking and revitalizing the Petition Clause. After canvassing the history of petitioning, including its transformation in the American system into a form of mass politics, he argues the right to petition is a "qualified right of access to seek redress of grievances on a public street or sidewalk within the personal hearing and seeing of incumbent government and political party officials."[9] Thus, he argues, "federal courts should require that any and all restrictions on protest activity proximate to government officials should be justified by actual – as opposed to merely hypothetical – risks, and that government should be required to use the least restrictive means possible to address these security concerns."[10]

Highlighting these other rights does not entail giving up on free speech doctrinal reforms. But so far, the Supreme Court has chosen not to revisit doctrines that allow governments to require permits, charge certain fees, and restrict the location, manner, and time of protest. If it had independent force, as Inazu suggests, the Assembly Clause might provide another or alternative basis for protecting protest groups subject to government surveillance, regulations that inhibit assembly, aggressive law enforcement tactics, and some forms of civil liability. Krotoszynski's right to "proximate" petitioning, though narrower in scope, might provide an independent basis for striking down free speech zones and other restrictions that prevent protesters from being seen and heard by target official audiences. Having and wielding these independent constitutional rights could shore up and supplement existing free speech protest rights.

Even if courts cannot be convinced to treat these rights as independently enforceable, there is value in recognizing that when protesters organize and march in the streets, the First Amendment contemplates that activity under not *one* but *three* separate provisions. The Supreme Court has recognized that freedoms of speech, assembly, and petition are "cognate" First Amendment rights.[11] The kindred provisions share common textual and historical foundations. One thing that unites them is their commitment to extending maximum protection to protest and dissent.

This provides yet another reason to reject the Court's skepticism that protest is a form of "speech-plus," a form of communicating the Court has suggested is not entitled to full First Amendment protection. A thicker account of the First Amendment might help courts recognize public protest is not just about communicating a message through a putative "mob." Organizing, participating in, and supporting public protest are about joining, solidarity, self-governance, and ensuring governmental transparency.

To facilitate and preserve public protest, one other "cognate" First Amendment right should also be broadly interpreted and vigorously enforced. As recent protests have confirmed, reporters and other observers must have the freedom to chronicle protest activities and governmental responses to them.[12] Freedom of the press ensures that reporters and members of the public have a First Amendment right not only to be present during protests but also to record what is happening there, so long as they do not interfere with legitimate law enforcement activities.[13]

Individuals reporting on and recording protest events as they transpire ought not to be targeted by law enforcement, swept into police dragnets, or have their recording equipment damaged or confiscated.[14] Public recording of law enforcement should now be considered a "clearly established" First Amendment right, the violation of which subjects law enforcement to civil liability. Strengthening "press" protections will facilitate protest and dissent by informing the public of protest griev-ances, checking law enforcement abuses, and improving the transparency of the democratic process.

PRESERVING THE PUBLIC FORUM

Public protest cannot survive without adequate public space for engaging in demon-strations, rallies, and other activities. Preserving the public forum is a critical com-ponent of the agenda to shore up and protect public protest rights. Governments hold public forums "in trust" for the people. One of the lessons of the book is that governments too often breach that duty of trust. A critical part of the preservation agenda must be to preserve and indeed add to the public places available for protest.

As discussed in Chapter 3, protesters can resort to forms of self-help to ensure that public forums continue to function as essential venues for speech and assembly. If they better understand the law of public protest and the system of managed dissent, protest organizers and participants can avoid some of their obstacles and pitfalls. They can comply with existing First Amendment and other laws, take advantage of permitting exceptions for spontaneous protests, and sometimes invoke state anti-SLAPP laws. These and other forms of self-help can lead to fewer arrests, reductions in the costs of dissent, and avoidance of certain forms of civil liability.

The principal responsibility for preserving the public forum rests with the govern-ment, which again holds public places "in trust" for the people. The notion that only *three* categories of public property exist where free speech and assembly rights are presumptively protected is inconsistent with both tradition and a national com-mitment to robust expressive freedoms. The Supreme Court is not likely to recon-sider the public forum doctrine in any significant respect. However, there are steps courts can take within that doctrine to preserve the public forum and the expressive topography from further deterioration.

Courts can preserve at least minimal access to "traditional" public forums by ensuring regulations do not ban or suppress assembly and speech in such places. Governments also sometimes "designate" public properties for expressive uses. Plaintiffs can present and courts can find the requisite governmental "intent" to open additional public properties to expression and assembly. Even within the stingy confines of the public forum doctrine, there are some opportunities for pres-ervation and expansion.

Courts can also review purportedly content-neutral "time, place, and man-ner" regulations in ways that recognize their considerable effect on protest rights. "Reasonableness" review generally ignores the vocality of place and the connec-tion between time, manner, and message. Courts should engage in a stricter review of the governmental interests underlying spatial restrictions, their tailor-ing, and the adequacy of so-called alternative channels of communication. For example, as explained in Chapter 3, suppressive "free speech zones" (wherever they are used) and targeted place regulations (TPRs) ought to be subject to more rigorous judicial scrutiny.

Onerous permitting requirements can likewise stifle dissent. Courts should require that all permitting provisions be narrowly tailored to the government's interests in public order and safety.[15] They should be especially skeptical of measures that price protesters out of the market for "free" expression. Legislatures and local policymakers should preserve and create additional opportunities for spontaneous protests. Responses to the murder of George Floyd, the Trump Administration's Muslim travel ban, and congressional proposals to "reform" the nation's immigration laws all demonstrated the necessity of allowing for unpermitted assemblies.

The militarization of public forums and militarized policing, which have long suppressed peaceful protest, must finally come to an end. Aggressive law enforcement "command-and-control" tactics intimidate protesters, chill lawful assembly and speech, and often lead to the use of escalated force and violence. Instead of keeping protesters and the public safe and protecting First Amendment rights, militarizing public forums and police forces imperils both safety and protest.

REFORMING PROTEST POLICING

Policing presents an existential threat to the preservation of public protest. Far too often, law enforcement agencies police protest through broad access restrictions, escalated force, and violence. Reform of protesting policing is critical and long overdue.

Militarized protest policing is an offshoot of the "escalated force" model of policing, which was prevalent in the U.S. through the 1970s. As discussed in Chapter 2, many police departments have turned to a "command-and-control" approach, which incorporates some of the worst elements of the "escalated force" model.[16] Command-and-control emphasizes "the micromanagement of all aspects of demonstrations," including efforts to control public space through the use of barricades, police lines, and other means of surrounding, subdividing and directing the flow of protesters.[17] Police exhibit "a willingness to use force against even minor violations of law."[18]

The problem of protest policing has received renewed attention.[19] Still, it persists. Command-and-control methods were used during the BLM protests in 2020 and more recently at pro-choice public protests. Press accounts and court cases have unearthed a disturbing record of instances in which peaceful protesters and members of the press were beaten with batons, run over by officers on bicycles and in patrol cars, shot with rubber bullets, and tear gassed.[20] These were not isolated incidents; they were *common* methods of policing protest activities throughout the nation.[21]

Public protests can be volatile and sometimes disorderly events. Some in-the-moment judgment calls regarding the use of force and other policing methods are difficult. But we are not talking about hard cases. Rather, the problem is the general impulse to come out of the gate armed to the teeth and firing non-lethal, but still very dangerous, projectiles to "maintain order."

Protesters face a daunting array of impediments to organizing and participating in public events. The specter of escalated force and police violence has a chilling effect on the willingness of all but the most courageous to attend and participate. There are also longstanding concerns, borne out by recent examples, that the most aggressive protest policing methods are applied to Black and other marginalized individuals and protesters with certain viewpoints.

If public protest is to be preserved, escalated force and command-and-control tactics must be abolished. Police departments need to devote far more time and other resources to educating officers about the substance of offenses such as "unlawful assembly" and "conspiracy to riot," methods of de-escalation, the protections afforded to protest under the First Amendment, and their duty to protect *all* speakers and groups from violence and other impediments to effective public protest.[22]

At the same time, police departments ought to spend far fewer resources on the acquisition of the latest military equipment. One of the lessons of the 2020 racial justice protests is that law enforcement must internalize the perspective that the public square is a traditional forum for speech, assembly, and petition, not a "battlespace" they are deputized to dominate. Robust and uninhibited public protest cannot occur when protesters fear that those who are duty-bound to protect their expressive rights are part of a militarized and aggressive resistance to their effective exercise.

REASSESSING PUBLIC DISORDER LAWS

Part of the problem with protest policing, and the law of public protest more generally, is the vagueness and breadth of criminal laws often enforced against protesters. Statutory offenses such as "unlawful assembly," "disorderly conduct," and "failure to disperse" grant law enforcement enormous discretion to arrest and detain protest organizers, participants, and supporters. These tools can effectively nip protests in the bud by halting processions and breaking up otherwise lawful and peaceful protest groups. They can also prevent protesters from engaging in valuable forms of non-violent civil disobedience.[23]

As Rachel Harmon has observed, "whatever policing strategy a department chooses, it is largely the police department rather than the law that determines what constitutes permissible protest and what instead represents a sufficient threat to public order to justify a forceful response."[24] In addition to over-reliance on aggressive protest policing, law enforcement has been given too much discretion to enforce loosely worded public order laws.

Commentators have catalogued the many problems associated with the over-criminalization of speech through vaguely worded laws and regulations.[25] One answer to this problem is to properly train law enforcement to apply the laws in ways that preserve speech, assembly, and petition rights. However, that approach glosses over more fundamental substantive problems relating to the criminalization of minor breaches of peace – especially in the context of the exercise of First Amendment rights.

As Rachel Moran has observed, those problems include not only the violation of constitutional speech and assembly rights but also the harms from discriminatory enforcement of such laws against people of color and those with unpopular views and, more broadly, the exercise of social control over members of marginalized communities who are disparately harassed over and jailed for these offenses.[26] Moran adds that disorderly conduct laws "ensnare thousands of people in the criminal legal system each year," waste taxpayer funds that could be better spent elsewhere, "traumatize people whose conduct caused very little harm," and "exacerbate[] inequities for people already living on the margins of society."[27]

Responding to these and other concerns, some scholars have proposed narrowing or repealing public disorder offenses frequently enforced against public protesters. For example, John Inazu has proposed reconsidering and narrowing the crime of "unlawful assembly," which criminalizes gathering with others for the purpose of committing an unlawful act. Inazu has argued that state laws defining this offense cede too much discretion to law enforcement to punish assemblies even when there is no evidence of a plan to commit a violent act.[28] Like Moran, Inazu has observed that some unlawful assembly laws constitute a form of "social control" owing to the threat of criminal prosecution of even non-violent and in some cases entirely lawful assemblies.[29] Their application, he has argued, "stifles dissent, mutes expression, and ultimately weakens the democratic experiment."[30]

Inazu has proposed that such laws, which have been applied to protesters across the ideological spectrum, be amended to apply only when there is proof of a plan to engage in *forceful* and *violent* lawbreaking that is likely to cause *imminent* and *severe* harm.[31] By contrast, he has asserted non-violent forms of civil disobedience should not be prosecuted as "unlawful assembly," though law enforcement can arrest lawbreakers after the fact.[32] Under this approach, a group gathering near an intersection, for example, would not be subject to arrest for "unlawful assembly" but participants could be punished for obstructing passage.[33]

Narrowing the terms of unlawful assembly laws protects the expressive interests of protesters by making it less likely law enforcement will disperse participants "based on speculative concerns over insignificant damage."[34] As Inazu stresses, "The exigency of an unlawful assembly means that the social control resulting from dispersals and arrests may often be more important to authorities than a successful prosecution. This concern is plausibly heightened when the purpose of the assembly is to protest the very authorities who have the power to order its dispersal."[35]

Limiting the contexts in which unlawful assembly can be charged removes a degree of the discretion law enforcement has often used to interrupt, contain, or suppress otherwise lawful and non-violent assemblies. As Inazu has noted, rehabilitating the offense of unlawful assembly would not entail giving protesters a license to commit violent or destructive acts. But it would protect what Inazu has referred to as "the First Amendment moments that can never be replicated" – non-violent assemblies and protests cut short and silenced by the application of "unlawful assembly" laws.[36]

Taking matters a step further, Moran has advocated outright *repeal* of the crime of "disorderly conduct."[37] As applied to speech and assembly, Moran has contended many such laws are vague, overbroad, disparately enforced against racial and religious minorities, and applied in ways that suppress communication of unpopular views and criticism of public officials.[38] On balance, Moran has concluded the costs of enforcement of disorderly conduct laws far outweigh its benefits. As we have seen, public disorder laws are a dangerous tool to place in the hands of undertrained officers who too often seek order at the expense of First Amendment rights to peacefully protest.

Nick Robinson has made similar claims about "rioting" and "incitement to riot" offenses.[39] Like Moran, he has presented a case for outright repeal of these laws. But like Inazu, Robinson has argued riot laws should at least be narrowed in ways that make them less likely to undermine the First Amendment and other constitutional rights of protesters. Like unlawful assembly and disorderly conduct laws, riot offenses sweep up protesters who may not themselves be engaged in any unlawful activity. "Incitement to riot" offenses can be brought against protesters who communicate provocative, but still protected, messages. Finally, like other public order laws, crimes of "riot" and "incitement to riot" are sufficiently discretionary to invite discriminatory abuses against certain racial and political groups.

Narrowing or repealing these public disorder laws are not the only options.[40] Commentators have also argued courts should grant limited First Amendment protection to non-violent acts of civil disobedience. The idea would not be to license acts of violence or riotous behavior, but to respond to excessive punishment of peaceful unlawful conduct in two ways: introducing "penalty sensitivity analysis" into criminal prosecutions of non-violent civil disobedience and limiting the civil liability of organizers of protests involving such activity.[41] The proposals respond to two recent phenomena discussed in the book. The first is the recent protest backlash in state legislatures, which have adopted or increased criminal penalties for even non-violent forms of protest. The second, examined in Chapter 4, is the attempt to impose derivative liability on protesters for violent conduct that occurs at protests.

Separately and together, these proposed reforms are all well worth considering. Although proponents for repeal make strong cases, narrowing existing offenses and bringing penalty sensitivity claims strike me as more viable than outright repeal. Some people do engage in disorderly and riotous conduct, including at public protests. The central problems in enforcement appear to be the discretion granted under loose public order laws and the lack of proper training with respect to protest policing. Amending and narrowing public disorder laws responds directly to these concerns, without throwing out the offense altogether. Along with penalty sensitivity analysis, statutory narrowing would also preserve space for non-violent acts of civil disobedience.

Narrowing public order offenses would also help preserve protesters' remedies in the event of First Amendment violations. As discussed in Chapter 8, under current law when officers have probable cause to arrest protesters for *any* offense, including unlawful assembly or disorderly conduct, the protesters generally cannot bring First Amendment claims that the officer retaliated against them because of their speech.[42] Given the ease with which officers can currently establish probable cause to arrest someone for unlawful assembly and other inchoate crimes, protesters are likely to be denied a remedy even if they can demonstrate their arrest was in retaliation for protected speech. Narrowing public disorder laws could make it more difficult for law enforcement to justify some of these retaliatory arrests.

Narrowing law enforcement authority to arrest protesters under public disorder laws is critical to protecting lawful protest. Unfortunately, it also runs against the tide of states *increasing* criminal penalties. In response to high-profile public protests, many states have ratcheted up the criminal and civil penalties for engaging in public disorder, unlawful assembly, obstruction of thoroughfares, and other acts. This backlash endangers public protest and dissent. Enacting additional vague and punitive offenses is the wrong response to the mostly peaceful public protests that occurred in 2020 and others that preceded them. The state backlash threatens to further encumber protest, ensnare dissenters, discriminate against protesters of color, and suppress legitimate political and other expression.

REDUCING THE COSTS OF DISSENT

Chapter 4 explained that organizing and participating in public protests has become increasingly costly. Policymakers have been stacking up fees and costs due and payable by protest organizers. Meanwhile, lawmakers have enacted new civil penalties that apply to protest organizers, participants, and supporters. In court, plaintiffs have been previewing new civil liability theories, including "negligent protest organizing" and "aiding and abetting defamation." Raising the costs of dissent chills protest by making it more expensive and subjecting protesters to unclear liability rules.

The Supreme Court has said little about the fees federal, state, and local officials can charge protesters to access a public forum. It has indicated they can charge flat fees ($300–$500) for cleanup and security but are prohibited from varying fees based on the predicted reaction of the crowd to the speaker's views.[43] The scope of protesters' civil liabilities also remains uncertain. During the Civil Rights Movement, opponents of desegregation frequently resorted to defamation lawsuits to chill civil rights advocacy. The Supreme Court responded to that tactic by altering state laws in ways that make it more difficult for public officials to recover damages.[44] In a case involving a civil rights boycott, the Court also refused to allow

businesses to recover millions of dollars in damages from organizers or participants unless they could show their harms were directly caused by the defendants'
acts or communications.[45]

These precedents leave considerable space for bureaucrats, legislators, and litigants to impose new fees and costs, enact new civil causes of action, and bring
novel civil actions against protesters and their supporters. To ensure access to the
public forum, courts need to strictly review common law claims, liability insurance,
indemnification, and other cost-shifting mechanisms. Given the rising costs of dissent, a Supreme Court ruling clarifying the First Amendment limits and safeguards
applicable to protest costs is long overdue.

Courts should be particularly skeptical of efforts to expand protesters' civil liabilities through tort lawsuits. Although the Supreme Court has not said much concerning the scope of protesters' civil liability, its decisions support narrowing, not
expanding, protesters' exposure to civil damages. Precedents do not support derivative liability actions, including "negligent protest organizing" and "riot boosting."
Under the First Amendment, protest organizers' liability must be limited to their
specific acts or any imminent unlawful acts they intended to incite. In response
to white supremacists in Charlottesville and the recent political insurrection, it is
tempting to try to stretch conspiracy and other laws to impose civil liability. However,
some applications of conspiracy liability also raise serious First Amendment issues.
As with other civil claims, courts should exercise special care before authorizing
such suits to proceed or upholding civil damages awards.

Enactment of new civil causes of action and statutory damage enhancements
are aspects of a broader protest backlash discussed earlier. Like courts, lawmakers
should endeavor to *reduce* protest costs and resist the urge to sanction civil actions
targeting protest organizers, participants, and supporters.

EXPANDING PROTESTERS' REMEDIES

While getting the costs of dissent under control is important, so too is ensuring
that protesters who suffer constitutional injuries can obtain compensation and other
remedies. As discussed in Chapter 8, protesters and others who suffer injuries at the
hands of law enforcement face a significant uphill battle in terms of recovery.

Legal immunities granted to law enforcement and other officials pose a serious,
and often insurmountable, obstacle to making protesters whole. My own data suggest that at summary judgment, sixty percent of actions brought by protesters under
federal civil rights law fail based on qualified immunity. Under the Court's for-
giving standard, only the most egregious violations of protesters' First Amendment
and Fourth Amendment rights defeat officers' immunity claims.[46] Further, only
proof that a municipal employer adopted and applied a policy or had a "custom"
of violating fundamental rights suffices to hold it liable.[47] Further, the Court has
significantly narrowed protesters' rights to bring civil claims alleging that officers

retaliated against them for their speech in violation of the First Amendment.[48] Finally, Supreme Court precedents strongly suggest, if not hold, that protesters cannot seek civil damages against *federal* officials for First Amendment violations.[49]

Protesters can and should continue to fight for civil remedies under the Court's limiting doctrines. As we have seen, in the most obvious and egregious cases governments will enter significant civil settlements with protesters. Even assuming some successes, however, large numbers of protesters will still be without any recourse to civil damages remedies.

As others have argued, for a variety of reasons, the Court's immunity doctrines and rules must be repealed or reformed.[50] As Joanna Schwartz has observed, "The Justices can end qualified immunity in a single decision, and they should end it now."[51] If the Supreme Court and lower courts are not willing to find room for compensating protesters for constitutional injuries, then the political branches must do so. Congress should reform qualified immunity under federal civil rights laws by loosening the "clearly established" liability standard and providing broader recourse against municipalities. It should reverse the Court's presumption against First Amendment retaliation claims under the federal civil rights statute. And Congress should codify remedies against federal law enforcement agents for First Amendment and other constitutional violations.

Absent federal action, which at this writing seems unlikely, state legislatures and city councils will need to continue their ongoing reform efforts concerning qualified immunity.[52] Rather than enacting new restrictions on public protest, states could instead create additional causes of action against officers who violate protesters' First Amendment and other rights.[53] In addition, states can also bring lawsuits on behalf of protesters whose First Amendment and Fourth Amendment rights have been violated.[54] If they are to be made whole for constitutional injuries, protesters will likely need to look to state constitutions and laws.

PROTECTING CAMPUS DISSENT

As discussed in Chapter 5, some claim there is an existential free speech crisis on the nation's university campuses. One concern is that students – and some faculty – are no longer committed to free and open inquiry. While some view the claim of "crisis" as overblown, there have been some worrying signs that free speech and dissent on campus are under strain.[55] Some of that strain concerns campus protests. Universities have traditionally been sites of political activism. Whether they will remain so depends on the preservation of protest rights on campuses.

University campuses are not the same as public streets and parks.[56] The university's principal mission relates to the production and dissemination of knowledge.[57] However, universities also serve broader democratic functions.[58] Campuses function as unique marketplaces of ideas.[59] They are also places where young adults learn to be independent and self-governing citizens.

Steps must be taken to preserve student, faculty, and staff protest rights on campus. The most significant challenges to protest and dissent on campus today relate to campus facilities, student conduct, and "free expression" policies. Public and private university administrators should do a thorough review of their campus free expression policies to ensure there is ample breathing space for protest and dissent. To facilitate that review, administrators and other policymakers should receive basic instruction regarding First Amendment standards, principles, and values. They might also consider establishing a campus free speech committee or "ombudsman" to collect information about protests on campus and conduct periodic reviews of free speech and assembly policies.

Vague public university policies implicate the due process rights of students and other speakers. Protesters and others should be clear about where, when, and how they may speak and assemble on campus. Poorly written policies, and those that retain prohibitions on fully protected expression, chill campus protest and dissent.

Requirements that campus speakers receive advance permission to assemble and speak may operate as unlawful prior restraints on expression.[60] Campus "free speech zones" are generally objectionable for the same reasons they offend the First Amendment outside campus gates. Too frequently these "zones" have been small (especially relative to otherwise expansive campuses), out-of-the-way venues where speakers have a hard time reaching audiences. Evidence that zoning has decreased on campuses is welcome news; however, campus free speech zoning remains a concern.

Universities should facilitate campus protest by making sure there are ample spaces for protest activity. Uncertainty regarding whether campus quadrangles, sidewalks, and other spaces constitute "public forums" for First Amendment purposes should not deter universities from adopting a default standard that common areas on campus are available for public expression. Of course, universities can still limit protest activities in classrooms, offices, and other areas used for professional purposes. They can also impose content-neutral time, place, and manner restrictions on protest.

Universities should not attempt to wall themselves off from the world outside campus gates. The First Amendment allows them to draw distinctions between speakers who are part of the university community (students, faculty, staff, administrators) and members of the public who wish to use campus facilities.[61] But the First Amendment obviously does not dictate that universities adopt stringent bans on non-university entity access and participation. Consistent with its obligations to community members, universities ought to provide opportunities for non-university entities to come to campus and engage with students, faculty, and staff.

One recent point of contention regards invitations to outside speakers. The considerations relevant to inviting speakers are varied and complex.[62] The way some communities have reacted to controversial speakers has raised difficult questions about free expression. Whether or not such speakers have any First Amendment *right* to be invited to speak on campus, once they are invited campus officials cannot "dis-invite" them based on their viewpoints.[63] They should be prepared to facilitate not just the visitor's expression but also meaningful protest of the speaker. As Greg Magarian has explained, First Amendment standards and values apply differently to violent, "preemptive," and "shouting down" protests.[64] Violent protest is never protected. However, preemptive protest, when it takes the form of seeking to convince others not to listen to a speaker, is fully protected counter-speech. Students and others who "shout down" a scheduled speaker are participating in an act of civil disobedience but can be disciplined for their actions.

It is not always or entirely clear that student shouting, for example, constitutes the sort of conduct that can be punished under the First Amendment. Given the uncertainty, as reflected in the Supreme Court's jurisprudence relating to the concept of the "heckler's veto," administrators should proceed with caution when drafting disciplinary policies for student protest. Severe punishments may chill valid campus protest and dissent. The Goldwater Institute's model "Campus Free Speech Act" is not the model to follow.[65] Its vague terms (focusing on "infringing the expressive rights of others") and draconian penalties (including expulsion) lack the sort of clarity and flexibility speech restrictions should exhibit.

Like other officials, university administrators must also contend with issues of cost and security relating to protests aimed at outside speakers. Universities could perhaps refuse to invite *any* outside speakers to campus. However, that would deprive students and others of opportunities to engage with important speakers and viewpoints.[66] For similar reasons, even if the First Amendment allows it, universities should not shift all or a significant portion of the costs of securing speakers and protesters to outside speakers or to students themselves. The First Amendment requirements for providing security and incurring other protest-related costs are frustratingly unclear.[67] It may be possible to develop some content-neutral system for allocating scarce funds for campus speakers. But that system would also limit engagement with the world beyond the university and would likely raise questions about whether the system disadvantages certain campus constituencies. As the Berkeley "Free Speech Week" debacle shows, universities may simply have to pay a steep price to maintain their character as marketplaces of ideas.

Managed dissent arrived on university campuses decades ago, in response to the actions of civil rights and anti-war protesters. It exhibits many of the same pathologies there as it does elsewhere on the expressive topography. It is important to remember campuses are places where a "spirit of rebellion" once flourished. When universities over-manage protest, they place that tradition in jeopardy.

Universities have other goals and priorities, including the creation of a welcoming and inclusive educational community. But that should not lead administrators to treat any speech that upsets students or disrupts the rhythms of campus life as unwelcome or subject to discipline. On public university campuses, the First Amendment denies administrators the power to manage political and social protests according to their content. On private university campuses, exercising that kind of managerial power is inconsistent with a commitment to the free exchange of ideas.

DISARMING THE PUBLIC SQUARE

As discussed in Chapter 6, the arming of the public square has significant implications for the preservation of public protest. Empirical and other evidence demonstrates that individuals are far less likely to participate in public protests if they
believe firearms will be present.[68] The combustible summer of 2020 showed what
can happen when individuals carry firearms at public protests. Arming protests is not
just dangerous. It is fundamentally incompatible with the values of free speech and
the exercise of First Amendment rights.[69]

Fortunately, there are several steps lawmakers and officials can take to protect
protesters from the intimidation and potential violence associated with public carry.
The Supreme Court has held there is a Second Amendment right to carry firearms
(and presumably other "arms") in some public places. That right has long been protected by statute in most states. But it has also been subject to limits on how, when,
and where individuals can bear arms. Future litigation will focus on whether these
limits contravene the Second Amendment.

Several restrictions on armed protests have solid historical and precedential support.
For example, states and localities can ban armed groups and other assemblies, including self-styled "militias," from parading in public while bearing arms. Bans on public
carry near all permitted events – including parades, protests, and demonstrations – may
withstand Second Amendment scrutiny. They can also proscribe the carrying of arms
at or near what the Court has called "sensitive places" – including polling places, state
capitols, courthouses, and university campuses – where many demonstrations and rallies occur. Law enforcement can enforce state laws that ban "going armed to the terror
of the public," brandishing weapons in threatening ways, and openly carrying dangerous and unusual weapons such as semi-automatic rifles with large capacity magazines
and dangerous projectiles.

By adopting a "history and tradition" approach, the Court has made it more difficult to defend firearms regulations. The foregoing examples fall within the scope of
what the Court has identified as the nation's regulatory tradition. Further, the Court
has indicated that a ban on *open* carry may be constitutional, so long as the law preserves the right to carry a *concealed* weapon. Although a decidedly second-best solu-
tion insofar as preserving public protests is concerned, that distinction would allow
policymakers to exclude some of the most intimidating kinds of firearms displays
during protests and other public events.

CLARIFYING – AND LIMITING – EMERGENCY POWERS

As recent events have highlighted, public emergencies give rise to special legal
authorities. During the Covid-19 pandemic state and local officials placed severe
restrictions on public protest activities, which some officials characterized as
"non-essential." Similarly, the civil unrest that followed the murder of George

Floyd produced a flurry of curfews and other measures aimed at managing public protest. If protest during pandemics, civil unrest, and other extraordinary circumstances is to be preserved, we need to clarify the scope and limits of governmental emergency powers

The pandemic and civil unrest exposed a lack of clarity concerning governmental power and its limits during emergencies. Civil liberties are always "essential" and cannot be suspended, even during a public emergency.[70] Indeed, the value of dissent may never be greater than when governments assert extraordinary powers – including the authority to exclude protesters from public streets and other thoroughfares.

Courts should reject the "suspension model," under which courts broadly defer to policymakers during emergencies. They can, of course, take public health and civil unrest conditions into account when assessing the government's purported interest in adopting restrictions and the relationship between the restrictions and that interest. But they should remain skeptical of broad curfews, bans on public assembly, and other measures that effectively suppress public protest.

As Karen Loor has observed, "Emergency officials view protests as law-enforcement-centric events, which means that before and after a legal emergency is declared, officials give the police free rein to control protesters."[71] By contrast, Chapter 7 argued in favor of modeling a "pathological" approach to emergency-related public protest restrictions.[72] That approach focuses on guarding against pretextual and overbroad restrictions on fundamental rights.

Courts should treat protest restrictions with skepticism, just as they would during ordinary periods, and to the extent practicable apply ordinary First Amendment standards to them. Recognizing that no emergency is of the same character or duration, they should not treat precedents set during previous emergencies as dispositive when the "next emergency" arises. During public health emergencies, courts should insist that restrictions on public protest be evidence-based and narrowly tailored to public health concerns. A similar approach should apply during periods of civil unrest, again with the understanding that the exigency can be factored in when judging the necessity and tailoring of protest restrictions.

Consideration of federal authority to address emergencies raises complex jurisdictional and constitutional concerns. Regarding public protest, some federal intervention may be necessary to coordinate responses and quell civil unrest. Presidents have on several occasions called out military personnel to address such concerns. However, presidents should seek to cooperate with state and local authorities when taking such drastic measures. Further, federal agents and U.S. Armed Forces should not be dispatched to actively police public protests. Finally, considering recent events, it is unfortunately necessary to emphasize that federal officials should never characterize or treat the nation's streets as "battlespaces" to be "dominated" and the nation's highest law enforcement officer should not suggest protesters be shot or harmed to quell civil unrest (or for any other reason).

In terms of federal law enforcement, prosecutors should tread very carefully when pursuing actions against protesters under the Insurrection Act, Anti-Riot Act, Civil Obedience Act, and sedition laws.[73] Some of these laws contain broad terms that can potentially reach even non-violent forms of political protest. Federal prosecutors should not treat disruptive protest and dissent as unpatriotic violence against the state. If prosecutors pursue cases under these federal authorities, courts must continue to limit their application in ways that preserve First Amendment protest rights.

Most of the foregoing are reactionary proposals. They rely primarily on courts to hold the line on First Amendment rights during declared and undeclared emergencies. Protest and other rights could also be preserved proactively. Federal and state authorities should develop plans that address how to preserve fundamental constitutional rights while at the same time dealing with public health and civil unrest exigencies. For instance, Loor has proposed a "council," consisting of police representatives, local civil rights attorneys, and others, which would establish protocols for responding to emergencies – including measures that preserve protest and other rights during an emergency.[74] Recent pandemic and civil unrest protests provide additional evidence that this kind of prophylactic work is critically important.

****

As this book demonstrates, countless laws, legal doctrines, norms, and customs affect people's ability to speak and assemble in public. In many respects, the current law of public protest is an affront to "the principle that in a free nation citizens must have the right to gather and speak with other persons in public places."[75]

My agenda for preserving public protest addresses various aspects of the law of public protest, from permitting, to protest policing and enforcement of state public disorder laws, to the public carry of firearms, to the scope of federal emergency powers. As broad as it is, the agenda is likely incomplete. The book has hopefully addressed the most significant restrictions on public protest. There are surely others worth considering.

Preserving public protest requires more than legal and constitutional reforms. It also entails a widespread change in public and official attitudes about public protest, which is often messy and disruptive of ordinary routines. As Harry Kalven wrote in 1965, "Among the many hallmarks of an open society, surely one must be that not every group of people on the streets is 'a mob.'"[76] As noted in the Introduction, opinion polling about public protest suggests that the public's overall attitude toward mass demonstrations ranges from skepticism to condemnation. Even the most popular protest events have support levels that hover below half, and positive responses are rarely higher than negative ones.[77] Public officials do not help matters when they refer to *every* public protest as an "angry mob," characterize public streets as a "battlespace" to be "dominated," and even suggest (as former President Trump allegedly did) that protesters be shot to prevent them from peacefully demonstrating.

If respect for protest and dissent are hallmarks of an open society, we have much work to do.

Perhaps the most intriguing, or surprising, thing about the subject of public protest is that people are still willing to participate. Indeed, the 2020 BLM protests were likely the largest in the nation's history. Their level of organization, participation, and commitment provides some hope that regardless of what impediments exist people will try to overcome them.

The concern is that at some point, even those strongly committed to public contention will stand down – out of concerns regarding unlawful arrest, police violence, armed counter-protesters, civil liability, or some combination of these and other factors. So far, however, reports of the death of public protest – particularly since the dawn of the digital age – have been greatly exaggerated. Hopefully, protest and dissent will not only persist but prosper. In a nation in which so many prize liberty and freedom of expression, there is no more appropriate tribute than to uphold its venerable tradition of public protest.

Notes

1 Packingham v. North Carolina, 137 S. Ct 1730, 1735, 1732 (2017).
2 Timothy Zick, *Speech Out of Doors: Preserving First Amendment Liberties in Public Places* (Cambridge: Cambridge Univ. Press, 2009).
3 Gregory P. Magarian, "Kent State and the Failure of First Amendment Law," 65 *Wash. U. J. L. & Pol'y* 41 (2021).
4 Larry Buchanan, Quoctrung Bui & Jugal K. Patel, "Black Lives Matter May Be the Largest Protest Movement in U.S. History," *N.Y. Times* (July 3, 2020), www.nytimes.com/interactive/2020/07/03/us/george-floyd-protests-crowd-size.html.
5 See Everytown Research and Policy, "Armed Assembly: Guns, Demonstrations, and Political Violence in America," joint research report between Everytown for Gun Safety Support Fund and the Armed Conflict Location & Event Data Project (August 23, 2021), https://everytownresearch.org/report/armed-assembly-guns-demonstrations-and-political-violence-in-america/.
6 See Zick, *Speech Out of Doors*; Tabatha Abu El-Haj, "Defining Nonviolence as a Matter of Law and Politics," in Melissa Schwartzberg (ed.), *Protest and Dissent: Nomos LXII* (New York: New York Univ. Press, 2020).
7 Ralph Young, *Dissent: The History of an American Idea* (New York: New York Univ. Press, 2015), 3.
8 Erica Chenoweth & Jeremy Pressman, "This Summer's Black Lives Matter Protesters Were Overwhelmingly Peaceful, Our Research Finds," *Wash. Post* (October 16, 2020), www.belfercenter.org/publication/summers-black-lives-matter-protesters-were-overwhelmingly-peaceful-our-research-finds.
9 See Missy Ryan & Dan Lamothe, "Trump Administration to Significantly Expand Military Response in Washington amid Unrest," *Wash. Post* (June 1, 2020), www.washingtonpost.com/national-security/defense-secretary-pledges-pentagon-support-to-help-dominate-the-battlespace-amid-unrest/2020/06/01/7c5b4630-a449-11ea-8681-7d471bf20207_story.html.
10 Norah O'Donnell, "Former Defense Secretary Mark Esper: President Trump Suggested Shooting Protesters, Missile Strikes in Mexico," *CBS News* (May 9, 2022), www.cbsnews.com/news/donald-trump-mark-esper-sacred-oath-60-minutes-2022-05-08.
11 Erum Salam, "Fears of Violence Against Pro-Choice Protests Intensify amid Wave of Attacks," *The Guardian* (June 28, 2022), www.theguardian.com/us-news/2022/jun/28/peaceful-pro-choice-protests-violence-attacks-police.
12 Ibid.

13 For a report on a study finding 139 instances over sixteen months, see Andy Campbell, "Political Violence Is the New American Normal," *Politico* (July 9, 2022), www.huffpost .com/entry/political-violence-the-new-american-normal_n_62c07c37e4b0ffe00a1260a6.

14 See, e.g., Christian Davenport, Sarah A. Soule & David A. Armstrong II, "Protesting While Black? The Differential Policing of American Activism, 1960–1990," 76 *Am. Socio. Rev.* 152 (2011); Maggie Koerth, "The Police's Tepid Response to the Capitol Breach Wasn't an Aberration," *FiveThirtyEight* (January 7, 2021), https://fivethirtyeight.com/ features/the-polices-tepid-response-to-the-capitol-breach-wasnt-an-aberration/.

15 See Nick Robinson & Elly Page, "Protecting Dissent: The Freedom of Peaceful Assembly, Civil Disobedience, and Partial First Amendment Protection," 107 *Cornell L. Rev.* 229, 244–47 (2021) (describing some of the post-BLM protest legislation).

16 See Mark Tushnet, "Spontaneous Demonstrations and the First Amendment," 71 *Ala. L. Rev.* 773, 790 (2020).

17 See Amber Baylor, "Unexceptional Protest," *UCLA L. Rev.* (forthcoming) (arguing that anti-protest legislation, which is often defended as a response to mass protest, increases everyday policing burdens in targeted communities).

INTRODUCTION

1 Cox v. Louisiana, 379 U.S. 536, 554–55 (1965).

2 One notable exception is Kevin Francis O'Neill, "Disentangling the Law of Public Protest," 45 *Loyola L. Rev.* 411 (1999). As discussed, my conception of the "law of public protest" is broader than O'Neill's, which is essentially limited to certain "regulatory contexts" – the issuance of permits for public protests; imposition of time, place, and manner and public forum restrictions; judicial speech injunctions; and protest policing. My conception includes all these contexts but also considers, among other things, the costs imposed on protesters, the remedies available to them for constitutional violations, emergency governmental powers that affect protest, and the presence of firearms at protests.

3 Ibid., 416 (suggesting the law of public protest can be clarified by attending to these "regulatory players").

4 The book is primarily about the law that applies to protests rather than, for example, the social science or political theory of protest. However, from time to time, the analysis will draw from these important disciplines.

5 See Seattle Affiliate of Oct. 22 Coalition v. City of Seattle, 550 F.3d 788, 798–800 (9th Cir. 2008) (invalidating parade ordinance that granted the Chief of Police broad discretion to determine location of parades and demonstrations).

6 See, e.g., John D. Inazu, "Unlawful Assembly as Social Control," 64 *UCLA L. Rev.* 2 (2017).

7 See Risa Goluboff, *Vagrant Nation: Police Power, Constitutional Change, and the Making of the 1960s* (Oxford: Oxford University Press, 2016), 118–19, 125 (describing the use of public disorder laws to harass civil rights protesters during the 1950s and 1960s).

8 See Rachel Moran, "Doing Away with Disorderly Conduct," 63 *B.U. L. Rev.* 65, 90–107 (2022).

9 See Gregory P. Magarian, "Conflicting Reports: When Gun Rights Threaten Free Speech," 83 *Law & Cont. Probl.* 169, 175 (2020) ("Police protection is a crucial (if often underappreciated) aspect of a meaningful right to expressive freedom.").

10 See Rachel A. Harmon, "The Problem of Policing," 110 *Mich. L. Rev.* 761 (2012).

11 See Lesley J. Wood, *Crisis and Control: The Militarization of Protest Policing* (London: Pluto Press, 2014).

12 See, e.g., Doe v. Mckesson, 945 F.3d 818 (5th Cir. 2019) (allowing tort claim against protest organizer to proceed on the theory that the organizer was negligent in organizing a demonstration), rev'd 141 S. Ct. 48, 51 (2020) (per curiam).

13 Jeff Reeves, "Raleigh Police Release Statement After Department Tweets 'Protesting Is a Non-Essential Activity'," *CBS17.com* (updated April 14, 2020), www.cbs17.com/news/local-news/wake-county-news/raleigh-police-release-statement-after-department-tweets-protesting-is-a-non-essential-activity/(reporting that Raleigh Police Department's Twitter account stated that "protesting is a non-essential activity").

14 See Nick Robinson & Elly Page, "Protecting Dissent: The Freedom of Peaceful Assembly, Civil Disobedience, and Partial First Amendment Protection," 107 *Cornell L. Rev.*229, 244 (2021) (describing "critical infrastructure" protest laws).

15 See John D. Inazu, *Liberty's Refuge: The Forgotten Freedom of Assembly* (New Haven, CT: Yale University Press, 2012); Ronald J. Krotoszynski, *Reclaiming the Petition Clause: Seditious Libel, "Offensive" Protest, and the Right to Petition the Government for a Redress of Grievances* (New Haven, CT: Yale University Press, 2012).

16 See Timothy Zick, "Arming Public Protests," 104 *Iowa L. Rev.* 233 (2018).

17 See Rodney A. Smolla, *Confessions of a Free Speech Lawyer: Charlottesville and the Politics of Hate* (Ithaca, NY: Cornell University Press, 2020), 275–76 (discussing the complexities of policing armed demonstrations).

18 See Shawn E. Fields, "Protest Policing and the Fourth Amendment," 55 *U.C. Davis L. Rev.* 347 (2021).

19 Harry Kalven, Jr., "The Concept of the Public Forum: Cox v. Louisiana," 1965 *Sup. Ct. Rev.* 1, 12 (1965).

20 Gregory P. Magarian, *Managed Speech: The Roberts Court's First Amendment* (Oxford: Oxford University Press, 2017), xv.

21 See Tabatha Abu El-Haj, "The Neglected Right of Assembly," 56 *UCLA L. Rev.* 543 (2009); Tabatha Abu El-Haj, "Changing the People: Legal Regulation and American Democracy," 86 *N.Y.U. L. Rev.* 1 (2011).

22 Tabatha Abu El-Haj, "Defining Nonviolence as a Matter of Law and Politics," in Melissa Schwartzberg (ed.), *Protest and Dissent: Nomos LXII* (New York: New York University Press, 2020), 205.

23 Clayton Bohnet, *Toward a Philosophy of Protest: Dissent, State Power, and the Spectacle of Everyday Life* (Lanham, MD: Lexington Books, 2020), 22.

24 See Timothy Zick, "Managing Dissent," 95 *Wash. U. L. Rev.* 1423 (2018).

25 See, e.g., Cantwell v. Connecticut, 310 U.S. 296, 306 (1940) (overturning a breach of peace conviction in part because the speaker's "deportment" was not "noisy, truculent, overbearing or offensive"); Chaplinsky v. New Hampshire, 315 U.S. 568, 573 (1942) (upholding a conviction for communicating "fighting words" to a police officer).

26 See Brandenburg v. Ohio, 395 U.S. 444, 445–46 (1969) (invalidating a conviction of members of the KKK for criminal syndicalism, where there was no evidence that speech was likely to lead to imminent violence).

27 See Maggie Astor, "Why Protest Movements Are 'Civil' Only in Retrospect," *N.Y. Times* (June 16, 2020), www.nytimes.com/2020/06/16/us/politics/us-protests-history-george-floyd.html.

28 Edwards v. South Carolina, 372 U.S. 229, 238 (1963) (invalidating breach of peace convictions of civil rights protesters). See also Cox, 379 U.S. 536, 545 (1965) (same).

29 See, e.g., Cox, 379 U.S. 536, 555.

30 Kalven, Jr., "The Concept of the Public Forum," 1, 8.

31 See John D. Inazu, "The First Amendment's Public Forum," 56 *Wm. & Mary L. Rev.* 1159 (2015) (critiquing time and manner restrictions).

32 See Nicole Goodkind, "Republican Anti-Protest Laws Sweep Across the U.S.," *Fortune* (August 13, 2021), https://fortune.com/2021/08/13/republican-anti-protest-laws-black-lives-matter/.

33 See Jeremy Waldron, "What Demonstrations Are, and What Demonstrations Mean," https://papers.ssrn.com/sol3/papers.cfm?abstract_id=3664849 (last revised November 6, 2020), 27.

34 See, e.g., Paul Herrnson & Kathleen Weldon, "Going Too Far: The American Public's Attitude Toward Protest Movements," *Huffington Post* (October 22, 2014; updated December 6, 2017), www.huffpost.com/entry/going-too-far-the-america_b_6029998.

35 Emily Ekins, "The State of Free Speech and Tolerance in America," *CATO Inst.* (October 31, 2017), https://perma.cc/FK4D-PZCR.

36 Statista Research Department (March 4, 2019), www.statista.com/statistics/758000/political-public-protest-participation-in-us/.

37 R. J. Reinhart, "One in Three Americans Have Felt Urge to Protest," *Gallup.com* (August 24, 2018), https://news.gallup.com/poll/241634/one-three-americans-felt-urge-protest.aspx.

38 Audra D.S. Burch, Weiyi Cai, Gabriel Gianordoli, Morrigan McCarthy & Jugal K. Patel, "How Black Lives Matter Reached Every Corner of America," *N.Y. Times* (June 13, 2020), www.nytimes.com/interactive/2020/06/13/us/george-floyd-protests-cities-photos.html.

39 Gregory P. Magarian, "When Audiences Object: Free Speech and Campus Speaker Protests," 90 *U. Colo. L. Rev.* 551, 559 (2019).

40 Ibid., 559–60.

41 Ibid., 560.

42 See Matt Perez, "Trump Tells Governors To 'Dominate' Protesters, 'Put Them in Jail For 10 Years," *Forbes* (June 1, 2020), www.forbes.com/sites/mattperez/2020/06/01/trump-tells-governors-to-dominate-protesters-put-them-in-jail-for-10-years/?sh=63c67ad913fb.

43 Magarian, "Conflicting Reports," 75.

44 See Cass R. Sunstein, *Why Societies Need Dissent* (Cambridge, MA: Harvard University Press, 2003).

45 Stephen D. Solomon, *Revolutionary Dissent: How the Founding Generation Created the Freedom of Speech* (New York: St. Martin's Press, 2016).

46 Regarding these and other First Amendment values and justifications, see generally Frederick F. Schauer, *Free Speech: A Philosophical Enquiry* (Cambridge: Cambridge University Press, 1982).

47 Whitney v. California, 274 U.S. 357, 372 (1927).

48 Edwards, 372 U.S. 229, 235.

49 NAACP v. Alabama ex rel Patterson, 357 U.S. 449, 460 (1958).

50 Whitney, 274 U.S. 257, 372 (Brandeis, J., concurring).

51 Ibid.

52 See, e.g., Alexander Meikeljohn, *Free Speech and Its Relation to Self-Government* (New York: Harper Bros., 1948). See also Lucy G. Barber, *Marching on Washington: The Forging of an American Political Tradition* (Berkeley: University of California Press, 2004) (examining the relationship between citizenship and public protest).

53 Nick Suplina, "Crowd Control: The Troubling Mix of First Amendment Law, Political Demonstrations, and Terrorism," 73 *Geo. Wash. L. Rev.* 395, 409 (2005).

54 Mari Matsuda, *Where Is Your Body? And Other Essays on Race, Gender, and the Law* 75 (Boston, MA: Penguin Random House, 1996).

55 McCullen v. Coakley, 573 U.S. 464, 476 (2014).

56 Ibid.

57 Magarian, *Managed Speech*, xi.

58 See Richard Ford, "Protest Fatigue," in Melissa Schwartzberg (ed.), *Protest and Dissent: Nomos LXII* (New York: New York University Press, 2020).

59 Malley v. Briggs, 475 U.S. 335, 341 (1986).

1 PROTEST, DISSENT, AND DEMOCRACY

1 Gregory P. Magarian, "Conflicting Reports: When Gun Rights Threaten Free Speech," 83 *Law & Cont. Probl.* 169, 175 (2020) ("The idea of a 'protest' does not define a legal category.").

2 See Max Weber, "'Objectivity' in Social Science and Social Policy," in E. A. Shils and H. A. Finch (eds.) *Max Weber: The Methodology of the Social Sciences* 90–100 (Glencoe, Ill: Routledge, 1949), 50–113.

3 "Protest," in *Merriam-Webster Online Dictionary*.

4 Ronald K. Collins & David M. Skover, *On Dissent: Its Meaning in America* (Cambridge: Cambridge University Press, 2013), 2–4.

5 Ibid., 6.

6 Ibid.

7 Steven H. Shiffrin, *Dissent, Injustice, and the Meaning of America* (Princeton, NJ: Princeton University Press, 1999).

8 Ibid., 77.

9 Collins & Skover, *On Dissent*, xi.

10 Ibid., 5.

11 Ralph Young, *Dissent: The History of an American Idea* (New York: New York University Press, 2015), 1–2.

12 Ibid., 2–3. See also Shiffrin, *Dissent*, xii (describing dissent as "an important part of our national identity").

13 Collins & Skover, *On Dissent*, 21.

14 Ibid., 115.

15 Steven H. Shiffrin, *The First Amendment, Democracy, and Romance* (Cambridge, MA: Harvard University Press, 1990), 91.

16 Cass R. Sunstein, *Why Societies Need Dissent* (Cambridge, MA: Harvard University Press, 2003), 110.

17 Ibid., 112.

18 Ibid.

19 Ibid., 110.

20 See John Rawls, *A Theory of Justice* (Cambridge, MA: Harvard University Press, 1971), 320 (defining civil disobedience as "conscientious, respectful breaches of law intended to protest and call for reform of a law or policy, and for which the agent takes full responsibility").

21 See generally Candice Delmas, "Uncivil Disobedience," in Melissa Schwartzberg (ed.), *Protest and Dissent, Nomos LXII* (New York: New York University Press, 2020), 9–44.

22 See Collins & Skover, *On Dissent*, 69 (examining reasons not to treat violence – particularly against persons – as legitimate dissent).

23 See generally Nick Robinson & Elly Page, "Protecting Dissent: The Freedom of Peaceful Assembly, Civil Disobedience, and Partial First Amendment Protection," 107 *Cornell L. Rev.* 229 (2021) (proposing limited First Amendment protection for non-violent acts of civil disobedience).

24 Ibid.

25 Ibid., 116.

26 Juliet Hooker, "Disobedience in Black: On Race and Dissent," in Melissa Schwartzberg (ed.), *Protest and Dissent, Nomos LXII* (New York: New York University Press, 2020), 45–63, 46.

27 Ibid.

28 Ibid., 50–52.

29 Ibid., 58.

30 Ibid., 59.

31 See Timothy Zick, *Speech Out of Doors: Preserving First Amendment Liberties in Public Places* (Cambridge:Cambridge University Press, 2008), 13–19 (discussing how public places facilitate public protest).

32 "Protest … means to make a solemn declaration. The protester addresses a public, or at least testifies in public." Clayton Bohnet, *Toward a Philosophy of Protest: Dissent, State Power, and the Spectacle of Everyday Life* (Lanham, MD: Lexington Books, 2020), 28.

33 See Jeremy Waldron, "What Demonstrations Are, and What Demonstrations Mean," unpublished manuscript, available at https://papers.ssrn.com/sol3/papers.cfm?abstract_id=3664849 (last revised November 6, 2020), 18.

34 Ibid., 14. See also Bohnet, *Toward a Philosophy of Protest*, 17 (describing protest as "a process of persuasion").

35 For a criticism of the Supreme Court's Civil Rights Era protest decisions on this ground, see Harry Kalven, Jr., "The Concept of the Public Forum: Cox v. Louisiana," 1965 *Sup. Ct. Rev.* 1, 8 (1965).

36 See Bohnet, *Toward a Philosophy of Protest*, 37 ("protest can be designed to impact the course of a people's deliberations, to change their minds").

37 Ibid., 22.

38 Ibid.

39 John Rawls, *A Theory of Justice, Revised Edition* (Cambridge, MA: Harvard University Press 1999), 330.

40 Waldron, "What Demonstrations Are," 19.

41 Ibid., 21.

42 Ibid., 24.

43 John Berger, "The Nature of Mass Demonstrations," 1 *International Socialism* 11 (Autumn 1968).

44 Bohnet, *Toward a Philosophy of Protest*, 49.

45 Ibid.

46 Waldron, "What Demonstrations Are," 23.

47 Ibid., 27.

48 Ibid.

49 For a discussion of confrontational tactics that disrupt social life and put pressure on social agents, see Jose Medina, "No Justice, No Peace: Uncivil Protest and the Politics of Confrontation," in Melissa Schwartzberg (ed.), *Protest and Dissent, Nomos LXII* (New York: New York University Press, 2020), 122–60.

50 Nick Suplina, "Crowd Control: The Troubling Mix of First Amendment Law, Political Demonstrations, and Terrorism," 73 *Geo. Wash. L. Rev.* 395, 409 (2005).

51 Amna Akbar, "The Radical Possibilities of Protest," in Melissa Schwartzberg (ed.), *Protest and Dissent: Nomos LXII* (New York:New York University Press, 2020), 57,64–79.

52 Ibid., 67.

53 Ibid., 68.

54 Mari Matsuda, *Where Is Your Body? And Other Essays on Race, Gender, and the Law* (New York: Penguin Random House, 1996), 75.

55 Waldron, "What Demonstrations Are," 16.

56 Ibid., 36 ("A protest is most obviously addressed to those against whom one protests. It can be addressed to a particular person in power who does something the protester finds worth publicly objecting to.").

57 Berger, "The Nature of Mass Demonstrations," 11–12.
58 Ibid.
59 Bohnet, *Toward a Philosophy of Protest*, 39.
60 See generally Alexander Meiklejohn, *Political Freedom* (New York: Harper, 1960).
61 See William P. Marshall, "In Defense of the Search for Truth as a First Amendment Justification," 30 *Ga. L. Rev.* 1 (1995).
62 New York Times Co. v. Sullivan, 376 U.S. 254, 270 (1964).
63 See Whitney v. California, 274 U.S. 357 (1927) (Brandeis, J., concurring).
64 Ibid.
65 Gregory P. Magarian, *Managed Speech: The Roberts Court's First Amendment xi* (Oxford: Oxford University Press, 2017).
66 Bohnet, *Toward a Philosophy of Protest*, 117.
67 See generally Zackary Okun Dunivin, Harry Yaojun Yan, Jelani Ince, & Fabio Rojas, "Participation in Public Political protests in the U.S. in the Last Two Years 2017," 119 *Proc. Natl. Acad. Sci.* (September 30, 2022), www.pnas.org/doi/10.1073/pnas.2117320119.
68 See Timothy Zick, "Speech and Spatial Tactics," 84 *Tex. L. Rev.* 581 (2006).
69 Waldron, "What Demonstrations Are," 28–29.
70 Ibid., 29.
71 Ibid., 31.
72 Ibid., 28.
73 Bohnet, *Toward a Philosophy of Protest*, 50.
74 Ibid., 51.
75 Timothy Zick, "The Costs of Dissent: Protest and Civil Liabilities," 89 *Geo. Wash. L. Rev.* 233 (2021).
76 Ibid.
77 Brian Martin, "Protest in a Liberal Democracy," 20 *Philosophy and Social Action* 13 (January–June 1994).
78 Ibid.
79 New York Times Co., 376 U.S. 254, 270. See NAACP v. Claiborne Hardware Co., 458 U.S. 886, 915–17 (1982) (emphasizing that non-violent but aggressive civil rights boycott was protected speech and assembly).
80 Tabatha Abu El-Haj, "Defining Nonviolence as a Matter of Law and Politics," in Melissa Schwartzberg (ed.), *Protest and Dissent, Nomos LXII* (New York: New York University Press, 2020), 201–36, 205.
81 Ibid., 204.
82 Ibid., 205.
83 Ibid., 204.
84 See Vincent Blasi, "The Checking Value in First Amendment Theory," 2 *Am. B. Found. Research J.* 521, 526 (1977).
85 Lee C. Bollinger, *The Tolerant Society* (Oxford: Oxford University Press, 1986).
86 Young, *Dissent*, 9.
87 See Gregory P. Magarian, "When Audiences Object: Free Speech and Campus Speaker Protests," 90 *U. Colo. L. Rev.* 551, 560 (2019) (describing the actions of "black bloc" activists who engaged in violence at a campus protest against Milo Yiannopoulos).
88 See Nick Robinson, "Rethinking the Crime of Rioting,"107 *Minn. L. Rev.* 77 (2022).
89 See Martin, "Protest in a Liberal Democracy."
90 Magarian, "When Audiences Object," 559.
91 See Douglas M. McLeod, "News Coverage and Social Protest: How the Media's Protest Paradigm Exacerbates Social Conflict," 2007 *J. Disp. Resol.* 185, 186–87 (2007).

92 Magarian, "When Audiences Object," 559–60.

93 Ibid., 560.

94 Ibid.

95 Waldron, "What Demonstrations Are," 28.

96 Berger, "The Nature of Mass Demonstrations."

97 Ibid.

98 Ibid.

99 Bohnet, *Toward a Philosophy of Protest*, 65.

100 Waldron, "What Demonstrations Are," 28.

101 Abu El-Haj, "Defining Nonviolence," 206. See also Andreas Madestam, Daniel Shoag, Stan Verger, & David Yanagizawa-Drott, "Do Political Protests Matter? Evidence from the Tea Party Movement," 128 *Q.J. Econ.* 1633, 1665 (2013) (finding that Tea Party protests increased turnout and voting for Republican candidates).

102 Susan Stokes, "Are Protests Good or Bad for Democracy?" in Melissa Schwartzberg (ed.), *Protest and Dissent, Nomos LXII* (New York: New York University Press, 2020), 269–83, 269.

103 Ibid., 273.

104 Ibid., 273–75.

105 Daniel Q. Gillion, *The Loud Minority: Why Protests Matter in American Democracy* (Princeton, NJ: Princeton University Press, 2020).

106 Ibid., 7.

107 Ibid.

108 Ibid., 11.

109 Ibid., 19. See also Taeku Lee, *Mobilizing Public Opinion: Black Insurgency and Racial Attitudes in the Civil Rights Era* (Chicago: University of Chicago Press, 2002).

110 See Soumyajit Mazumder, "The Persistent Effect of U.S. Civil Rights Protests on Political Attitudes," 62 *Am. J. Pol. Sci.* 922, 923 (2018) (demonstrating that white people in counties that witnessed historical civil rights protests are more likely to support liberal policies including affirmative action, to identify as Democrats, and to have less resentment toward Black people).

111 Richard Thompson Ford, "Protest Fatigue," in Melissa Schwartzberg (ed.), *Protest and Dissent, Nomos LXII* (New York: New York University Press, 2020), 161–88, 163.

112 Ibid.

113 Ibid., 164.

114 Ibid., 164.

115 Ibid., 166–67.

116 Ibid.

117 Ibid., 167

118 Ibid.

119 See Susan J. Brison, "'No Ways Tired': An Antidote to Protest Fatigue in the Trump Era," in Melissa Schwartzberg (ed.), *Protest and Dissent, Nomos LXII* (New York: New York University Press, 2020), 189–98, 192–195 (observing that protest dignifies dissent energizes participants, and unites movements).

120 Ford, "Protest Fatigue," 169.

121 Ibid., 175.

122 Mark Lilla, *The Once and Future Liberal: After Identity Politics* (New York: Harper Collins, 2017), 111.

123 Gillion, *The Loud Minority*, 26.

2 THE MANAGERIAL SYSTEM

1 See Timothy Zick, "Managing Dissent," 95 *Wash. U. L. Rev.* 1423 (2018).
2 Gregory P. Magarian, *Managed Speech: The Roberts Court's First Amendment* (Oxford: Oxford Univ. Press, 2017), xv.
3 See generally Tabatha Abu El-Haj El-Haj, "The Neglected Right of Assembly," 56 *UCLA L. Rev.* 543 (2009); Tabatha Abu El-Haj, "Changing the People: Legal Regulation and American Democracy," 86 *N.Y.U. L. Rev.* 1 (2011).
4 See Timothy Zick, *Speech Out of Doors: Preserving First Amendment Liberties in Public Places* (Cambridge: Cambridge Univ. Press, 2008), 32–33.
5 See ibid., 34–35.
6 See Hague v. Committee for Industrial Organization, 307 U.S. 496, 515 (1939) (recognizing a First Amendment right to assemble and speak in public streets and parks).
7 Davis v. Massachusetts, 167 U.S. 43, 47 (1897).
8 See, e.g., Schneider v. State, 308 U.S. 147, 160 (1939) (striking down a ban on handbilling); Cox v. New Hampshire, 312 U.S. 569 (1941) (upholding a flat permit fee).
9 Cantwell v. Connecticut, 310 U.S. 296, 308 (1940).
10 Ibid., 308, 310, 309.
11 Chaplinsky v. New Hampshire, 315 U.S. 568, 673 (1942).
12 See Cohen v. California, 403 U.S. 15, 25 (1971) (overturning the conviction of a speaker who wore a jacket emblazoned with the words "Fuck the Draft" into a courthouse corridor).
13 Terminiello v. City of Chicago, 337 U.S. 1 (1949).
14 Ibid., 4.
15 Ibid., 25 (Jackson, J., dissenting).
16 Ibid., 32.
17 See Feiner v. New York, 340 U.S. 315, 320 (1951).
18 See Frederick Schauer, "Costs and Challenges of the Hostile Audience," 94 *Notre Dame L. Rev.* 1671, 1684–89 (2019) (discussing the obligations of law enforcement in response to hostile audience reactions).
19 Ibid., 1697.
20 NAACP v. Alabama, 357 U.S. 449, 460 (1958).
21 See Edwards v. South Carolina, 372 U.S. 229, 238 (1963) (invalidating breach of peace convictions of civil rights protesters); Cox v. Louisiana, 379 U.S. 536, 545 (1965), (same).
22 Edwards, 372 U.S. 229, 235; Cox, 379 U.S. 536, 562.
23 Cox, 379 U.S. 536, 555.
24 Ibid., 578 (Black, J., dissenting).
25 Ibid., 584 (Black, J., dissenting).
26 Harry Kalven, Jr., "The Concept of the Public Forum: Cox v. Louisiana," 1965 *Sup. Ct. Rev.* 1, 8 (1965).
27 New York Times Co. v. Sullivan, 376 U.S. 254, 270 (1964).
28 Kalven, "The Concept of the Public Forum," 8.
29 Brandenburg v. Ohio, 395 U.S. 444 (1969).
30 NAACP v. Claiborne Hardware Co., 458 U.S. 886 (1982).
31 Kalven, "The Concept of the Public Forum," 22.
32 See C. Edwin Baker, "Unreasoned Reasonableness: Mandatory Parade Permits and Time, Place, and Manner Regulations," 78 *Nw. L. Rev.* 937, 941 (1984) (expressing concern that the Court's speech-conduct dichotomy "immediately relegates assemblies to a lesser constitutional status than speech").

33 See, e.g., Truax v. Corrigan, 257 U.S. 312 (1921) (upholding an injunction on picketing on the grounds that it caused economic harms through psychological and moral coercion); American Steel Foundries v. Tri-City Central Trades Council, 257 U.S. 184 (1921) (enjoining picketers from approaching people in groups); Giboney v. Empire Storage & Ice Co., 336 U.S. 490 (1949) (enjoining peaceful picketing where its purpose was to compel the employer to violate antitrust laws); Cox, 379 U.S. 536, 578 (1965) (Black, J., concurring in the judgment in part and dissenting in part) ("Picketing, though it may be utilized to communicate ideas, is not speech, and therefore is not of itself protected by the First Amendment.").

34 Claiborne Hardware, 458 U.S. 886, 889, 932.

35 Brown v. Louisiana, 383 U.S. 131, 143 (1966).

36 Ibid., 136.

37 Ibid., 140.

38 Tinker v. Des Moines Indep. Sch. Dist., 393 U.S. 503, 508 (1969).

39 See Adderley v. Florida, 405 U.S. 39, 46 (1966) (upholding the trespass convictions of civil rights protesters located in the curtilage of a jailhouse).

40 See Garner v. Louisiana, 368 U.S. 157, 163 (1961) (invalidating breach-of-peace convictions in sit-in cases on due process grounds).

41 See United States v. O'Brien, 391 U.S. 367, 371 (1968) (upholding a conviction for the public destruction of a draft card by burning). See also Clark v. Cmty. For Creative Non-Violence, 468 U.S. 288 (1984) (upholding restrictions on overnight camping at Lafayette Square Park and the National Mall).

42 McCullen v. Coakley, 573 U.S. 464, 490 (2014).

43 Ibid., 489.

44 Ibid.

45 Madsen v Women's Health Center, 512 U.S. 753, 772–73 (1994). See also Frisby v. Schultz, 487 U.S. 474 (1988) (upholding an ordinance banning the "targeted picketing" of residences).

46 Snyder v. Phelps, 562 U.S. 443, 449 (2011).

47 See Zick, "Managing Dissent."

48 Collin v. Smith, 578 F.2d 1197 (7th Cir. 1978).

49 Smith v. Collin, 439 U.S. 916 (1978).

50 The last case to expressly invoke the Assembly Clause was Claiborne Hardware. See also El-Haj, "The Neglected Right of Assembly."

51 See Ronald J. Krotoszynski, *Reclaiming the Petition Clause: Seditious Libel, "Offensive" Protest, and the Right to Petition the Government for a Redress of Grievances* (New Haven, CT: Yale University Press 2012).

52 See Magarian, *Managed Speech*, xv (emphasis in original).

53 See Nick Robinson & Elly Page, "Protecting Dissent: The Freedom of Peaceful Assembly, Civil Disobedience, and Partial First Amendment Protection," 107 *Cornell L. Rev.* 229, 232 (2021) ("Despite the centrality of civil disobedience at many demonstrations, the courts have traditionally not provided such disobedience First Amendment protection.").

54 Ibid., 254.

55 See ibid., 259–68 (arguing for a penalty-sensitive approach to peaceful acts of civil disobedience).

56 See O'Brien, 391 U.S. 367, 371 (1968) (upholding a federal conviction for destroying draft card).

57 See Claiborne Hardware, 458 U.S. 886, 915–17 (1982).

58 See Spence v. Washington, 418 U.S. 405 (1974).

59 See Timothy Zick, "Arming Public Protests," 104 *Iowa L. Rev.* 223, 253 (2018).

60 See Hurley v. GLIB, 515 U.S. 557 (1995).

61 Texas v. Johnson, 491 U.S. 397, 405 (1989) (invalidating a state law conviction for "desecrating" the U.S. flag).

62 See, e.g., Clark, 468 U.S. 288 (1984) (upholding restrictions on overnight camping at Lafayette Square Park and the National Mall).

63 1VAC30-150, Regulations for Public Use of Robert E. Lee Monument, Richmond, VA.

64 See Rachel Moran, "Doing Away with Disorderly Conduct," 63 B.C. L. Rev. 65 (2022).

65 See generally John Inazu, "Unlawful Assembly as Social Control," 64 *UCLA L. Rev.* 2 (2017); Nick Robinson, "Rethinking the Crime of Rioting," 107 *Minn. L. Rev.* 77 (2022).

66 See Robinson & Page, "Protecting Dissent," 240–42.

67 Tabatha Abu El-Haj, "Defining Peaceably: Policing the Line Between Constitutionally Protected Protest and Unlawful Assembly," 80 *Mo. L. Rev.* 961, 966 (2015).

68 Robinson & Page, "Protecting Dissent," 242–43.

69 See Jocelyn Simonson, "Beyond Body Cameras: Defending a Robust Right to Record the Police," 104 *Geo. L. J.* 1559 (2016). See also Fields v. City of Phila., 862 F.3d 353 (3d Cir. 2017); Am. Civil Liberties Union v. Alvarez, 679 F.3d 583, 608 (7th Cir. 2012) (striking down an Illinois eavesdropping statute as applied to recording of police); Glik v. Cunniffe, 655 F.3d 78, 82 (1st Cir. 2011) (holding that the arrest of a bystander who recorded police violated the First Amendment).

70 Amanda Holpuch, "Arizona Law Bans People from Recording Police Within Eight Feet," N.Y. *Times* (July 9, 2022), https://www.nytimes.com/2022/07/09/us/arizona-recording-police-8-feet.html.

71 See Brandenburg, 395 U.S. 444 (1969) (defining the category of unprotected incitement to unlawful action).

72 See Sines v. Kessler, 324 F.Supp.3d 765 (W.D. Va. 2018) (denying a motion to dismiss a federal action against Charlottesville "Unite the Right" marchers).

73 See Watts v. United States, 394 U.S. 705, 708 (1969) (holding that threats are not covered by the Free Speech Clause); Virginia v. Black, 538 U.S. 343, 360 (2003) ("Intimidation in the constitutionally proscribable sense of the word is a type of true threat, where a speaker directs a threat to a person or group of persons with the intent of placing the victim in fear of bodily harm or death.").

74 See Claiborne Hardware, 458 U.S. 886, 915–17 (1982).

75 Chaplinsky, 315 U.S. 568, 573 (1942) (upholding a conviction for communicating "fighting words" to a police officer).

76 New York Times Co., 376 U.S. 254, 278 (1964).

77 See Milkovich v. Lorain Journal Co., 497 U.S. 1 (1990).

78 See Schauer, "Costs and Challenges."

79 See generally Zick, *Speech Out of Doors*.

80 Hudgens v. NLRB, 424 U.S. 507 (1976).

81 See Hague, 307 U.S. 496, 515 (1939) (recognizing a First Amendment right to speak and assemble in public streets and parks).

82 See Perry Educ. Ass'n v. Perry Local Educators' Ass'n, 460 U.S. 37, 45 (1983) (describing public forum categories).

83 Hague, 307 U.S. 496, 515.

84 Perry, 460 U.S. 37, 45.

85 Cornelius v. NAACP Legal Defense & Educ. Fund, 473 U.S. 788 (1985).

86 See Hodge v. Talkin, 799 F.3d 1145 (D.C. Cir. 2015) (concluding that the Supreme Court plaza is a limited public forum and upholding a ban on assemblies at the plaza);

Oberwetter v. Hilliard, 639 F.3d 545 (D.C. Cir. 2011) (upholding speech restrictions at the Jefferson Memorial, which the court characterized as a "non-public" forum).

87 See, e.g., Santa Monica Food Not Bombs v. City of Santa Monica, 450 F.3d 1022, 1039 (9th Cir. 2006) ("As the cautionary language in our earlier opinions indicates, the significant governmental interest justifying the unusual step of requiring citizens to inform the government in advance of expressive activity has always been understood to arise only when large groups of people travel together on streets and sidewalks."); Cox v. City of Charleston, 416 F.3d 281, 285 (4th Cir. 2005) (the "[u]nflinching application" of a permitting requirement "to groups as small as two or three renders it constitutionally infirm"); Douglas v. Brownell, 88 F.3d 1511, 1524 (8th Cir. 1996) ("[A]pplying the permit requirement to groups as small as ten persons compounds our conclusion that the parade permit ordinance is not narrowly tailored [to advance the government's interest in protecting the safety and convenience of users of public sidewalks and streets.]"); American-Arab Anti-Discrimination Committee v. City of Dearborn, 418 F.3d 600, 608 (6th Cir. 2005) (striking down a permit requirement as "hopelessly overbroad" on the grounds that the requirement could conceivably apply to groups as small as "two or more persons").

88 See Nathan W. Kellum, "Permit Schemes: Under Current Jurisprudence, What Permits Are Permitted?" 56 *Drake L. Rev.* 381 (2008).

89 1VAC30-150, Regulations for Public Use of Robert E. Lee Monument, Richmond, VA.

90 Ibid.

91 Ibid.

92 See John McCarthy & Clark McPhail, "The Institutionalization of Protest in the United States," in D.S. Meyer & S. Tarrow (eds.), *The Social Movement Society: Contentious Politics for a New Century* (Lanham, MD: Rowman & Littlefield, 1998), 83–110; Clark McPhail, David Schweingruber, & John McCarthy, "Policing Protest in the United States: 1960–1995," in Donatella della Porta & Herbert Reiter (eds.), *Policing Protest: The Control of Mass Demonstrations in Western Democracies,* (Minneapolis: University of Minnesota Press, 1998), 49–69.

93 See 36 C.F.R. §7.96 ("National Capitol Region" permit requirements).

94 Timothy Zick, "Speech and Spatial Tactics," 84 *Tex. L. Rev.* 581 (2006).

95 See Timothy Zick, "The Costs of Dissent: Protest and Civil Liabilities," 89 *Geo. Wash. L. Rev.* 233 (2021).

96 See Cox, 312 U.S. 569 (1941) (upholding a flat permit fee); Forsyth County v. Nationalist Movement, 505 U.S. 123, 134–36 (1992) (invalidating a variable permitting fee).

97 Rachel A. Harmon, "Policing, Protesting, and the Insignificance of Hostile Audiences," *Knight First Amendment Institute at Columbia University* (November 13, 2017), https://knightcolumbia.org/content/policing-protesting-and-insignificance-hostile-audiences.

98 Ibid.

99 Ibid.

100 Ibid.

101 See Atwater v. Lago Vista, 532 U.S. 318 (2001).

102 See Whren v. United States, 517 U.S. 806 (1996).

103 See Graham v. Connor, 490 U.S. 390, 396 (1989).

104 Nieves v. Bartlett, 139 S. Ct. 1715 (2019).

105 Harmon, "Policing."

106 See Tate Ryan-Mosley & Sam Richards, "The Secret Police: Cops Built a Shadowy Surveillance Machine in Minnesota after George Floyd's Murder," *MIT Technology Review* (March 3, 2022), www.technologyreview.com/2022/03/03/1046676/police-surveillance-minnesota-george-floyd/.

107 Laird v. Tatum, 408 U.S. 1 (1972).
108 Ibid., 13–14.
109 See Tyler Valeska, "First Amendment Limitations on Public Disclosure of Protest Surveillance," 121 *Colum. L. Rev. Forum* 241 (2021).
110 See McCarthy & McPhail, "Institutionalization of Protest," 49.
111 Ibid.
112 See Lesley J. Wood, *Crisis and Control: The Militarization of Protest Policing* (London: Pluto Press, 2014).
113 See Edward R. Maguire, "New Directions in Protest Policing," 35 *S.L.U. Pub. L. Rev.* 67 (2015).
114 Ibid., 83 (quoting A. Vitale, "The Command and Control and Miami Models at the 2004 Republican National Convention: New Forms of Policing Protests," 12 *Mobilization* 403, 404 (2007)).
115 Ibid., quoting Vitale, "Command and Control," 406.
116 See Radley Balko, *Rise of the Warrior Cop: The Militarization of America's Police Forces* (New York: PublicAffairs, 2014).
117 See Zick, "The Costs of Dissent."
118 These and other examples are reported in Christopher Ingraham, "Republican Lawmakers Introduce Bills to Curb Protesting in at Least 18 States," *Wash. Post* (February 24, 2017), www.washingtonpost.com/news/wonk/wp/2017/02/24/republican-lawmakers-introduce-bills-to-curb-protesting-in-at-least-17-states/. See also Traci Yoder, "New Anti-Protesting Legislation: A Deeper Look," *Nat'l Law. Guild* (March 2, 2017), https://perma.cc/P5UT-6MMV. The laws and bills are tracked and described by the International Center for Not for Profit Law, "U.S. Protest Law Tracker" (updated September 23, 2022), www.icnl.org/usprotestlawtracker/?location=&status=enacted&issue=&date=&type=legislative.
119 See New York State Rifle & Pistol Assn. v. Bruen, 142 S.Ct. 2111 (2022) (recognizing a right to bear arms in public places).
120 See Zick, "Arming Public Protest." See also Nicolle Okoren, "The Birth of a Militia: How an Armed Group Polices Black Lives Matter Protests," *Guardian* (July 27, 2020), https://perma.cc/R28B-5C5X.
121 Jeff Reeves, "Raleigh Police Release Statement after Department Tweets 'protesting is a non-essential activity'," *CBS17.com* (updated April 14, 2020), www.cbs17.com/news/local-news/wake-county-news/raleigh-police-release-statement-after-department-tweets-protesting-is-a-non-essential-activity/ (reporting that the Raleigh Police Department's Twitter account stated, "protesting is a non-essential activity").
122 See Lindsay F. Wiley & Stephen I. Vladeck, "Coronavirus, Civil Liberties, and the Courts: The Case Against 'Suspending' Judicial Review," 133 *Harv. L. J. F.* 179, 194 (2020) (highlighting the "unique checking role of an independent judiciary and the costs of its absence" during declared emergencies).
123 18 U.S.C. § 2101.

3 DISPLACING DISSENT

1 I developed this argument at length in Timothy Zick, *Speech Out of Doors: Preserving First Amendment Liberties in Public Places* (Cambridge: Cambridge University Press, 2009).
2 Gordon S. Wood, *The Creation of the American Republic, 1776–1787* (Chapel Hill: University of North Carolina Press, 1998), 319–28.

3 Alexis de Tocqueville, *Democracy in America* (1835) (Chicago: University of Chicago Press, 2002).

4 International Society for Krishna Consciousness v. Lee, 505 U.S. 672, 696 (1992) (Kennedy, J., concurring).

5 Hague v. Committee for Industrial Organization, 307 U.S. 496, 515 (1939).

6 See Kent Greenawalt, "Free Speech Justifications," 89 *Colum. L. Rev.* 119 (1989); Alexander Mieklejohn, *Free Speech and Its Relation to Self-Government* (New York: Harper & Bros., 1948); C. Edwin Baker, "Unreasoned Reasonableness: Mandatory Parade Permits and Time, Place, and Manner Regulations," 78 *Nw. U. L. Rev.* 937 (1983).

7 John D. Inazu, "The First Amendment's Public Forum," 56 *Wm. & Mary L. Rev.* 1159 (2015).

8 NAACP v. Button, 371 U.S. 415, 433 (1963).

9 Cass R. Sunstein, *Republic.com* (Princeton, NJ: Princeton University Press, 2001).

10 See McCullen v. Coakley, 573 U.S. 464, 476 (2014) (observing that on public streets "a listener often encounters speech he might otherwise tune out").

11 See Terminiello v. City of Chicago, 337 U.S. 1, 4 (1949) (noting that speech "may indeed best serve its high purpose when it induces a condition of unrest, creates dissatisfaction with conditions as they are, or even stirs people to anger").

12 See William Kaplan, *State and Salvation: The Jehovah's Witnesses and Their Fight for Civil Rights* (Toronto: University of Toronto Press, 1989).

13 See, e.g., Taylor Branch, *Pillar of Fire: America in the King Years 1963–1965* (New York: Simon & Schuster, 1998).

14 See Baker, "Unreasoned Reasonableness," 972 (noting that "often the most important and most valued consequence of a demonstration is its impact on the demonstrators themselves in terms of building spirit, commitment, and solidarity").

15 Marcel Henaff & Tracy B. Strong (eds.), *Public Space and Democracy* 5 (Minneapolis: University of Minnesota Press, 2001).

16 See Zick, *Speech Out of Doors*, 257 (discussing media coverage of protests).

17 See ibid., 8–9 (criticizing First Amendment doctrine's conception of place as property).

18 See ibid., 9–12 (discussing the expressive characteristics of place).

19 Schneider v. State of New Jersey, 308 U.S. 147, 151–52 (1939).

20 Martin v. City of Struthers, 319 U.S. 141, 146 (1943).

21 See Eugene Volokh, "Cheap Speech and What It Will Do," 104 *Yale L. J.* 1805, 1806–07 (1995) (arguing that the Internet would democratize and diversify the media environment).

22 Reno v. ACLU, 521 U.S. 844 (1997).

23 Harry Kalven, Jr., "The Concept of the Public Forum: Cox v. Louisiana," 1965 *Sup. Ct. Rev.* 1, 12 (1965).

24 Zick, *Speech Out of Doors*, 5–8 (explaining the concept of the "expressive topography"). See also Ronald J. Krotoszynski, Jr., "Our Shrinking First Amendment: On the Growing Problem of Reduced Access to Public Property for Speech Activity and Some Suggestions for a Better Way Forward," 78 *Ohio St. L. J.* 779 (2017).

25 See U.S. v. Kokinda, 497 U.S. 720 (1990) (holding that a sidewalk used to enter U.S. Post Office property is not a traditional public forum because it does not function like an ordinary public sidewalk).

26 Calvin Massey, "Public Fora, Neutral Governments, and the Prism of Property," 30 *Hastings L. J.* 309, 319 (1999).

27 Ibid., 310.

28 See Boardley v. U.S. Dept. of Interior, 615 F.3d 508, 515 (D.C. Cir. 2010) ("Thus, to establish that a national park (in whole or part) is a traditional public forum, Boardley must show that, like a typical municipal park, it has been held open by the government for the purpose of public discourse.").

29 Harry Kalven, Jr., *The Negro and the First Amendment* (Chicago: University of Chicago Press, 1964), 6.

30 See Tabatha Abu El-Haj, "All Assemble: Order and Disorder in Law, Politics and Culture," 16 *U. Penn. J. Const'l Law* 949, 956–68 (2014) (describing the many legal and constitutional challenges Occupy protesters faced).

31 Zick, *Speech Out of Doors*, 6–7. See also Ronald J. Krotoszynski, Jr., *The Disappearing First Amendment* (Cambridge: Cambridge University Press, 2019) (lamenting the loss of protest space and proposing more limits on government's managerial powers with regard to place).

32 See generally Krotoszynski, "Our Shrinking First Amendment."

33 See Don Mitchell, *The Right to the City: Social Justice and the Fight for Public Space* (New York: The Guilford Press, 2003), 130.

34 Kalven, "The Concept of the Public Forum," 12.

35 See El-Haj, "All Assemble."

36 See C. McPhail, D. Schweingruber, & J. McCarthy, "Policing Protest in the United States: 1960–1995," in Donatella della Porta & H. Reiter (eds.), *Policing Protest: The Control of Mass Demonstrations in Western Democracies* (Minneapolis, MN: University Of Minnesota Press, 1998), 49–69.

37 Cox v. New Hampshire, 312 U.S. 569 (1941).

38 Thomas v. Chicago Park Dist., 534 U.S. 316, 322 (2002).

39 See Inazu, "The First Amendment's Public Forum," 1181 ("One of the problems with the content-neutrality inquiry is that it misses the expressive connection between speech and the time, place, and manner in which it occurs.").

40 For a critical analysis of permits and other time, place, and manner requirements, see Baker, "Unreasoned Reasonableness," 972.

41 See Zick, *Speech Out of Doors*, 191–92 (describing examples).

42 New York City Admin. Code, § 10-110 (a)(1) (emphasis added).

43 Ibid., § 10-110 (a)(2).

44 Ibid., § 10-110 (a)(3).

45 Int'l Action Ctr. v. City of New York, 522 F. Supp.2d 679, 684–91 (S.D. N.Y. 2007).

46 Ibid.

47 New York City Admin. Code, § 10-110 (b)(3).

48 Ibid., § 10-110 (a)(4).

49 Zick, *Speech Out of Doors*, 203–04.

50 See National Council of Arab Americans v. City of New York, 331 F. Supp.2d 258 (S.D. N. Y. 2004).

51 This was recognized as a world record. See www.guinnessworldrecords.com/world-records/74335-largest-anti-war-rally.

52 See, e.g., See Bl(a)ck Tea Society v. City of Boston, 378 F.3d 8, 14 (1st Cir. 2004).

53 Marcavage v. City of New York, 2010 WL 3910355 *9 (S.D. N.Y. 2010), aff'd 689 F.3d 98 (2nd Cir. 2012).

54 See Don Mitchell & Lynn A. Staeheli, "Permitting Protest: Parsing the Fine Geography of Dissent in America," 29.4 *Int. J. Urban Reg. Res.* 796–813 (December 2005).

55 Olivia Paschal, "The Backlash to New Rules on Protests in D.C.," *The Atlantic* (October 13, 2018), www.theatlantic.com/politics/archive/2018/10/new-rules-could-curb-protests-dc/572944/.

56 See Mark Tushnet, "Spontaneous Demonstrations and the First Amendment," 71 *Ala. L. Rev.* 773 (2020).

57 See Baker, "Unreasoned Reasonableness," 1010–11.

58 Vodak v. City of Chicago, 639 F.3d 738, 746 (7th Cir. 2011). See generally Tabatha Abu El-Haj, "The Neglected Right of Assembly," 56 *UCLA L. Rev.* 543, 548–52 (2009); Vince Blasi, "Prior Restraints on Demonstrations," 68 *Mich. L. Rev.* 1481, 1524–27, and n. 170 (1970).

59 See Cox, 312 U.S. 569, 574 (1941) ("The authority of a municipality to impose regulations in order to assure the safety and convenience of the people in the use of public highways has never been regarded as inconsistent with civil liberties but rather as one of the means of safeguarding the good order upon which they ultimately depend.").

60 See generally Timothy Zick, "Speech and Spatial Tactics," 84 *Tex. L. Rev.* 581 (2006).

61 See David Rabban, *Free Speech in Its Forgotten Years 1870–1920* (Cambridge: Cambridge University Press, 1999).

62 See, e.g., Susan Rachel Nanes, "Constitutional Infringement Zones, Protest Pens and Demonstration Zones at the 2004 National Political Conventions," 66 *La. L. Rev.* 189 (2005).

63 See Ward v. Rock Against Racism, 491 U.S. 781, 791 (1989).

64 See, e.g., Serv. Employee Int'l Union v. City of Los Angeles, 114 F. Supp.2d 966, 968–69 (C.D. Cal. 2000) (invalidating the original protest zoning plan for the 2000 Democratic National Convention in Los Angeles on the ground that no meaningful protest was possible within the zone).

65 Coal. To Protest the Democratic Nat'l Convention v. City of Boston, 327 F. Supp. 2d 61, 67 (D. Mass. 2004).

66 Ibid., 74–75.

67 See Bl(a)ck Tea Society, 378 F.3d 8 (1st Cir. 2004).

68 Keith E. Whittington, *Speak Freely: Why Universities Must Defend Free Speech* (Princeton, NJ: Princeton University Press, 2018), 97.

69 Inazu, "The First Amendment's Public Forum," 1182.

70 See Susan H. Williams, "Content Discrimination and the First Amendment," 139 *U. Pa. L. Rev.* 615, 644 (1991) (noting substantial deference to authorities under the time, place, and manner doctrine).

71 See Zick, *Speech Out of Doors,* ch. 7.

72 See Lesley J. Wood, *Crisis and Control: The Militarization of Protest Policing* (London: Pluto Press, 2014).

73 Missy Ryan & Dan Lamothe, "Trump Administration to Significantly Expand Military Response in Washington amid Unrest," *Wash. Post* (June 1, 2020), www.washingtonpost .com/national-security/defense-secretary-pledges-pentagon-support-to-help-dominate-the-battlespace-amid-unrest/2020/06/01/7c5b4630-a449-11ea-8681-7d471bf20207_story .html.

74 See Zick, *Speech Out of Doors,* 197–98 (discussing research on protest policing). See also E. Maguire, "New Directions in Protest Policing," 35 *S.L.U. Pub. L. Rev.* 67, 83 (2015) (quoting A. Vitale, "The Command and Control and Miami Models at the 2004 Republican National Convention: New Forms of Policing Protests," 12 *Mobilization* 403, 404, 406 (2007)); John D. McCarthy & Clark McPhail, "The Institutionalization of Protest in the United States," in David S. Meyer & Sydney Tarrow (eds.), *The Social Movement Society,* (Lanham, MD: Rowman & Littlefield, 1998).

75 Talia Buford, Lucas Waldron, Mois Syed, & Al Shaw, "We Reviewed Police Tactics Seen in Nearly 400 Protest Videos. Here's What We Found," *ProPublica* (July 16, 2020), https://projects.propublica.org/protest-police-tactics/.

76 See Stephen Gandel, "At Least 40 Lawsuits Claim Police Brutality at George Floyd Protests across U.S.," *CBS News* (June 23, 2020), www.cbsnews.com/news/george-floyd-protests-police-brutality-settlements-lawsuits/.

77 See Kim Barker, Mike Baker, & Ali Watkins, "In City After City, Police Mishandled Black Lives Matter Protests," *N.Y. Times* (Mar. 20, 2021), www.nytimes.com/2021/03/20/us/protests-policing-george-floyd.html.

78 Sarah A. Soule & Christian Davenport, "Velvet Glove, Iron Fist, or Even Hand? Protest Policing in the United States, 1960–1990," 14(1) *Mobilization* 1 (February 2009).

79 See Chun Hin Jeffrey Tsoi, "Seizing §1983 After Your Protest Today: Fourth Amendment and Protest Policing post-*Torres*," 59 *Am. Crim. L. Rev. Online* 98 (2022); Shawn E. Fields, "Protest Policing and the Fourth Amendment," 55 *U.C. Davis L. Rev.* 347 (2021).

80 See Zick, "Speech and Spatial Tactics."

81 See 36 C.F.R. §7.96.

82 Oberwetter v. Hilliard, 639 F.3d 545 (D.C. Cir. 2011).

83 See Cox v. Louisiana, 379 U.S. 559 (1965) (rejecting a First Amendment challenge to a Louisiana law prohibiting picketing or parades "in or near" courthouses if aimed to impede the administration of justice or influence a court officer).

84 See 40 U.S.C. § 6135 (making it unlawful "to parade, stand, or move in processions or assemblages in the Supreme Court Building or grounds, or to display in the Building and grounds a flag, banner, or device designed or adapted to bring into public notice a party, organization, or movement"). See also Hodge v. Talkin, 799 F.3d 1145 (D.C. Cir. 2015) (upholding speech and assembly restrictions applicable to the Supreme Court plaza).

85 See Heffron v. International Society for Krishna Consciousness, Inc., 452 U.S. 640 (1981) (upholding "booth rule" at the Minnesota State Fair); Hill v. Colorado, 530 U.S. 703 (2000) (upholding "buffer zone" near abortion clinics); McCullen, 573 U.S. 464 (2014) (upholding 35-foot buffer zone outside state "reproductive health care facilities"); Frisby v. Schultz, 487 U.S. 474 (1988) (upholding ban on "targeted picketing" of residences); Burson v. Freeman, 504 U.S. 191 (1992) (upholding ban on campaign speech near polling places); Clark v. Cmty. For Creative Non-Violence, 468 U.S. 288 (1984) (upholding ban on overnight camping at Lafayette Park and the National Mall in Washington. D.C.).

86 See Snyder v. Phelps, 562 U.S. 443 (2011).

87 See ibid., 456–57 (observing "Westboro's choice of where and when to conduct its picketing is not beyond the Government's regulatory reach.").

88 Ibid., 457.

89 See 18 U.S.C. § 1507 (banning pickets or parades "in or near a building or residence occupied or used by such judge, juror, witness, or court officer ... with the intent of influencing any judge, juror, witness, or court officer, in the discharge of his duty.").

90 See, e.g., Mary Sell, "Bill Aims to Stop Protests Outside Alabama Homes," *Alabama Daily News* (May 30, 2022), www.aldailynews.com/bill-aims-to-stop-protests-outside-alabama-homes/.

91 See DeAndria Turner, "Lauderdale County Activist Group Believes Protest Bill Targets Them," *WAFF 48* (April 29, 2022) (describing Alabama bill limiting location of protests following demonstrations over removal of Confederate monuments), www.waff.com/2021/04/29/lauderdale-county-activist-group-believes-local-protest-bill-targets-them/.

92 See Cal. Penal Code §594.39 (imposing various restrictions on First Amendment activity within 100 feet of the entrance of any "vaccination site," defined to include any space or site where vaccines are provided, including hospitals, physician's offices, clinics, and any retail space or pop-up location).

93 See, e.g., Arkansas Code § 5-38-101; Indiana Code § 35-31.5-2-79.7; K.S.A. 2020 Supp. § 21-5818.

94 See Center for Constitutional Rights, "New Lawsuit Challenges Anti-Protest Trespass Law," Press Release (May 22, 2019) (describing a challenge to "a Louisiana law that makes it a felony punishable by up to five years in prison to be anywhere on the 125,000 miles of pipelines that run throughout the state without permission"), https://ccrjustice .org/home/press-center/press-releases/new-lawsuit-challenges-anti-protest-trespass-law.

95 McCullen, 573 U.S. 464, 480.

96 Burson, 504 U.S. 191, 207.

97 McCullen, 573 U.S. 464, 501–03 (Scalia, J., concurring).

98 Ibid., 490–91 (holding that the 35-foot buffer zone was not narrowly tailored to the state's interests in order and access).

99 See ibid., 503 ("although the statute applies to all abortion clinics in Massachusetts, only one is known to have been beset by the problems that the statute supposedly addresses").

100 Hill, 530 U.S. 703 (2000).

101 See ibid., 744 (Scalia, J., dissenting). See also Colo. Rev. Stat. § 18–9–122(1) (1999).

102 See Reed v. Town of Gilbert, 576 U.S. 155, 170 (2015) (observing that speaker- or identity-based restrictions can be content-based).

103 See United States v. O'Brien, 391 U.S. 367, 383–84 (1968) (declining to review congressional committee reports to determine whether regulation of the destruction of draft cards was based on content).

104 See Inazu, "The First Amendment's Public Forum," 1181 ("Indeed, content-neutral laws can still devastate expressive content.").

105 Zolan Kanno-Youngs, "A Battle over How to Battle *Roe*: Protests at Justices' Homes Fuel Rancor, *N.Y. Times* (May 12, 2022), www.nytimes.com/2022/05/12/us/politics/abortion-protests-supreme-court-justices.html.

106 See United States v. Grace, 461 U.S. 171 (1983) (invalidating restrictions on the display of signs on sidewalks near the Supreme Court).

107 18 U.S.C. § 1507.

108 See, e.g., Md. Code, Criminal Law, § 3-904.

109 Carey v. Brown, 447 U.S. 455 (1980).

110 Frisby, 487 U.S. 474, 483.

111 See Madsen v. Women's Health Center, Inc., 512 U.S. 753, 775 (1994) (invalidating 300-foot zones around the residences of abortion clinic workers).

112 See Montgomery County Ordinance, § 32-23 (banning "picketing a private residence").

113 Maria Kramer & Jesus Jimenez, "Armed Man Traveled to Justice Kavanaugh's Home to Kill Him, Officials Say," *N.Y. Times* (June 8, 2022), www.nytimes.com/2022/06/08/us/brett-kavanaugh-threat-arrest.html.

114 Packingham v. North Carolina, 137 S. Ct. 1730, 1735 (2017).

115 Ibid.

116 Ibid., 1737.

117 Ibid., 1735 (citation omitted).

118 See ibid. (noting that seven in ten adults use at least one social networking site and the low costs of digital communication).

119 Ibid.

120 John D. Inazu, "Virtual Assembly," 98 *Cornell L. Rev.* 1093 (2013).

121 See Zick, *Speech Out of Doors*, 322–24 (addressing public protest in "networked" public places).

122 See Howard Rheingold, *Smart Mobs: The Next Social Revolution* (Cambridge, MA: Basic Books, 2002), ch. 7.

123 See Fields v. City of Philadelphia, 862 F.3d 353, 360 (3rd Cir. 2017) ("[J]ust the act of recording, regardless [of] what is recorded, may improve policing.").

124 See generally Zeynep Tufekci, *Twitter and Tear Gas: The Power and Fragility of Networked Protest* (New Haven, CT: Yale University Press, 2018).

4 THE RISING COSTS OF DISSENT

1 See Aimee Edmondson, *In Sullivan's Shadow: The Use and Abuse of Libel Law During the Long Civil Rights Struggle* (Amherst, MA: University of Massachusetts Press, 2019). See also Anthony Lewis, *Make No Law: The Sullivan Case and the First Amendment* (New York: Vintage, 1992).

2 New York Times Co. v. Sullivan, 376 U.S. 254, 278 (1964).

3 Edmondson, *In Sullivan's Shadow*, 5.

4 New York Times Co., 376 U.S. 254, 276.

5 NAACP v. Claiborne Hardware Co., 458 U.S. 886 (1982).

6 Ibid., 894.

7 Ibid., 895.

8 Maxwell v. Southern Christian Leadership Conference, 414 F.2d 1065 (5th Cir. 1969).

9 Ibid., 1067.

10 Ibid.

11 See, e.g., Bell v. Maryland, 378 U.S. 226 (1964) (black students arrested for criminal trespass for refusing to leave a restaurant).

12 Maxwell, 414 F.2d 1065, 1068.

13 Michael J. Klarman, *From Jim Crow to Civil Rights: The Supreme Court and the Struggle for Racial Equality* 383 (Oxford: Oxford University Press, 2004).

14 See NAACP v. Alabama *ex rel.* Patterson, 357 U.S. 449, 453 (1958).

15 Klarman, *From Jim Crow to Civil Rights*, 383.

16 Gibson v. Florida Legislative Investigation Committee, 372 U.S. 539 (1963).

17 See Eric Neisser, "Charging for Free Speech: User Fees and Insurance in the Marketplace of Ideas," 74 *Geo. L. J.* 257, 269–72 (1985) (describing various costs).

18 Cox v. New Hampshire, 312 U.S. 569, 577 (1941). See David Goldberger, "A Reconsideration of *Cox v. New Hampshire*: Can Demonstrators Be Required to Pay the Costs of Using America's Public Forums?" 62 *Tex. L. Rev.* 403 (1983).

19 See, e.g., Long Beach Area Peace Network v. City of Long Beach, 522 F.3d 1010, 1015–17 (9th Cir. 2008) (noting that the total estimated charges for a planned march totaled $7,041).

20 See International Center for Not-For-Profit Law, "US Protest Law Tracker," www.icnl .org/usprotestlawtracker/?location=&status=enacted&issue=&date=&type=legislative.

21 See, e.g., Utah Admin. Code R920-4-5 (requiring proof of liability insurance and execution of indemnification form for the issuance of a permit authorizing a parade on a Utah state highway). See also Neisser, "Charging for Free Speech," 300–29 (analyzing insurance requirements); Long Beach Area Peace Network, 574 F.3d 1011, 1042 (9th Cir. 2009); Santa Monica Food Not Bombs v. City of Santa Monica, 450 F.3d 1022, 1047 (9th Cir. 2006).

22 Utah Admin. Code R920-4-5.

23 Marissa J. Lang, "The Government Might Ask Activists to Repay the Costs of Securing Protests. Experts Say It Could Price Them Out," *Wash. Post* (September 28, 2019), www .washingtonpost.com/local/the-government-might-ask-activists-to-repay-the-costs-of-securing-protests-experts-say-it-could-price-them-out/2019/09/28/66f7785a-e07b-11e9-8dc8-498eabc129a0_story.html.

24 Ibid.

25 Ibid.

26 Ibid.

27 Frederick Schauer, "Costs and Challenges of the Hostile Audience," 94 *N.D. L. Rev.* 1671, 1686 (2019).

28 Christopher Ingraham, "Republican Lawmakers Introduce Bills to Curb Protesting in at Least 18 States," *Wash. Post* (February 24, 2017), www.washingtonpost.com/news/wonk/wp/2017/02/24/republican-lawmakers-introduce-bills-to-curb-protesting-in-at-least-17-states/.

29 See, e.g., Steven Wishnia, "D.A. Goes After BART Shutdown Protesters for $70,000 Fine," Oakland Post (Jan. 9, 2015), www.postnewsgroup.com/d-goes-bart-shutdown-protesters-70000-fine/amp/.

30 See Lang, "Government Might Ask Activists to Repay" (noting that for large protests, organizers "can already expect to stare down a budget of more than $100,000").

31 On the actionable creation of a public nuisance as encompassing obstructing free passage, see Cal. Civ. Code §§ 3479, 3480 (West 2018).

32 On the tort of false imprisonment, see *Restatement (Second) of Torts* § 42 (Am Law Inst. 1965); William L. Prosser, "False Imprisonment: Consciousness of Confinement," 55 *Colum. L. Rev.* 847 (1955).

33 See, e.g., Marcavage v. City of New York, 689 F.3d 98 (2nd Cir. 2012) (upholding the arrest of political protesters under an obstruction of free passage ordinance); Lewry v. Town of Standish, 984 F.2d 25 (1st Cir. 1993) (discussing a Maine statute prohibiting the obstruction of public ways and the obstruction of free passage).

34 See, e.g., Huntington Life Sciences, Inc. v. Stop Huntington Animal Cruelty, 71 A.D.3d 734 (N.Y. App. 2010). See also Highland Enterprises, Inc. v. Barker, 133 Idaho 330 (Idaho 1999) (upholding an award of approximately $1 million based on environmental protest activities, including spiking trees and obstructing roadways). The typical "interference with advantageous relations" tort action is premised on interference with commercial, economic, or contractual relations. See Shawsheen River Estates Assocs. v. Herman, No. 95–1557, 1995 WL 809834 (Mass. Super. Ct. April 11, 1995). There does not appear to be a reported decision applying such a cause of action to interference with the exercise of a constitutional right.

35 New York Times Co., 376 U.S. 254, 276.

36 See ibid., 279.

37 Mckesson v. Doe, 945 F.3d 818 (5th Cir. 2019).

38 Mckesson v. Doe, 141 S. Ct. 48 (2020).

39 Doe v. Mckesson, 339 So.3d 524 (La. Sup. Ct. 2022).

40 Mckesson, 945 F.3d 818, 823.

41 SDCL § 20-9-54(1)-(3). See Andrew Malone & Vera Eidelman, "The South Dakota Legislature Has Invented a New Legal Term to Target Pipeline Protesters," *ACLU.org.* (April 1, 2019), www.aclu.org/blog/free-speech/rights-protesters/south-dakota-legislature-has-invented-new-legal-term-target.

42 Monica Krup, "'Riot Boosting': South Dakota's Integration of Environmental, Indigenous, and First Amendment Concerns and the Rhetoric on Protest," 22 *Rutgers Race & L. Rev.* 293 (2021).

43 See Malone & Eidelman, "South Dakota Legislature Has Invented."

44 See Brandenburg v. Ohio, 395 U.S. 444, 447 (1969) (holding that speakers may be held liable for advocacy of violence where they intend to incite imminent lawless acts and those acts are likely to occur).

45 See Nwanguma v. Trump, 903 F.3d 604, 612 (6th Cir. 2018).
46 See Jeanine Santucci, "10 House Members Sign on to NAACP Lawsuit Accusing Trump of Inciting Capitol Riot," *USA Today* (April 7, 2021), www.usatoday.com/story/news/politics/2021/04/07/10-democrats-join-lawsuit-against-trump-giuliani-over-capitol-riot/7124759002/; Mike Ives, "Two Capitol Police Officers Sue Trump Over January Riot," *N.Y. Times* A18 (April 1, 2021), www.nytimes.com/2021/03/31/us/politics/capitol-police-lawsuit-trump.html.
47 Sines v. Kessler, 324 F.Supp.3d 765 (W.D. Va. 2018). The federal law, passed in the wake of the Ku Klux Klan's violent reign of terror and referred to as the "Klan Act," is codified at 42 U.S. C. § 1985(3).
48 City of Keene v. Cleveland, 167 N.H. 731 (2015).
49 Hurchalla v. Lake Point Phase I, LLC, 2019 WL 2518748 (Ct. App. Fla. 2019).
50 Gertz v. Robert Welch, Inc., 418 U.S. 323 (1974).
51 Gibson Bros Inc. v. Oberlin College, 2019 WL 7556252 (Ohio Com.Pl.) (Trial Order) (June 27, 2019). See Brian Pascus, "Oberlin College President Carmen Twillie Ambar on the $44 Million Ruling Against the School," *CBSNews.com* (June 27, 2019), www.cbsnews.com/news/oberlin-college-president-defamation-lawsuit-verdict-gibsons-bakery-44-million-libel/.
52 Gibson Bros Inc. v. Oberlin College, 187 N.E.3d 629 (Ohio Ct. App. 2022).
53 See Virginia v. Black, 538 U.S. 343, 359 (2003) ("'True threats' encompass those statements where the speaker means to communicate a serious expression of an intent to commit an act of unlawful violence to a particular individual or group of individuals.").
54 Planned Parenthood of the Columbia/Willamette, Inc. v. American Coalition of Life Activists, 290 F.3d 1058 (9th Cir. 2002) (en banc).
55 See Racketeering Influenced and Corrupt Organizations Act (RICO), 18 U.S.C. §§ 1961–1968.
56 See National Organization for Women, Inc. v. Scheidler, 510 U.S. 249, 262 (1994) (holding that a federal racketeering law contains no economic motive requirement precluding its application to pro-life protesters); Scheidler v. National Organization for Women, Inc., 537 U.S. 393, 409–10 (2003) (concluding that abortion protesters did not "obtain" property by their actions, and thus did not commit the predicate act of extortion).
57 18 U.S.C. § 1964 (c).
58 FACE, § 248(b).
59 See Leslie Gielow Jacobs, "Applying Penalty Enhancements to Civil Disobedience: Clarifying the Free Speech Clause Model to Bring the Social Value of Political Protest into the Balance," 50 *Ohio St. L. J.* 185 (1998).
60 See, e.g., Huffman & Wright Logging Co. v. Wade, 317 Or. 445, 458 (Sup. Ct. Oregon 1993) (upholding a punitive damages award in connection with environmental protest involving trespass to chattels tort).
61 Christopher Ingraham, "Republic Lawmakers Introduce Bills"; Traci Yoder, "New Anti-Protesting Legislation: A Deeper Look, *Nat'l Law. Guild* (March 2, 2017), https://perma.cc/P5UT-6MMV.
62 New York Times Co. v Sullivan, 276 U.S. 254, 277 (1964).
63 See Anna Stolley Persky, "Protesters May Pay the Price When Civil Disobedience Becomes Costly," *A.B.A.J.* (November 1, 2015).
64 Timbs v. Indiana, 139 S. Ct. 682, 689 (2019).
65 See, e.g., Ashcroft v. Free Speech Coal., 535 U.S. 234, 244 (2002) ("The Constitution gives significant protection from overbroad laws that chill speech within the First Amendment's vast and privileged sphere.").

66 See Phila. Newspapers, Inc. v. Hepps, 475 U.S. 767 (1986) (clarifying "falsity" requirement).
67 Snyder v. Phelps, 562 U.S. 443, 458–59 (2011).
68 Claiborne Hardware, 458 U.S. 886, 916.
69 Ibid., 919.
70 Mark Tushnet, "Spontaneous Demonstrations and the First Amendment," 71 *Ala. L. Rev.* 773, 790 (2020).
71 Ibid., 788.
72 Ibid.
73 George Pring & Penelope Canan, *SLAPPs: Getting Sued for Speaking Out* (Philadelphia, PA: Temple University Press, 1996).
74 See Reporters Committee for Freedom of the Press, "Overview of Anti-SLAPP Laws," www.rcfp.org/introduction-anti-slapp-guide/#:~:text=As%20of%20April%202022%2C%2032,Mexico%2C%20New%20York%2C%20Oklahoma%2C.
75 See, e.g., Geiser v. Kuhns, 2020 WL 967456 (Cal. Ct. App. February 28, 2020) (applying California's anti-SLAPP law to protest activity).
76 Energy Transfer Equity, LP v. Greenpeace Int'l et al., 2018 WL 4677788 (D.N.D. July 25, 2018).
77 Compare Adelson v. Harris, 774 F.3d 803, 809 (2nd Cir. 2014) (finding the application of Nevada's anti-SLAPP provisions in federal court "unproblematic") with Carbone v. Cable News Network, Inc., 910 F.3d 1345, 1351 (11th Cir. 2018) (finding that the motion-to-strike procedure in Georgia anti-SLAPP law conflicted with federal rules and could not apply in federal court).
78 See Cox, 312 U.S. 569, 577 (1941) (upholding a flat $500 permit fee).
79 See ibid. For arguments that even flat permit fees violate the First Amendment, see C. Edwin Baker, "Unreasoned Reasonableness: Mandatory Parade Permits and Time, Place, and Manner Regulations," 78 *Nw. L. Rev.* 937 (1983); Goldberger, "A Reconsideration of *Cox v. New Hampshire.*"
80 See Forsyth County v. Nationalist Movement, 505 U.S. 123, 133–34 (1992).
81 Ibid., 134. See The Nationalist Movement v. City of York, 481 F.3d 178, 186 (3rd Cir. 2007) (invalidating a reimbursement provision that allowed the city to charge speakers for costs relating to the audience's reaction to their speech).
82 See, e.g., Church of the American Knights of the Ku Klux Klan v. City of Gary, 334 F.3d 676, 681–82 (7th Cir. 2003) (invaliding a $4,935 fee charged to cover the costs of police protection as a condition for the group's rally on city hall grounds).
83 See Neisser, "Charging for Free Speech," 330–42 (discussing various First Amendment problems associated with police service fees); ibid., 343–44 (arguing against cleanup deposits on First Amendment grounds).
84 Decisions requiring an indigency exception include *Nationalist Movement*, 481 F.3d 178, 183–86 and Cent. Fla. Nuclear Freeze Campaign v. Walsh, 774 F.2d 1515, 1523–24 (11th Cir. 1985). But see Sullivan v. City of Augusta, 511 F.3d 16, 43–45 (1st Cir. 2007) ("Where, as here, … there are ample alternative forums for speech, we see insufficient justification for the district court's ruling that the Constitution mandates an indigency exception"); Stonewall Union v. City of Columbus, 931 F.2d 1130, 1137 (6th Cir. 1991) ("Because we believe the availability of the sidewalks and parks provides a constitutionally acceptable alternative for indigent paraders, we find that the lack of an indigency exception does not render the ordinance constitutionally invalid."); iMatter v. Njord, 774 F.3d 1258, 1264 (10th Cir. 2014) (agreeing that "so long as there are ample alternative forums for speech, the Constitution does not mandate an indigency exception to an otherwise-valid permit requirement").

85 See, e.g., Sullivan, 511 F.3d 16, 45.

86 See, e.g., ibid., 41. See also iMatter, 774 F.3d 1258, 1265 (concluding that city sidewalks were adequate alternatives to city streets).

87 Murdock v. Pennsylvania, 319 U.S. 105, 111 (1943).

88 See, e.g., Clements v. Fashing, 457 U.S. 957, 964 (1982) (upholding a Texas law regarding the eligibility of officials to run for another public office by distinguishing cases requiring fees from candidates that may unconstitutionally burden candidates of a lower economic status); Lubin v. Panish, 415 U.S. 709, 718 (1974) (ruling that the selection of candidates solely on the ability to pay filing fees unconstitutionally excludes candidates unable to pay).

89 Ibid., 113–14.

90 See Tushnet, "Spontaneous Demonstrations," 781n29 (reaching the same conclusion, although acknowledging a lack of judicial authority).

91 See, e.g., Long Beach Area Peace Network, 522 F.3d 1010, 1032–34 (upholding some costs but holding that charges for "litter abatement" and "traffic control" were invalid); Central Florida Nuclear Freeze Campaign, 774 F.2d 1515 (rejecting shifting of some policing costs to protesters).

92 See, e.g., Stonewall Union, 931 F.2d 1130, 1131 (6th Cir. 1991) (upholding fees for permit processing and traffic control); Sullivan, 511 F.3d 16, 21 (upholding an ordinance requiring permit applicants to pay both a processing fee of $100 and "the cost of the extra police officers and police vehicles needed to control and divert traffic during the event").

93 See Michael C. Dorf, "Reconsidering the Heckler's Veto Principle," *Dorf on Law* (November 22, 2017), www.dorfonlaw.org/2017/11/reconsidering-hecklers-veto-principle .html (suggesting there may be a threshold amount that would qualify as a "compelling interest" for limiting campus speech).

94 See Neisser, "Charging for Free Speech," 301–02 (discussing the First Amendment implications of insurance requirements).

95 Ibid.

96 See Claiborne Hardware, 458 U.S. 886, 916–17. See also iMatter, 774 F.3d 1258, 1270 (invalidating an insurance liability requirement in part on the grounds that the First Amendment does not allow protesters to be held liable for the acts of third parties); Long Beach Area Peace Network, 574 F.3d, 1039–40 (invalidating an indemnification requirement on similar grounds).

97 Neisser, "Charging for Free Speech," 308–10.

98 Ibid., 312.

99 See iMatter, 774 F.3d 1258, 1269 (holding Utah's liability insurance requirement was not narrowly tailored to the government's liability concerns).

100 See ibid., 1271 (invalidating an indemnification requirement).

101 See Dorf, "Reconsidering the Heckler's Veto" (discussing the campus cost-shifting problem).

102 Neisser, "Charging for Free Speech," 297.

103 See Alexander Sammon, "A History of Native Americans Protesting the Dakota Access Pipeline," *Mother Jones* (September 9, 2016), www.motherjones.com/environment/ 2016/09/dakota-access-pipeline-protest-timeline-sioux-standing-rock-jill-stein/ (examining the events that led to the pipeline protests); Monica Davey & Julie Bosman, "Protests Flare After Ferguson Police Officer Is Not Indicted," *N.Y. Times* (November 24, 2014), www.nytimes.com/2014/11/25/us/ferguson-darren-wilson-shooting-michael-brown-grand-jury.html(explaining the events that led to the Ferguson protests); Gregory Krieg, "Police Injured, More than 200 Arrested at Trump Inauguration Protests in DC," *CNN*

(January 21, 2017), www.cnn.com/2017/01/19/politics/trump-inauguration-protests-womens-march/index.html (examining the events surrounding the arrests of protesters at Donald Trump's inauguration).

104 Claiborne Hardware, 458 U.S. 886, 915.

105 See, e.g., Huffman & Wright Logging Co. v. Wade, 857 P.2d 101, 105 (Or. 1993) (en banc) (finding protesters climbed on and chained themselves to plaintiff's logging equipment without permission).

106 See generally Jacobs, "Applying Penalty Enhancements," 54 (challenging the distinction between speech and conduct in context of expressive lawbreaking, including acts of civil disobedience).

107 Cf. Wisconsin v. Mitchell, 508 U.S. 476, 487 (1993) (upholding hate crimes enhancement because the enhancement was not tied to the message of the crime but rather the underlying conduct). In *Mitchell*, the conduct in question was a criminal assault, which does not itself express any message entitled to First Amendment consideration or protection. In the environmental or political protest context, the protest itself is entitled to free speech and assembly protection, even if the underlying trespass is not.

108 See Nick Robinson & Elly Page, "Protecting Dissent: The Freedom of Peaceful Assembly, Civil Disobedience, and Partial First Amendment Protection," 107 *Cornell L. Rev.* 229 (2021).

109 Claiborne Hardware, 458 U.S. 886, 909.

110 See New York Times Co., 276 U.S. 254, 265 (concluding that the First Amendment applied to states' enforcement of common law defamation standards). See also Daniel J. Solove & Neil M. Richards, "Rethinking Free Speech and Civil Liability," 109 *Colum. L. Rev.* 1650, 1689 (2009) (proposing the "duty-defining power" theory of First Amendment limits on civil liability, which focuses on governmental use of power to influence expression).

111 Claiborne Hardware, 458 U.S. 886, 916–17 ("[T]he presence of activity protected by the First Amendment imposes restraints on the grounds that may give rise to damages liability and on the persons who may be held accountable for those damages.").

112 Ibid., 915; See NAACP v. Button, 371 U.S. 415, 438 (1963).

113 Button, 371 U.S. 415, 438.

114 Claiborne Hardware, 458 U.S. 886, 912.

115 See ibid., 913 (observing that political expression "has always rested on the highest rung of the hierarchy of First Amendment values") (quoting Carey v. Brown, 447 U.S. 455, 467 (1980)). See also Garrison v. Louisiana, 379 U.S. 64, 74–75 (1964) ("[S]peech concerning public affairs is more than self-expression; it is the essence of self-government.").

116 Mckesson, 945 F.3d 818, 826.

117 Ibid., 827–28.

118 Ibid., 823.

119 Ibid., 827.

120 Ibid.

121 Ibid., 827–28.

122 Doe, 339 So.3d 524, 532.

123 Claiborne Hardware, 458 U.S. 886, 927.

124 Doe, 339 So.3d 524, 533.

125 See Brandenburg, 395 U.S. 444, 447 (holding that speakers may be held liable for advocacy of violence where they intend to incite imminent lawless acts and those acts are likely to occur).

126 Claiborne Hardware, 458 U.S. 886, 908.

127 Ibid., 918–19.

128 Ibid., 920.
129 NAACP v. Overstreet, 384 U.S. 118, 122 (1966) (Douglas, J., dissenting from denial of certiorari).
130 Mckesson, 945 F.3d 818, 827.
131 See, e.g., Herceg v. Hustler Magazine, Inc., 814 F.2d 1017, 1024 (5th Cir. 1987) ("Mere negligence, therefore, cannot form the basis of liability under the incitement doctrine any more than it can under libel doctrine."); Valenzuela v. Aquino, 800 S.W. 2d 301, 309 (Tx. Ct. App. 1990) (dismissing a negligent infliction of emotional distress claim brought by an abortion provider whose home was picketed). See also N.Y. Times Co., 376 U.S. 254, 279–80 (holding that proof of "actual malice" is required in libel suits brought by public officials).
132 Valenzuela, 800 S.W. 2d 301, 309.
133 Snyder, 562 U.S. 443, 458–59.
134 See Timothy Zick, *Speech Out of Doors: Preserving First Amendment Liberties in Public Places* (Cambridge: Cambridge University Press, 2008), 191–96 (describing the development and content of detailed permitting regimes applicable to public protests).
135 Nieves v. Bartlett, 139 S. Ct. 1715, 1730 (2019) (Gorsuch, J., concurring in part and dissenting in part).
136 See Doe, 339 So.3d 524, 548 (Griffin, J., dissenting) ("the finding of a duty in this case will have a chilling effect on political protests in general as nothing prevents a bad actor from attending an otherwise peaceful protest and committing acts of violence").
137 Mckesson, 945 F.3d 818, 822.
138 See Maxwell, 414 F.2d 1065, 1068.
139 See Tinker v. Des Moines Independent Community School District, 393 U.S. 503, 508 ("Any word spoken … that deviates from the views of another person may start … a disturbance."); Terminiello v. City of Chicago, 337 U.S. 1, 4 (1949) (observing that free speech may best serve its functions "when it induces a condition of unrest").
140 See Julie Bosman, Sabrina Tavernise, & Mike Baker, "Why These Protesters Aren't Staying Home for Coronavirus Orders," N.Y. *Times* (April 23, 2020), www.nytimes.com/2020/04/23/us/coronavirus-protesters.html.
141 Mckesson, 945 F.3d 818, 828 (quoting NAACP, 458 U.S. 886, 916).
142 Claiborne Hardware, 458 U.S. 886, 918.
143 SDCL § 20-9-54(1)-(3).
144 Dakota Rural Action v. Noem, 416 F.Supp.3d 874, 884–86 (D.S.D. 2019).
145 Ibid., 884–85.
146 Ibid., 886–87.
147 Ibid., 889.
148 Ibid., 883–84.
149 See Brandenburg, 395 U.S. 444, 447 (describing incitement standard); Claiborne Hardware, 458 U.S. 886, 908 (limiting protesters' liability for the acts of third parties). See also Scales v. United States, 367 U.S. 203, 229 (1961) ("[Q]uasi-political parties or other groups that may embrace both legal and illegal aims differ from a technical conspiracy, which is defined by its criminal purpose.").
150 See Sines, 324 F. Supp.3d 765 (W.D. Va. 2018) (rejecting a motion to dismiss a suit against Unite the Right rally organizers).
151 Chris Gelardi, "Detroit Is Suing Black Lives Matter Protesters for 'Civil Conspiracy,'" *The Intercept* (December 21, 2020), https://theintercept.com/2020/12/21/detroit-black-lives-matter-lawsuit/.
152 See generally, David B. Filvaroff, "Conspiracy and the First Amendment," 121 *U. Penn. L. Rev.* 189 (1972).

153 Claiborne Hardware, 458 U.S. 886, 933.

154 Ibid., 934.

155 Brandenburg, 395 U.S. 444, 447.

156 Claiborne Hardware, 458 U.S. 886, 908.

157 Ibid., 916.

158 Sines, 324 F. Supp.3d 765, 783–84.

159 Claiborne Hardware, 458 U.S. 886, 908.

160 Ibid.

161 Ibid., 924.

162 Ibid., 925.

163 Ibid., 915 (noting "the nonviolent elements of petitioners' activities are entitled to the protection of the First Amendment").

164 Ibid., 925.

165 Sines, 324 F. Supp.3d 765, 784.

166 See, e.g., ibid., 787 (allegations that defendant Cantwell personally attacked counter-protesters with mace and committed assault); ibid., 790 (allegation that defendant Damigo assaulted counter-protesters).

167 Claiborne Hardware, 458 U.S. 886, 916.

168 Ibid., 920.

169 See Sines, 324 F. Supp.3d 765, 784 (applying for a permit and inviting participants); ibid., 785 (inviting participants and organizing participation); ibid., 787 (telling participants to march in formation); ibid. (using social media to "coordinate attendance" and instructing marchers to wear specific attire); ibid., 789 (publishing content "in support of the rally" and contributing to planning of the rally); ibid., 790 (meeting with other defendants to organize the rally); ibid., 791 (using website to plan rallies); ibid., 792 (using social media to communicate with participants); ibid., 793 (meeting with other defendants to march in formation at rally); ibid., 794 (promotion of event).

170 See, e.g., ibid., 788 (interpreting defendant Vanguard America's rhetoric while considering *later* acts of violence); ibid., 790 (reasoning that defendant Damigo's arrest for violent acts at the rally demonstrated conspiratorial intent).

171 Claiborne Hardware, 458 U.S. 886, 918.

172 Ibid., 902.

173 Ibid., 926. The Court did note that "If that language had been followed by acts of violence, a substantial question would be presented whether Evers could be held liable for the consequences of that unlawful conduct;" ibid., 928. However, the only acts of violence occurred weeks after Evers' speeches, ibid.

174 Ibid., 928.

175 Ibid.

176 Ibid., 929.

177 Ibid.

178 Ibid., 923.

179 Sines, 324 F.Supp.3d 765, 790, 786, 787.

180 Ibid., 789, 786.

181 See, e.g., Hess v. Indiana, 414 U.S. 105, 107–08 (1973) (per curiam) (reversing a disorderly conduct conviction based on a protester stating a group should "take the fucking street later" or "take the fucking street again"); Watts v. United States, 394 U.S. 705, 708 (1969) (reversing a conviction for threatening the president and observing, "The language of the political arena, like the language used in labor disputes, is often vituperative, abusive, and inexact.").

182 Sines, 324 F.Supp.3d 765, 785.
183 See Nicholas Fandos, Michael S. Schmidt, and Maggie Haberman, "144 Constitutional Lawyers Call Trump's First Amendment Defense 'Legally Frivolous,'" N.Y. *Times* A19 (February 6, 2021), https://www.nytimes.com/2021/02/05/us/politics/trump-impeachment-defense.html.
184 See Thompson v. Trump, 2022 WL 503384 *33–36 (D.C.C. 2022).
185 Ibid., *40.
186 Ibid., *39. See also ibid., *44 (concluding that President Trump's January 6 rally speech met the incitement standard).
187 See Detroit Will Breathe v. City of Detroit, 524 F.Supp.3d 704, 712 (E.D. Mich. 2021) (dismissing the city's civil conspiracy counterclaim, noting the city's evidence of a conspiracy was based primarily on evidence the protest group was "organizing and publicizing public protests, albeit with occasional strident and passionate language").
188 See, e.g., Chip Gibbons, "The Prosecution of Inauguration-Day Protesters Is a Threat to Dissent," *The Nation* (October 20, 2017) (describing "conspiracy to riot" charges brought against hundreds of inauguration day protesters, based on protected expression such as chanting and marching).
189 For a thorough discussion of the First Amendment's Petition Clause, see Ronald J. Krotoszynski, *Reclaiming the Petition Clause* (New Haven, CT: Yale University Press, 2012).
190 New York Times Co., 376 U.S. 254, 276.
191 See United States v. Alvarez, 567 U.S. 709 (2012) (rejecting the theory that falsehoods are categorically unprotected speech but allowing that speakers can be liable for falsehoods that cause tangible harms).
192 See ibid., 723 (opinion of Kennedy, J.) ("Where false claims are made to effect a fraud or secure moneys or other valuable considerations, say offers of employment, it is well established that the Government may restrict speech without affronting the First Amendment."); ibid., 734–35 (Breyer, J., concurring) (referring to perjury and false statements made to government officials).
193 New York Times Co., 376 U.S. 254, 276.
194 Hurchalla, 2019 WL 2518748, * 4–5.
195 New York Times Co., 376 U.S. 254, 270.
196 See, e.g., Eastern Railroad Presidents Conference v. Noerr Motor Freight, Inc., 365 U.S. 127, 138 (1961) (holding that antitrust laws do not apply to businesses combining to lobby the government, even where such conduct has an anticompetitive purpose and effect, because the alternative "would raise important constitutional questions" under the First Amendment).
197 The appeals court concluded there was evidence the dean of students, who was at the protest, handed a flyer to a journalist and that faculty members advised students they could place flyers on car windshields. Gibson Bros., 187 N.E.3d 629, 646–48.
198 Ibid., 646.
199 Ibid., 646–47.
200 See *Restatement of Torts (Second)*, § 577 (1), comment f.

5 MANAGING CAMPUS PROTEST

1 See William & Mary, First Amendment Rights on Campus, Committee Charge, www .wm.edu/about/administration/provost/committees/firstamendmentrights/charge/index .php. The views expressed in the chapter and elsewhere in this book are my own and should not in any way be attributed to the university.

2 Healy v. James, 408 U.S. 169 (1972) (Douglas, J., concurring).

3 See Seymour Martin Lipset, *Rebellion in the University* (New Brunswick, NJ: Transaction Publishers, 1976), chs. 4–5 (describing campus activism from the Revolution through the 1950s).

4 Don Mitchell, *A Right to the City: Social Justice and the Fight for Public Space* (New York: Guilford Press, 2003), ch. 3.

5 See generally, Robert Cohen and Reginald E. Zelnik (eds.), *The Free Speech Movement: Reflections on Berkeley in the 1960s* (Berkeley: University of California Press, 2002).

6 Ibid., 92–93.

7 Kenneth J. Heineman, *Put Your Bodies Upon the Wheel: Student Revolt in the 1960s* (Lanham, MD: Rowman & Littlefield, 2001).

8 Healy, 408 U.S. 169, 171.

9 Charles Alan Wright, "The Constitution on the Campus," 22 *Vand. L. Rev.* 1027 (1969).

10 Ibid.

11 See Healy, 408 U.S. 169, 180 (holding the denial of a local SDS chapter violated the First Amendment).

12 John Kenneth Galbraith, "An Adult's Guide to New York, Washington and Other Exotic Places," 4 *New York* 52 (November 5, 1971).

13 See Ronald L. Rowland, "An Overview of State Legislation Responding to Campus Disorders," 1 *J. L. & Educ.* 231 (1972).

14 Keith E. Whittington, *Speak Freely: Why Universities Must Defend Free Speech* 13 (Princeton, NJ: Princeton University Press, 2018).

15 John Inazu, "The Purpose (and Limits) of the University," 5 *Utah L. Rev.* 943, 947 (2018).

16 Healy, 408 U.S. 169, 197.

17 Inazu, "Purpose (and Limits) of the University," 950.

18 Healy, 408 U.S. 169, 180–81.

19 See Robert Post, "The Classic First Amendment Tradition Under Stress: Freedom of Speech and the University," in Lee C. Bollinger & Geoffrey R. Stone (eds.), *The Free Speech Century* (New York: Oxford University Press2018), 106, 112.

20 Ibid., 108.

21 See, e.g., Greg Lukianoff, *Freedom from Speech* (New York: Encounter Books, 2014), 29–36 (discussing "disinvitation season" on many university campuses). See also Greg Lukianoff & Jonathan Haidt, "The Coddling of the American Mind," *Atlantic* (September 2015), https://www.theatlantic.com/magazine/archive/2015/09/the-coddling-of-the-american-mind/399356/; Abby Jackson, "'Disinvitations' for College Speakers Are on the Rise – Here's a List of People Turned Away This Year," *Business Insider* (July 28, 2016), www.businessinsider.com/list-of-disinvited-speakers-at-colleges-2016-7.

22 As I will discuss, the Supreme Court has assumed the First Amendment applies on campus, at least to some activities. See Erwin Chemerinsky & Howard Gillman, *Free Speech on Campus* (New Haven, CT: Yale University Press, 2017), 77 (positing a "free speech zone" outside formal educational settings in which "the only restrictions are those of the society at large").

23 Healy, 408 U.S. 169, 180–81.

24 Ibid.

25 Keyishian v. Bd. Of Regents, 385 U.S. 589, 592 (1967).

26 Rosenberger v. Rector, University of Virginia, 515 U.S. 819, 836 (1995).

27 See UWM Post, Inc. v. Bd. Of Regents, 774 F. Supp. 1163, 1179–80 (E.D. Wis. 1991); Doe v. Univ. of Mich., 721 F. Supp. 852, 866–67 (E.D. Mich. 1989). See also IOTA XI Chapter of Sigma Chi Fraternity v. George Mason Univ., 993 F.2d 386, 393 (4th Cir. 1993) (invalidating the university's punishment of a fraternity based on disapproval of its viewpoint).

28 Post, "The Classic First Amendment Tradition," 112.

29 Thomas Healy, "Return of the Campus Speech Wars," 117 *Mich. L. Rev.* 1063, 1075 (2019).

30 See Inazu, "The Purpose (and Limits) of the University," 949 ("The democratic university must also strive to protect minority, dissenting, or unpopular views – an aspiration that draws its inspiration from the First Amendment."). See also Whittington, *Speak Freely*, 98–99 (discussing truth-seeking and self-government principles in the context of campus protest); Chemerinsky & Gillman, *Free Speech on Campus*, 77 (highlighting the importance of preserving free speech on campuses).

31 See Sweezy v. New Hampshire, 354 U.S. 234, 250 (1957) ("No one should underestimate the vital role in a democracy that is played by those who guide and train our youth."); Inazu, "The Purpose (and Limits) of the University," 949–53 (discussing the democratic functions of universities).

32 Mahanoy Area Sch. Dist. v. B.L., 141 S. Ct 2038, 2046 (2021).

33 See Timothy Zick, *Speech Out of Doors: Preserving First Amendment Liberties in Public Places* (Cambridge: Cambridge University Press, 2008), 273–76 (describing common elements of the "campus order management system").

34 Ibid., 273.

35 Ibid., 274.

36 See ibid.

37 See Roberts v. Haragan, 346 F. Supp. 2d 853 (N.D. Tex. 2004).

38 See PLC v. University of Houston, 259 F. Supp. 2d 575 (S.D. Tex. 2003); see also Brandenburg v. Ohio, 395 U.S. 444 (1969) (narrowly defining the category of unprotected incitement to unlawful action).

39 See Healy, 408 U.S. 169, 181 (holding that "denial [to particular groups] of use of campus facilities for meetings and other appropriate purposes" must be subjected to the level of scrutiny appropriate to any form of prior restraint).

40 Zick, *Speech Out of Doors*, 274.

41 See Freedman v. Maryland, 380 U.S. 51 (1965) (defining procedural protections applicable in cases of prior restraint).

42 Zick, *Speech Out of Doors*, 274.

43 Ibid., 275.

44 See ibid., 276.

45 Post, "The Classic First Amendment Tradition," 118–19.

46 Robert C. Post, "There Is No 1st Amendment Right to Speak on a College Campus," *Vox* (December 31, 2017), www.vox.com/the-big-idea/2017/10/25/16526442/first-amendment-college-campuses-milo-spencer-protests.

47 Rosenberger, University of Virginia, 515 U.S. 819, 836.

48 Widmar v. Vincent, 454 U.S. 263, 267n5 (1981).

49 Healy, 408 U.S. 169, 180–81.

50 See Hague v. Comm. for Indus. Org., 307 U.S. 496, 515 (1939) (recognizing the traditional availability of public streets and parks for expressive activity).

51 Inazu, "The Purpose (and Limits) of the University," 954.

52 See Derek P. Langhauser, "Free and Regulated Speech on Campus: Using Forum Analysis for Assessing Facility Use, Speech Zones, and Related Expressive Activity," 31 *J. C. & U. L.* 481, 483 (2005). See also Bowman v. White, 444 F.3d 967, 976–77 (8th Cir. 2006) (reviewing spaces on typical campus).

53 See Perry Educ. Ass'n v. Perry Local Educators' Ass'n, 460 U.S. 37, 45 (1983) (describing public forum categories).

54 See, e.g., Widmar, 454 U.S. 263 (applying forum doctrine to university facility policy); Rosenberger, 515 U.S. 819, 836 (applying forum doctrine to university policy on funding student publications).

55 Gilles v. Garland, 281 F. App'x 501, 511 (6th Cir. 2008).

56 American Civil Liberties Union v. Mote, 423 F.3d 438, 444 (4th Cir. 2005).

57 Bloedorn v. Grube, 631 F.3d 1218, 1233–34 (11th Cir. 2011).

58 Hays County Guardian v. Supple, 969 F.2d 111.117 (5th Cir. 1992).

59 See, e.g., Bloedorn, 631 F.3d 1218, 1232 ("A university campus will surely contain a wide variety of fora on its grounds."); Bowman, 444 F.3d 967, 976–77 ("[L]abeling the campus as one single type of forum is an impossible, futile task."); Justice for All v. Faulkner, 410 F.3d 760, 766 (5th Cir. 2005) (rejecting the argument that the public forum doctrine requires the court to choose between the polar extremes of treating an entire campus as a designated public forum or a limited public forum).

60 Cf. Widmar, 454 U.S. 263 (holding that a state university could not exclude a student group from campus facilities opened to other student groups).

61 See, e.g., McGlone v. Bell, 681 F.3d 718, 733 (6th Cir. 2012) ("Because the perimeter sidewalks at [Tennessee Tech University] blend into the urban grid and are physically indistinguishable from public sidewalks, they constitute traditional public fora.").

62 See generally Zick, *Speech Out of Doors*.

63 See State v. Spingola, 136 Ohio App. 3d 136, 736 N.E.2d 48 (1999) (reasoning that campus sidewalks and other areas are non-public fora where students have limited expressive rights).

64 See, e.g., Paul Horwitz, "Universities as First Amendment Institutions: Some Easy Answers and Hard Questions," 54 *U.C.L.A. L. Rev.* 1497 (2007).

65 Widmar, 454 U.S. 263, 268n5 (emphasis added).

66 Rosenberger, 515 U.S. 819, 836; Healy, 408 U.S. 169, 180–81.

67 See Joseph D. Herrold, "Capturing the Dialogue: Free Speech Zones and the 'Caging' of First Amendment Rights," 54 *Drake L. Rev.* 949, 955–59 (2006) (describing campus free speech zoning). See also Thomas J. Davis, "Assessing Constitutional Challenges to University Free Speech Zones Under Public Forum Doctrine," 79 *Ind. L. J.* 267 (2004).

68 See Timothy Zick, "Speech and Spatial Tactics," 84 *Tex. L. Rev.* 581 (2006).

69 Zick, *Speech Out of Doors*, 277.

70 See Roberts, 346 F. Supp. 2d 853.

71 See PLC, 259 F. Supp. 2d 575.

72 See Foundation for Individual Rights in Education, "Modesto Junior College Free Speech Area" (September 19, 2013), www.thefire.org/modesto-junior-college-free-speech-zone/.

73 See Zick, *Speech Out of Doors*, 281 (describing a policy limiting access on a 168-acre campus to a single area for a total of two hours per day).

74 FIRE, "Free Speech Zones" (May 24, 2019), www.thefire.org/issues/free-speech-zones/.

75 Ibid.

76 See ibid. (reporting that as of 2018, eleven states had banned campus speech zoning). See also American Association of University Professors, "Campus Free-Speech Legislation: History, Progress, and Problems" (April 2018), https://www.aaup.org/report/campus-free-speech-legislation-history-progress-and-problems.

77 Uzuegbunam v. Preczewski, 141 S. Ct. 792 (2021).

78 The dean of students at the University of Mississippi defended his campus's free speech zone policy on the grounds that it would "make[] it easier to have areas where people know something is going on, so they can choose to listen or to avoid it." Mary M. Kershaw, "Free Speech Has Its Place – or Several – on USA's Campuses," *USA Today* (May 13, 2002).

79 For a discussion of the evidence for and against the proposition that campuses are experiencing a speech "crisis," see Healy, "Return of the Campus Speech Wars."

80 See generally, Mary-Rose Papandrea, "The Free Speech Rights of University Students," 101 *Minn. L. Rev.* 1801 (2017).

81 See Tinker v. Des Moines Indep. Comm. Sch. Dist., 393 U.S. 503 (1969); Bethel Sch. Dist. V. Fraser, 478 U.S. 675 (1986); Hazelwood Sch. Dist. v. Kuhlmeier, 484 U.S. 260 (1988); Morse v. Frederick, 551 U.S. 393 (2007).

82 See Tinker, 393 U.S. 503, 511; Bethel Sch. Dist., 478 U.S. 675, 683.

83 See Inazu, "The Purpose (and Limits) of the University," 957–58, n.66 (collecting and discussing lower court cases).

84 Bd. of Regents of the University of Wisconsin System v. Southworth, 529 U.S. 217, 238n.4 (2000) (Souter, J., concurring).

85 Tilton v. Richardson, 403 U.S. 672, 688 (1971). See also Widmar, 454 U.S. 263, 274n.14 ("University students are, of course, young adults. They are less impressionable than younger students.").

86 See Clay Calvert, "Reconsidering Incitement, *Tinker* and the Heckler's Veto on College Campuses: Richard Spencer and the Charlottesville Factor," 112 *Nw. U. L. Rev. Colloquy* 109, 117 (2018) (arguing that the *Tinker* "disruption" standard should not be applied on college campuses); Frank D. LoMonte, "'The Key Word Is Student': *Hazelwood* Censorship Crashes the Ivy-Covered Gates," 11 *First Amend. L. Rev.* 305, 311 (2013) (lamenting that some lower courts often begin analyses of college students' free speech rights with the secondary school "disruption" standard).

87 See Papandrea, "Free Speech Rights of University Students," 1840–41 (critiquing lower courts' application of the "disruption" standard).

88 See Chemerinsky & Gillman, *Free Speech on Campus*, 76 (arguing that all members of the academic community must have the freedom "to use campus grounds for the broad expression of ideas, even if those ideas are expressed in ways that run contrary to the norms of professional conduct").

89 See Rumsfeld v. Forum for Academic and Institutional Rights, 547 U.S. 47, 65 (2006) ("We have held that high school students can appreciate the difference between speech a school sponsors and speech the school permits because legally required to do so .... Surely students have not lost that ability by the time they get to law school.").

90 See Papandrea, "Free Speech Rights of University Students," 1819–26.

91 Doe, 721 F. Supp. 852; Corry v. Stanford, No. 740309 (Cal. Super. Ct. February 27, 1995).

92 Foundation for Individual Rights in Education, "Spotlight on Speech Codes in 2006: The State of Free Speech on Our Nation's Campuses" (December 6, 2006), www .thefire.org/presentation/wp-content/uploads/2016/05/17121607/Spotlight-on-Speech-Codes-2006.pdf.

93 See Zick, *Speech Out of Doors*, 272.

94 Foundation for Individual Rights in Education, "Spotlight on Speech Codes in 2022," https://d28htnjz2elwuj.cloudfront.net/wp-content/uploads/2022/02/11105334/fire-spotlight-on-speech-codes-2022.pdf.

95 See Speech First, Inc. v. Schlissel, 939 F.3d 756, 765 (6th Cir. 2019).

96 See R.A.V. v. City of St. Paul. 505 U.S. 377 (1992) (invalidating a municipal ordinance that banned expression that was likely to offend).

97 See Chemerinsky & Gillman, *Free Speech on Campus*, 77 (distinguishing between a "professional zone" and a "larger free speech zone" on campuses).

98 See Eliza Gray, "Civil Libertarians Say Expelling Oklahoma Frat Students May Be Illegal," *Time* (March 10, 2015), https://time.com/3739268/sigma-alpha-epsilon-university-of-oklahoma-expel-free-speech/.

99 Rosenberger, 515 U.S. 819, 836. See also Papish v. University of Missouri Curators, 410 U.S. 667 (1973) (overturning the expulsion of a student for distribution of an allegedly indecent newspaper).

100 See Chemerinsky & Gillman, *Free Speech on Campus*, 137–40 (discussing "safe spaces"); ibid., 146–50 (suggesting university officials sometimes use their own voices to push back against messages antithetical to institutional values).

101 See Papandrea, "Free Speech Rights of University Students," 1803 (arguing that "the authority of public universities to restrict student speech is, or at least should be, quite narrow").

102 See Pickering v. Bd. of Educ., 391 U.S. 563, 574 (1968) (balancing a public school teacher's right to speak on matters of public concern with the school's interest in efficient operation).

103 See, e.g., Connick v. Myers, 461 U.S. 138, 154 (1983) ("Our holding today is grounded in our longstanding recognition that the First Amendment's primary aim is the full protection of speech upon issues of public concern, as well as the practical realties involved in the administration of a government office.").

104 Widmar, 454 U.S. 263, 267n5; Healy, 408 U.S. 169, 169.

105 See Zick, *Speech Out of Doors*, 276, 290–92 (discussing restrictions on campus access for non-university entities).

106 Bloedorn, 631 F.3d 1218, 1235. See also Students for Life USA v. Waldrop, 162 F. Supp. 3d 1216, 1224 (S.D. Ala. 2016) ("[T]he Court accepts that the Perimeter could theoretically be a designated public forum as to students despite being a limited public forum as to the general public.").

107 See, e.g., Bowman, 444 F.3d 967, 981 (8th Cir. 2006) (upholding a general permit requirement); Gilles, 281 F. App'x 501, 511 (upholding a student-sponsorship requirement as applied to a campus evangelist).

108 See Brister v. Faulkner, 214 F.3d 675, 682–83 (5th Cir. 2000) (invalidating restrictions on speech and assembly on sidewalks bordering a campus); McGlone, 681 F.3d 718, 734–35 (finding the requirement that potential speakers obtain advance permission to access sidewalks bordering a campus to be an unconstitutional restriction on an evangelist's speech rights).

109 See, e.g., Bowman, 444 F.3d 967, 981–82 (finding a five-day cap on permits was not narrowly drawn to achieve an interest in "fostering a diversity of viewpoints and avoiding the monopolization of space" because "the space will go unused even if Bowman still wants to use the space" after his five days are over).

110 Healy, 408 U.S. 169, 197 (Douglas, J., concurring).

111 See, e.g., Lukianoff, *Freedom from Speech*, 29–36 (discussing "disinvitation season" on many university campuses). See also Lukianoff & Haidt, "The Coddling of the American Mind"; Jackson, "'Disinvitations' for College Speakers."

112 See Gregory P. Magarian, "When Audiences Object: Free Speech and Campus Speaker Protests," 90 *U. Colo. L. Rev.* 551 (2019).

113 Rosie Gray, "How Milo Yiannopoulos's Berkeley 'Free Speech Week' Fell Apart," *The Atlantic* (September 22, 2017), www.theatlantic.com/politics/archive/2017/09/how-milo-yiannopoulos-berkeley-free-speech-week-fell-apart/540867/.

114 Peter Beinart, "A Violent Attack on Free Speech at Middlebury," *The Atlantic* (March 6, 2017), www.theatlantic.com/politics/archive/2017/03/middlebury-free-speech-violence/518667/.

115 Katherine Mangan, "After a Speaker Is Shouted Down, William & Mary Becomes New Flashpoint in Free-Speech Fight," *Chronicle of Higher Education* (October 5, 2017), www.chronicle.com/article/after-a-speaker-is-shouted-down-william-amp-mary-becomes-new-flash-point-in-free-speech-fight/.

116 See Healy, "Return of the Campus Speech Wars," 1064–70 (expressing skepticism about a "free speech crisis" on American campuses).

117 See Frederick Schauer, "Costs and Challenges of the Hostile Audience," 94 *Notre Dame L. Rev.* 1671, 1672 (2019) (noting a trend at colleges and elsewhere of speakers being targeted by "often-large groups of often-disruptive counterprotesters").

118 See Healy, "Return of the Campus Speech Wars," 1079–80.

119 See generally Schauer, "Costs and Challenges." See also Magarian, "When Audiences Object," 557.

120 Magarian, "When Audiences Object," 557.

121 See Brandenburg, 395 U.S. 444, 448.

122 Magarian, "When Audiences Object," 560.

123 Ibid.

124 Ibid.

125 See ibid., 560–61 (describing the conflation of protest and violence in media coverage of the 2015 protests against institutional racism at the University of Missouri).

126 See, e.g., FIRE: Foundation for Individual Rights in Education, "User's Guide to FIRE's Disinvitation Database" (June 9, 2016), https://www.thefire.org/research-learn/campus-disinvitation-database.

127 Magarian, "When Audiences Object," 564.

128 See ibid., 564–65 (noting power imbalance between students and institutions).

129 Ibid., 571.

130 Ibid., 572.

131 See In re Kay, 464 P.2d 142, 147 (Cal. 1970) (positing that even though these forms of dissent "may be impolite and discourteous" they can "nonetheless advance the goals of the First Amendment").

132 See Whittington, *Speak Freely*, 100–01 (discussing the distinction between "actual" and "staged" disruptions).

133 Admittedly, it may be difficult for administrators to distinguish between temporary and symbolic disruptions and those intended as actual disruptions. See ibid., 101 (giving the example of protesters temporarily blocking the motorcade of a university president).

134 See Thomas Emerson, *The System of Freedom of Expression* (New York: Random House, 1970), 338. See also Heidi Kitrosser, "Free Speech, Higher Education, and the PC Narrative," 101 *Minn. L. Rev.* 1987, 2040 (2017) (arguing that shouting down "plainly crosses the line from protest and counter-speech to naked exercise of force").

135 Magarian, "When Audiences Object," 572.

136 Ibid., 573.

137 Whittington, *Speak Freely*, 94.

138 See Schauer, "Costs and Challenges," 1695.

139 See ibid. ("Although it is plain that heckler's do have free speech rights, the argument that they have rights to drown out other speakers seems strained.").

140 See Todd Richmond, "University of Wisconsin Approves Policy That Punishes Student Protesters," *Chicago Tribune* (October 6, 2017), http://perma.cc/UC34-HPH9.

141 See Nick Robinson & Elly Page, "Protecting Dissent: The Freedom of Peaceful Assembly, Civil Disobedience, and Partial First Amendment Protection," 107 *Cornell L. Rev.* 229 (2021) (proposing penalty sensitivity for minor legal infractions associated with civil disobedience).

142 Goldwater Institute, "Campus Free Speech Act," § 1(J).

143 See Schauer, "Costs and Challenges," 1696 (positing that "questions about what forms of behavior are to count as interference persist, although they are as much questions of cognitive science as they are of law").

144 Ibid., 1697.

145 See generally Schauer, "Costs and Challenges."

146 See ibid., 1676–83 (reviewing the Supreme Court's "hostile audience" decisions).

147 Ibid., 1687. See Stephen Holmes & Cass R. Sunstein, *The Costs of Rights: Why Liberty Depends on Taxes* (New York: W.W. Norton & Company, 1999) (examining the various costs of rights protection).

148 See Brandenburg, 395 U.S. 444, 448 (invalidating an Ohio statute that allowed criminal punishment for mere advocacy of violence, even if the violence was not imminent or likely to occur). See also Calvert, "Reconsidering Incitement," 116 (arguing that past violence in places like Charlottesville does not justify university decisions to censor future speech).

149 Padgett v. Auburn University, 2017 WL 10241386 *1 (M.D. Ala., April 18, 2017).

150 I have already ruled out the application of the "substantial disruption" standard used in secondary schools, which seems to allow officials to rely on *anticipated* disruption.

151 One might argue that if a particular speaker, for example Richard Spencer, has been involved in incidents in which campus audiences have reacted violently to his message, other universities should be able to rely on those incidents when denying a permit to speak. By the same token, if, as was the case at the University of Florida, Spencer's speech did not result in violence, a court would presumably also take that into account in making "imminence" and "likelihood" determinations. The Supreme Court has not defined the quantum of evidence needed to demonstrate when unlawful activity will "imminently" and "likely" follow speech. It is possible a court would credit such evidence, assuming the circumstances were as described – i.e., the same speaker, scheduled to deliver essentially the same remarks. However, that assumes all campus audiences would react the same way to the speech. Further, preemptively restraining a speaker based on the unlawful acts of the audience remains a serious problem.

152 See University of California, Berkeley, "Report of the Chancellor's Commission on Free Speech" (2018), https://chancellor.berkeley.edu/sites/default/files/report_of_the_commission_on_free_speech.pdf.

153 Claire McNeill, "UF Security Costs Top $500,000 for Richard Spencer's Talk on White 'Separation,'" *Tampa Bay Times* (October 11, 2017), https://www.tampabay.com/news/education/college/uf-security-costs-top-500000-for-richard-spencers-talk-on-white-separation/2340689/.

154 Forsyth Cty. v. Nationalist Movement, 505 U.S. 123, 124 (1992).

155 Ibid., 134–35.

156 Schauer, "Costs and Challenges," 1690.

157 See Calvert, "Reconsidering Incitement," 29, n133 (suggesting *Forsyth County* may allow campus administrators to develop content-neutral criteria for charging security fees). But see Schauer, "Costs and Challenges," 1682 (positing "it is at least plausible to speculate that in 1992 all members of the Supreme Court believed it a violation of the First Amendment to impose upon demonstrators the cost of police protection and related security to control a hostile audience whose hostility was in response to the content of an otherwise constitutionally protected speech, protest, march, demonstration, or rally").

158 See Erica Goldberg, "Must Universities 'Subsidize' Controversial Ideas?: Allocating Security Fees When Student Groups Host Divisive Speakers," 21 *Geo. Mason U. C. R. L. J.* 349, 405 (2011) ("Violent responses to controversial speech are unfortunate, but penalizing speakers for the misdeeds of their listeners is a far greater injustice."); Macklin W. Thornton, "Laying Siege to the Ivory Tower: Resource Allocation in Response to the Heckler's Veto on University Campuses," 55 *S.D. L. Rev.* 674 (2018) ("In confronting a heckler's veto, public universities should afford speakers the positive right to speak.").

159 Shelton v. Tucker, 364 U.S. 479, 487 (1960).

160 Gallup, "Free Expression on Campus: A Survey of U.S. College Students and U.S. Adults" 12 (2016), https://knightfoundation.org/wp-content/uploads/2016/04/FreeSpeech_campus-1.pdf.

161 See Healy, "Return of the Campus Speech Wars," 1064–70 (reviewing evidence concerning university students' attitudes toward controversial speech and concluding the "crisis" narrative is overstated).

162 Inazu, "The Purpose (and Limits) of the University."

163 Ibid., 947.

164 Ibid., 949.

165 Whittington, *Speak Freely*, 7.

166 Healy, 408 U.S. 169, 169 (Douglas, J., concurring).

6 ARMING PUBLIC PROTESTS

1 Luke Morgan, "Leave Your Guns at Home: The Constitutionality of a Prohibition on Carrying Firearms at Political Demonstrations," 68 *Duke L. J.* 175, 181 (2018).

2 District of Columbia v. Heller, 554 U.S. 570 (2008); McDonald v. City of Chicago, 561 U.S. 742 (2010).

3 New York State Rifle & Pistol Association v. Bruen, 142S. Ct. 2111 (2022).

4 Although this chapter focuses on the public carrying of firearms, these are not the only "arms" at issue. See Eric Ruben, "The Law of the Gun," 107 *Iowa L. Rev.* 173 (2021) (analyzing the right to keep and bear *non-firearms* weapons).

5 Heller, 554 U.S. 570, 626.

6 Ibid., 627.

7 Ibid., 626–27. These limits on the Second Amendment right were reaffirmed in McDonald, 561 U.S. 742, 786.

8 Heller, 554 U.S. 570, 620–21.

9 Ibid., 626.

10 See ibid., 613–14 (reviewing early laws banning concealed carry but retaining open carry).

11 See ibid., 613.

12 The Court affirmed this understanding in *Bruen*. See ibid., 2150 (concluding that early history showed "States could lawfully eliminate one kind of public carry – concealed carry – so long as they left open the option to carry openly.").

13 Bruen, 142 S. Ct. 2111, 2133.

14 Ibid., 2124; see also ibid., 2162 (Kavanaugh, J., concurring) (observing that the Court's decision did not call these licensing laws, currently used in 43 states, into question).
15 Ibid., 2126.
16 Ibid., 2133.
17 Eric Tirschwell & Alla Lefkowitz, "Prohibiting Guns at Public Demonstrations: Debunking First and Second Amendment Myths After Charlottesville," 65 *UCLA L. Rev. Disc.* 172, 178 (2018).
18 See Everytown for Gun Safety, "Armed Assembly: Guns, Demonstrations, and Political Violence in America," (August 23, 2021), https://everytownresearch.org/report/armed-assembly-guns-demonstrations-and-political-violence-in-america/.
19 Vera Bergenbruen, "Armed Demonstrators and Far-Right Groups Are Escalating Tensions at Abortion Protests," *Time* (July 8, 2022), https://time.com/6194085/abortion-protests-guns-violence-extremists.
20 See Katlyn E. DeBoer, "Clash of the First and Second Amendments: Proposed Regulation of Armed Protests," 45 *Hastings Const. L. Q.* 333, 337–40 (2018) (describing several recent examples of armed protests).
21 See Andrew Leonatti, "Why Was Kyle Rittenhouse Acquitted?" *FindLaw* (November 23, 2021), www.findlaw.com/legalblogs/courtside/why-was-kyle-rittenhouse-acquitted/.
22 My initial view was that public carry was not *wholly* incompatible with public protest, in the literal sense that an individual could attend a public rally without necessarily undermining others' First Amendment rights. See Timothy Zick, "Arming Public Protests," 104 *Iowa L. Rev.* 223 (2018). For the reasons discussed, I have come to view the two activities as both inherently and fundamentally incompatible.
23 David Frum, "The Chilling Effects of Openly Displayed Firearms," *The Atlantic* (August 16, 2017), www.theatlantic.com/politics/archive/2017/08/open-carry-laws-mean-charlottesville-could-have-been-graver/537087/.
24 John Feinblatt, "Ban the Open Carry of Firearms," N.Y. *Times* (August 17, 2017) (op-ed arguing for ban on open carry at public protests and in public places), www.nytimes.com/2017/08/17/opinion/open-carry-charlottesville.html.
25 Mary Anne Franks, *The Cult of the Constitution: Our Deadly Devotion to Guns and Free Speech* 102 (Stanford, CA: Stanford University Press, 2019).
26 Ibid.
27 See generally Darrell A. H. Miller, "Guns as Smut: Defending the Home-Bound Second Amendment," 109 *Colum. L. Rev.* 1278 (2009) (arguing for a "home-bound" Second Amendment).
28 Ibid., 1308.
29 Ibid.
30 Ibid., 1310.
31 Ibid.
32 Ibid. (quoting Jack M. Balkin, "Constitutional Hardball and Constitutional Crises," 26 *Quinnipiac L. Rev.* 579, 592 (2008)).
33 Gregory P. Magarian, "Speaking Truth to Firepower: How the First Amendment Destabilizes the Second," 91 *Tex. L. Rev.* 49, 95 (2012).
34 Ibid.
35 See Whitney v. California, 274 U.S. 357, 375 (1927) (Brandeis, J. concurring) ("the fitting remedy for evil counsels is good ones").
36 Joe Palazzolo, "ACLU Will No Longer Defend Hate Groups Protesting With Firearms," *Wall St. Journal* (August 17, 2017), www.wsj.com/articles/aclu-changes-policy-on-defending-hate-groups-protesting-with-firearms-1503010167.

37 Eugene Volokh, "The First and Second Amendments," 109 *Colum. L. Rev. Online* 97, 102–03 (2009).

38 Ibid., 102.

39 Ibid.

40 See Paul Duggan, "Militiamen Came to Charlottesville as Neutral First Amendment Protectors, Commander Says," *Wash. Post* (August 13, 2017).

41 See Everytown for Gun Safety, "Armed Assembly."

42 Ibid.

43 Ibid.

44 See Bergenbruen, "Armed Demonstrators and Far Right Groups" (reporting on ACLED study concerning firearms at abortion protests).

45 Diana Palmer, "Fired Up or Shut Down: The Chilling Effect at Armed Protests" (April 2021) (doctoral dissertation on file with author), www.northeastern.edu/rise/presentations/fired-up-or-shut-down-the-chilling-effect-at-armed-protests.

46 Ibid., ch. 4.

47 Ibid.

48 See Zick, "Arming Public Protests," 253 (expressing doubts about assertion of a First Amendment-based right based solely on state allowance of public carry). But see Monica Youn, "The Chilling Effect and the Problem of Private Action," 66 *Vand. L. Rev.* 1473 (2013) (arguing that private deterrence of the exercise of constitutional rights ought to be a cognizable injury).

49 See Cox v. Louisiana, 379 U.S. 536, 551 (1965); Gregory v. City of Chicago, 394 U.S. 111, 117–20 (1969) (Black, J., concurring); Police Dep't of Chicago v. Mosley, 408 U.S. 92, 97 (1972); Forsyth County v. Nationalist Movement, 505 U.S. 123, 134–36 (1992).

50 See Zack Beauchamp, "Why Police Encouraged a Teenager with a Gun to Patrol Kenosha's Streets," *Vox* (August 27, 2000) (noting police said "we appreciate you guys" to armed militias), www.vox.com/2020/8/27/21404117/kenosha-kyle-rittenhouse-police-gun-populism.

51 Matt Cohen, "Armed Protesters Stormed the Michigan Statehouse This Afternoon," *Mother Jones* (April 30, 2020), www.motherjones.com/coronavirus-updates/2020/04/lansing-michigan-capitol-protests-stay-at-home-order-whitmer/.

52 See Tirschwell & Lefkowitz, "Prohibiting Guns at Public Demonstrations," 189 ("[E]lected officials have wide latitude within the First and Second Amendments to prohibit and punish the open carry of weapons where such conduct is likely to intimidate, alarm, or terrify the public, or cause civil disorder.").

53 Young v. State, 992 F.3d 765, 813 (9th Cir. 2021) (en banc).

54 To ensure First Amendment content neutrality, the law or regulation would apply to any event that requires a permit, including public protests.

55 Hague v. Comm. For Indus. Org., 307 U.S. 496, 515 (1939).

56 Miller, "Guns as Smut," 475.

57 See Ala. Code § 13A-11-59; Cal. Pen. Code § 17510; D.C. Code § 7-2509.07(a)(14); 430 Ill. Comp. Stat. § 66/65(a)(10); 720 Ill. Comp. Stat. § 5/24-1(a)(8); Md. Code Ann. Criminal Law § 4-208; N.C. Gen. Stat. § 14-277.2. Alabama law defines "demonstration" as follows:

> Demonstrating, picketing, speechmaking or marching, holding of vigils and all other like forms of conduct which involve the communication or expression of views or grievances engaged in by one or more persons, the conduct of which has the effect, intent or propensity to draw a crowd or onlookers. Such term shall not include casual use of property by visitors or tourists which does not have an intent or propensity to attract a crowd or onlookers.
> § 13A-11-59(a)(1).

58 See, e.g., D.C. Code § 7-2509.07(a)(14). See also Ala. Code § 13A-11-59.

59 N.C. Gen. Stat. § 14-277.2(a) (emphasis added).

60 See Gregory S. Schneider, "Richmond City Council Ban on Firearms at Public Events," *Wash. Post* (September 9, 2020), www.washingtonpost.com/local/virginia-politics/richmond-council-firearms-ban/2020/09/09/aa61b53a-f2e8-11ea-b796-2dd09962649c_story.html.

61 See, e.g., Kendall Burchard, "Your 'Little Friend' Doesn't Say 'Hello': Putting the First Amendment Before the Second in Public Protests," 104 *Va. L. Rev. Online* 30 (2018); Tirschwell & Lefkowitz, "Prohibiting Guns at Public Demonstrations."

62 Bruen, 142 S. Ct. 2111, 2133.

63 Ibid.

64 See Darrell A. H. Miller, "Constitutional Conflict and Sensitive Places," 28 *Wm. & Mary. Bill of Rts. J.* 459, 476 (2019).

65 Statute of Northampton 1328, 2 Edw. 3 c.3 (Eng.).

66 Bruen, 142 S. Ct. 2111, 2139-42 (discussing Northampton law).

67 Ibid., 2142.

68 See David B. Kopel & Joseph G. S. Greenlee, "The 'Sensitive Places' Doctrine: Locational Limits on the Right to Bear Arms," 13 *Charleston L. Rev.* 205, 229 (2018) (noting that by the time of American independence, there was "great suspicion about large armed assemblies").

69 See ibid., 244. See also Tirschwell & Lefkowitz, "Prohibiting Guns at Public Demonstrations," 178n25.

70 *Public Statutes of the State of Tennessee, Since the Year 1858: Being in the Nature of a Supplement to the Code* 108 (2nd ed. Supp. 1972).

71 1870 Tex. Laws 63 (emphasis added).

72 1879 Mo. Laws § 1274.

73 *General Statutes of Oklahoma: A Compilation of All the Laws of a General Nature Including the Session Laws of 1907*, 451 (1908).

74 See Kopel & Greenlee, "'Sensitive Places' Doctrine," 290 (arguing that "public assembly" bans are not supported under the "sensitive places" doctrine and violate broad Second Amendment right to public carry).

75 See Heller, 554 U.S. 570, 582, 595, 606, 618, 634-35; Bruen, 142 S. Ct. 2111, 2139-42.

76 See White House Vigil for ERA Comm. V. Clark, 746 F.2d 1518, 1534 (D.C. Cir. 1984) (upholding sign regulation under the First Amendment's standard for "time, place, and manner" regulations).

77 Heller, 554 U.S. 570, 626.

78 See Morgan, "Leave Your Guns at Home."

79 See Carina Bentata Gryting & Mark Anthony Frasetto, "NYSRPA v. Bruen and the Future of the Sensitive Places Doctrine: Rejecting the Ahistorical Government Security Approach," 63 *B.C. L. Rev. E.Supp.* I.-60 (2022), https://lawdigitalcommons.bc.edu/cgi/viewcontent.cgi?article=4076&context=bclr&_ga=2.49292003.458692541.1657038627-623047687.1653340792.

80 Heller, 554 U.S. 570, 626.

81 Bruen, 142 S. Ct. 2111, 2133.

82 Adderley v. Florida, 385 U.S. 39, 49 (1966) (Douglas, J., dissenting).

83 See Miller, "Constitutional Conflict," 470–72.

84 Ibid., 471–72.

85 See Kopel & Greenlee, "'Sensitive Places' Doctrine," 250–52.

86 Bruen, 142 S. Ct. 2111, 2134.

87 See, e.g., Va. Code Ann. § 18.2-287.4 (2014) (prohibiting open carry of handguns in certain populous cities and counties); 18 Pa. Cons. Stat. Ann. § 6108 (open carrying of handguns is freely allowed everywhere in the state of Pennsylvania, except Philadelphia, where a person must be licensed to carry a firearm in order to openly carry); ibid. (open carry of long guns prohibited in Philadelphia).

88 See Heller, 554 U.S. 570, 684–87(Breyer, J., dissenting) (discussing gun powder and other firearms regulations in large cities).

89 Miller, "Guns as Smut," 478. See also Gregory P. Magarian, "Conflicting Reports: When Gun Rights Threaten Free Speech," 83 Law & Cont. Probs. 169, 189–91 (2020) (distinguishing between Second Amendment autonomy and First Amendment collective interests).

90 Tirschwell & Lefkowitz, "Prohibiting Guns at Public Demonstrations," 180 n36 (collecting sources).

91 Mass Gen, Laws. ch. 33, §129. The Massachusetts Supreme Judicial Court upheld this law in Commonwealth v. Murphy, 44 N.E. 138, 138 (Mass. 1896).

92 30 R.I. Gen Laws § 30-12-7.

93 Presser v. Illinois, 116 U.S. 252 (1886).

94 Heller, 554 U.S. 570, 620 (citing Presser, 116 U.S. 252, 264–65).

95 Tirschwell & Lefkowitz, "Prohibiting Guns at Public Demonstrations," 181n43, (collecting laws).

96 See Vietnamese Fishermen's Ass'n v. Knights of the Ku Klux Klan, 543 F. Supp. 198 (S.D. Tex. 1982); Person v. Miller, 854 F.2d 656 (4th Cir. 1988).

97 See John Early, "3 Militia Groups Connected to Unite the Right Rally Settle Lawsuits" (May 16; updated May 30, 2018), https://web.archive.org/web/20190214121756/ https://www.nbc29.com/story/38204693/settlements-from-unite-the-right-05-16-2018. See also City of Charlottesville v. Pennsylvania Light Foot Militia, Case No. 17000560–00 (Consent Decrees and Default Judgments), www.law.georgetown.edu/icap/wp-content/uploads/sites/32/2018/08/All-Consent-Decrees-and-Default-Judgments-without-photos.pdf.

98 Va. Code. Ann. § 18.2-433.2(1) (2014).

99 See Institute for Constitutional Advocacy and Protection, "Prohibiting Private Armies at Public Rallies," 2 (3rd ed., September 2020), www.law.georgetown.edu/icap/wp-content/uploads/sites/32/2018/04/Prohibiting-Private-Armies-at-Public-Rallies.pdf.

100 Ibid., 5–7.

101 Michael C. Dorf, "Constitutional Arithmetic Post-Charlottesville: Sometimes One Plus One Equals Zero," Dorf on Law (August 21, 2017), www.dorfonlaw.org/2017/08/constitutional-arithmetic-post.html.

102 Michael C. Dorf, "When Two Rights Makes a Wrong: Armed Assembly Under the First and Second Amendments," 116 Nw. L. Rev. 111 (2021).

103 See Tabatha Abu El-Haj, "The Neglected Right of Assembly," 56 UCLA L. Rev. 543, 560–70 (2009) (recounting the early American understanding of the right of "peaceable" assembly).

104 See Zick, "Arming Public Protests," 250–52 (discussing expressive association claim).

105 See generally John D. Inazu, Liberty's Refuge: The Forgotten Freedom of Assembly (New Haven, CT: Yale University Press, 2010). See also Boy Scouts of America v. Dale, 530 U.S. 640, 653–54 (2000) (invalidating an anti-discrimination law on the ground that it violated the First Amendment right to associate for expressive purposes).

106 See Dale, 530 U.S. 640, 653 ("As we give deference to an association's assertions regarding the nature of its expression, we must also give deference to an association's view of what would impair its expression.").

107 New York State Rifle & Piston Ass'n v. City of New York, 883 F.3d 45, 67–68 (2nd Cir. 2018).

108 See, e.g., S.C. Code § 22-5-150 (prohibiting any person from going "armed offensively, to the terror of the people").

109 See William Blackstone, *Commentaries on the Laws of England*, Book the Fourth (Oxford: Clarendon Press, 1769) 148–49 ("The offence of riding or going armed with dangerous or unusual weapons is a crime against the public peace, by terrifying the good people of the land; and is particularly prohibited by the Statute of Northampton."). See also State v. Huntly, 25 N.C. 418, 418 (1843); State v. Staten, 32 N.C. App. 495, 496–97 (1977); Simpson v. State, 13 Tenn. (5 Yer.) 356 (1833); O'Neill v. State, 16 Ala. 65, 67 (1849); Saul Cornell, "The Right to Keep and Carry Arms in Anglo-American Law: Preserving Liberty and Keeping the Peace," 80 *Law & Cont. Prob.* 11 (2017) (discussing early common law concerning public arms-bearing); Saul Cornell & Nathan DeDino, "A Well Regulated Right: The Early American Origins of Gun Control," 73 *Fordham L. Rev.* 487 (2004) (examining a number of early American restrictions on public carry).

110 See Bruen, 142 S. Ct. 2111, 2144–45.

111 See Mark Anthony Frassetto, "To the Terror of the People: Public Disorder Crimes and the Original Public Understanding of the Second Amendment," 43 *S. Ill. U. L. J.* 61, 67 (2018) (interpreting the Statute of Northampton to generally preclude public carry).

112 See Chune v. Piott, 80 Eng. Rep. 1161, 1162 (K.B. 1615) ("Without all question, the sheriffe hath power to commit … if contrary to the Statute of Northampton, he sees any one to carry weapons in the high-way, in terrorem populi Regis; he ought to take him, and arrest him, notwithstanding he doth not break the peace in his presence.").

113 Queen v. Soley, 88 Eng. Rep. 935, 936–37 (Q.B. 1701).

114 See 1 William Hawkins, *A Treatise of the Pleas of the Crown; Or, A System of the Principal Matters Relating To That Subject, Digested Under Proper Heads* (8th ed., by John Curwood) (London:Printed for S. Sweet, R. Pheney, A. Maxwell, and R. Stevens and Sons, 1824) 516 (including among the things likely to strike terror in the people "the Shew of Armour"). But see Bruen, 142 S. Ct. 2111, 2144-45 (citing Hawkins for a narrower interpretation of the offense).

115 See Bruen, 142 S. Ct. 2111, 2145 (reviewing English and early American history). See also Zick, "Arming Public Protests," 59 (discussing possible limits of armed to the terror offense).

116 Bruen, 142 S. Ct. 2111, 2145.

117 See State v. Dawson, 272 N.C. 535, 541–42 (1968) (describing elements of the crime). See ibid., 549 (upholding a conviction where the defendant, armed with a carbine and four pistols, drove on the public highways at night, firing bullets into a store and two homes).

118 See Virginia Bridges, "A Durham Man Brought a Semi-Automatic Rifle to a Rumored KKK Rally. Did He Break the Law?" *The Herald Sun* (September 6, 2017) (reporting North Carolina officers arrested a would-be counter-protester for "going armed to the terror" when he appeared at the public site of a rumored KKK rally in Durham openly displaying a semi-automatic rifle), www.heraldsun.com/news/local/counties/durham-county/article171511767.html.

119 Tirschwell & Lefkowitz, "Prohibiting Guns at Public Demonstrations," 183–84.

120 See Joseph Blocher, Samuel W. Buell, Jacob D. Charles & Darrell A. H. Miller, "Pointing Guns," 99 *Tex. L. Rev.* 101, 123 (2021) (concluding that Heller does not jeopardize brandishing and other firearms offenses).

121 Ibid., 103.
122 Ibid., 107.
123 Ibid.
124 See, e.g., Kolbe v. Hogan, 849 F.3d 114 (4th Cir.), cert. denied, 138 S. Ct. 469 (2017).
125 Duncan v. Becerra, 970 F.3d 1133, 1147 (9th Cir. 2020), rev'd, Duncan v. Bonta, 19 F.4th 1087 (9th Cir. 2021) (en banc).
126 See, e.g., ILL. Comp. Stat. 5/24–1(a)(3) (West 2010 & Supp. 2018).
127 See David M. Shapiro, "Guns, Speech, Charlottesville: The Semiotics of Semiautomatics," 106 *Geo. L. J. Online* 1, 4–6 (2017) (proposing "open-carry zones" as a means of regulating open carry at public protests); Bruen, 142 S. Ct. 2111, 2145 (discussing early state surety laws). These options have serious drawbacks or limits. See Zick, "Arming Public Protests," 247–48 (critiquing open-carry zone proposal on safety and other grounds); Magarian, "Speaking Truth to Firepower," 174–75 (raising potential First Amendment content neutrality concerns with open-carry zoning); Bruen, 142 S. Ct. 2111, 2145 (concluding surety laws required a showing of reasonable cause to fear injury or breach of peace by the arms bearer).
128 Police Dept. of the City of Chicago, 408 U.S. 92, 95.
129 Ward v. Rock Against Racism, 491 U.S. 781, 791 (1989).
130 See Dorf, "When Two Rights Make a Wrong," 10 (concluding "[a] carefully crafted restriction on armed assembly should satisfy" First Amendment time, place, and manner standards).
131 See Texas v. Johnson, 491 U.S. 397, 405 (1989) (invalidating a state law conviction for "desecrating" the U.S. flag).
132 United States v. O'Brien, 391 U.S. 367, 376 (1968).
133 Rumsfeld v. Forum for Academic and Institutional Rights, 547 U.S. 47, 66 (2006).
134 See Chesney v. City of Jackson, 171 F.Supp.3d 605, 618 (E.D. Mich. 2016) (concluding that the most common audience reaction to seeing public carry is fear); Northrup v. Toledo Police Div., 58 F. Supp. 3d 842, 848 (N.D. Ohio 2014), rev'd on other grounds, 785 F.3d 1128 (6th Cir. 2015) (rejecting the argument that the defendant, who was carrying a firearm in a holster when arrested, was engaged in expressive conduct); Deffert v. Moe, 111 F. Supp. 3d 797, 814 (W.D. Mich. 2015); Baker v. Schwarb, 40 F. Supp. 3d 881, 895 (E.D. Mich. 2014) (observing that the audience did not appear to understand the message the armed defendant was seeking to convey); Nordyke v. King, 319 F.3d 1185, 1190 (9th Cir. 2003) ("Typically a person possessing a gun has no intent to convey a particular message, nor is any particular message likely to be understood by those who view it."). See also Burchard, "Your Little Friend Doesn't Say Hello," 44 ("Guns don't speak. Although they may command attention and fear, the objects themselves are not inherently expressive."); Tirschwell & Lefkowitz, "Prohibiting Guns at Public Demonstrations," 188 (concluding that open carry is not expressive).
135 O'Brien, 391 U.S. 367, 376. See also Forum for Academic and Institutional Rights, 547 U.S. 41, 66 (rejecting the claim that requiring law schools to send emails and provide other forms of equal access for military employers violated rights of expressive conduct).
136 See Nordyke, 319 F.3d 1185, 1190 (observing that "a gun supporter waving a gun at an anti-gun control rally" may be engaged in expressive conduct); Burgess v. Wallingford, 2013 WL 4494481, *9 (D. Conn. May 15, 2013) ("Gun possession may, in some contexts, … invoke First Amendment analysis.").
137 O'Brien, 391 U.S. 367, 376–77.

138 See Watts v. United States, 394 U.S. 705, 708 (1969) (holding that "true threats" are not protected by the Free Speech Clause); Virginia v. Black, 538 U.S. 343, 360 (2003) ("Intimidation in the constitutionally proscribable sense of the word is a type of true threat, where a speaker directs a threat to a person or group of persons with the intent of placing the victim in fear of bodily harm or death.").

139 Joseph Blocher & Reva Siegel, "Guns Are a Threat to the Body Politic," *The Atlantic* (March 8, 2021), www.theatlantic.com/ideas/archive/2021/03/guns-are-threat-body-politic/618158/.

140 Joseph Blocher & Reva B. Siegel, "When Guns Threaten the Public Sphere: A New Account of Public Safety Regulation under *Heller*," 116 *Nw. L. Rev.* 139 (2021).

141 Ibid.

142 Ibid., 165.

143 Blocher & Siegel, "When Guns Threaten the Public Sphere."

7 PUBLIC PROTEST AND EMERGENCY POWERS

1 Nev. Rev. Stat. § 414.060.

2 James G. Hodge, Jr., Jennifer L. Piatt, Hanna N. Reinke, & Emily Carey, "COVID's Constitutional Conundrum: Assessing Individual Rights in Public Health Emergencies," 88 *Tenn. L. Rev.* 837 (2021).

3 See Lawrence O. Gostin & James G. Hodge, "US Emergency Legal Responses to Novel Coronavirus: Balancing Public Health and Civil Liberties," 323 *Am. Med. Ass'n* 1131 (2020).

4 See Sarah Mervosh et al., "See Which States and Cities Have Told Residents to Stay at Home," *N.Y. Times* (April 20, 2020), www.nytimes.com/interactive/2020/us/coronavirus-stay-at-home-order.html.

5 See Geller v. de Blasio, No. 20-cv-3566, 2020 WL 2520711 * 1 (S.D.N.Y. May 18, 2020) (discussing New York City's prohibition on public gatherings, which included protests); @RaleighPolice, Twitter (April 14, 2020), https://twitter.com/raleighpolice/status/1250111779574894594? ("Protesting is a non-essential activity"); Nat'l Coal. Against Censorship, "The Right to Protest During the Pandemic, https://ncac .org/news/dissent-protest-pandemic. A few state orders classified protest as "essential." See Ohio Dep't of Health, Amended Director's Stay At Home Order 12(g) (April 2, 2020), https://coronavirus.ohio.gov/static/publicorders/Directors-Stay-At-Home-Order-Amended-04-02-20.pdf; Nico Perrino, "The Constitution in the Age of the Coronavirus," *So to Speak*, podcast, The Fire (April 28, 2020) (describing Ohio's stay-at-home order exempting protest as an essential activity), www.thefire .org/news-and-media/so-to-speak/.

6 See generally Jeremy Pressman & Erica Chenoweth, "Crowd Estimates April 2020," https://docs.google.com/spreadsheets/d/138XK6Cc9-1GdVL12Kef-fQto6pzoGlwI-Eyea8r_XwI/edit#gid=1538635238; Jeremy Pressman & Erica Chenoweth, "Crowd Estimates May 2020," https://docs.google.com/spreadsheets/d/1pZo5p9EKZJ87IvPVjIp5onQQPET_ucV8vKVfZ6NpOvg/edit#gid=1538635238.

7 See Pressman & Chenoweth, "Crowd Estimates May 2020."

8 Toluse Olorunnipa et al., "Rallies against Stay-at-Home Orders Grow as Trump Sides with Protesters," *Wash. Post* (April 17, 2020), www.washingtonpost.com/national/rallies-against-stay-at-home-orders-grow-as-trump-sides-with-protesters/2020/04/17/1405ba54-7f4e-11ea-8013-1b6da0e4a2b7_story.html.

9 See Pressman & Chenoweth, "Crowd Estimates May 2020."

10 Sam Stanton, "CHP Bans Protests at California Capitol After Rally Against Newsom's Stay-at-Home Order," *The Sacramento Bee* (April 22, 2020), www.sacbee.com/article242198781.html.

11 Michael Nowels, "Want to Hold a Protest in California? Here Are the Strict New Rules from Gov. Gavin Newsom," *The Mercury News*, www.mercurynews.com/2020/05/26/want-to-hold-a-protest-in-california-here-are-strict-new-rules-from-gov-gavin-newsom/.

12 See Janelle Griffith, "Nurses are Protesting Working Conditions Under Coronavirus – and Say Hospitals Aren't Protecting Them," *NBS News.com* (April 20, 2020), www.nbcnews.com/news/us-news/nurses-are-protesting-working-conditions-under-coronavirus-say-hospitals-aren-n1181321.

13 See Rachel Lerman & Nitasha Tiku, "Amazon, Instacart Workers Launch May Day Strike to Protest Treatment During Coronavirus Pandemic," *Wash. Post* (May 1, 2020), www.washingtonpost.com/technology/2020/05/01/amazon-instacart-workers-strike/.

14 Angela Fortuna, "Protesters Fight for Prisoners to Be Released Because of Coronavirus," *NBC Connecticut* (April 12, 2020), www.nbcconnecticut.com/news/local/protesters-fight-for-prisoners-to-be-released-because-of-coronavirus/2254444/.

15 Ross Ketschke, "'Honking Protest' Calls for Detained Migrants to Be Released Amid Pandemic," *NBC 5* (April 17, 2020), www.mynbc5.com/article/honking-protest-calls-for-detained-migrants-to-be-released-amid-pandemic/32193366.

16 Ibid.

17 Tori Lynn Schneider, "Protesters Line Old Capitol Steps with Body Bags, Urge Florida Governor Not to Rush Re-Opening," *Tallahassee Democrat* (May 12, 2020), www.tallahassee.com/story/news/2020/05/12/protesters-line-old-capitol-steps-body-bags-urge-florida-governor-not-rush-re-opening/3114218001/.

18 Marina Pitofsky, "Immunocompromised NC Man Fights Back Against Reopen Protesters with Message from Plane," *The Hill* (May 14, 2020), https://thehill.com/blogs/blog-briefing-room/news/497881-immunocompromised-nc-man-fights-back-against-reopen-protesters.

19 Geller, 2020 WL 2520711, at * 1.

20 Ibid.

21 Derrick Bryson Taylor, "George Floyd Protests: A Timeline," *N.Y. Times* (June 22, 2020), www.nytimes.com/article/george-floyd-protests-timeline.html.

22 Ava Wallace & Roman Stubbs, "Louisville Protesters Decry Police Shooting That Killed Breonna Taylor in Her Apartment," *Wash. Post* (May 29, 2020), www.washingtonpost.com/politics/louisville-protestors-decry-police-shooting-that-killed-apartment-resident/2020/05/29/f7dd8e72-a1fo-11ea-b5c9-570a91917d8d_story.html.

23 Larry Buchanan, Quoctrung Bui, & Jugal K. Patel, "Black Lives Matter May Be the Largest Movement in U.S. History," *N.Y. Times* (July 4, 2020), www.nytimes.com/interactive/2020/07/03/us/george-floyd-protests-crowd-size.html.

24 Ibid.

25 Audra D.S. Burch, Weiyi Cai, Gabriel Gianordoli, Morrigan McCarthy, & Jugal K. Patel, "How Black Lives Matter Reached Every Corner of America," *N.Y. Times* (June 13, 2020), www.nytimes.com/interactive/2020/06/13/us/george-floyd-protests-cities-photos.html.

26 *CBS News*, "Minneapolis Police Precinct and Businesses Set on Fire as Protests over George Floyd's Death Rage on" (May 29, 2020), www.cbsnews.com/news/george-floyd-protests-minneapolis-police-third-precinct/.

27 See Jack Arnholz, Ivan Pereira, & Christina Carrega, "US Protests Map Shows Where Curfews and National Guard Are Active," *ABC News* (June 4, 2020),

https://abcnews.go.com/US/locations-george-floyd-protests-curfews-national-guard-deployments/story?id=70997568.

28 Ibid.

29 See, e.g., Sharon Coolidge, Alexander Coolidge, & Ian Mckenzie, "Saturday Night Protest Arrests: No Outside Agitators, most Charged with Curfew Violations," *Cincinnati Enquirer* (June 1, 2020), www.cincinnati.com/story/news/2020/06/01/saturday-night-protest-arrests-most-charged-curfew-violations/5304020002/.

30 See Kim Barker, Mike Baker, & Ali Watkins, "In City After City, Police Mishandled Black Lives Matter Protests," *N.Y. Times* (April 6, 2021), www.nytimes.com/2021/03/20/us/protests-policing-george-floyd.html.

31 See Mark Berman & Emily Wax-Thibodeaux, "Police Keep Using Force Against Peaceful Protesters, Prompting Sustained Criticism About Tactics and Training," *Wash. Post* (June 4, 2020), www.washingtonpost.com/national/police-keep-using-force-against-peaceful-protesters-prompting-sustained-criticism-about-tactics-and-training/2020/06/03/5d2f51d4-a5cf-11ea-bb20-ebf0921f3bbd_story.html.

32 K.K. Rebecca Lai, "Here Are the 100 U.S. Cities Where Protesters Were Tear Gassed," *N.Y. Times* (June 18, 2020), www.nytimes.com/interactive/2020/06/16/us/george-floyd-protests-police-tear-gas.html.

33 Liz Szabo, Jay Hancock, Kevin McCoy, Donovan Slack, & Dennis Wagner, "Fractured Skulls, Lost Eyes: Police Break their Own Rules When Shooting Protesters with 'Rubber Bullets'," *USA Today* (June 22, 2020), www.usatoday.com/in-depth/news/nation/2020/06/19/police-break-rules-shooting-protesters-rubber-bullets-less-lethal-projectiles/3211421001/.

34 Katelyn Burns, "Police Targeted Journalists Covering George Floyd Protests," *Vox* (May 31, 2020), www.vox.com/identities/2020/5/31/21276013/police-targeted-journalists-covering-george-floyd-protests; ACLU Oregon, "ACLU of Oregon Files Class Action Lawsuit Against Police in Portland for Attacking Journalists and Legal Observers," (June 28, 2020), www.aclu-or.org/en/press-releases/aclu-oregon-files-class-action-lawsuit-against-police-portland-attacking-journalists.

35 Anita Snow, "AP Tally: Arrests at Widespread U.S. Protests Hit 10,000," *AP News* (June 4, 2020), https://apnews.com/bb2404f9b13c8b53b94c73f818f6a0b7.

36 See Katelyn Burns, "The Racist History of Trump's 'When the Looting Starts, the Shooting Starts' Tweet," *Vox* (May 9, 2020), www.vox.com/identities/2020/5/29/21274754/racist-history-trump-when-the-looting-starts-the-shooting-starts.

37 Matt Perez, "Trump Tells Governors to 'Dominate' Protesters, 'Put Them in Jail for 10 Years'," *Forbes* (June 1, 2020), www.forbes.com/sites/mattperez/2020/06/01/trump-tells-governors-to-dominate-protesters-put-them-in-jail-for-10-years/?sh=27ca95b013fb.

38 Meghann Myers, "Esper Encourages Governors to 'Dominate the Battlespace' to Put Down Nationwide Protests," *Military Times* (June 1, 2020), www.militarytimes.com/news/your-military/2020/06/01/secdef-encourages-governors-to-dominate-the-battlespace-to-put-down-nationwide-protests/.

39 See Emily Badger, "How Trump's Use of Federal Forces in Cities Differs from Past Presidents," *N.Y. Times* (July 23, 2020) (discussing constitutional concerns regarding the use of federal forces for local law enforcement purposes), www.nytimes.com/2020/07/23/upshot/trump-portland.html?referringSource=articleShare.

40 *ABC News*, "Transcript: Trump to Mobilize Federal Resources to Stop Violence, Restore Security," (June 1, 2020), https://abcnews.go.com/Politics/transcript-trump-mobilize-federal-resources-stop-violence-restore/story?id=71008802.

41 Ibid.

42 Ibid.

43 See 18 U.S.C. §§ 251–253.

44 Peter Baker et al., "How Trump's Idea for a Photo Op Led to Havoc in the Park," N.Y. *Times* (June 2, 2020), www.nytimes.com/2020/06/02/us/politics/trump-walk-lafayette-square.html.

45 Domenico Montanaro, "Watchdog Report Says Police Did Not Clear Protesters to Make Way for Trump Photo-Op," NPR (June 9, 2021), www.npr.org/2021/06/09/1004832399/watchdog-report-says-police-did-not-clear-protesters-to-make-way-for-trump-last-.

46 See Sergio Olmos et al., "Federal Agents Unleash Militarized Crackdown on Portland," N.Y. *Times* (July 21, 2020), www.nytimes.com/2020/07/17/us/portland-protests.html.

47 See Exec. Order. No. 13933, "Executive Order on Protecting American Monuments, Memorials, and Statues Combatting Recent Criminal Violence" (June 26, 2020), www.whitehouse.gov/presidential-actions/executive-order-protecting-american-monuments-memorials-statues-combating-recent-criminal-violence/.

48 Katie Shepherd & Mark Berman, "'It Was Like Being Preyed Upon': Portland Protesters Say Federal Agents in Unmarked Vans Are Detaining Them," *Wash. Post* (July 17, 2020), www.washingtonpost.com/nation/2020/07/17/portland-protests-federal-arrests/; Alex Ward, "The Unmarked Federal Agents Arresting People in Portland, Explained," *Vox* (July 20, 2020), www.vox.com/2020/7/20/21328387/portland-protests-unmarked-arrest-trump-wold.

49 See Mike Baker, "Chaotic Scenes in Portland as Backlash to Federal Deployment Grows," N.Y. *Times* (July 23, 2020), www.nytimes.com/2020/07/21/us/portland-protests.html.

50 See Emily Gillespie & Rachel Siegel, "Oregon Attorney General Sues Federal Agencies for Allegedly Violating Protesters' Civil Rights," *Wash. Post* (July 19, 2020), www.washingtonpost.com/nation/2020/07/18/portland-oreland-ag-lawsuit/. The lawsuit was later dismissed on the grounds that the state lacked the legal standing to assert claims on behalf of protesters.

51 See Badger, "Trump's Use of Federal Forces."

52 See 18 U.S.C. §§ 2101–02; 18 U.S.C. § 231.

53 18 U.S.C. § 2384. See Katie Benner, "Barr Told Prosecutors to Consider Sedition Charges for Protest Violence," N.Y. *Times* (September 17, 2020), www.nytimes.com/2020/09/16/us/politics/william-barr-sedition.html.

54 See International Center for Non-Profit Law, "US Protest Law Tracker," www.icnl.org/usprotestlawtracker/.

55 See Aymann Ismail, "The Anti-Lockdown Protests Prove Police Know How to Treat Protesters Fairly," *Slate* (May 28, 2020), https://slate.com/news-and-politics/2020/05/police-response-george-floyd-minneapolis-shutdowns.html; Li Zhou & Kainaz Amaria, "These Photos Capture the Stark Contrast in Police Response to the George Floyd Protests and the Anti-lockdown Protests," *Vox* (May 27, 2020), www.vox.com/2020/5/27/21271811/george-floyd-protests-minneapolis-lockdown-protests.

56 See Lesley J. Wood, *Crisis and Control: The Militarization of Protest Policing* (London: Pluto Press, 2014), 41–42 ("[P]olice and intelligence agents are much more likely to label protesters from poor or racially marginalized communities, ideologically oriented protesters, and youthful protesters [as uncooperative and threatening].").

57 See, e.g., Paul L. Murphy, *The Constitution in Crisis Times, 1918–1969* (New York: Harper & Row, 1972); Michal R. Belknap, "The New Deal and the Emergency Powers Doctrine," 62 *Tex. L. Rev.* 67 (1983); David Bonner, *Emergency Powers in Peacetime* (London: Sweet & Maxwell, 1985); Jules Lobel, "Emergency Power and the Decline of Liberalism," 98 *Yale L. J.* 1385, 1386 (1989); Michael Linfield, *Freedom Under Fire: U.S.*

Civil Liberties in Times of War (Boston, MA: South End Press, 1990); William H. Rehnquist, *All the Laws But One* (New York: Alfred A. Knopf, 1998); David Cole, "Judging the Next Emergency: Judicial Review and Individual Rights in Times of Crisis," 101 *Mich. L. Rev.* 2565 (2003); Bruce Ackerman, "The Emergency Constitution," 113 *Yale L. J.* 1029 (2004).

58 See Keith E. Whittington, "Yet Another Constitutional Crisis?," 43 *Wm. & Mary L. Rev.* 2093, 2096–98 (2002) (describing the problems associated with defining "crisis").

59 See U.S. Const., art. I, § 9, cl. 2.

60 Ibid., art. IV, § 4.

61 Ibid., art. I, § 8, cl. 15.

62 Ibid., art. I, § 8, cl. 16.

63 See James G. Hodge, Jr. et al., "Legal Crises in Public Health," 47 *J.L. Med. Ethics* 778, 782 (2019) (noting the propensity of state and federal officials to declare public health emergencies).

64 Owen Gross, "Chaos and Rules: Should Responses to Violent Crises Always Be Constitutional?," 112 *Yale L. J.* 1011, 1096 (2003).

65 Kennedy v. Mendoza-Martinez, 372 U.S. 144, 160 (1963) ("[W]hile the Constitution protects against invasions of individual rights, it is not a suicide pact.").

66 See Gross, "Chaos and Rules" ("Experience shows that when grave national crises are upon us, democratic nations tend to race to the bottom as far as the protection of human rights and civil liberties, indeed of basic and fundamental legal principles, is concerned.").

67 See, e.g., Schenck v. United States, 249 U.S. 47 (1919) (upholding an Espionage Act conviction for political pamphleteering); Dennis v. United States, 341 U.S. 494 (1951) (upholding a federal conviction for conspiracy to advocate for the overthrow of the government); Holder v. Humanitarian Law Project, 561 U.S. 1 (2010) (upholding a conviction for providing "material support" to foreign terrorist organizations). During World War I, the Supreme Court failed to overturn even one of the more than 1,000 convictions for protesting the war or the draft. Cole, "Judging the Next Emergency," 2569.

68 See generally, Karen J. Pita Loor, "When Protest Is the Disaster: Constitutional Implications of State and Local Emergency Power," 43 *Seattle U. L. Rev.* 1 (2019) (examining executive and judicial responses to the 2016 North Dakota Access Pipeline, 2014 Ferguson, and 1999 Seattle World Trade Organization protests).

69 John Hart Ely, *Democracy and Distrust: A Theory of Judicial Review* 109 (Cambridge, MA: Harvard University Press, 1980). See also Vincent Blasi, "The Pathological Perspective and the First Amendment," 85 *Colum. L. Rev.* 449, 457 (1985) ("Most constitutional commitments are fragile in the sense that they embody ideals that are easily abandoned or tempered in times of stress. Certain distinctive features of the commitment to free speech enhance that fragility."); Lucas A. Powe, Jr., "Situating Schauer," 72 *Notre Dame L. Rev.* 1519, 1531–32 (1997) (describing speech as "a good times civil liberty").

70 See Geoffrey Stone, *Perilous Times: Free Speech in Wartime, From the Sedition Act of 1798 to the War on Terrorism* (New York: WW. Norton, 2005).

71 See Cole, "Judging the Next Emergency," 2566 (arguing that judicial review has "established important constraints on the exercise of emergency powers and has restricted the scope of what is acceptable in future emergencies").

72 Gross, "Chaos and Rules," 1029.

73 See Aaron Perrine, "The First Amendment Versus the World Trade Organization: Emergency Powers and the Battle in Seattle," 76 *Wash. L. Rev.* 635 (2001) (arguing that protest restrictions imposed pursuant to the emergency declaration during the World Trade Organization gathering in Seattle in 1999 violated the First Amendment).

74 See Cole, "Judging the Next Emergency," 2570–71 (reviewing reasons why the courts are likely to perform poorly in terms of defending civil liberties during times of crisis).

75 See Gross, "Chaos and Rules," 1023 (arguing executive officials should be allowed to act extraconstitutionally during certain emergency circumstances). See also Mark Tushnet, "Defending *Korematsu?*: Reflections on Civil Liberties in Wartime," *Wis. L. Rev.* 273 (2003).

76 See Cole, "Judging the Next Emergency," 2590 ("The public is easily scared, and quick to approve of security measures launched in its name, especially if the measures do not directly affect the rights of the majority.").

77 See Lindsay F. Wiley & Stephen I. Vladeck, "Coronavirus, Civil Liberties, and the Courts: The Case Against 'Suspending' Judicial Review," 133 *Harv. L. J. F.* 179, 194 (2020) (highlighting the "unique checking role of an independent judiciary and the costs of its absence" during declared emergencies).

78 See Gross, "Chaos and Rules," 1021–23 (describing several typical responses to "acute national crises"). See also Hodge et al., "Legal Crises in Public Health."

79 See generally Linda A. Sharp, "COVID-19 Related Litigation: Constitutionality of Stay-at-Home, Shelter-in-Place, and Lockdown Orders," 55 *A.L.R Fed. 3d Art.* 3 (2020) (cataloguing cases involving civil liberties challenges, including complaints based on religious freedom, the right to travel, abortion, and free expression); Laurie Sobel & MaryBeth Musumeci, "Litigation Challenging Mandatory Stay at Home and Other Social Distancing Measures," *Kaiser Fam. Found* (June 5, 2020), www.kff.org/coronavirus-covid-19/issue-brief/litigationchallenging-mandatory-stay-at-home-and-other-social-distancing-measures/. Free speech, assembly, and petition challenges were brought in the following and other cases: Legacy Church, Inc. v. Kunkel, 455 F. Supp. 3d 1100 (D. N.M. 2020); Givens v. Newsom, 459 F. Supp. 3d 1302 (E.D. Cal. 2020); Lebanon Valley Auto Racing Corp. v. Cuomo, 478 F. Supp. 3d 389 (N.D.N.Y. 2020); County of Butler v. Wolf, 486 F.Supp.3d 883 (W.D. Pa. 2020); Geller, 2020 WL 2520711; Antietam Battlefield KOA v. Hogan, 461 F.Supp.3d 214 (D. Md. May 20, 2020); Benner v. Wolf, 461 F.Supp.3d 154 (M.D. Pa. 2020); Republican Party of Illinois v. Pritzker, No. 20-C-3489, 470 F.Supp.3d 813 (N.D. Ill. 2020); Binford v. Sununu, No. 217-2020-CV-00152 (N.H. Super. Ct. March 25, 2020); Ramsek v. Beshear, 2020 U.S. Dist. LEXIS 89602 (E.D. Ky. May 21, 2020), vacated and remanded, 989 F.3d 494 (6th Cir. 2020). The Sixth Circuit vacated the decision in *Ramsek* because the challenged executive order had been repealed.

80 As were their other fundamental rights, including the right to in-person religious worship. Roman Catholic Diocese of Brooklyn v. Cuomo, 141 S. Ct. 63, 69 (2020) (Gorsuch, J., concurring) (criticizing New York's restrictions on religious worship).

81 Givens, 459 F. Supp. 3d 1302, 1313.

82 Ibid.

83 Geller, 2020 WL 2520711, *3–4.

84 Ibid., *4.

85 Ibid.

86 See Hodge, et al., "Legal Crises in Public Health," 15–16 (describing judicial approaches to a variety of constitutional claims challenging pandemic-related restrictions).

87 Binford, slip op., 13.

88 Ramsek, 2020 U.S. Dist. LEXIS 89602, at *21.

89 Wiley & Vladeck, "Coronavirus, Civil Liberties, and the Courts," 180.

90 See, e.g., In re: Abbott, 954 F.3d 772 (5th Cir. 2020) (upholding a ban on surgical abortions); Binford, slip. op., 13 (upholding a statewide ban on large gatherings).

91 Jacobson v. Massachusetts, 197 U.S. 11 (1905).

92 Ibid., 31.
93 Smith v. Avino, 91 F.3d 105, 109–110 (11th Cir. 1996).
94 Ibid., 109.
95 Ibid.
96 Wiley & Vladeck, "Coronavirus, Civil Liberties, and the Courts," 182–83.
97 Ibid., 184.
98 The Supreme Court has made a similar assumption. See Pleasant Grove City, Utah v. Summum, 555 U.S. 460 (2009) ("Speakers, no matter how long-winded, eventually come to the end of their remarks; persons distributing leaflets and carrying signs at some point tire and go home; monuments, however, endure.").
99 Wiley & Vladeck, "Coronavirus, Civil Liberties, and the Courts," 182.
100 Ibid., 188.
101 Ibid., 183.
102 For a critique of broad readings of governmental authority under *Jacobson*, see Josh Blackman, "The Irrepressible Myth of *Jacobson v. Massachusetts*," 70 *Buffalo L. Rev.* 131 (2022).
103 See Jacobson, 197 U.S. 11, 29 (noting that constitutional rights can be "subjected to such restraint, to be enforced by reasonable regulations, as the safety of the general public may demand.").
104 Ibid., 38.
105 Wiley & Vladeck, "Coronavirus, Civil Liberties, and the Courts," 190.
106 Ibid., 193.
107 Korematsu v. United States, 323 U.S. 214, 216–18 (1944).
108 See Jamal Greene, "The Anticanon," 125 *Harv. L. Rev.* 379, 387–90 (2011) (describing *Korematsu* as part of the constitutional "anticanon").
109 See Blasi, "The Pathological Perspective and the First Amendment," 457 ("Most constitutional commitments are fragile in the sense that they embody ideals that are easily abandoned or tempered in times of stress. Certain distinctive features of the commitment to free speech enhance that fragility.").
110 Ibid., 459.
111 Ibid., 468.
112 Ibid., 466–76.
113 Ibid., 456–58.
114 Goss, "Chaos and Rules," 1058. See also Hodge, et al., "Legal Crises in Public Health" (advocating for an accommodationist model based on evidence-based public health responses, flexible conceptions of rights, and the government's duty to preserve public health).
115 Wiley & Vladeck, "Coronavirus, Civil Liberties, and the Courts," 189.
116 Ibid.
117 Cole, "Judging the Next Emergency," 2575–76.
118 See Loor, "When Protest Is the Disaster," 1 ("The emergency management one-size-fits-all approach, however, does not differentiate between political activism, a flood, a terrorist attack, or a loose shooter.").
119 Roman Catholic Diocese of Brooklyn, 141 S. Ct. 63, 70 (Gorsuch, J., concurring).
120 See Loor, "When Protest Is the Disaster," 13–22 (describing state executive emergency powers).
121 Ibid., 6.
122 Ashley Southall, "N.Y Attorney General Sues NYPD over Protests and Demands Monitor," *N.Y. Times* (January 14, 2021), www.nytimes.com/2021/01/14/nyregion/nypd-police-protest-lawsuit.html.

123 See Timothy Zick, *Speech Out of Doors: Preserving First Amendment Liberties in Public Places* (Cambridge: Cambridge University Press, 2008), ch. 7 (describing militarized protest policing during these and other critical democratic moments). See also Wood, *Crisis and Control*.

124 See "Report of the WTO Accountability Review Committee of the Seattle City Council" (September 14, 2020). See also U.S. Dept. of Justice, "After-Action Assessment of the Police Response to the August 2014 Demonstrations in Ferguson, Missouri" (2015), https://cops.usdoj.gov/ric/Publications/cops-p317-pub.pdf.

125 For further discussion, see Heidi Boghosian, *The Policing of Political Speech: Constraints on Mass Dissent in the U.S.* (New York: National Lawyers Guild, 2010), www.nlg.org/wp-content/uploads/2016/09/PolicingPolSpeechCoverAndBody.pdf.

126 See, e.g., Abay v. City of Denver, 445 F.Supp.3d 1286 (D. Colo. 2020) (granting a temporary restraining order (TRO) against police use of chemical agents and projectiles); Don't Shoot Portland v. City of Portland, 465 F.Supp.3d 1150 (D. Or. 2020) (granting a TRO against police use of tear gas against peaceful protesters); Black Lives Matter Seattle-King County v. City of Seattle, 466 F.Supp.3d 1206 (W.D. Wash. 2020) (granting a TRO against police use of tear gas and pepper spray as crowd control measures).

127 Index Newspapers LLC v. U.S. Marshals Service, 977 F.3d 817 (9th Cir. 2020).

128 See Sasso v. City of Dallas, No. 3:20-CV-1398, 2020 WL 2839217 (N.D. Tex. June 1, 2020). But see NAACP v. Peterman, 2020 WL 4572848 (M.D. N.C. July 6, 2020) (granting a TRO prohibiting the enforcement of several curfew orders).

129 Va. Student Power Network v. City of Richmond, 105 Va. Cir. 259 (Va. Cir. Ct. June 30, 2020) (order denying temporary injunction), https://acluva.org/sites/default/files/field_documents/2020.06.29_vspnv.richmondetal.order.pdf.

130 Black Lives Matter D.C. v. Donald Trump, 544 F.Supp.3d 15 (D.D.C. 2021).

131 Daniel Politi, "Jury Awards $14 Million to George Floyd Protesters Injured by Cops in Denver," *Slate* (March 26, 2022), https://slate.com/news-and-politics/2022/03/jury-awards-14-million-george-floyd-protesters-denver.html.

132 See Loor, "When Protest Is the Disaster," 14–15 (noting the lack of publicly available resources).

133 See ibid., 14 (noting that state authorities do not provide for the preservation of individual liberties during declared emergencies). See also Mo. Rev. Stat. § 44.101 (2007) (protecting the right to keep and bear arms during declared emergencies).

134 Luis Martinez, Elizabeth McLaughlin, & Matt Seyler, "What the National Guard Can and Cannot Do in Minneapolis," *ABC News* (May 29, 2020), https://abcnews.go.com/US/national-guard-minneapolis/story?id=70953206.

135 See Kent State University, "Kent State Shootings: Digital Archive," *Kent State Univ. Librs. Special Collections & Archives*, https://omeka.library.kent.edu/special-collections/kent-stateshootings-digital-archive [https://perma.cc/H5AA-XK86].

136 See Loor, "When Protest Is the Disaster," 5 (noting that an emergency declaration "aggravates violations of protesters' rights").

137 For examples of curfews upheld during "emergency" periods of civil unrest, see United States v. Chalk, 441 F.2d 1277, 1280 (4th Cir. 1971) (addressing a curfew imposed in response to racial violence and observing that "[i]nvocation of emergency powers necessarily restricts activities that would normally be constitutionally protected"); In re Juan C., 33 Cal. Rptr. 2d 919 (Ct. App. 1994) (noting that "[a]n insurrection or riot presents a case in which the government's interest in safety outweighs the individual's right to assemble, speak or travel in public areas so long as an imminent peril of violence exists").

138 See Loor, "When Protest Is the Disaster," 42–47 (describing an array of spatial restrictions used to quell protests during emergencies).

139 See Menotti v. City of Seattle, 409 F.3d 1113, 1143 (9th Cir. 2005).

140 See Loor, "When Protest Is the Disaster," 50–55 (describing ad hoc emergency rules during recent demonstrations, including orders to "keep moving" and to stay away from downtown areas upon release).

141 See Jonathan Berlin & Kori Rumore, "12 Times the President Called in the Military Domestically," *Chicago Tribune* (June 1, 2020), www.chicagotribune.com/news/ct-national-guard-deployments-timeline-story.html.

142 See 10 U.S.C. §§ 251–53. See also Michael S. Schmidt & Maggie Haberman, "Trump Aides Prepared Insurrection Act Order During Debate over Protests," *N.Y. Times* (June 25, 2021), www.nytimes.com/2021/06/25/us/politics/trump-insurrection-act-protests.html.

143 See 18 U.S.C. § 1385 (generally restricting state or federal governments from utilizing US military personnel for civilian law enforcement).

144 For discussion, see Scott R. Anderson & Michael Paradis, "Can Trump Use the Insurrection Act to Deploy Troops to American Streets," *Lawfare Blog* (June 3, 2020), www.lawfareblog.com/can-trump-use-insurrection-act-deploy-troops-american-streets; Jennifer K. Elsea, "Defense Primer: Legal Authorities for the Use of Military Forces," *Congressional Research Service* (January 3, 2020), https://crsreports.congress.gov/product/pdf/IF/IF10539.

145 See 10 U.S.C. §§ 251–53.

146 Ian Shapira, "For 200 Years, the Insurrection Act Had Given Presidents the Power to Deploy the Military to Quell Unrest," *Wash. Post* (June 3, 2020), www.washingtonpost.com/history/2020/06/03/insurrection-act-trump-history/.

147 Sean McGrane, "Katrina, Federalism, and Military Law Enforcement: A New Exception to the Posse Comitatus Act," 108 *Mich. L. Rev.* 1309, 1318–19 (2010). Congress later passed the Warner Amendment to the Insurrection Act, granting presidents explicit authority "to deploy military for law enforcement purposes following a natural disaster, with or without a governor's consent." Ibid., 1330. The Warner Amendment gave rise to significant federalism objections. Congress repealed it just a year and a half after passage. Ibid., 1331–32.

148 See Badger, "Trump's Use of Federal Forces" (discussing the reactions of several history and constitutional scholars to Trump's intervention in domestic protests).

149 See Anthony J. Ghiotto, "Defending Against the Military: The Posse Comitatus Act's Exclusionary Rule," 11 *Harv. Nat'l Sec. J.* 359, 382–86 (2020); Congressional Research Service, "The Posse Comitatus Act and Related Matters: The Use of the Military to Execute Civilian Law" (updated November 6, 2018).

150 See Arthur Rizer, "Trading Police for Soldiers: Has the Posse Comitatus Act Helped Militarize Our Police and Set the Stage for More Fergusons?" 16 *Nev. L.J.* 467, 505–11 (2016).

151 Nicole Sganga, "Federal Agents Sent to Portland in 2020 Were 'Unprepared' to Quell Unrest Watchdog Finds," *CBS News* (April 21, 2021), www.cbsnews.com/news/portland-protests-2020-federal-agents-unprepared/.

152 Ibid.

153 For an insightful account of the federal government's response to the BLM protests, see Karen J. Greenberg, *Subtle Tools: The Dismantling of American Democracy from the War on Terror to Donald Trump* (Princeton, NJ: Princeton University Press, 2022), ch. 8.

154 Ibid., 146, 149.

155 Ibid., 151.

156 See ibid., 152–53, 159–661, 70–71.
157 See Marvin Zalman, "The Federal Anti-Riot Act and Political Crime: The Need for Criminal Law Theory," 20 *Vill. L. Rev.* 897, 910, 916 (1975) (discussing legislative history).
158 18 U.S.C. § 2101(a).
159 See "Recent Cases, First Amendment – Federal Anti-Riot Act – Fourth Circuit Finds the Anti-Riot Act Partially Unconstitutional – United States v. Miselis, 972 F.3d 518 (4th Cir. 2020)," 134 *Harv. L. Rev.* 2614 (2021).
160 Brandenburg v. Ohio, 395 U.S. 444 (1969) (per curiam).
161 United States v. Miselis, 972 F.3d 518 (4th Cir. 2020); United States v. Rundo, 990 F.3d 709 (9th Cir. 2021).
162 I8 U.S.C. §231(a)(3).
163 Conrad Wilson, "DOJ Uses Civil Rights-Era Law to Charge Protesters and Insurrectionists," *NPR* (May 22, 2021), www.npr.org/2021/05/22/999180144/doj-uses-civil-rights-era-law-to-charge-protesters-and-insurrectionists.
164 United States of America v. Tia Deyon Pugh, Crim. Act. No. 1:20-cr-73-TFM (S. D. Ala. May 13, 2021).
165 See, e.g., Schenck, 249 U.S. 47 (upholding an Espionage Act conviction for political pamphleteering).
166 Debra Cassens Weiss, "Alito: COVID-19 Restrictions Highlight Disturbing Trend of 'Lawmaking by Executive Fiat,'" *ABA Journal* (November 13, 2020). For a critique of judicial responses to restrictions on worship and other religious activities during the height of the COVID-19 pandemic, see Josh Blackman, "The 'Essential' Free Exercise Clause," 4 *Har. J. L. Pub. Pol'y* 637 (2021).
167 See Loor, "When Protest Is the Disaster," 66–70.

8 PROTESTERS' REMEDIES

1 Harlow v. Fitzgerald, 457 U.S. 800 (1982).
2 Bivens v. Six Unknown Fed. Narcotics Agents, 408 U.S. 388 (1971).
3 42 U.S.C. § 1983 provides:

> Every person who, under color of any statute, ordinance, regulation, custom, or usage, of any State or Territory or the District of Columbia, subjects, or causes to be subjected, any citizen of the United States or other person within the jurisdiction thereof to the deprivation of any rights, privileges, or immunities secured by the Constitution and laws, shall be liable to the party injured in an action at law, suit in equity, or other proper proceeding for redress.

4 Owen v. City of Independence, 445 U.S. 622, 651 (1980).
5 Pierson v. Ray, 386 U.S. 547 (1967).
6 Harlow, 457 U.S. 800.
7 Ibid., 818.
8 Ibid.
9 Malley v. Briggs, 474 U.S. 335, 341 (1986).
10 Harlow, 457 U.S. 800, 819.
11 Ashcroft v. al-Kidd, 563 U.S. 731, 741 (2011).
12 White v. Pauly, 137 S. Ct. 548, 551 (2017) (per curiam).
13 Ashcroft, 563 U.S. 731, 742.
14 Hope v. Pelzer, 536 U.S. 730, 741 (2002).
15 Saucier v. Katz, 533 U.S. 194 (2001).

16 Pearson v. Callahan, 555 U.S. 223 (2009).
17 See Reuters Investigates, "For Cops Who Kill, Special Supreme Court Protection" (examining 252 cases from 2015–2019), www.reuters.com/investigates/special-report/usa-police-immunity-scotus/.
18 Malley v. Briggs, 475 U.S. 335 (1986).
19 Messerschmidt v. Millender, 132 S. Ct. 1235 (2012).
20 See Scott Michelman, "The Branch Best Qualified to Abolish Qualified Immunity," 93 *Notre Dame L. Rev.* 1999 (2018).
21 Ibid. (emphasis added)
22 Harlow, 457 U.S. 800, 814.
23 Ibid.
24 Ibid., 200.
25 Mitchell v. Forsyth, 472 U.S. 511, 526 (1985) (emphasis in original).
26 Ibid. (quoting Gregoire v. Biddle, 177 F.2d 579, 581 (2nd Cir. 1949)).
27 Pierson, 386 U.S. 547.
28 Harlow, 457 U.S. 800, 818.
29 Brosseau v. Haugen, 543 U.S. 194 (2000). See also Saucier, 533 U.S. 194, 202.
30 Al-Kidd, 563 U.S. 731.
31 See, e.g., Joanna C. Schwartz, "The Case Against Qualified Immunity," 93 *Notre Dame L. Rev.* 1797 (2018).
32 Monell v. Department of Social Services, 436 U.S. 658, 694 (1978).
33 Edward C. Dawson, "Replacing Monell Liability with Qualified Immunity for Municipal Defendants in 42 U.S.C. § 1983 Litigation," 86 *U. Cinn. L. Rev.* 483, 486 (2018) (citations omitted).
34 See Joanna Schwartz, "Backdoor Municipal Immunity," *Yale L. J. Forum* (October 14, 2022), 136–62, www.yalelawjournal.org/forum/backdoor-municipal-immunity.
35 City of Canton v. Harris, 489 U.S. 378, 388 (1989). See, e.g., Est. of Jones by Jones v. City of Martinsburg, W. Virginia, 961 F.3d 661, 671–72 (4th Cir. 2020) ("If the City's failure to train reflects such a deliberate or consciously indifferent 'policy,' then its failure can fairly be said to be the 'moving force [behind] the constitutional violation.'").
36 See Connick v. Thompson, 563 U.S. 51 (2011).
37 See Schwartz, "Backdoor Municipal Immunity" (criticizing this "backdoor" form of municipal immunity).
38 Fred Smith, "Local Sovereign Immunity," 116 *Colum. L. Rev.* 409 (2016).
39 Hartman v. Moore, 547 U.S. 250, 256 (2006).
40 Ibid., 259.
41 Ibid., 260.
42 Nieves v. Bartlett, 139 S. Ct. 1715 (2019).
43 Ibid., 1723.
44 Ibid., 1725.
45 Ibid.
46 Ibid.
47 Ibid., 1727 (emphasis added).
48 Lozman v. City of Rivera Beach, Fla., 138 S. Ct. 1945, 1954 (2018).
49 See ibid. (plaintiff alleged "that the City, through its legislators, formed a premeditated plan to intimidate him in retaliation for his criticisms of city officials and his open-meetings lawsuit").
50 Bivens, 408 U.S. 388 (1971).
51 Hernandez v. Mesa, 140 S. Ct. 735, 741 (2020) (internal quotation marks omitted).

52 Ibid.
53 Ibid., 743.
54 Ziglar v. Abbasi,137 S.Ct. 1843, 1857–58 (2017). The Court applied the same approach
    in its most recent *Bivens* decisions. See Hernández v. Mesa, 140 S. Ct. 735, 743 (2020);
    Egbert v. Boule, 142 S. Ct 1793, 1803–04 (2022).
55 Hernandez, 140 S. Ct. 735, 743.
56 Ibid.
57 Ziglar, 137 S. Ct. 548, 1857.
58 Hernandez, 140 S. Ct. 735, 743.
59 Ibid.
60 Ibid.
61 Egbert, 142 S. Ct. 1793, 1803.
62 Ibid., 1805 (quoting Ziglar, 137 S.Ct. 548, 1858).
63 Ziglar, 137 S. Ct. 548, 1856.
64 See Wood v. Moss, 572 U.S. 744, 757 (2014); Reichle v. Howards, 566 U.S. 658, 663n4
    (2012) ("We have never held that *Bivens* extends to First Amendment claims"); Ashcroft
    v. Iqbal, 556 U.S. 662, 675 (2009) (assuming, without deciding, that a free exercise claim
    was available because the issue was not raised on appeal, but noting that the reluctance
    to extend *Bivens* "might well have disposed of respondent's First Amendment claim of
    religious discrimination" because "we have declined to extend *Bivens* to a claim sound-
    ing in the First Amendment"); Bush v. Lucas, 462 U.S. 367 (1983) (declining to extend
    Bivens to a claim sounding in the First Amendment).
65 Egbert, 142 S. Ct. 1793, 1807.
66 Ibid., 1807.
67 Consistent with the book's focus, my research involved cases in which individuals
    and groups participated in traditional forms of public protest. Thus, most of the cases
    involved demonstrations, parades, and rallies. A few involved restrictions on leaflet-
    ting, and one case was initiated because a protester projected images onto a govern-
    ment building. My data set excludes First Amendment claims resulting from prisoner
    litigation, employment-related actions, actions filed after ordinary traffic stops or
    domestic disturbance calls, and speech that occurs at town hall and other municipal
    meetings.
68 See Schwartz, "The Case Against Qualified Immunity," 1808–11 (concluding that
    qualified immunity screens out very few filed cases).
69 My results include claims against individual officers and officials but generally excludes
    claims of municipal liability under *Monell*. As indicated, my data set includes only
    judicial decisions, not dispositions that did not result in published or unpublished
    opinions and orders. See Joanna C. Schwartz, "How Qualified Immunity Fails," 127
    Yale L. J. 2 (2017) (studying *dockets* in over 1,000 Section 1983 cases).
70 See Schwartz, "The Case Against Qualified Immunity."
71 See generally Shawn E. Fields, "Protest Policing and the Fourth Amendment," 55 *U.C.
    Davis L. Rev.* 347 (2021).
72 Nieves, 139 S. Ct. 1715, 1727.
73 I included only cases in which *Nieves* applies, is cited, and is discussed by the court.
    Some lower courts have not addressed First Amendment retaliation claims as *Nieves*
    dictates.
74 While the focus here is on First Amendment claims, an arrest based on probable
    cause will also likely defeat common law tort claims such as false arrest or wrongful
    imprisonment.

75 Ballentine v. Tucker, 28 F.4th 54 (9th Cir. 2022).
76 Nieves, 139 S. Ct. 1715, 1730 (Gorsuch, J., concurring in part and dissenting in part) (quoting Houston v. Hill, 482 U.S. 451, 463 (1987)).
77 Nieves, 139 S. Ct. 1715, 1741 (Sotomayor, J., dissenting).
78 Ibid., 1737.
79 Ibid., 1738.
80 Ibid., 1741.
81 Ibid., 1740.
82 Ibid.
83 See Katherine Grace Howard, "You Have the Right to Free Speech: Retaliatory Arrests and the Pretext of Probable Cause," 51 *Ga. L. Rev.* 607, 614 (2017).
84 Ibid., 1731.
85 See John S. Clayton, "Policing the Press: Retaliatory Arrests of Newsgatherers After Nieves v. Bartlett," 120 *Colum. L. Rev.* 2275 (2020).
86 See Michael Mills, "The Death of Retaliatory Arrest Claims: The Supreme Court's Attempt to Kill Retaliatory Arrest Claims in Nieves v. Bartlett," 105 *Cornell L. Rev.* 2059 (2020).
87 For lower court decisions recognizing First Amendment *Bivens* claims or assuming their viability, see, e.g., Hartley v. Wilfert, 918 F. Supp. 2d 45, 50–51 (D.D.C. 2013) (recognizing a *Bivens* claim against Secret Service agents in the context of public demonstration); Mendocino Envtl. Ctr. v. Mendocino Cnty., 14 F.3d 457, 464 (9th Cir.1994) (plaintiffs made a *Bivens* claim where complaint contained specific factual allegations that tended to show FBI agents intended to interfere with plaintiffs' First Amendment rights to demonstrate and communicate their message about the environment); Korb v. Lehman, 919 F.2d 243, 248 (4th Cir. 1990) (stating that "[w]e believe a *Bivens* action should … exist" in a First Amendment retaliation context but affirming dismissal on qualified-immunity grounds); Gibson v. United States, 781 F.2d 1334 (9th Cir. 1986) (action against FBI agents for conspiracy to violate civil rights); Dellums v. Powell, 566 F.2d 167, 194 (D.C. Cir. 1977) (protest case). Decisions refusing to recognize First Amendment *Bivens* claims include Vega v. United States, 2018 WL 740184 (9th Cir. February 27, 2018) (prisoner case); Davis v. Billington, 681 F.3d 377 (D.C. Cir. 2012) (discharge of a federal employee); Feit v. Ward, 886 F.2d 848 (7th Cir. 1989) (employment case).
88 See, e.g., Dyer, 2021 WL 694811, * 5–6 (applying "special factors" and concluding that a First Amendment claim against TSA agents who interfered with videotaping of a pat-down search could proceed under *Bivens*); ACLU of Nevada v. U.S. General Services Admin., 2014 WL 135219 (D. Nev. January 10. 2014) (holding under "special factors" analysis that *Bivens* did not apply to permitting requirement for demonstration).
89 See Black Lives Matter D.C. v. Trump, 544 F.Supp.3d 15 (DDC 2021); Index Newspapers LLC v. U.S. Marshals Svc., 977 F.3d 817 (9th Cir. 2020); Bond v. Hughes, 2017 WL 1347884 (D. Md. 2017); Lash v. Lemke, 786 F.3d 1 (D.C. Cir. 2015); ACLU of Nevada, 2014 WL 135219; Bloem v. Unknown Dept. of Interior Employees, 920 F.Supp.2d 154 (D.D.C. 2013); Pahls v. Thomas, 718 F.3d 1210 (10th Cir. 2013); Tobey v. Jones, 706 F.3d 379 (4th Cir. 2013); Hartley v. Wilfert, 918 F.Supp.2d 45 (D.D.C. 2013); Marcavage v. NPS, 666 F.3d 856 (3rd Cir. 2012); Oberwetter v. Hilliard, 639 F.3d 545 (D.C. Cir. 2011); Weise v. Casper, 593 F.3d 1163 (10th Cir. 2010); Lederman v. U.S., 291 F.3d 36 (D.C. Cir. 2002); Mendocino Env. Ctr. 14 F.3d 457; Dellums, 566 F.2d 167.
90 Dellums, 566 F.2d 167.
91 Ibid., 194–95.
92 Ibid. (quoting Edwards v. South Carolina, 372 U.S. 229, 235 (1963)).

93 Dellums, 566 F.2d 167, 195. Applying the then-applicable subjective "good faith" standard, the court also held that the federal defendants were not entitled to qualified immunity. The court vacated the judgments for plaintiffs because the jury was not properly
instructed as to the amount of damages they sustained. Ibid., 196.

94 Black Lives Matter D.C., 544 F.Supp.3d 15.

95 Ibid., 30–31.

96 Ibid.

97 Ibid., 31–32.

98 Ibid., 32–33.

99 Ibid., 33–34.

100 For information about settlements and consent decrees relating to protest policing in
cities across the United States, see Heidi Boghosian, "Punishing Protest: Government
Tactics That Suppress Free Speech (2007)," Nat'l Lawyers Guild, www.nlg.org/
punishing-protest/.

101 Patrick McGreevy, "Lawsuit from 2000 Protest Settled," *L.A. Times* (May 8, 2004), www
.latimes.com/archives/la-xpm-2004-may-08-me-demo8-story.html. See also Brittnee Bui,
"Class Actions as a Check on LAPD: What Has Worked and What Has Not," 67 *UCLA
L. Rev.* 432, 451–59 (2020).

102 NYCLU, "Victory in Unlawful Mass Arrest During 2004 RNC the Largest Protest Settlement
in History," (January 15, 2014), www.nyclu.org/en/press-releases/victory-unlawful-mass-
arrest-during-2004-rnc-largest-protest-settlement-history. See also Conor Friedersdorf,
"What Bloomberg Did to Peaceful Protesters," *The Atlantic* (February 25, 2020), www
.theatlantic.com/ideas/archive/2020/02/what-bloomberg-did-rnc-protesters/607030/.

103 Colin Moynihan, "City Settles Occupy Protesters' False-Arrest Lawsuit," *N.Y. Times*
(June 10, 2014), www.nytimes.com/2014/06/11/nyregion/new-york-settles-suit-over-arrests-
of-occupy-wall-street-protesters.html; Associated Press, "New York City Settles with
6 Occupy Wall Street Protesters Pepper-Sprayed by the Police," *N.Y. Times* (July 6, 2015),
www.nytimes.com/2015/07/07/nyregion/new-york-city-reaches-settlements-for-6-pepper-
sprayed-occupy-wall-street-protesters.html.

104 See Schwartz, "Backdoor Municipal Immunity." See also Nancy Leong, "Municipal
Failures," 108 *Cornell L. Rev.* (forthcoming).

105 See Leong, "Municipal Failures" (concluding that in cases decided from 2010 through
2021, plaintiffs prevailed on such claim in seven circuits, with some obtaining large jury
awards).

106 See Clayton, "Policing the Press," 2307–08 (arguing for both relaxed "similarly situated"
standard and exception for discretionary misdemeanors).

107 See Ending Qualified Immunity Act, H.R. 7085, 116th Cong. (2020), www.congress.gov/
bill/116th-congress/house-bill/7085/text. See also Christina Prignano, "Ayanna Pressley,
Justin Amash Introduce Bill to End Prohibition on Lawsuits Against Police Officers,"
The Boston Globe (June 4, 2020), www.bostonglobe.com/2020/06/04/nation/ayanna-
pressley-justin-amash-introduce-bill-end-prohibition-lawsuits-against-police-officers/.

108 See, e.g., Schwartz, "The Case Against Qualified Immunity"; William Baude, "Is
Qualified Immunity Unlawful?" 106 *Cal. L. Rev.* 45 (2018); Michael L. Wells, "Qualified
Immunity After Ziglar v. Abassi: The Case for a Categorical Approach," 68 *Am. U.
L. Rev.* 379 (2018); Aaron L. Nielson & Christopher J. Walker, "The New Qualified
Immunity," 89 *S. Cal. L. Rev.* 1 (2015).

109 See Ilya Somin, "States Can Reform Qualified Immunity on Their Own," *The
Volokh Conspiracy* (June 26, 2020), https://reason.com/volokh/2020/06/26/states-can-
reform-qualified-immunity-on-their-own/.

110 Emma Tucker, "States Tackling 'Qualified Immunity' for Police as Congress Squabbles Over the Issue," *CNN* (April 23, 2021), www.cnn.com/2021/04/23/politics/qualified-immunity-police-reform/index.html.

111 Jeffery C. Mays & Ashley Southall, "It May Soon Be Easier to Sue the N.Y.P.D. for Misconduct," *N.Y. Times* (March 25, 2021), www.nytimes.com/2021/03/25/nyregion/nyc-qualified-immunity-police-reform.html.

112 See Fields, "Protest Policing and the Fourth Amendment," 21–22 (describing actions by Oregon Attorney General in response to the Trump administration's use of federal agents in Portland and New York Attorney General in response to the alleged policing abuses during Black Lives Matter protests).

113 Ibid., 23–37.

114 Ibid., 33–34.

9 PRESERVING PUBLIC PROTEST

1 See NAACP ex rel. Patterson v. Alabama, 357 U.S. 449 (1958) (recognizing the right of expressive association); Borough of Duryea, Pa. v. Guarnieri, 564 U.S. 379 (2011) (asserting that the "rights of speech and petition share substantial common ground").

2 John Inazu, "Unlawful Assembly as Social Control," 64 *UCLA L. Rev.* 2, 8 (2017).

3 Ibid.

4 John D. Inazu, *Liberty's Refuge: The Forgotten Freedom of Assembly* (New Haven, CT: Yale University Press, 2012).

5 Ibid., 5.

6 Tabatha Abu El-Haj, "The Neglected Right of Assembly," 56 *UCLA L. Rev.* 543 (2009).

7 Ronald J. Krotoszynski, Jr., *Reclaiming the Petition Clause* (Newhaven, CT, and London: Yale University Press, 2012).

8 Timothy Zick, *Speech Out of Doors: Preserving First Amendment Liberties in Public Places* (Cambridge: Cambridge University Press, 2009).

9 Krotoszynski, *Reclaiming the Petition Clause*, 183.

10 Ibid.

11 Thomas v. Collins, 323 U.S. 516. 530 (1945).

12 See Tyler Valeska, "A Press Clause Right to Cover Public Protests," 65 *Wash. U. J. L. & Pub. Pol'y* 151 (2021).

13 Regarding the right to record under the First Amendment, see Margot E. Kaminski, "Privacy and the Right to Record," 97 *B.U. L. Rev.* 167 (2017). For cases concerning the right to record actions of law enforcement and other public officials in public places, see Glik v. Cunniffe, 655 F.3d 78, 83 (1st Cir. 2011) ("[T]he First Amendment protects the filming of government officials in *public* spaces"); Smith v. City of Cumming, 212 F.3d 1332, 1333 (11th Cir. 2000) ("The First Amendment protects the right to gather information about what public officials do on *public* property, and specifically, a right to record *matters of public interest.*").

14 See Valeska, "A Press Clause Right" (arguing for media exemptions from curfew and equipment ordinances, heightened protections against arrest and detainment, and special access to spaces cleared by dispersal orders).

15 See, e.g., Cox v. City of Charleston, 416 F.3d 281, 285 (4th Cir. 2005) ("[U]nflinching application" of a permitting requirement "to groups as small as two or three renders it constitutionally infirm."); Douglas v. Brownell, 88 F.3d 1511, 1524 (8th Cir. 1996) ("[A]pplying the permit requirement to groups as small as ten persons compounds our conclusion that the parade permit ordinance is not narrowly tailored.").

16 See Edward R. Maguire, "New Directions in Protest Policing," 35 *S.L.U. Pub. L. Rev.* 67 (2015).

17 Ibid., 83 (quoting A. Vitale, "The Command and Control and Miami Models at the 2004 Republican National Convention: New Forms of Policing Protests," 12 *Mobilization* 403, 404 (2007)).

18 Ibid. (quoting Vitale, "Command and Control," 406).

19 See Lesley J. Wood, *Crisis and Control: The Militarization of Protest Policing* (London: Pluto Press, 2014). See also Radley Balko, *Rise of the Warrior Cop: The Militarization of America's Police Forces* (New York: Public Affairs, 2014).

20 See Katelyn Burns, "Police Targeted Journalists Covering the George Floyd Protests," *Vox* (May 31, 2020), www.vox.com/identities/2020/5/31/21276013/police-targeted-journalists-covering-george-floyd-protests; Jan Wolfe & Ismail Shakil, "U.S. Settles with Black Lives Matter Protesters Violently Cleared from White House Park," *Reuters.com* (April 13, 2022), www.reuters.com/world/us/us-justice-dept-settles-cases-related-police-response-dc-anti-racism-protests-2022-04-13/; Troy Closson, "NYPD Should Discipline 145 Officers for Misconduct, Watchdog Says," *N.Y. Times* (May 11, 2022), www.nytimes.com/2022/05/11/nyregion/nypd-misconduct-george-floyd.html?referringSource=articleShare.

21 Talia Buford, Lucas Waldron, Moiz Syed, & Al Shaw, "We Reviewed Police Tactics Seen in Nearly 400 Protest Videos. Here's What We Found," *ProPublica* (July 16, 2020), https://projects.propublica.org/protest-police-tactics/.

22 See Yuri R. Linetsky, "What the Police Don't Know May Hurt Us: An Argument for Enhanced Legal Training of Police Officers," 48 *N.M. L. Rev.* 1 (2018).

23 See Nick Robinson & Elly Page, "Protecting Dissent: The Freedom of Peaceful Assembly, Civil Disobedience, and Partial First Amendment Protection," 107 *Cornell L. Rev.* 229 (2021).

24 Rachel A. Harmon, "Policing, Protesting, and the Insignificance of Hostile Audiences," Knight First Amendment Institute at Columbia University (November 13, 2017), https://knightcolumbia.org/content/policing-protesting-and-insignificance-hostile-audiences.

25 See, e.g., Dan T. Coenen, "Freedom of Speech and the Criminal Law," 97 *B.U. L. Rev.* 1533 (2017).

26 Rachel Moran, "Doing Away with Disorderly Conduct," 63 *B.U. L. Rev.* 65, 90–107 (2022).

27 Ibid., 68.

28 Inazu, "Unlawful Assembly as Social Control."

29 Ibid., 7.

30 Ibid., 8–9.

31 Ibid., 9-10.

32 Ibid., 10.

33 Inazu also suggests, in the alternative, a "two-tier" system in which assemblies contemplating violence are subject to criminal liability while those contemplating only non-violent actions are subject only to a civil fine. Ibid., 51.

34 Ibid., 29.

35 Ibid., 34.

36 Ibid., 52.

37 Moran, "Doing Away with Disorderly Conduct," 66 ("Disorderly conduct laws cause more harm than good and should be abolished.").

38 Ibid., 67; 82–85.

39 Nick Robinson, "Rethinking the Crime of Rioting," 107 *Minn. L. Rev.* 77 (2022).

40 See Coenen, "Freedom of Speech and the Criminal Law," 1588–1602 (making various proposals for de-criminalizing speech and assembly).

41 See Robinson & Page, "Protecting Dissent," 236.

42 See Nieves v. Bartlett, 139 S. Ct. 1715 (2019).

43 See Cox v. New Hampshire, 312 U.S. 569, 577 (1941) (upholding flat fee to cover costs of protest); Forsyth Cty. v. Nationalist Movement, 505 U.S. 123, 130–34 (1992) (striking down variable fee).

44 New York Times Co. v. Sullivan, 376 U.S. 254, 278 (1964).

45 NAACP v. Claiborne Hardware, 458 U.S. 886 (1982).

46 Harlow v. Fitzgerald, 457 U.S. 800 (1982).

47 Monell v. Department of Social Serv., 436 U.S. 658 (1978).

48 Nieves, 139 S. Ct. 1715.

49 See Wood v. Moss, 572 U.S. 744, 757 (2014). See also Reichle v. Howards, 566 U.S. 658, 663n4 (2012) ("We have never held that *Bivens* extends to First Amendment claims.").

50 See William Baude, "Is Qualified Immunity Unlawful?" 106 *Cal. L. Rev.* 45 (2018); Michael L. Wells, "Qualified Immunity After Ziglar v. Abassi: The Case for a Categorical Approach," 68 *Am. U. L. Rev.* 379 (2018); Aaron L. Nielson & Christopher J. Walker, "The New Qualified Immunity," 89 *S. Cal. L. Rev.* 1 (2015); Joanna C. Schwartz, "The Case Against Qualified Immunity," 93 *Notre Dame L. Rev.* 1797 (2018).

51 Schwartz, "The Case Against Qualified Immunity," 1800.

52 See Ilya Somin, "States Can Reform Qualified Immunity on Their Own," *The Volokh Conspiracy* (June 26, 2020), https://reason.com/volokh/2020/06/26/states-can-reform-qualified-immunity-on-their-own/.

53 See, e.g., Inazu, "Unlawful Assembly as Social Control," 51 (suggesting the enactment of civil remedies against law enforcement officials "who disperse or arrest protesters without the requisite level of reasonable suspicion" required under unlawful assembly laws).

54 See Shawn E. Fields, "Protest Policing and the Fourth Amendment," 55 *U.C. Davis L. Rev.* 347 (2021).

55 For a discussion of the evidence for and against such a crisis, see Thomas Healy, "Return of the Campus Speech Wars," 117 *Mich. L. Rev.* 1063 (2019).

56 See Bloedorn v. Grube, 631 F.3d 1218, 1233–34 (11th Cir. 2011) ("[T]he purpose of a university is strikingly different from that of a public park. Its essential function is not to provide a forum for general public expression and assembly.").

57 Keith E. Whittington, *Speak Freely: Why Universities Must Defend Free Speech* (Princeton, NJ: Princeton University Press, 2018), 13.

58 See John D. Inazu, "The Purpose (and Limits) of the University," 5 *Utah L. Rev.* 943, 968 (2018).

59 See Healy v. James, 408 U.S. 169, 180–81 (1972) (observing that the university classroom "with its surrounding environs is peculiarly the 'marketplace of ideas'").

60 See, e.g., McGlone v. Bell, 681 F.3d 718, 734–35 (6th Cir. 2012) (invalidating advance permission requirement as invalid prior restraint).

61 See, e.g., Bloedorn, 631 F.3d 1218, 1235 (concluding that an evangelist not associated with a university was not part of the class for whom the campus forum was created).

62 See Gregory P. Magarian, "When Audiences Object: Free Speech and Campus Speaker Protests," 90 *U. Colo. L. Rev.* 551, 80 (2019).

63 See Erwin Chemerinsky & Howard Gillman, *Free Speech on Campus* (New Haven, CT: Yale University Press, 2017), 70.

64 Magarian, "When Audiences Object," 557.

65 See Michael Hiltzik, "How a Right-Wing Group's Proposed 'Free Speech' Law Aims to Undermine Free Speech on Campus," *L.A. Times* (May 30, 2018), www.latimes.com/business/hiltzik/la-fi-hiltzik-free-speech-20180530-story.html.

66 See Healy, "Return of the Campus Speech Wars," 1080 (noting that "a university that invites no outside speakers would be a boring place, and students might choose not to attend").

67 See Frederick Schauer, "Costs and Challenges of the Hostile Audience," 94 *Notre Dame L. Rev.* 1671 (2019).

68 See Diana Palmer, "Fired Up or Shut Down: The Chilling Effect at Armed Protests," doctoral dissertation on file with author (April 2021), https://www.northeastern.edu/rise/presentations/fired-up-or-shut-down-the-chilling-effect-at-armed-protests.

69 See Gregory P. Magarian, "Speaking Truth to Firepower: How the First Amendment Destabilizes the Second," 91 *Tex. L. Rev.* 49, 95 (2012).

70 Cf. Josh Blackman, "The 'Essential' Free Exercise Clause," 4 *Har. J. L. Pub. Pol'y* 637 (2021) (arguing that free exercise of religion remains a "fundamental" right even during public health emergencies).

71 Karen J. Pita Loor, "When Protest Is the Disaster: Constitutional Implications of State and Local Emergency Power," 43 *Seattle U. L. Rev.* 1, 6 (2019).

72 Vincent Blasi, "The Pathological Perspective and the First Amendment," 85 *Colum. L. Rev.* 449, 457 (1985).

73 See Timothy Zick, "Seditious Conspiracy Charge Against Oath Keepers Founder and Others in Jan. 6 Riot Faces First Amendment Hurdle," *The Conversation* (January 14, 2022), https://theconversation.com/seditious-conspiracy-charge-against-oath-keepers-founder-and-others-in-jan-6-riot-faces-first-amendment-hurdle-174958.

74 See Loor, "When Protest Is the Disaster," 66–70.

75 International Society for Krishna Consciousness v. Lee, 505 U.S. 672, 696 (Kennedy, J., concurring).

76 Harry Kalven, Jr., "The Concept of the Public Forum: Cox v. Louisiana," 1965 *Sup. Ct. Rev.* 1, 32 (1965).

77 See, e.g., Paul Herrnson & Kathleen Weldon, "Going Too Far: The American Public's Attitude Toward Protest Movements," *Huffington Post* (October 22, 2014; updated December 6, 2017), www.huffpost.com/entry/going-too-far-the-america_b_6029998.

Index

Printed in the USA
CPSIA information can be obtained
at www.ICGtesting.com
LVHW021657050124
768120LV00005B/447